Legacy of Beauty: A Festschrift in Honor of Jo Ann Davidson

Edited by A. Rahel Wells and Iriann Marie Irizarry

Adventist Theological Society
Berrien Springs, Michigan

Legacy of Beauty: A Festschrift in Honor of
Jo Ann Davidson

Printed in the United States of America

Published by the Adventist Theological Society
Berrien Springs MI 49103

Edited by A. Rahel Wells and Iriann Marie Irizarry
Cover design by Melissa Sharley
Text layout by April Younker

ISBN: 978-0-9831147-6-5 (paperback)

Table of Contents

Contributors

C. Adelina Alexe, PhD Candidate, Independent Scholar, Seventh-day Adventist Theological Seminary, Andrews University, Berrien Springs, Michigan.

Sarah Gane Burton, MA, Independent Scholar.

Christie G. Chadwick, PhD, Professor of Old Testament and Biblical Languages, Adventist University of São Paulo (UNASP), Engenheiro Coelho SP, Brazil.

Mathilde Frey, PhD, Professor of Hebrew Bible and Old Testament, Walla Walla University, Walla Walla, Washington.

Anna M. Galeniece, DMin, BCC, Professor of Chaplaincy; Director of Seminary Chaplaincy Study Center, Seventh-day Adventist Theological Seminary, Andrews University, Berrien Springs, Michigan.

Constance Clark Gane, PhD, Research Professor of Archaeology and Old Testament, Seventh-day Adventist Theological Seminary, Andrews University, Berrien Springs, Michigan.

Daniela Gelbrich, PhD, Professor of Biblical Hebrew and Old Testament, Adventist University of France, Collonges-sous-Salève, France.

Angelika Kaiser, Dr. Phil., Instructor of Linguistics and Philology, Seventh-day Adventist Theological Seminary, Andrews University, Berrien Springs, Michigan.

Marla A. Samaan Nedelcu, PhD, Adjunct Professor of Religion, Southern Adventist University, Collegedale, Tennessee; Adjunct Professor of Religion, AdventHealth University online.

Carina Prestes, PhD, Professor of Religion and Biblical Archaeology, Adventist University of São Paulo (UNASP), Engenheiro Coelho SP, Brazil.

Dragoslava Santrac, PhD, Managing Editor of the *Encyclopedia of Seventh-day Adventists*, General Conference of Seventh-day Adventists, Silver Spring, Maryland.

A. Rahel Wells, PhD, Professor of Hebrew Bible and Old Testament, Andrews University, Berrien Springs, Michigan.

Hyveth Williams, DMin, PhD, Professor of Homiletics; Director of Doctor of Ministry program, Seventh-day Adventist Theological Seminary, Andrews University, Berrien Springs, Michigan.

Acknowledgements

This book would not have happened without so many people working together. First of all, we want to thank the authors. They worked so hard to produce such excellent essays to honor Jo Ann, in the midst of so many other responsibilities and life emergencies. We are also grateful to the tribute contributors for being willing to share touching testimonies about Jo Ann, as well as words of encouragement and good wishes.

We also want to thank Richard M. Davidson, Jo Ann's husband, who collected and formatted her prodigious bibliography. He also reviewed every paper, and supported and encouraged us in a myriad of other ways, including by keeping this a secret from Jo Ann!

In the production of the final volume, April Younker, a long-time friend of Jo Ann's, served as copy editor and provided lots of technical help. Melissa Sharley, who knows and loves Jo Ann as well, designed the book cover to reflect the beauty and godly simplicity of her life, as well as her love of the color red. The Adventist Theological Society sponsored this project, and we are very grateful for the support of all those on the executive committee.

We are also thankful for our husbands, Bill Wells and Nick Hausted, who put up with our editing and festschrift conversations at all hours of the day and night over the last two years, especially during the final months. Their support and love is beyond compare.

Most of all, we praise God, not only for giving us the strength to see this project through to completion, but also for being the author of all beauty. And for being Jo Ann's Creator and Redeemer, inspiring her legacy of beauty that she continues to share with the world.

A. Rahel Wells and Iriann Marie Irizarry

Introduction

Legacy of Beauty is a fitting title for a Festschrift honoring Dr. Jo Ann Davidson. Not only did she write her dissertation on the theology of beauty, but she also exhibits a beautiful spirit in her character and a love of beauty in her everyday life.

In addition, she has left a beautiful legacy of courage to many female scholars who have been inspired and able to study theology because of her trailblazing path. This includes myself (Rahel Wells), her daughter, as I grew up watching both my parents teach theology and the Bible. As a result I did not think twice about following God's call down the same path, even though it came after many years of study in the sciences. Jo Ann's love for animals and the beauty of creation inspired me from a young age to care for God's creatures. I ended up writing my dissertation on that topic and dedicating it to my parents, as my dad inspired my love for the Old Testament, and my mom inspired my love for God's creation and creatures.

I (Iriann Irizarry) met her in Puerto Rico when she visited us at Antillean Adventist University for a week of prayer. That was such a pivotal moment in my life and in my decision to pursue further theological studies. As a comparative literature graduate considering a transition to theological studies, it was deeply impactful to meet a female theologian in Adventism. I had just found out that I could receive formal theological training shortly before meeting Jo Ann, but seeing her in person (teaching, preaching, ministering) solidified my awareness and encouraged my hope that, yes, women are called to be in that line of work in our church! I still hold vivid memories of that event. Little did I know that through the years I would grow to cherish and admire her as a professor, thinker, writer, and mentor.

All contributors to this volume are female Adventist scholars, and many have similar stories of their direct or indirect inspiration by Jo Ann. Some are her seminary colleagues, others are former students, and still others are those who have been impacted by Jo Ann in some other way. Many others who would also fit into these categories were not able to contribute a chapter, but in many cases wrote tributes to Jo Ann that can be found in the appendix.

We asked each contributor to reflect on how beauty is manifested in the Bible in some way. The first section of chapters is concerned with the beauty of narrative and literary artistry, another of Jo Ann's great loves. In fact, C. Adelina Alexe writes how she learned her love for narrative analysis from Jo Ann, and showcases this in her examination of how Jesus and other supporting characters interact in his struggle in Gethsemane. Angelika Kaiser analyzes 2 Sam 9 and considers the emotional nature of David in his interactions with Mephibosheth. Mathilde Frey finds beauty even in the narrative of Jephthah's daughter in Judges 11. Finally, Dragoslava Santrac delineates beautiful structures in the Psalms, specifically highlighted by a close examination of divine speeches.

The next section focuses on beauty in archaeology and culture. Sarah Gane Burton and Constance Clark Gane investigate the cultural-historical background of the Esther narrative and her relationship with the king, offering a fresh reading in light of textual material from the Old Testament and ancient Near East. Carina Prestes examines archaeological and cultural evidence for women leaders in the early New Testament church, using Lydia as a test case to compare with women in the Greco-Roman world. Christie G. Chadwick uses a similar lens as she considers how women lived and operated in the ancient societies of Israel. Finally, Hyveth Williams wrestles with various issues surrounding clothes and adornment in the Bible, especially in light of her appreciation for Jo Ann's elegant taste.

The final section contains contributions related to theology and beauty in God's character. Daniela Gelbrich looks at the beauty of God's vulnerability and commitment. Marla A. Samaan Nedelcu explores God's beauty in the Eden narrative, especially as it relates to humans made in God's image. Anna M. Galeniece considers the ministry of presence, as manifested by three biblical women, who ultimately reflect God's ministry of presence in their lives. Finally, A. Rahel Wells considers God's love for his non-human animal creation, specifically in light of the connections between how God views animals and the poor.

We have been blessed by editing these chapters, and we hope that Jo Ann will also find their content insightful and engaging, as we all carry on her legacy of beauty.

A. Rahel Wells and Iriann Marie Irizarry

Dedicated to Jo Ann Davidson

Life Sketch

Jo Ann Davidson, PhD
Professor of Systematic Theology

Jo Ann Mazat was born to missionary parents and is a fourth generation Seventh-day Adventist. She recalls her mother saying to her, "the blessings of being a Seventh-day Adventist have surely seeped into your genes and chromosomes by now!" Growing up in Singapore with her 3 siblings gave her a love for helping other people understand God better. After returning to the States, she attended Campion Academy in Colorado, and pursued a music major with an emphasis in violin performance at La Sierra College (now University).

While at La Sierra, she met Richard Davidson, and they married soon after college. When they moved to Andrews University for him to attend seminary, Jo Ann completed her Bachelor of Arts degree in violin performance with a minor in speech. Richard pastored for six years in Arizona, during which time Jo Ann not only gave private music lessons and served in various capacities in the Flagstaff SDA church, but also performed in the Flagstaff Symphony orchestra, earned a minor in nutrition at Northern Arizona University, and gave nutrition classes as part of the church outreach to the community. When they returned to Andrews for Richard to pursue a PhD in Old Testament, Jo Ann earned a Master's degree in music history, while also working as an administrative assistant in the Seminary, as well as typing her husband's papers. Through these jobs, and discussing Scripture together with Richard in their seven-mile walk to and from campus every day, she fell in love with theology. While raising and homeschooling their two children, she began to take a class at the Seminary every semester, just for the joy of it.

She did so well in her classes, that she was offered a position teaching at the Seminary, contingent upon earning a PhD in Systematic Theology. She commuted to Trinity Evangelical Divinity School in Deerfield, IL, for several years, while continuing to care for her teenage children, working long into the night to complete her degree in 2000. God brought together all of her previous training and experiences to enable her to write her dissertation masterpiece on the theology of beauty (aesthetics) from a biblical perspective.

There were many hurdles she had to face along the way, including teachers and then students, who said to her face that a woman should never be teaching theology. But Jo Ann persevered and won many of them over with her winsome ways and keen mind.

Throughout her life and ministry, Jo Ann Davidson has carved a path that contemporary women are now able to traverse and widen. Jo Ann is the first woman to earn a PhD in Systematic Theology and to teach full-time at the Seventh-day Adventist Theological Seminary as a tenured full professor. She also served as the first female president of the Adventist Theological Society. Her trailblazing contributions to the theological dialogue, as well as what her example means to other aspiring women in the field, will remain as landmarks in Adventist theology.

She has written over 100 scholarly/professional articles/chapters which have appeared in various *Festschriften* honoring other scholars, and in such journals as the *Andrews University Seminary Studies*, the *Journal of the Adventist Theological Society,* the *Adventist Review,* and the *Signs of the Times,* along with a column, "Let's Face It," in the journal

Perspective Digest. She has also authored the books *Jonah: The Inside Story* (Review and Herald), *Toward a Theology of Beauty: A Biblical Perspective* (University Press of America), *Glimpses of Our God* (Pacific Press), and *Rediscovering the Glory of the Sabbath* (Pacific Press).

Jo Ann has also read over 75 scholarly papers in various academic venues, including presenting a paper at almost every annual meeting of the Evangelical Theological Society and the Adventist Theological Society during the entire course of her teaching career. She has lectured at several hundred different venues—in virtually every state or province in the USA and Canada and some twenty countries outside of North America—including women's retreats, pastors' meetings, Bible conferences, and local churches. She has written numerous magazine articles popularizing theology for general readership, including two Sabbath School Lesson quarterly Bible Study Guides, making clear that her impact goes far beyond the academy.

Jo Ann has made significant and unique contributions to theology in areas largely overlooked by other Adventist (and Christian) theologians till recently. Her published dissertation provided the first major theology of aesthetics from a biblical, not Greek, perspective. She was already writing and lecturing widely on creation care and ecological concerns long before it was fashionable to study these issues in Adventist circles. Her book and Sabbath School Bible Guides on the "inside story" of Jonah introduced to Adventism the new discipline of narrative theology. Her numerous writings and lectures on the "glory" of the Sabbath, culminating in her newest book, highlighted the beauty and joy of the Sabbath at a time when little had been written emphasizing its positive experiential aspect. Jo Ann's studies of the biblical narratives dealing with women forged a new path in Adventist studies, upholding the elevated status of women in the Bible, and giving hope to many struggling women through her writings on the subject and her scores of women's retreats held throughout North America during the last several decades.

Jo Ann is beloved by her students because of her enthusiastic teaching, passion for Scripture, and empathetic and caring heart. She is known for sharing her home in hospitality and feasting, inviting each class over for a gourmet meal and sweet fellowship. Though her career has been cut short, showcasing the fragility of the position of women in theology, her influence and dynamic impact on the field will continue. This Festschrift is one such example of how her love of beauty and biblical aesthetics has deepened the appreciation of many for the complexity and beauty found in the narratives of Scripture, in the natural world, and in the character of God the Master Aesthete. Each of the studies in this volume in some way pays tribute to the value of beauty, which Jo Ann has sought so diligently to uphold.

In addition to her teaching and academic ministry, Jo Ann finds great fulfillment in her many roles as wife, mother, daughter, sister, auntie, teacher, musician, student, and Seventh-day Adventist Christian. As she transitions to the new academic status of Senior Research Professor at the Theological Seminary, we know that she will continue to bless the world.

A. Rahel Wells and Richard M. Davidson

A Selected Bibliography of Jo Ann Davidson

DISSERTATION

"Toward a Theology of Beauty: A Biblical Aesthetic." PhD dissertation, Trinity Evangelical Theological Seminary, 2000.

BOOKS

Rediscovering the Glory of the Sabbath. Nampa, ID: Pacific Press, 2020.

Glimpses of Our God. Nampa, ID: Pacific Press, 2011.

Toward a Theology of Beauty: A Biblical Perspective. Lanham, MD: University Press of America, 2008.

Jonah: The Inside Story. Hagerstown, MD: Review & Herald, 2003.

CHAPTERS CONTRIBUTED TO BOOKS/VOLUMES

"Shaken in Shechem." Pages 16–19 in *Strength for the Journey.* Edited by Donna Jackson. Columbia, MD: North American Division Ministerial Association, 2020.

"Ruth (Introduction and Commentary)." Pages 418–426 in *Andrews Bible Commentary.* Edited by Ángel Manuel Rodríguez. Berrien Springs, MI: Andrews University Press, 2020.

"The Second Coming of Christ: Is There a 'Delay'?" Pages 253–270 in *God's Character and the Last Generation*. Edited by Jiří Moskala and John C. Peckham. Nampa, ID: Pacific Press, 2018.

"Wind and the 'Holy Wind': Divine Assurance of Salvation." Pages 361–374 in *Salvation: Contours of Adventist Soteriology*. Edited by Martin F. Hanna, Darius W. Jankiewicz, and John W. Reeve. Andrews University Press, 2018.

"La mayordomía y su relación con el medio ambiente." Pages 139–157 in *El señorío de Cristo y la Mayordomía Cristiana: Aspectos bíblicos, teológicos y prácticos*. Edited by Benjamín Rojas and Cristian S. Gonzales. Lima, Perú: Universidad Peruana Unión, 2016.

"The Creator and Creation: God's Affection for This World." Pages 505–515 in *Meeting with God on the Mountains: Essays in Honor of Richard M. Davidson*. Edited by Jiří Moskala. Berrien Springs, MI: Old Testament Department of the Seventh-day Adventist Theological Seminary, Andrews University, and Adventist Theological Society, 2016.

"¿Cómo considera Dios a su creación?" Pages 5–14 in *Custodios del Planeta: Ecoteología y Ambientalismo*. Edited by Stephen Dunbar, L. James Gibson, and Humberto M. Rasi. Libertador San Martín: Universidad Adventista del Plata; Nuevo León: Adventus, Editorial Universitaria Iberoamericana; Ciudad Autónoma de Buenos Aires: Asociación Casa Editora Sudamericana, 2016.

"Women in the Old Testament: Leadership Principles." Pages 259–275 in *Servants & Friends: A Biblical Theology of Leadership*. Edited by Skip Bell. Berrien Springs, MI: Andrews University Press, 2014.

"The Word Made Flesh: The Inspiration of Scripture." Pages 1–14 in *The Word: Searching, Living, Teaching*. Volume 1. Edited by Artur A. Stele. Silver Spring, MD: Biblical Research Institute, Review and Herald, 2015.

"Women in Scripture: A Survey and Evaluation." Pages 121–142 in *Women and Ordination: Biblical and Historical Studies*. Nampa, ID: Pacific Press, 2015.

"Behold, I Come Quickly . . . But We Are Still Here." Pages 275–284 in *The Great Controversy and the End of Evil: Biblical and Theological Studies in Honor of Ángel Manuel Rodríguez in Celebration of His Seventieth Birthday*. Edited by Gerhard Pfandl. Silver Spring, MD: Review and Herald, Biblical Research Institute; Nampa, ID: Pacific Press, 2015.

"How Does God Regard His Creation?" Pages 3–12 in *Entrusted: Christians and Environmental Care*. Edited by Stephen Dunbar, L. James Gibson, and Humberto M. Rasi. San Martín, Entre Ríos, Argentina: Adventus-International University Publishers, 2013.

"The Word Speaks for Itself: A Theology of Scripture." Pages 44–54 in *In the Beginning*. Edited by Bryan Ball. Nampa, ID: Pacific Press, 2012.

"What Does it Mean to Say that the Bible is Inspired?" Pages 27–37 in *Always Prepared: Answers to Questions About Our Faith*. Edited by Humberto M. Rasi and Nancy J. Vyhmeister. Nampa, ID: Pacific Press, 2011.

"Finding True Rest in Jesus." Pages 43–50 in *Really Living: People Whose Lives Have Been Changed by Jesus*. Edited by Don Schneider. Nampa, ID: Pacific Press, 2010.

"Ellen White and Environmental Ethics." Pages 21–78 in *Ellen White and Current Issues Symposium*, vol. 5. Edited by Merlin D. Burt. Berrien Springs, MI: Center for Adventist Research, Andrews University, 2009 (copyright 2010).

"The Inspiration of Scripture: Word Made Flesh." Pages 44–65 in *Christ in the Classroom: Adventist Approaches to the Integration of Faith and Learning*, vol. 34-B. Edited by Humberto M. Rasi. Silver Spring, MD: General Conference of SDA, 2007.

"Deep Breathing." Pages 51–58 in *"For You Have Strengthened Me": Biblical and Theological Studies in Honor of Gerhard Pfandl in Celebration of His Sixty-fifth Birthday.* Edited by Martin Pröbstle with assistance of Gerald A. Klingbeil and Martin G. Klingbeil. St. Peter am Hart, Austria: Seminar Schloss Bogenhofen, 2007.

"La expiación según Moisés." Pages 247–272 in *Volviendo a los Orígenes: Entendiendo el Pentateuco.* Edited by Merling Alomía, Segundo Correa, Víctor Choroco and Edgard Horna. Lima, Perú: Universidad Peruana Union, 2006.

"Jonas: lições de um profeta para os últimos dias." Pages 27–39 in *O futuro: a visão adventista dos últimos acontecimentos*. Edited by Alberto R. Timm, Amin A. Rodor and Vanderlei Dorneles. Engenheiro Coelho, Brazil: UNASPress, 2004.

"Seventh-day Adventists and Ecology." Pages 359–378 in *The Word of God for the People of God: A Tribute to the Ministry of Jack J. Blanco.* Edited by Ron du Preez, Philip G. Samaan, and Ron E. M. Clouzet. Collegedale, TN: School of Religion, Southern Adventist University, 2004.

"The Last Days and the Prophet Jonah." Pages 275–292 in *The Cosmic Battle for Planet Earth: Essays in Honor of Norman R. Gulley.* Edited by Jiří Moskala and Ron du Preez. Berrien Springs, MI: Andrews University, 2003.

"The Bible and Aesthetics." Pages 201–265 in *Christ in the Classroom: Adventist Approaches to Integration of Faith and Learning*, vol. 26-B. Edited by Humberto M. Rasi. Silver Spring, MD: Institute for Christian Teaching, Education Department, General Conference of Seventh-day Adventists, 2000.

"Abraham, Akedah and Atonement." Pages 49–72 in *Creation, Life and Hope: Essays in Honor of Jacques B. Doukhan.* Edited by Jiří Moskala. Berrien Springs, MI: Old Testament Department, Andrews University Theological Seminary, 2000.

"Women in Scripture: A Survey and Evaluation." Pages 157–186 in *Women in Ministry: Biblical and Historical Perspectives.*" Edited by Nancy Vyhmeister. Berrien Springs, MI: Andrews University Press, 1998.

REFEREED JOURNAL ARTICLES

"Joseph, Judah and Jesus: Revisiting Genesis 37–50." *Journal of the Adventist Theological Society* 30.1–2 (2019 [published in 2021]): 179–199.

"A Power or Person: The Nature of the Holy Spirit." *Journal of the Adventist Theological Society* 27.1 (2016): 24–26.

"Deep Breathing of the Soul: Honesty in Prayer." *Ministry: International Journal for Pastors* 88.7 (July 7, 2016): 21–23.

"Women Bear God's Image: Considerations from a Neglected Perspective." *Andrews University Seminary Studies* 54.1 (Spring 2016): 31–50.

"Love and Judgment: God's Triumph—Part 2." *Ministry: International Journal for Pastors* 86.5 (May 2014): 18–20.

"Love and Judgment: God's Triumph—Part 1." *Ministry: International Journal for Pastors* 86.3 (March 2014): 15–18.

"Biblical Narratives: Their Truth *and* Beauty." *Andrews University Seminary Studies* 49.1 (2011): 149–158.

"The Decalogue Predates Mount Sinai: Indicators from the Book of Genesis." *Journal of the Adventist Theological Society* 19.1–2 (2008): 61–81.

"Creator, Creation and Church: Restoring Ecology to Theology." *Andrews University Seminary Studies* 45.1 (2007): 101–122.

"The Well Women of Scripture Revisited." *Journal of the Adventist Theological Society* 17.11 (Spring 2006): 209–228.

"John 4: Another Look at the Samaritan Woman." *Andrews University Seminary Studies* 43.1 (Spring 2005): 159–168.

"Word Made Flesh: The Inspiration of Scripture." *Journal of the Adventist Theological Society* 15.1 (Spring 2004): 21–33.

"World Religions and the Vegetarian Diet." *Journal of the Adventist Theological Society* 14.2 (Autumn 2003): 114–130.

"Toward a Scriptural Aesthetic." *Andrews University Seminary Studies* 41.1 (Spring 2003): 101–111.

"Genesis Matriarchs Engage Feminism." *Andrews University Seminary Studies* 40.2 (Autumn 2002): 169–178.

"'Even if Noah, Daniel, and Job' (Ezekiel 14:14, 20)—Why These Three?" *Journal of the Adventist Theological Society* 12.2 (Fall 2001): 132–144.

"Modern Feminism and Religious Pluralism." *Journal of the Adventist Theological Society* 10.2 (Autumn 1999): 401–440.

"Eschatology and Genesis 22." *Journal of the Adventist Theological Society* 11.1–2 (Spring and Autumn 2000): 232–247.

"Modern Feminism, Religious Pluralism, and Scripture." *Journal of the Adventist Theological Society* 10.1–2 (1999): 401–440.

PROFESSIONAL JOURNALS/PERIODICAL ARTICLES

"Offensive Grace." Former Presidents' Forum. *Perspective Digest* 27.2 (April 1, 2022): electronic journal, https://www.perspectivedigest.org/archive/27-2/offensive-grace.

"Joseph, Judah, and Jesus." *Perspective Digest* 26.4 (October 1, 2021): electronic journal, https://www.perspectivedigest.org/archive/26-4/joseph-judah-and-jesus.

"The Gospel and a Queen." *Perspective Digest* 26.2 (April 1, 2021): electronic journal, https://www.perspectivedigest.org/archive/26-2/the-gospel-and-a-queen.

"Love the Law? Really?" Former Presidents' Forum. *Perspective Digest* 26.1 (January 1, 2021): electronic journal, https://www.perspectivedigest.org/archive/26-1/love-the-law-really.

"Judgment and Other Good News: Clarifying the Nature of the Everlasting Gospel." *Adventist Review* 97.10 (October 2020): 54-55.

"The Creator and Creation: God's Affection for This World, Part 2." *Messenger: Journal of the Seventh-day Adventist Church in the United Kingdom and Ireland* 125.22 (November 9, 2020): 8-9.

"The Creator and Creation: God's Affection for This World, Part 1." *Messenger: Journal of the Seventh-day Adventist Church in the United Kingdom and Ireland* 125.21 (October 26, 2020): 8–9.

"An Atheist Confirms Ellen White's Counsel." *Adventist World* 15.3 (March 2019): 22–23.

"The Aesthetic Nature of God." *Perspective Digest* 24.3 (July 1, 2019): electronic journal, https://www.perspectivedigest.org/archive/24-3/the-aesthetic-nature-of-god.

"What Does 'Inspired' Mean?" *Perspective Digest* 22.1 (January 1, 2019) electronic journal, https://www.perspectivedigest.org/archive/22-1/what-does-inspired-mean.

"A Strange Anomaly." Former Presidents' Forum. *Perspective Digest* 21.2 (April 1, 2016), electronic journal, https://www.perspectivedigest.org/archive/21-2/a-strange-anomaly.

"The Church, Stewardship and Ecology." *Dynamic Steward* 19.3 (2015): 24.

"An Ancient Honor Roll." *College and University Dialogue* 26.3 (2014): 5–8.

"Christians and Creation Care." *Lake Union Herald* 106.10 (Nov-Dec 2014): 14–17.

"Let Them Praise the Name of the Lord." *Dynamic Steward* 17.2 (Apr-Jun 2013): 6–7.

"Toward a Theology of Beauty." *Perspective Digest* 18.3 (June 28, 2013), electronic journal, https://www.perspectivedigest.org/archive/18-3/toward-a-theology-of-beauty

"God and Aesthetics: Exploring Beauty's True Source." *Adventist Review* 189.32 (November 15, 2012): 20–22.

"God in Three Persons—Blessed Trinity." *Adventist World* 7.3 (March 2011): 28–29.

"Worshiping God in Truth and Beauty." *Best Practices for Adventist Worship*, November 2010 (NAD Church Resource Center newsletter on-line).

"The Word Made Flesh." *Perspective Digest* 15.3 (July 1, 2010): 21–25.

"Sabbath is for Love." *Signs of the Times* 137.8 (August 2010): 43–46.

"Voices from the Dome: Jo Ann Davidson." *Adventist Review* on-line, July 1, 2010.

"Hagar: Hope for the Disenfranchised," "Rebekah: More than the 'Little Woman,'" "Rachel and Leah: A Lesson in R-e-s-p-e-c-t," & "Another Stop at the Well." *LEAD* magazine 3.2 (Apr-June 2010): 20–22, 82.

"The Decalogue Before Mount Sinai." *Perspective Digest* 15.1 (January 1, 2010): 7–23.

"God's Wonderful World." *Record* 114.41 (October 24, 2009): 6.

"Fun Facts on Ecology." *Shabbat Shalom: A Journal for Jewish-Christian Reconciliation* 56.2 (2009): 16–17.

"Jo Ann Davidson: Interview." *Shabbat Shalom: A Journal for Jewish-Christian Reconciliation* 56.2 (2009): 10–15.

"Who Cares? Environmental Ethics and the Christian." *Adventist Review* 186.18 (June 25, 2009): 51–54.

"Creation Care and the Christian." *Perspective Digest* 14.1–2 (2009): 1–3.

"And It Was Good." *Adventist Review* 185.23 (August 21, 2008): 8–11.

"The Sabbath: A Royal Delight." *New England Pastor*, March–April 2008, 6–7.

"World Religions and the Vegetarian Diet." *Perspective Digest* 12.1 (2007): 25–39.

"Well Women Revisited." *Perspective Digest* 12.4 (2007): 7–20.

"Behold the Lamb." *Adventist Review* 182.27 (July 2005): 21–23.

"Old Testament Honor Roll." *Adventist Review* 182.18 (May 2005): 28–31.

"Inspiration and Science." *Perspective Digest* 10.4 (2005): 11–23.

"Those Who Revise and Those Who Revolt." *Perspective Digest* 10.2 (2005): 34–46.

"Anticipating Shabbat, Anticipating Heaven." *Shabbat Shalom: A Journal for Jewish-Christian Reconciliation* (Spring 2004): 30–31.

"The Pain That Opens Our Hearts to Search for God is Deep (Let's Face It)." *Perspective Digest* 9.3 (2004): 42–44.

"Lightning on the Mountain (Let's Face It)." *Perspective Digest* 9.2 (2004): 61–62.

"A Great Disappointment (Let's Face It)." *Perspective Digest* 8.1 (2003): 50–52.

"God's Word: Its Origin and Authority." *Ministry: International Journal for Pastors* 75.1 (January 2003): 5–9.

"Passing the Gavel (The President's Page)." *Perspective Digest* 7.2 (2002): 10–12.

"Praise the Lord and Pass the Ammunition (The President's Page)." *Perspective Digest* 7.1 (2002): 10–12.

"Sabbath: Palace in Time." Pages 12–14 in *You're a Seventh-day Adventist: Welcome to the Family,* 12–14. Special magazine bound in *Lake Union Herald* 92.2 (February 2002): between pages 8 and 9.

"Ellen White and the Cities: Was She a Fearmonger? (The President's Page)." *Perspective Digest* 6.4 (2001): 10–12.

"The President's Page." *Perspective Digest* 6.2 (2001): 11.

"Of Daunting Challenges and Breathless Dreams (The President's Page)." *Perspective Digest* 6.1 (2001): 11–13.

"A Rest Designed for Royalty." *Adventist Review* 178.35 (August 30, 2001): 6-10.

"The Great Sabbath Welcome." *Perspective Digest* 5.4 (2000): 9–11.

"Plain Truth from a Mad Cowboy and Others (The President's Page)." *Perspective Digest* 5.3 (2000): 9–11.

"A Tale of Three Mountains (Let's Face It)." *Perspective Digest* 5.1 (2000): 1–3.

"All Generations Shall Call Her Blessed." *Perspective Digest* 4.4 (1999): 49–51.

"The Breaker of Prophetic Silence (Let's Face It)." *Perspective Digest* 4.3 (1999): 57–58.

"Finding God (Let's Face It)." *Perspective Digest* 4.1 (1999): 58–60.

"Deep Breathing." *Adventist Review* 176.18 (May 6, 1999): 36–38.

"Prayers that Make One Shudder (Let's Face It)." *Perspective Digest* 3.4 (1998): 53–55.

A Time for Extravagant Love (Let's Face It)." *Perspective Digest* 3.3 (1998): 46–48.

"A Trip to Dark Gethsemane: The Ultimate Prayer (Let's Face It)," *Perspective Digest* 3.2 (1998): 71–73.

"A Pre-eminent Prayer Warrior (Let's Face It)." *Perspective Digest* 3.1 (1998): 52–55.

"The God Who Calls Again." *Adventist Review* 174.23 (June 12, 1997): 8–13.

"Something's Gonna Happen. . . When the People of the Lord Get Down To Pray. . . (Let's Face It)." *Perspective Digest* 2.4 (1997): 52–54.

"The Problematic Judgment on Eve (Let's Face It)." *Perspective Digest* 2.3 (1997): 53–55.

"The Genesis Narratives are Not Mere Tales for Children (Let's Face It)." *Perspective Digest* 2.2 (1997): 54–56.

"Sabbath is for Love." *Signs of the Times* (May 1997): electronic journal, https://signsofthetimes.org.au/2010/08/Sabbath-is-for-love/.

"Creating Sabbath Delight." Featured cover picture of Jo Ann Davidson and article/interview. *Women of Spirit* 3:3 (May/June 1997): 16–19.

"The Garden of Eden Has a Terrible Litter Problem. It Is Knee Deep in Our Prejudices and Preconceptions (Let's Face It)." *Perspective Digest* 2.1 (1996): 53-56.

"Why Me? My Gender Surely Figured Largely–and Rightly So: Women, As a Best-selling Author Points Out, Are From Venus, Men From Mars (Let's Face It)." *Perspective Digest* 1.3 (1996): 39–41.

ENCYCLOPEDIA ARTICLES

"Beauty." Pages 642–643 in *Ellen G. White Encyclopedia.* Edited by Denis Fortin and Jerry Moon. Hagerstown, MD: Review & Herald, 2013.

"Sabbath, Observance of." Pages 1118–1120 in *Ellen G. White Encyclopedia.* Edited by Denis Fortin and Jerry Moon. Hagerstown, MD: Review & Herald, 2013.

STUDY BIBLE COMMENTARY ARTICLES

"Women in the Bible: General Introduction." Page 15 in *Woman's Bible, NKJV*. Edited by SDA General Conference Women's Ministries Department and Editorial Safeliz. Madrid, Spain: Editorial Safeliz, 2014.

"Women in the Five Books of Moses." Pages 19–22 in *Woman's Bible, NKJV*. Edited by SDA General Conference Women's Ministries Department and Editorial Safeliz. Madrid, Spain: Editorial Safeliz, 2014.

"Women in the Time of the Judges." Pages 291–292 in *Woman's Bible, NKJV*. Edited by SDA General Conference Women's Ministries Department and Editorial Safeliz. Madrid, Spain: Editorial Safeliz, 2014.

"Women in the Historical Books." Pages 367–370 in *Woman's Bible, NKJV*. Edited by SDA General Conference Women's Ministries Department and Editorial Safeliz. Madrid, Spain: Editorial Safeliz, 2014.

"Women in Wisdom Literature." Page 666 in *Woman's Bible, NKJV*. Edited by SDA General Conference Women's Ministries Department and Editorial Safeliz. Madrid, Spain: Editorial Safeliz, 2014.

"Women in the Books of the Prophets." Page 874 in *Woman's Bible, NKJV*. Edited by SDA General Conference Women's Ministries Department and Editorial Safeliz. Madrid, Spain: Editorial Safeliz, 2014.

"Women in the Gospels." Pages 1211–1220 in *Woman's Bible, NKJV*. Edited by SDA General Conference Women's Ministries Department and Editorial Safeliz. Madrid, Spain: Editorial Safeliz, 2014.

"Women in the Book of Acts." Page 1389 in *Woman's Bible, NKJV*. Edited by SDA General Conference Women's Ministries Department and Editorial Safeliz. Madrid, Spain: Editorial Safeliz, 2014.

"Women in the Letters and Epistles." Pages 1438–1440 in *Woman's Bible, NKJV*. Edited by SDA General Conference Women's Ministries Department and Editorial Safeliz. Madrid, Spain: Editorial Safeliz, 2014.

"Women in the Apocalypse." Page 1582 in *Woman's Bible, NKJV*. Edited by SDA General Conference Women's Ministries Department and Editorial Safeliz. Madrid, Spain: Editorial Safeliz, 2014.

MANUALS/ACADEMIC ESSAYS/TREATISES

(Principal contributor), *Glimpses of Our God.* Adult Sabbath School Bible Study Guide for January–March 2012. Silver Spring, MD: General Conference of Seventh-day Adventists, 2012.

(Principal contributor), *Jonah: The Inside Story*. Adult Sabbath School Bible Study Guide for October–December 2003. Silver Spring, MD: General Conference of Seventh-day Adventists, 2003.

Proverbs. Adult Sabbath School/Bible Study Guide for January –March, 2015, Teachers Edition. Teachers Helps for Lessons 10-13. Silver Spring, MD: General Conference of Seventh-day Adventists, 2015.

RECORDINGS OR FILM PRODUCTIONS

"God as Presence in the Bible." Adventist Theological Society, *Life with God*, Season 2, Episode 8. April 15, 2021.

(with Kendra Arsenault). "Christianity and the Artist." *Advent Next* Podcast. December 5, 2019.

(with Kendra Arsenault). "Aesthetics: A Theology of Beauty." *Advent Next* Podcast. November 28, 2019.

Interview for 3ABN. November 8, 2018.

(with Teresa Reeve). "The Final Kingdom: Life as It Was Meant to Be, Forever." *Faith and Life*, Season 2, Hope Channel, Recorded May 3, 2018.

(with Ante Jerončić). "The World Is Ending: The Hope of the Second Coming." *Faith and Life*, Season 2. Hope Channel, Recorded May 2, 2018.

(Davidson, Jo Ann; Felix H. Cortez; E. Edward Zinke; Andrea Jakobsons). "God, The Father: God and Us: How Does Revelation and Inspiration Work? (Part 1)." *Faith and Life,* Season 1, program 2, Hope Channel, recorded August 21, 2017.

(Davidson, Jo Ann; Felix H. Cortez; E. Edward Zinke; Andrea Jakobsons). "God, The Father: God and Us: How Does Revelation and Inspiration Work? (Part 2)." *Faith and Life,* Season 1, program 3, Hope Channel, recorded August 21, 2017.

(Davidson, Jo Ann; Felix H. Cortez; Jiří Moskala; and Andrea Jakobsons). "The Law of God: The Sabbath: Rest and Reconnection. (Part 1)." *Faith and Life,* Season 1, program 24, Hope Channel, recorded August 22, 2017.

(Davidson, Jo Ann; Felix H. Cortez; Jiří Moskala; and Andrea Jakobsons). "The Law of God: The Sabbath: Rest and Reconnection. (Part 2)." *Faith and Life,* Season 1, program 25, Hope Channel, recorded August 22, 2017.

Filmed interview for HOPE CHANNEL/Brazil. July 26, 2017.

"World Religions and the Vegetarian Diet." Thirty-minute Interview on RADIO GASTROPOD, January, 2017.

"Stewardship." General Conference DVD on Stewardship, September 28, 2015.

"The God We Worship." Project Trinity, part 5. Andrews University Seminary Online Seminar, recorded May 28, 2013, published May 12, 2014.

Filmed interview for NAD Ordination Study Committee, April 15, 2013.

Filmed interview for NAD Ministerial e-magazine, February 26, 2013.

Interview with Dave Gemmell for Women Clergy Educational Resource, NAD production, September 25, 2012.

Live interview with Brad Thorp on Hope Channel's "Beginnings" program, April 4, 2012.

Filmed interview for documentary on the nature of man and hell, with Jim Wood of LLT Productions. Filmed at Andrews University, January 25, 2011.

"Creation." Radio interview on Hope Channel, October 20, 2010.

"The Sabbath." Radio interview by Phil Follett on LifeTalk Radio, Collegedale, TN, April 20, 2010.

"Aesthetics" and "Creation Care." Filmed interviews on Romanian National Television, June 29, 2009.

Interview for documentary on creation care. Filmed at Samford University, Beeson Divinity School, Birmingham, AL, March 5–6, 2009.

SCHOLARLY/PROFESSIONAL PAPERS READ

"Does the Psalmist Solve Paul? Psalm 119 as a Background to Romans 7." Paper presented at the Annual Meeting of the Evangelical Theological Society. Virtual, November 2020.

"Old Testament Law and Justice." Paper presented at the Law and Justice Conference, Atlanta, Georgia, September 27, 2019.

"Gospel and Queen: Esther's Christological Narrative Theology." Paper presented at the Annual Meeting of the Evangelical Theological Society. San Diego, CA, November 20, 2019.

"Joseph, Judah, and Jesus: Revisiting Genesis 37–50." Paper presented at the Annual Meeting of the Evangelical Theological Society. Denver, CO, November 13, 2018.

"Power or Person: Nature of the Holy Spirit." Paper presented at the Annual Meeting of the Evangelical Theological Society. San Antonio, TX, November 16, 2016.

"Aesthetics and Faith." Andrews Research Conference. Berrien Springs, MI, May 7, 2016.

"The Great Communicator: God is Not Silent." Keynote presentation to the Global Adventist Internet Network Conference. Washington, DC, February 26, 2016.

"Women Bear God's Image: Considerations from a Neglected Perspective." Paper presented at the Annual Meeting of the Adventist Theological Society. San Diego, CA, November 20, 2014.

"Dialogue Part1"; "Dialogue Part 2"; "God–Lover of the Beautiful"; "SON"; "God is Holy." Four papers presented at the Music, Worship, and Theology Seminar: "The Holiness of God." Manchester, UK, October 30–November 2, 2014.

"Seventh-day Adventists and Creation Care." Paper presented at the Stewardship Online Conference, Silver Spring, MD, September 19, 2014.

"Why I Believe the Bible"; "Authority of the Bible"; "Authority of Scripture II"; "Non-biblical Concepts of Scripture I"; "Non-biblical Concepts of Scripture II"; "A Biblical Basis for Environmental Care." Six Papers presented at the International Conference on the Bible & Science: Affirming Creation. St. George, UT: August 15–24, 2014.

"Word Made Flesh: The Authority of Scripture"; "Biblical Foundation to Aesthetics." Two papers presented at the Biblical Foundations of the Academic Disciplines Conference. Montemorelos University, Montemorelos, Mexico, January 14, 2014.

"The Word Speaks for Itself: Issues of Revelation and Inspiration." Paper presented at the Annual Meeting of the Evangelical Theological Society. Baltimore, MD, November 19, 2013.

"God's Care for His Creation." Celebration of Creation. Walla Walla, WA, November 9, 2013.

"For the Beauty of the Earth: A Pastoral Response to Climate Change." DMin Forum *Reflections on Christian Theology*. Berrien Springs, MI, November 6, 2013.

"Needed: A More 'Worldly' Attitude." Paper presented at the *Entrusted: Christians and Environmental Care* Conference. Loma Linda, CA, April 26, 2013.

"Abraham, Isaac and Akedah: The Atonement According to Moses." Paper presented at the Regional Meeting of the Adventist Theological Society. Loma Linda, CA, April 20, 2013.

"Creation Care and the Sabbath." Paper presented at the Annual Meeting of the Adventist Theological Society. Milwaukee, WI, November 14, 2012.

"Old Testament Women in Ministry" and "Biblical Matriarchs Engage Feminism." Two Papers presented at the University of Southern Caribbean Conference on Ordination Issues. Trinidad, West Indies, October 26, 2012.

"Authority of Scripture," "Non-Biblical Concepts of Scripture," and "Biblical Foundation to Aesthetics." Three papers presented at the Biblical Foundations Conference. Bloemfontein, South Africa, July 26–August 5, 2012.

"God is Three Persons: Blessed Trinity." Paper presented at the Plenary Session of the III Conferencia Bíblica–Trinidad. Montemorelos University, Montemorelos Mexico, July 4–7, 2012.

"The Human Nature of the Third Person of the Trinity in the Writings of Ellen White." Paper presented at the III Conferencia Bíblica—Trinidad. Montemorelos University, Montemorelos, Mexico, July 4–7, 2012.

"The Human Nature of Christ: Reflections by Ellen White." Paper presented at the Third International Bible Conference. Jerusalem, Israel, June 11–21, 2012.

"The Nature of the Holy Spirit." Paper presented at the South American Division Ministerial Council. Foz do Iguaçu, Brazil, May 21, 2011.

"Biblical Narratives: Their Beauty AND Truth." Paper presented at the Seminary Scholarship Symposium. Andrews University, Berrien Springs, MI, February 4, 2011.

"Believing the Creation Reveals God's Love." Paper presented at the Internationally-broadcasted Celebration of Creation. Andrews University, Berrien Springs, MI, October 23, 2010.

"Interpreting Biblical Narratives." Paper presented at the Professional Conference for Pastors of Spain and Portugal. Sagunto, Spain, September 10, 2010.

"And It WAS Good: Creation Care and the Christian." Paper presented at the "Yes, Creation!" Lecture Series of the General Conference of Seventh-day Adventists. Atlanta, GA, June 29, 2010.

"Needed: A More Worldly Attitude." Paper presented at the Southern Adventist University "Earth Day." Collegedale, TN, April 22, 2010.

"Artistic Nature of God." Paper presented at the Andrews University Creative Arts Festival. Berrien Springs, MI, March 3, 2010.

"The Sabbath and Environmental Ethics." Paper presented at the Seminary Scholarship Symposium. Andrews University, Berrien Springs, MI, February 5, 2010.

"The Sabbath and Environmental Ethics." Paper presented at the Annual Meeting of the Evangelical Theological Society. New Orleans, LA, November 19, 2009.

"Sabbath, a Day of Delight." Paper presented at the Adventist Military Chaplains National Convention. Berrien Springs, MI, Andrews University, June 4, 2009.

"Ellen White and Environmental Ethics." Paper presented at the Ellen White and Current Issues Symposium. Andrews University, Berrien Springs, MI, April 6, 2009.

"A Theology of Beauty." Paper presented to the Music and Worship Conference plenary session. Andrews University, Berrien Springs, March 27, 2009.

"Creation Care and the Christian." Paper presented to the Student Chapel of Samford University. Birmingham, AL, March 5, 2009.

"Joy of the Judgment: A Canonical Study." Paper presented to the Annual Seminary Scholarship Symposium. Andrews University, Berrien Springs, MI, February 6, 2009.

"Joy of the Judgment: A Canonical Study." Paper presented to the Annual Meeting of the Evangelical Theological Society. Providence, RI, November 20, 2008.

"Jonah: Passionate Preacher." Paper presented to the General Conference Annual Ministry Seminar. Walla Walla University, Walla Walla, WA, April 22, 2008.

"Sabbath and Ecology." Paper presented to the Biblical Research Institute Committee of the General Conference. Loma Linda, CA, April 14, 2008.

"Creation Care and the Christian." Paper presented to the Doctoral Colloquium. Andrews University, Berrien Springs, MI, March 27, 2008.

"The Law is Not Jewish: Indicators from the Book of Genesis." Paper presented to the Annual Seminary Scholarship Symposium. Andrews University, Berrien Springs, MI, Andrews University, February 5, 2008.

"The Law is Not Jewish: Indicators from the Book of Genesis." Paper presented to the Annual Meeting of the Evangelical Theological Society. San Diego, CA, November 15, 2007.

"Creator, Creation and Church: Restoring Ecology to Theology." Paper presented to the Annual Seminary Scholarship Symposium. Andrews University, Berrien Springs, MI, February 8–9, 2007.

"Creator, Creation, and Church: Restoring Ecology to Theology." Paper presented to the Annual Meeting of the Evangelical Theological Society. Washington, DC, November 15, 2006.

"The Well Women of Scripture Revisited." Paper presented at the Annual Seminary Scholarship Symposium. Andrews University, Berrien Springs, MI, February 3, 2006.

"Gott gebraucht Menschen." Paper presented at the International Bible Study Conference. Bogenhofen, Austria, July 25, 2005.

"The Well Women of Scripture Revisited." Paper presented at the Annual Wheaton Theology Conference. Wheaton College, Wheaton, IL, April 7, 2005.

"Truth is Beauty, and Beauty is Truth, with Apologies to Yeats." Paper presented at the SDA Theological Seminary Scholarship Fair. Andrews University, Berrien Springs, MI, February 4, 2005.

"Truth is Beauty and Beauty is Truth, with Apologies to Yeats." Paper presented at the Annual Meeting of the Evangelical Theological Society. San Antonio, TX, November 18, 2004.

"The Atonement According to Moses." Paper presented at the Seventh South-American Biblical-Theological Symposium. Lima, Peru, July, 2004.

"The Word and His Word." Paper presented at the Annual Meeting of the Adventist Theological Society. Atlanta, GA, November 2003.

"The Inspiration of Scripture." Paper presented at the meeting of the Midwest Region of the Adventist Theological Society. Eau Claire, MI, November 2003.

"Word Made Flesh: The Inspiration of Scripture." Paper presented at the NAD Faith and Science Conference. Glacier View, CO, August 2003.

"World Religions and Vegetarian Diet." Paper presented at the Annual Meeting of the Adventist Theological Society. Toronto, Canada, November 22, 2002.

"The Prophet Jonah and the Gospel." Paper presented at the meeting of the Midwest Chapter of the Evangelical Theological Society. Wheaton College, Wheaton, IL, March 22, 2002.

"Issues in Biblical Narratives: The Woman at the Well (John 4)." Paper presented at the Annual Meeting of the Evangelical Theological Society. Colorado Springs, CO, November 14, 2001.

"Toward a Theology of Beauty: A Biblical Aesthetic." Paper presented at the Annual Meeting of the Evangelical Theological Society. Nashville, TN, November 16, 2000.

"Eschatology in Genesis 22." Paper presented at the Annual Meeting of the Evangelical Theological Society. Danvers, MA, November 17, 1999.

"Biblical Sarah and Rebecca Engage Feminism." Paper presented at the Annual Meeting of the Evangelical Theological Society. Orlando, Florida, November, 1998.

"Biblical Matriarchs and Feminism." Paper presented at the meeting of the Midwest Chapter of the Society of Biblical Literature. Milwaukee, WI, Spring, 1997.

"The Mission of the Church." Paper presented as a Plenary Address at the 1996 Annual Council General Conference Message and Mission Commission. Alajuela, Costa Rica, 1996.

Part 1:
Beauty in Narrative and Literary Analysis

When Jephthah's Daughter Spoke

Mathilde Frey

Abstract

This essay analyzes the somber story of Jephthah's daughter, focusing on the rhetoric and structure of the dialogue between father and daughter in Judg 11:34–40. The study further engages linguistic and contextual elements from other parts of the Hebrew Bible, such as Gen 22 and Exod 19, and thereby explores possibilities for intertextual readings as well as theological interpretations that go beyond the traditional. As a young woman who lives in a world of patriarchal power and oppression, the speeches of Jephthah's daughter show that she rejects the notion of being remembered as a victim to her father's vow. Her words unequivocally reveal her own assessment of the vow and her consciousness about her victimhood, yet she expresses agency in her own experience as a sacrifice of burnt offering. In speaking her own words, she destabilizes the patriarchal power structures of her world, and opens ways for the reader to hear those who have been silenced throughout history.[1]

Introduction

Between Jephthah's unsuccessful diplomacy message to the king of Ammon (Judg 11:12–28) and his successful battle (11:29, 32, 33) is Jephthah's vow to the Lord, "If You will indeed give the sons of Ammon into my hand, then it shall be that whatever comes out of the doors of my house to meet me when I return in peace from the sons of Ammon, it shall be the Lord's, and I will offer it up as a burnt offering" (11:30–31). Commentators have noted that these verses are some of the most controversial and debated in the Hebrew Bible. Some see a similarity between Jephthah, who persuades God to be with him in the battle against the Ammonites, and Barak who refused to lead the battle without Deborah going with him (Judg 4:6–9).

---

[1] It is my pleasure to contribute to this Festschrift honoring Jo Ann Davidson, whom I admire for her dedication to the aesthetic value of the Bible's narratives, poetry, and literary structures. Her enthusiasm in re-telling the ancient stories of the Sabbath and celebrating its beauty is a memory I will always cherish from my time at Andrews University.

There was also Gideon who tested God before agreeing to go to battle (Judg 6: 36–40). In his vow Jephthah bargained with God to give him victory over the Ammonites. He was on a dangerous mission and seems to think of the vow as an act of devotion to gain divine assurance and victory. Butler, in his commentary on the book of Judges, interprets Jephthah's vow making as an act of faith, "In the face of war with the Ammonites, Jephthah decides he needs more than faith."[2]

A vow (*neder*) in the Hebrew Bible and the surrounding Near Eastern world was a formal and solemn statement in which the speaker promised to give something to the deity or perform a certain act if the deity would act in favor of the petitioner.[3] Vow-making is widely present in the Hebrew Bible.[4] The seriousness of a vow is stated as follows, "When you make a vow to the Lord your God, you shall not delay to pay it, for it would be sin in you, and the Lord your God will surely require it of you" (Deut 23:21[22], NASB). One of the most prominent vows is in Hannah's prayer for a son with the promise to "give him to the Lord all the days of his life" (1 Sam 1:11) as a Nazarite. Hannah fulfilled her vow after Samuel was weaned but still very young and brought him to the sanctuary in

---

[2] Trent C. Butler, *Judges* (Vol. 8, WBC; Grand Rapids, MI: Zondervan, 2006), 287.

[3] O. Kaiser, "נָדַר *nadar*; נֶדֶר *neder*," in *Theological Dictionary of the Old Testament*, ed. G. Johannes Botterweck, Helmer Ringgren, and Heinz-Josef Fabry; (Grand Rapids, MI: Eerdmans, 2015), 9:244. Edwin M. Yamauchi and Marvin R. Wilson, *Dictionary of Daily Life: In Biblical and Post-Biblical Antiquity* (Peabody, MA: Hendrickson, 2017), 1329–41.

[4] See the vow in the account of Jacob (Gen 28:20–22; 31:13); in the Nazarite law (Num 6:1–21); in laws where the object of a vow is a human being claimed by monetary redemption (Lev 27:2–8); in vows where the object is an animal (Lev 7:16; 22:18, 21, 23; 23:38; 27:9–13; Num 15:3, 8; 29:39; Deut 12:6, 11, 17, 26; 23:18[19]), or a house or field (Lev 27:14–25); in a vow with a personal matter of a man (Num 30:2), and a personal matter of a woman (Num 30:3–15); in Israel's battle account against the Canaanites (Num 21:2); in the prayer of Hannah (1 Sam 1:11); and in the story of Absalom (2 Sam 15:7–8). The prophetic books of Isaiah (19:21), Jeremiah (44:24–25), Nahum 1:15[2:1], Jonah (1:16; 2:2), and Malachi (1:14) speak of vows made to God and other deities. Vows are integral to the Psalms (22:25 [26]; 50:14; 56:12 [13]; 61:5 [6], 8 [9]; 65:1 [2]; 66:13; 116:14, 18), and have a place in the wisdom literature in Proverbs (17:14; 20:25), Job (22:27) and Qohelet (5:4–5[3–4]).

Shiloh, where he served for all his life (1 Sam 1:24–28). Nevertheless, the Hebrew Bible contains one narrative where the fulfillment of an oath is prevented in order to spare the life of the king's son even though he was guilty (1 Sam 14:1–45). Saul, who considered it a sin to neglect his oath that he had imposed on his army (14:24), was ready to kill his son Jonathan (14:38–39, 43–44). But because the people intervened, Jonathan was spared, "the people rescued Jonathan, and he did not die" (14:45). Likewise, in texts of the ancient Near East, vows were made in times of crisis. They needed to be fulfilled, otherwise the gods would be angry and cause disaster on those who failed to obey.[5] The Ugaritic epic of King Keret (circa 1500–1200 BCE) contains a vow that remained unfulfilled and was followed by disaster on the king's family.[6]

A vow in the Hebrew Bible typically consists of a petition, a condition, and the promise.[7] The formulation of the vow has a protasis starting with the preposition "if" (Hebrew *'im*) and concluding with an apodosis in a promise in the sense of, "if you will do or give this to me, I will do or give this to you." Jacob's vow in Gen 28:20–21 (NASB) is a good example of the language and structure of a vow:

> If God will be with me
> and will keep me on this journey that I take,
> and will give me food to eat and garments to wear,

---

[5] Notable studies on vows in the Hebrew Bible and the ancient Near East include Alfred Wendel, *Das Israelitisch-Jüdische Gelübde* (Berlin: Philo-Verlag, 1931); Simon B. Parker, "The Vow in Ugaritic and Israelite Narrative Literature," in *Ugarit Forschungen* 11 (1979): 693–700; Tony W. Cartledge, *Vows in the Hebrew Bible and the Ancient Near East* (Journal for the Study of the Old Testament Supplement Series 147; Sheffield: JSOT Press, 1992). Some see parallels to Jephthah's vow in Greek literature. See A. C. Pearson, "Vows (Greek and Roman)" in *Encyclopedia of Religion and Ethics* 12 (Edinburgh: Bloomsbury T&T Clark, 2000), 641–43.

[6] Samuel Henry Hooke, *Middle Eastern Mythology* (Mineola, NY: Dover, 2004), 87–89; Cyrus H. Gordon, "Notes on the Legend of Keret," *Journal of Near Eastern Studies* 11/3 (1952): 212–13; Baruch Margalit, "The Legend of Keret," in *Handbook of Ugaritic Studies*, ed. Wilfried G. E. Watson and Nicolas Wyatt (Leiden: Brill, 1999), 203–33.

[7] Jack M. Sasson, *Judges 1–12*, The Anchor Yale Bible 6D (London: Yale University Press, 2014), 436.

and I return to my father's house in safety,
then the LORD will be my God.

Jephthah's Vow

"Jephthah made a vow to the Lord and said, 'If You will indeed give the sons of Ammon into my hand, then it shall be that whatever comes out of the doors of my house to meet me when I return in peace from the sons of Ammon, it shall be the Lord's, and I will offer it up as a burnt offering'" (Judg 11:30–31, NASB).

Jephthah's vow has been studied for its ambiguity in language in reference to the unidentified individual coming out of his house, in effect leaving it to the Lord to choose who should come out of his house.[8] Commentators hold that it was entirely possible for an animal to come out of the house and meet Jephthah.[9] The fact that archaeologists have uncovered some early Israelite domestic structures such as the four-room house, which included rooms for animals on the ground floor, seems to allow for a sheep or calf to get out of the animal enclosure if the door was left open.[10] Others have argued against the possibility of having an animal included in the vow based on the language, "whoever goes out of the doors of my

---

[8] David Marcus, *Jephthah and His Vow* (Lubbock: Texas Tech, 1986), 55. See also the extensive discussion on this part in Butler, *Judges*, 287–290.

[9] Robert G. Boling, *Judges* (The Anchor Bible; New York: Doubleday, 1975), 170; Terry L. Brensinger, *Judges*, Believers Church Bible Commentary (Scottdale, PA: Herald, 1999), 133; K. Lawson Younger, *Judges, Ruth*, The NIV Application Commentary (Grand Rapids, MI: Zondervan, 2020), 263; Roy Gane, *God's Faulty Heroes* (Hagerstown, MD: Review and Herald, 1996), 91.

[10] Gane, *God's Faulty Heroes*, 91; Ehud Netzer, "Domestic Architecture in the Iron Age," in *The Architecture of Ancient Israel: From the Prehistoric to the Persian Periods* (ed. Aharon Kempinski and Ronni Reich; Jerusalem: Israel Exploration Society, 1992), 193–201; Yigal Shiloh, "The Casemate Wall, the Four-Room House, and Early Planning in the Israelite City," *Bulletin of the American Schools of Oriental Research* 268 (1987): 3–15; Shlomo Bunimovitz and Avraham Faust, "The Four Room House: Embodying Iron Age Israelite Society," in *Near Eastern Archaeology* (Vol. 66; Atlanta, GA: Scholars Press, 2003), 22–31.

house to meet me,"[11] which seems to apply to a human member of Jephthah's household and could include a slave.[12]

After the vow is spoken, the following section in Judg 11:32–33 seems to imply that Jephthah's victory over the Ammonites is because God kept His part of the bargain.[13] Jephthah's military campaign crushed down on the Ammonites and took over the area from Aroer to Minnith and Abel-keramim, twenty cities. The text describes the battle in rather broad strokes without giving attention to details of the battle, but instead pointing to the outcome, "The sons of Ammon were subdued before the sons of Israel" (v. 33). Indeed, the book of Judges is not interested in the details of battle but in the stories of the leaders, how they were chosen, how they gained power, how they acted while in charge, and how they used their power.[14]

Jephthah's Daughter

Jephthah's daughter leaps into the story without any prior announcement. Nothing is said about her or her mother, and there is no name for her in the biblical text.[15] It is noteworthy how she is introduced: "Behold, his daughter coming out to meet him, with tambourines and dancing." The use of the emphatic Hebrew word *hinneh,* usually translated "behold," is followed directly by the subject, "his daughter" who is doing the very acts pledged for as "burnt offering," namely, "coming out (*yatsa'*) . . . to meet (*qara'*)

---

[11] Mieke Bal, *Death and Dissymmetry: The Politics of Coherence in the Book of Judges* (Chicago, IL: University of Chicago Press, 1988), 45; Sasson, *Judges 1–12*, 438–449.

[12] Dale S. DeWitt, "The Jephthah Traditions: A Rhetorical and Literary Study in the Deuteronomistic History" (PhD diss., Andrews University, 1987), 217.

[13] Gane, *God's Faulty Heroes*, 92.

[14] Tammy J. Schneider, *Judges*, Berit Olam: Studies in Hebrew Narrative and Poetry (Collegeville, MN: The Liturgical Press, 1999), 176.

[15] In Pseudo-Philo, Jephthah's daughter is named Seila, and her story is elaborated. See Philip S. Alexander, "Retelling the Old Testament," in *It Is Written: Scripture Citing Scripture,* ed. D. A. Carson and H. G. M. Williamson (Cambridge: Cambridge University Press, 1988); Frederick Murphy, *Pseudo-Philo: Rewriting the Bible* (New York, NY: Oxford, 1993); Pieter Van der Horst, "Portraits of Biblical Women in Pseudo-Philo's *Liber Antiquitatum Biblicarum,*" *Journal for the Study of Pseudepigrapha* 5 (1989): 29–46.

me" (Judg 11:31). Jephthah watched as "his daughter came out (*yatsa'*) to meet (*qara'*) him" (11:34). What was thought of as ambiguity in the vow, now turns into tragedy before the father's eyes. His daughter is the "burnt offering."

Commentators have often emphasized the image of a single woman with an instrument in her hand dancing toward her father all alone.[16] Jack M. Sasson argues that this is not what the biblical text and custom portray.[17] The Hebrew word for tambourines is plural, referring to handheld percussion instruments associated with dancing according to the custom of women who greet the men on their victorious return from war (1 Sam 18:6). The instruments were likely smaller drums without metal jingles. They consisted of a piece of goatskin leather stretched over a circular wood frame of about twenty-five centimeters (10 inches). The tambourines were held in one hand and struck with the other to make a beat and accompany string and wind instruments like the *kinnor*.[18] One person would hold only one tambourine in their hand. Exodus 15:20–21 describes how Miriam took the tambourine and the rest of the women followed with their tambourines and joined the group dance, responding to the beat of drums and the music of other instruments. A similar description is given in 1 Sam 18:6 on the festive atmosphere and large triumphal procession greeting and celebrating David, the hero, who returned from a military victory. When read with this context in mind the Mizpah greeting party of one would be a poor welcome for Jephthah on the celebration of his heroic victory over the Ammonites. "In contrast, the point of having a large party moving out of the compound is to accentuate the oddity of Jephthah fixing his sight just on his daughter when she was joined by other celebrants."[19]

The crucial information about the daughter's relation to her father is told in two ways in Judg 11:34. First, the narrative shows that she is his only child, literally "only she, an only one." In its parallel occurrence in Gen 22, the expression "an only one"

---

[16] Daniel I. Block, *Judges, Ruth*, New American Commentary 6 (Nashville, TN: Broadman & Holman, 1999), 371; Phyllis Trible, *Texts of Terror: Literary-Feminist Readings of Biblical Narratives*, Overture to Biblical Theology (Philadelphia, PA: Fortress, 1984), 101.

[17] Sasson, *Judges 1–12*, 439.

[18] See Carol Meyers, "Of Drums and Damsels: Women's Performance in Ancient Israel," *Biblical Archaeologist* 54/1 (1991): 16–27.

[19] Sasson, *Judges 1–12*, 439.

(*yehidah*) tells of Isaac not just as a single son of Abraham but as his father's "only one who you love" (Gen 22:2, 12, 16).[20] In Isaac's relationship to Abraham, singularity is qualified by love. In Jephthah's relationship with his daughter, love is not part of the recounted story. Instead, one learns about the father–daughter relationship from another angle, "beside her he had no son nor daughter," or in a more accurate phrasing, "of himself he had no one, son or daughter." The daughter who greeted him as a hero was all he had to secure offspring and ensure the future of his house. Over the course of the following events in Jephthah's story, his life will be portrayed in isolation and without offspring to carry his memory into the future. This is Jephthah's tragedy.[21]

Jephthah's Shocking Decision

Jephthah tore his garments as he recognized his daughter (Judg 11:35).[22] At the same time he shouted, "Alas, my daughter!" The immensity of his vow strikes him. The English interjection "Alas," which most often expresses regret or sadness, is not adequate to convey the depth of his agony. The accented Hebrew *'ahah* echoes in a long scream and is an onomatopoeic cry of distress,[23] "a guttural ejaculation which is here better transliterated than translated," so Boling.[24] Furthermore, twelve out of fifteen occurrences of the similar expressions of shock in the Hebrew Bible either explicitly or implicitly reference the "Lord God,"[25] such as Gideon being surprised when he recognized the Lord in the angel at the altar (Judg

---

[20] The Hebrew *yehidah* is used as a noun, not as an adjective, and "has to do with favoritism and love rather than singularity." See, Sasson, *Judges 1–12*, 439, and 531, note 16 pointing to Arnold B. Ehrlich, *Randglossen zur Hebräischen Bibel; Textkritisches, Sprachliches und Sachliches: Josua, Richter, I. u. II. Samuelis* (Vol 3; Hildesheim: Georg Olms Verlagsbuchhandlung, 1968), 121.

[21] Deborah W. Rooke, *Handel's Israelite Oratorio Libretti: Sacred Drama and Biblical Exegesis* (Oxford: Oxford University Press, 2012), 2008.

[22] This act is usually done in a tragic situation and in mourning (cf., Gen 37:29, 34; 2 Sam 1:2; 13:19).

[23] Sasson, *Judges 1–12*, 439.

[24] Boling, *Judges*, 208.

[25] Josh 7:7; Judg 6:22; 2 Kgs 3:10; Jer 1:6; 4:10; 14:13; 32:17; Ezek 4:14; 9:8; 11:13; 21:5; Joel 1:15.

6:22). For this reason, "*'ahah*, my daughter!" should be recognized as Jephthah's jolting AHA! moment that his only child is indeed the "burnt offering" he had pledged to the Lord.

Jephthah's subsequent words are filled with charges against his daughter, "You have truly brought me down to my knees" (Judg 11:35; my translation). The sentence emphasizes the action by doubling the verb *kara'* ("to bow down," "bend one's knee," "break down," "sink to the ground") in a causative verbal expression.[26] The intense use of language describes Jephthah's desolate feeling with the imagery of an animal that is forced into submission by bending its knees, lowering its legs, and sinking to the ground.[27] In effect, the father placed the blame for his calamity on his daughter. He then added to that a second accusation directly pointing at her, "you, you are among those who trouble me" (my translation). With the independent personal pronoun "you" (*'att*) he aimed at his daughter in the sense of pointing his finger at her. He repeated the "you" with the verb, "you are," making her out as one who joined those who ruin his life ("troublemakers," Hebrew *'achar* for "trouble," "calamity," "disaster," "ruin").[28] For the Hebrew audience, the intensity of the encounter is cast into a prominent play on words that prepares the audience for the father's long distressing exclamation: *'ahah* surrounded by words with the gutturals *k* and *r* which echo the *'ahah* in each of the following words with *k*, *ch*, and *r*, "When he saw her [*kiroto*; preposition *ki* is prefixed to the verb *ra'ah*], he tore [*yikrah*] his clothes and said, 'Ah [*'ahah*], my daughter! You, you have truly brought me down to my knees [*hachrea' hich'rati*], you are among those who trouble me [*'ochra*]'." If Jephthah was shocked to see his daughter, his aggressive accusations surely must have shocked her.

Jephthah concludes his speech, "I, I have opened my mouth to the Lord, and I cannot turn back" (my translation). Would it be a stretch to observe here that Jephthah, after he has cast the

---

[26] Ludwig Koehler and Walter Baumgartner, *Hebrew and Aramaic Lexicon of the Old Testament* (Leiden: Brill, 2001), 499. In Judg 11:35, the first use of the verb *kara'* is a Hiphil infinitive absolute and then followed by the same verb in a perfect tense.

[27] H. Eising, כָּרַע *kara'*, *Theological Dictionary of the Old Testament* 7:337.

[28] *HALOT*, 824; Mosis, עָכַר *'akar*, *TDOT* 11: 67–71.

daughter/woman with the adversary, he places himself, the man/father, unto the side of God? Again, a Hebrew audience would be well aware that opening one's mouth is not how one makes a vow to the Lord. Such an expression occurs only in the case of Jephthah. When one "opens the mouth" the circumstances often tell of distress, destruction, and death. The earth opened its mouth to receive Abel's blood (Gen 4:11) and to swallow the rebels among the Israelite tribes (Num 16:30–35; Deut 11:6). In poetic texts, those who open their mouth are enemies who threaten the life of the faithful (Ps 22:13[14]; Lam 2:16; 3:46).

Robert Alter has noted a crucial pun in Jephthah's language between the expression "I, I have opened (*patsah*) my mouth" and his name *yiftah* in Hebrew, which is based on the verb, *patah*, "he opens," which is a verb close in semantics and phonetics to *patsah*.[29] The irony is in his own words that have trapped him in the high-stakes negotiations of a vow to the Lord. Moses states in Deuteronomy that "If you refrain from vowing, it would not be sin in you. You shall be careful to perform what goes out from your lips, just as you have voluntarily vowed to the Lord your God, what you have promised" (Deut 23:22–23). The consequence of the father's open mouth is a threat to his daughter's life.

Was there truly no possibility for Jephthah to turn back on his vow? A significant instruction about a vow (*neder*), especially one that is made in a crisis situation, is found in Lev 27:2–8. Here, the promise or object of the vow is a human being, male or female. The text gives instruction how such a person who is pledged to God could be reclaimed. A fixed monetary value system was in place with details on gender and age and could be used to redeem the pledged individual. The value of a male between twenty and sixty years of age was fifty shekels, and a female of the same age group was thirty shekels; a male between five and twenty years was twenty shekels, and a female ten shekels; a male between one month and five years was five shekels, and a female three shekels; a male above sixty years of age was fifteen shekels, and a female ten shekels. Gane notes regarding this law, that "rather than human sacrifice (cf. Judg 11:30–31, 35–36, 39) or lifelong service at the sanctuary (1 Sam 1:11, 24–28; 2:11), the Lord will receive what amounts to a

[29] Robert Alter, *The Hebrew Bible: A Translation with Commentary* (New York, NY: W. W. Norton & Company, 2019), 125 (see note 35).

redemption price corresponding to the valuation of an individual."[30] Furthermore, Gane notes that Lev 27 also provides a solution for people who were pledged as sanctuary servants, but could not be put to service because there was not sufficient work for them. The law would then allow to exchange the pledged individual by giving redemption money to the sanctuary according to the fixed scale.[31] In light of this law, Jephthah would have had the possibility to redeem his daughter by paying the fixed amount according to her age to the sanctuary.

Connections with Mount Moriah

The daughter responds, "My father!" (Judg 11:36). The Hebrew vocative *'avi* echoes Isaac's voice when he interrupted the three-day silence on the journey with his father to the top of Mount Moriah. But then, note the differences between Moriah and Mizpah:

- On Mount Moriah, the father comforted the son, "Here I am, my son" (Gen 22:7).
- In the streets of Mizpah, the father does not offer his presence as comfort for his daughter.
- On Mount Moriah, the son trusts the father with his questions, "Behold, the fire and the wood, but where is the lamb for the burnt offering?" (Gen 22:7).
- In Mizpah, a daughter does not ask questions.
- On Mount Moriah, life and death is in the realm of God, "Abraham said, 'God will provide for Himself the lamb for the burnt offering, my son'" (Gen 22:8).
- In Mizpah, the daughter is fully aware that her life depended on the father's word, "So she said to him, 'My father, you have given your word to the Lord; do to me as you have said'" (Judg 11:36).
- On Mount Moriah, "the two of them walked together" (Gen 22:8).
- In Mizpah, the father "sent her away" (Judg 11:38).

[30] Roy Gane, *Leviticus, Numbers*, The NIV Application Commentary (Grand Rapids, MI: Zondervan, 2004), 464–68.

[31] Ibid., 469.

- On Mount Moriah, the angel of the Lord called from heaven, "Do not stretch out your hand against the lad, and do nothing to him" (Gen 22:12).
- In Mizpah, "her father did to her according to the vow which he had made" (Judg 11:39).[32]

With the sound of the tambourines coming to a shrill end the daughter's response to the father captures his arrogant and hasty vow and places his self-inflicted compulsion into the center of her speech. Note the stream of consciousness in her response as she picks up her father's words about opening his mouth to the Lord and then letting the audience in on her thought processes about the consequence of his vow and why he will have to execute what he has promised (Judg 11:36, my translation).[33]

My father!
You have opened your mouth to the Lord;
do to me as has come out from your mouth;
after the Lord has done for you vengeance from your enemies, from the sons of Ammon.

Unlike Isaac, Jephthah's daughter did not question her father nor hesitate about the consequences of his vow, especially as she recognized his pledge in the context of what God had done for him. This has given reason to characterize her as a "paragon of faithfulness"[34] even in the face of death, and one who is loyal to the standards of the Israelite covenant community.[35]

---

[32] See the exposition on Abraham and Jephthah in Søren Kierkegaard, *Fear and Trembling*, trans. Alastair Hannai (London: Penguin Books, 1985), 54–67.

[33] About "stream of consciousness" as a literary device, see Virginia Woolf, "Modern Fiction" in *The Essays of Virginia Woolf: Volume 4 1925–1928*, ed. Andrew McNeille (Orlando, FL: Houghton Mifflin Harcourt, 2008); William James, *The Principles of Psychology* (Vols. 1-2; Pantianos Classics; Cambridge, MA: Harvard University Press, 1983).

[34] Susan Ackerman, *Warrior, Dancer, Seductress, Queen: Women in Judges and Ancient Israel* (The Anchor Bible Reference Library; New York, NY: Doubleday, 1998), 110.

[35] J. A. Hackett, "In the Days of Jael: Reclaiming the History of Women in Ancient Israel" in *Immaculate and Powerful: The Female in*

The Daughter's Speech

Nonetheless, it is important to pay close attention to the daughter's spoken and unspoken words. First, she addressed him with an affectionate "my father" after he had just thrown a double-dosed onslaught and embraced him in her greeting with deep understanding for his agony. Such affection must have torn a hole in Jephthah's heart, especially after his attacks on her. The narrative does not portray him as a man who had experienced tenderness and love in his past life. Quite the opposite, as the son of a prostitute, his stepbrothers had rejected him. He fled from home and lived with "worthless fellows" (Judg 11:1–3). The people who made him their ruler hated him (vv. 6–11). The Ammonites were his greatest threat (vv. 12–28). "My father" may be the only expression of sympathy Jephthah ever received.

Even so, the daughter's affection toward her father should not be interpreted as capitulation to the inevitable. There is boldness in the young woman's reply when she speaks her father's words back to him.

> "I, I have opened my mouth to the Lord" (Judg 11:35)
> "You have opened your mouth to the Lord" (Judg 11:36)

It "tells us much about her knowledge of her father that she grasps at once that he had bargained something precious for his victory."[36] In addition, the father's words mirrored back to him reveal nothing less than his own peril (see above on the meaning of the expression "open mouth" in Judg 11:35; cf. Ps 22:14; 144:11; Lam 2:16; 3:46). In our time a person who "opens their mouth" would be considered foolish and labeled a "big mouth." In the biblical context one who opens his mouth is a threat and an enemy to God's faithful people. In effect, Jephthah became his own threat and enemy.

Sacred Image and Social Reality, eds. C. W. Atkinson, C. H. Buchanan, and M. R. Miles (Boston, MA: Beacon, 1985), 30; J. A. Hackett, "Women's Studies and the Hebrew Bible" in *The Future of Biblical Studies:The Hebrew Scriptures*, eds. R. E. Friedman and H. G. M. Williamson (Atlanta, GA: Scholars Press, 1987), 159.

[36] Sasson, *Judges 1–12*, 440.

The focus of the daughter's speech is forcefully direct, "Do to me as it came out from your mouth." Her appeal is without hesitation in an imperative voice, "Do to me!" (*'aseh li*). She holds her father to his vow not out of submissiveness, but because, "The young woman understands well. She knows that 'death and life are in the power of the tongue' (Prov. 18:21)."[37] And, it was her father who had spoken the word. The portrayal of the daughter as one who simply consents out of an overwhelming respect for a vow made to God, or who just accepts her fate and encourages her father to carry out the vow, misses the powerful expressions and deep insights her speech conveys. Sasson's interpretive question, "What, in fact, is there for an unmarried daughter to say when learning that both her father and her God had agreed to make her the price for her people's victory?," does not quite capture the assertiveness she shows in her speech. As a young woman keenly aware of her father's difficult circumstances, the daughter speaks loudly in a world of patriarchal dominance. If there is restraint in her words, there surely is subversive rebuke against the status quo of male-controlled authority.[38]

In her last line, the daughter sets the record straight about who Jephthah's real troublemaker or enemy is—the Ammonites; not her. She completely disregards his allegations against her and in turn instructs her father in a remedial statement of conviction about the place and role of God in the entire story, "the Lord has executed vengeance for you against your enemies." Sasson recognizes in the Hebrew noun *neqamot* ("vengeance" or "retribution") a "plural of amplification."[39] Boling argues for the meaning of "deliverance" or "salvation" instead of vengeance following Mendenhall's important study on the Hebrew word *naqam*,[40] in this case, which would then translate the daughter's words as, "the Lord has done deliverance for

---

[37] Trible, *Texts of Terror*, 103.

[38] Sasson, *Judges 1–12*, 448. See especially the excellent article by Katerina Koci, "Whose Story? Which Sacrifice? On the Story of Jephthah's Daughter," *Open Theology*, 7/1 (2021): 331–344. Retrieved from https://doi.org/10.1515 /opth-2020-0167 on 30 October 2023.

[39] Sasson, *Judges 1–12*, 440; E. Kautzsch, ed., *Gesenius' Hebrew Grammar* (Oxford: Clarendon Press, 1909), 398.

[40] George E. Mendenhall, "The Vengeance of Yahweh" in *The Tenth Generation* (Baltimore, MD: Johns Hopkins University Press, 1973), 69–104.

you from your enemies."[41] The reason for the notion of deliverance is based on the fact that God is the agent who acts on behalf of His covenant to deliver His people. In the covenant context between God and Israel, the Hebrew words *naqam* and *neqamah* do not carry the notion of vindictiveness, as a human action would, but they speak of God's attribute of divine justice in view of His redemptive and restorative purposes for His people.[42] When God comes with *naqam*, His reward is salvation (e.g., Isa 35:4), and the day of His *naqam* brings comfort to the people who mourn (e.g., Isa 61:2).

Jephthah's daughter speaks a second time, "She said to her father, 'Let this thing be done for me; let me alone two months, that I may go to the mountains and weep because of my virginity, I and my companions'" (Judg 11:37, NASB). This second speech counters the father's vow in Judg 11:30–31. It is important to note that, as the father made a pledge to Yahweh and expressed his wish, the daughter expressed her will to her father, not as a formal vow but in words that may challenge and undermine, if not invalidate, her father's vow. She starts out in a passive but firm voice, presses forward with an imperative, and continues in a crescendo of self-determination that will reverberate in the lamentations of sisterhood recurring yearly on top of the mountains (Judg 11:39, 40).

"Let this word/thing be done to me," she requests (*ye'aseh li hadavar hazeh*, Nifal with jussive meaning). What is this word/thing? A series of tragic events actually:

You let me alone for two months (*harpeh mimennih*, Hifil imperative)
And I will go (*ve'elkhah*, Qal cohortative)
And I will descend upon the mountains (*veyaradti al-heharim*, Qal perfect)
And I will weep upon my virginity (*ve'evkeh al-betulay*, Qal cohortative)
I and my companions

[41] Boling, *Judges*, 209.

[42] Joel Nobel Musvosvi, "The Concept of Vengeance in the Book of Revelation in its Old Testament and Near Eastern Context" (PhD diss.; Andrews University, 1986). Cf. Ken Brown, "Vengeance and Vindication in Numbers 31," *JBL* 134/1 (2015): 65–84.

The imperative, "you let me alone" (*harpeh mimenni*) is literally, "you let loose from me," or "you drop down from me."[43] In several passages the verb *harpeh* is linked with the hand and connotes the idea of relaxing the hand, letting it sink down, or fall limp (cf. 2 Sam 24:16; Isa 13:7; Jer 6:24; 50:43; Zeph 3:16). The father must loosen his grip, give up control of his daughter. The way the daughter used the idiom surely does not give the impression that she was begging her father to let her go or bargaining for alone time. Rather, after the father's admission to a pledge of poor judgment to Yahweh, she now takes charge of her life. She decides on the time frame, "two months," which is an unfamiliar time reference in biblical texts, virtually exclusive to this narrative (Judg 11:37, 38, 39).[44] The usual time period of mourning, which occurs eleven times in the Hebrew Bible, is three months.[45] The only other reference to a period where two months seem to have passed and the third month is marked with the phrase "on this day" reads, "In the third month after the sons of Israel had gone out of Egypt, on this day they came into the wilderness of Sinai" (Exod 19:1). It is on this occasion that Moses will go up to God, and the Lord will come down upon the mountain to declare His covenant with the people of Israel.[46] In the context of the daughter's unusual circumstances, the "two months" may be considered unusual as well. However, in the occasion of these two months, similar covenant overtones as in Exod 19 await the attentive reader.

Note how the daughter speaks of her actions: (a) she will go; (b) she will go down upon/over the mountains; (c) she will weep upon/over her virginity. The Hebrew verb, *yarad*, "to go down, descend," usually describes a movement that is downhill topographically. Medieval and modern interpreters have puzzled over the use of this verb as it does not seem to make much sense for

[43] *HALOT*, 1277.

[44] The only other text that contains the expression "two months" is 1 Kgs 5:14, a reference to forced laborers working for one month in Lebanon and for two months in Solomon's house.

[45] Gen 38:24; Exod 2:2; 2 Sam 6:11; 24:13; 2 Kgs 23:31; 24:8; 1 Chr 13:14; 21:12; 36:2, 9; Amos 4:7.

[46] See discussion on "the third month" in Exod 19:1 in William H. C. Propp, *Exodus 19–40*, The Anchor Bible (New York, NY: Doubleday, 2006), 154.

the daughter to go and then "go down upon the mountains."[47] For this reason, some translations take this expression as a reference to an undefined movement such as, "I will go and wander on the mountains" (KJV, NKJV). The ESV reads, "I will go up and down upon the mountains." Others ignore the expression altogether and translate, "I will go to the mountains" (NASB).

The daughter's wish, "I will descend upon the mountains" (Judg 11:37)[48] shows up elsewhere in the Hebrew Bible, which accentuates the significance of this clause in the overall biblical text and in the Jephthah narrative specifically. The combination of the verb "to descend" (*yarad*) with the prepositional clause "upon the mountain" (*'al-har*) is used in six other passages, each describing theophanic imagery of Yahweh descending upon the mountain(s) (Exod 19:11, 18, 20; Neh 9:13; Ps 133:3; Isa 31:4). Except for Judg 11:37, human beings never descend "upon" a mountain; they always descend "from" a mountain.[49] In Exod 19, Yahweh is the one descending upon Mount Sinai in fire and smoke and then speaking the commandments before the people (Exod 20). The confessional prayer of the Levites in Neh 9, recounts Yahweh's Sinai theophany, "He gave them just ordinances and true laws, good statutes and commandments" (v. 13). In Ps 133, the poet sings of Yahweh's dwelling with His people in pleasant unity and describes it like the dew of Hermon "coming down upon the mountains of Zion where Yahweh commanded the blessing—life forever" (v. 3). According to Isa 31, Yahweh of hosts "comes down" upon Mount Zion to wage war against Egypt and protect and deliver Jerusalem (v. 4).

The "figurative depiction of God's action in terms of human motion expresses at one and the same time God's infinite transcendence and His personal and intimate involvement with

---

[47] *HALOT*, 434; G. Mayer, יָרַד *yarad*, *TDOT* 6: 315–322. Some have proposed another Hebrew verb, *rud*, "to wander," as in Ps 55:3. See Alter, *Prophets*, 125 (note 37); Boling, *Judges*, 209. See the discussion in Sasson, *Judges 1–12*, 441.

[48] Sasson points out the odd Hebrew syntax in this verse with the verb *yarad* as a perfect conversive ("I descend," *veyaradti*) sandwiched between two cohortatives, which are volitional verbs expressing the daughter's strong will ("and I will go . . . and I will weep," *ve'elchah . . . ve'evkeh*). See Sasson, *Judges 1–12*, 441.

[49] See Exod 19:14; 32:1, 15; 34:29; Num 14:45; 20:28; Deut 9:15; 10:5; Josh 2:23; Judg 3:27; 4:14; 9:36.

humanity."[50] All passages cited above refer to Yahweh who pledges a covenant relationship based on the people's shared experiences of bondage and liberation. The words He speaks upon Mount Sinai are words for life, eternally binding for a covenant community that is carried forward by His steadfast love. Yahweh's covenant is the ultimate promise—His oath made to His people (Deut 9:5; 29:12) who in turn have "passed over into the covenant of the Lord your God and into His oath" (Deut 29:12 NASB). Thus, to make a vow and offer sacrifices, including the burnt offering, must function within Yahweh's covenantal oath with His people.

For Jephthah's daughter to speak in language that otherwise tells of Yahweh's descent upon Mount Sinai carries covenant notions within dimensions of sacred time and space as in the covenant context of Exod 19. The peculiar time is "two months," first in reference to people whose journey takes them to Mount Sinai where the Lord will descend, and then to a daughter who will "go and descend upon the mountains and weep." The space is "upon the mountains" in reference to Yahweh's descent upon Mount Sinai in fire and rising smoke (Exod 19:18) to establish His covenant by "the perpetual burnt offering, the one done on Mount Sinai" (Num 28:6, literal translation). In essence, the daughter's words render the vow of one who "opened his mouth to Yahweh" as inapt, if not sacrilegious, when he pledged a burnt offering to Yahweh. Rather, Yahweh's covenant commitment upon the mountain demonstrates that the burnt offering belongs in the sphere of His oath pledged to His people. Heschel identifies such complete and utter dedication as existence lived in the presence of a God who Himself is utterly dedicated to and cares about the human being. "Not only a vow or conversion, not only the focusing of the mind upon God, engages [the human being] to Him; all deeds, thoughts, feelings, and events are His concern"[51] (edited for inclusion).

The Fate of the Daughter

The daughter's descent "upon the mountains" does not come without pain and grief. She tells her father that she is going to weep

[50] Nahum M. Sarna, *Exodus*, The JPS Torah Commentary (New York, NY: The Jewish Publication Society, 1991), 105.

[51] Abraham Joshua Heschel, *Man Is Not Alone: A Philosophy of Religion* (New York, NY: Farrar, Straus and Giroux, 1979), 237.

over her "virginity" (*betulim*). The Hebrew term *betulah* is more complex than a simple reference to a "virgin," especially when one takes into account cognate languages such as Egyptian, Akkadian, and Ugaritic.[52] In the biblical context, the term *betulah* is used as a reference to a young girl's nubile stage of life, a girl in a marriageable age who is still under the guardianship of her father, a girl without sexual experience with men, and a bride to be married.[53] At the end of the narrative there is the additional note that, "she had not known a man" (Judg 11:39).

She will bewail her virginity, but to what end?[54] Is she in her youth preparing for a brutal end of life? Is she as a young woman preparing for lifelong cultic service in the temple and therefore, to remain without children? In Exod 38:8, the "serving women" were connected to the sanctuary, and according to 1 Sam 2:22, those who slept with them committed sin. Ancient Near Eastern temples had women dedicated to cultic service, some celibate, others not, but they should not have children.[55] As noted earlier, Jephthah had every right to turn back from his vow and redeem his daughter even from becoming one of the "serving women" in the temple (see Lev 27:2–8).

Again, it is important to note the daughter's speech about the two months "upon the mountains" when she will be weeping "upon" her virginity before drawing conclusions about the purpose and meaning of these words. The preposition *'al* "upon" shows its significance especially when one recognizes how it functions in the structural features in the text, namely in the parallelism between two lines in verse 37 and in the inverted parallelism in verse 38.

---

[52] Bergman-Ringgren and Tsevat, בְּתוּלָה *betulah*, בְּתוּלִים *betulim*, *TDOT* 2:338–343.

[53] Ibid. See also Gordon Wenham, "Betulah: 'A Girl of Marriageable Age,'" *Vetus Testamentum* 22, no. 3 (1972): 326–48.

[54] See a concise summary of feminist scholarship on the meaning of virginity in the ancient world and the Hebrew Bible, and the interpretation of Jephthah's daughter bewailing her virginity in Kimberly D. Russaw, "Daddy's Little Girls?: An Examination of Daughters in the Hebrew Bible" (PhD diss.; Vanderbilt University, 2016).

[55] Sasson, *Judges 1–12*, 449.

A I will descend upon the mountains (*'al-heharim*) (Judg 11:37)
B I will weep upon my virginity (*'al-betulay*)
B' She wept upon her virginity (*'al-betulayha*) (Judg 11:38)
A' Upon the mountains (*'al-heharim*)

The preposition "upon" or "over" (*'al*) is based on the Semitic root *'alah*, which carries the meaning of that which is above, high, and prominent by a rising upward movement. The "upward" meaning of the preposition *'al* is embedded in the verb *'alah*, "to go up," as well as in the noun *'olah* for a "rising offering" or "burnt offering."[56] The semantic, structural, and phonetic use of *'al* in the daughter's speech cannot be overlooked when one remembers the crucial cognate words in Jephthah's vow about the burnt offering, *'olah* (Judg 11:31). As Jephthah pledged to "bring up" (Hifil of *'alah*) a "rising offering" (*'olah*), the daughter determined in her request that she will descend "upon" (*'al*) the mountains and weep "upon" (*'al*) her virginity. Now, the daughter's determined speech (11:37) stands as the antithesis to the father's vow just by the use of small but meaningful linguistic elements.

Ultimately, the daughter's weeping "upon" (*'al*) her virginity "upon" (*'al*) the mountains, invites the audience to identify her as the burnt offering (*'olah*) even before she returned and Jephthah "did to her according to the vow which he had made" (11:39). She became the burnt offering by her own volition in the presence and intimacy of a lamenting sisterhood community.

Jephthah's response to the daughter's request is a single word, a straightforward imperative, "Go!" He does not comment on the daughter's powerful discourse. The narrator adds, "So he sent her away" (Judg 11:38). Robert Alter interprets Jephthah's extreme brevity as a choked emotional response of a man who is barely able to speak.[57] Sasson, on the other hand, considers the one-word response as a rather harsh reply, as one dismissing a servant,[58] which seems to be more coherent with the father's previous denouncing words. One wishes he had at least added "my daughter" after the

---

[56] H. F. Fuhs, עָלָה *'ala*, *TDOT* 11:76–95; D. Kellermann, עוֹלָה / עֹלָה *'ola*, *TDOT* 11:96–113.

[57] Alter, *The Hebrew Bible,* 125 (note 38).

[58] Sasson, *Judges 1–12*, 442.

imperative "Go!" as in Ruth's case (Ruth 2:2); it would have shown some fatherly tenderness at the end of his pitiful outburst. Instead, "For two months she went, she and her companions, and wept upon the mountains upon her virginity" (Judg 11:38). Time and place are now between father and daughter. At least, she was not alone; the young women, her friends, were with her.

Upon the daughter's return, the narrative again takes up the language of Jephthah's vow that included an actual physical act.

> "Do (*'asah*) to me according to what came out of your mouth" (Judg 11:36)
> "He did (*'asah*) to her according to the vow which he had made" (Judg 11:38)

An associated passage is Jeremiah 44:25, where the verb *'asah* is used in a prominent way to show the acting on a vow (*neder*) in a physical manner. The prophet speaks to God's people who have immigrated to Egypt after much of the population of Judah was exiled to Babylon, "As for you and your wives, you have spoken with your mouths and fulfilled *it* with your hands, saying, 'We will certainly perform (*'asoh na'aseh*) our vows (*neder*) that we have vowed, to burn sacrifices to the queen of heaven and pour out drink offerings to her.' Go ahead and confirm your vows, and certainly perform ('*asoh ta'asehna*) your vows!"

What Jephthah did to his daughter has been the subject of speculation and debate for centuries. Scholars have argued that since the daughter did not bewail her death as a burnt offering victim but rather her virginity, her father must have given her into lifelong service to the sanctuary.[59] This would fit better with the overall character of Jephthah as a faithful judge of Israel, one who had made an effort to avoid war against the Ammonites through negotiations (Judg 11:12–14, 27), as well as a man of principle who had learned

---

[59] David Kimchi (1160–1235) in *Genesis Rabbah* 60.3. David Marcus shows how Kimchi's interpretation was adopted by such traditional commentators as Levi ben Gershon (14th century), Abravanel (15th century), Yehiel Hillel Altschuler (18th century), Malbim (19th century) as well as by modern scholars such as Hengstenberg, Reinke, Auberlen, Keil, Delitsch, Köhler, and König (*Jephthah and His Vow*, 8–9, 17–18). Marcus himself holds to this interpretation (31).

to obey the Lord (v. 24). In addition, the epistle of Hebrews has Jephthah included in the list of heroes of faith (Heb 11:32). For these reasons, one could argue that it would be unlikely for Jephthah to have offered his daughter as a burnt offering sacrifice.[60] On the other hand, the footnote to Judg 11:39 in the *NKJV Cultural Backgrounds Study Bible* has the following to say:

> The statement should be interpreted in the light of the Canaanized Israelite society and culture to which Jephthah belonged. For these people, vows to sacrifice children were not rash or impulsive but deadly serious expressions of devotion (2 Kings 3:27). Though Yahweh would have found such an act to be abhorrent (Deut 12:31), He often allows His people to suffer the consequences of their bad choices.[61]

In 2 Kgs 3:27, Mesha king of Moab offered his son as burnt offering in a desperate attempt to ward off the Israelites. Contrary to clear commands where God condemns human sacrifices (Lev 18:21; 20:2–5; Deut 12:31; 18:10; cf. Mic 6:7), King Ahaz of Judah (2 Kgs 16:3) and King Manasseh sacrificed their sons (2 Kgs 21:6). Second Kings 17:17 lists the sacrifice of children among the reasons for Israel's downfall (cf. Jer 7:31; 19:3–6).

Jephthah's recital of Israelite history to the Ammonite king (Judg 11:14–27) gives reason to assume that he would have had sufficient knowledge about the Israelite God as one who did not accept human sacrifice. In that same vein, he would also be aware of Israel's sanctuary laws. In Lev 1, only male animals of the herd or flock, or birds could be offered as burnt offerings. The animals would be slaughtered and burnt on an altar to the Lord. Jephthah surely would also realize the violence involved in such an act even though death

---

[60] Angel Manuel Rodriguez, Biblical Research Institute of General Conference of Seventh-day Adventists. Retrieved from https://www.adventistbiblicalresearch.org/materials/bible-ot-texts/judges-1129-40 on 20 October 2017.

[61] *NKJV Cultural Backgrounds Study Bible: Bringing to Life the Ancient World of Scripture* (Grand Rapids, MI: Zondervan, 2017), 452; Block, *Judges, Ruth*, 364–79; idem, "The Period of the Judges: Religious Disintegration under Tribal Rule," in *Israel's Apostasy and Restoration: Essays in Honor of Roland K. Harrison* (ed. A. Gileadi; Grand Rapids, MI: Baker, 1988), 39–58.

would be quick: "The trussing is brutal, the bleating is shrill, blood spurts everywhere, limbs jerk, and the bowels let go. Then there is the cracking of bones, the ripping of organs, the screeching of fire, and the acrid stench of burning flesh."[62] Trible makes the point: "A vow led to victory; victory produced a victim; the victim died of violence; violence has, in turn, fulfilled the vow."[63]

Conclusions

Thereafter, the biblical writer has two things to say about the daughter. One, "she herself had not known a man." Second, "she became a custom in Israel," "a decree" (*choq*). Ironically, and in spite of having no name in the biblical story, she is the one who is remembered by the women with an annual ceremony (Judg 11:40). Death and silence are not the final words of the story. Even though nameless and childless, she is remembered. The meaning of this tradition was to decree that such a horror should never happen again in Israel. The *Targum of Jonathan to the Prophets* clarifies, "And it became a decree in Israel, so that no man should offer up his son or daughter as a burnt offering, as Jephthah the Gileadite without consulting Phineas the priest; for if he had consulted Phineas the priest, he would have redeemed her for money.[64] Likewise, Flavius Josephus, "Accordingly, when that time was over, [Jephthah] sacrificed his daughter as a burnt offering, offering such an oblation as was neither conformable to the law nor acceptable to God, not weighing with himself what opinion the hearers would have of such a practice."[65] Sasson refers to Rambam who long ago noted that "it would not do for the women of Israel to gather for four days a year to memorialize a young girl just because she was forced to die a spinster."[66]

Where will one recognize God in the nameless daughter's story? When comparing how God acted and intervened in the story of

---

[62] Sasson, *Judges 1–12*, 444.

[63] Trible, *Texts of Terror*, 105–6.

[64] Leivy Smolar and Moses Aberbach, *Studies in Targum Jonathan to the Prophets* (New York, NY: KTAV, 1983), 10 (cited in Lillian R. Klein, *The Triumph of Irony in the Book of Judges*, Journal for the Study of the Old Testament Supplement Series 68 [Sheffield: Almond Press, 1988], 93).

[65] *Ant.* 5.266.

[66] Ramban (Nachmanides), *Commentary on the Torah: Leviticus* (ed. C. Chavel; New York: Shilo, 1974), 479–83; Sasson, *Judges 1–12*, 449.

Abraham and Isaac on Mount Moriah (Gen 22), it is clear that in Jephthah's case God did not ask for a burnt offering in order to bring victory over the Ammonites. Furthermore, when Jephthah fulfilled his vow, "There is no last-minute intervention by the deity to save a child, no ram in the thicket."[67] There is, however, a place where one is able to capture a glimpse of the presence of God, and it is not in Jephthah's pledge but in Mizpah when the daughter speaks truth to power. Julia Claassens' seminal essay makes the point that it is "through patriarchy's power that Jephthah's daughter loses her life. And yet, . . . one sees an example of a woman, who even though she finds herself trapped in circumstances that violate their self-worth, resists the indignity that had befallen her."[68] God stands by as a witness in the streets of Mizpah. After all, Mizpah is Yahweh's "watchtower,"[69] where the Lord watches out for daughters (Gen 31:48–50):

> Laban said, "This heap is a witness between you and me this day." Therefore it was named Galeed, and Mizpah, for he said, "May the LORD watch between you and me when we are absent one from the other. If you mistreat my daughters, . . . see, God is witness between you and me."

The countless stories of unnamed daughters who continue to "go and descend upon the mountains and weep" (Judg 11:37) will be told "wherever this gospel is preached in the whole world," for "what this woman has done will also be spoken of in memory of her" (Matt 26:13).

---

[67] J. Cheryl Exum, "Murder They Wrote: Ideology and the Manipulation of Female Presence in Biblical Narrative," *Union Seminary Quarterly Review* 43 (1989): 22.

[68] L. Julia Claassens, "Female Resistance In Spite of Injustice: Human Dignity and the Daughter of Jephthah," *Old Testament Essays* 26/3 (2013): 607.

[69] *HALOT*, 624.

Unmoved Mover?
A Close Reading of 2 Samuel 9

Angelika Kaiser

Abstract

This narrative analysis of 2 Sam 9 provides a close reading of the pivotal story of David's behavior towards Saul's house, when he extended God's kindness (*ḥesed)* to Mephibosheth, Jonathan's son. Considering this benevolent act, commentators have interpreted David as being moved by political strategizing, fear, mere technical bureaucrat-like covenant-fulfillment, and like reasons. This study offers a close narrative analysis of the respective chapter and takes the backstory of David's relationship to Jonathan and to the Saulides into account. Literary features of this as well as other narratives are considered in detail, to find out, whether the text itself gives indications for the motives of David's benevolence towards Mephibosheth and how this benevolence relates to God's kindness, which David intended to show to anyone left of the house of Saul (2 Sam 9:3). The results of this narrative analysis not only show David as emotionally moved by and showing *ḥesed*, but doing so against the backdrop of the fierce enmity Saul displayed to him over several years. Second Samuel 9 also manifests strong typological echoes of God's own *ḥesed*-based actions towards humans as descendants of the earth's original fallen king (Adam). That God himself–just like David–is moved and emotionally involved with those He benefits, emerges as one main conclusion of this study of the elaborately told story in 2 Sam 9.[1]

---

[1] It happens that certain stories stick with us and we do not really know why. Maybe something about the time in life when we heard or read it, the place we were at when we encountered it, physically or in our life experience. Or maybe the way we found out about it. The real reason for our liking can elude us. Second Samuel 9 is one story that has stuck with me in a deep way for over eight years now. I know exactly why, though. It is beautiful in its brevity. It is beautiful in its complexity. It is beautiful in its message. It simply is beautiful. Thus, I am gratefully sharing my observations of this story in a *Festschrift* that honors the work of a colleague who dedicated her life to the study of a theology of beauty.

Introduction

David moves. From his father's home to the palace, from the palace to the desert, from the desert to an interim capital, and finally to a newly minted capital. Yet he also moves public opinion (2 Sam 3:36), people to die (2 Sam 4:12), the Israelite tribes (2 Sam 5:1–3), the capital itself (2 Sam 5:6–9), Philistine idols (2 Sam 5:21), and foreign dignitaries (2 Sam 5:11). He moves the ark of the covenant (2 Sam 6), his own plans for the temple-building (2 Sam 7), and foreign policy landscape (2 Sam 8).

The narrative in 2 Sam 9 is a rather moving story of David showing covenantal faithfulness and kindness to Jonathan's son Mephibosheth. The crippled descendant of a fallen king gets suddenly moved into the most positive phase of his life. By what is David moved, however? Does the text say anything about his intentions for this act of kindness? Was it political calculation? Even an act of cold fear? Was his motive affectionate, warm benevolence? Or was he emotionally unmoved and simply fulfilling his covenant duties, like a bureaucrat fulfills his preset tasks? This question is relevant not only for the portrayal of David in this narrative, but also for the portrayal of the kindness of God (חֶסֶד אֱלֹהִים) which David wants to show to anyone "still left of the house of Saul" (v. 3, NIV).[2]

Background, Problem, Purpose, and Method

The narrative of 2 Sam 9 is an elaborately crafted piece of literature. It is the first narrative within the traditionally so-called Succession History of David as seen in 2 Sam 9–1 Kgs 2, which many consider "extraordinarily good literature."[3] It follows the depiction of David having established his kingship over all of Israel and having gained significant military successes (ch. 8). Right after this, David is presented as contemplating whether anyone from Saul's house is left to which he may show *ḥesed* (חֶסֶד; "covenantal

---

[2] Hereafter the ESV will be used throughout the chapter unless otherwise noted.

[3] Greger Andersson, *Untamable Texts*, Library of Biblical Studies 514 (New York, NY: T & T Clark, 2009), 4. Andersson continues by saying that "it is commonly assumed that such sections should be regarded as historiography (perhaps the finest of antiquity) and apologetics" before he reflects on the current scholarly standpoints on and debate about the David narrative.

faithfulness, loyalty, [loving]kindness") for Jonathan's sake (9:1).[4] With *ḥesed* being a prominent concept in this narrative—it is mentioned three times in this rather short chapter (vv. 1, 3, 7)—and being specified as God's *ḥesed* (חֶסֶד אֱלֹהִים), readers are invited to not only inform their own picture of David but also the picture they hold of God.[5]

In 2 Sam 9, David remembers the covenant Jonathan made with him right before David had to part ways with Saul and the royal court for his own safety's sake (1 Sam 20:14–17, 42).[6] What follows is an intricate junction of several strands of the David-narrative, which come together to create a vivid picture of David as a person and king, as well as his understanding of kindness (חֶסֶד) or, as David rewords his initial question briefly thereafter, the kindness *of God* (2 Sam 9:3).

The encounter between David and Mephibosheth has been foreshadowed in multiple ways in previous narratives (1 Sam 20; 2 Sam 4) and will be taken up again in two subsequent chapters (chs. 16, 19).[7] It forms a part of the overall portrayal of David's relationship to the Saulides, which permeates David's entire ascension story.[8] The scholarly consensus has been that this narrative depicts David's direct fulfillment of the covenant made with his close friend Jonathan. The king demonstrates *covenantal faithfulness (ḥesed)* to the house of Saul for Jonathan's sake.[9]

---

[4] Hereafter the term *ḥesed* will be predominantly used in its Hebrew yet transliterated form, in order to use it as a term for the concept itself and not narrowing it down by favoring one English translation option only.

[5] Furthermore, the triple mentioning of חֶסֶד connects this narrative to 1 Sam 20, where this word appears three times as well (vv. 8, 14, 15). In both stories, חֶסֶד "is nothing less than the difference between life and death," as J. P. Fokkelman points out (*King David*, Studia Semitica Neerlandica 20 [Assen/Maastricht, Netherlands: Van Gorcum, 1981], 29). For a further study on loyalty, see Uriah Y. Kim, *Identity and Loyalty in the David Story*, Hebrew Bible Monographs 22 (Sheffield: Sheffield Phoenix, 2008).

[6] Instances of covenant confirmation between David and Jonathan are 1 Sam 23:18 and 24:21–22.

[7] Fritz Stolz, *Das erste und zweite Buch Samuel*, Zürcher Bibelkommentare 9 (Zürich: Theologischer Verlag, 1981), 229-230.

[8] Ibid., 230.

[9] Craig E. Morrison, *2 Samuel*, Berit Olam (Collegeville, MN: Liturgical Press, 2013), 120.

Conclusions regarding David's motives for this faithfulness/kindness, however, show how much these interpretations differ in the theological discussion. The *expressed* intention is clear and undisputable from the text: David wants to show kindness to remaining Saulides "for Jonathan's sake" (2 Sam 9:1), thus directly honoring the covenant he and Jonathan made (1 Sam 20) and confirmed repeatedly (e.g., 23:18). Throughout the centuries, however, commentators have surmised *implied* intentions for David's benevolence toward Jonathan's son. After all, David could have been driven by different motives, such as a friendship-based benevolence,[10] the need for dutiful albeit emotionally uninvolved covenant fulfillment,[11] political intentions (keeping an eye on Mephibosheth),[12] a desire to strategically demonstrate his (David's) trustworthiness to the people he now fully started to rule,[13] or simply by a combination of several of these reasons.[14] Commentators argue

---

[10] The French Calvinist theologian and jurist Lambert Daneau (1530-1595) considers David's act a positive emotionally engaged benevolence in honor of David's and Jonathan's friendship and considers it a role model for Christian friendships. See Lambert Daneau, *Tractatus Duo. . . De Amicitia Christiana* (Geneva, 1579). A similar argument is given by Kim, who sees the emphasis on David's actions driven predominantly, if not solely, by his friendship with Jonathan (Kim, *Identity and Loyalty in the David Story*, 114).

[11] Various commentaries portray the encounter between David and Mephibosheth in a rather stiff, bureaucratic manner, e.g., Walter Brueggemann, *First and Second Samuel*, Interpretation: A Bible Commentary for Teaching and Preaching (Louisville, KY: Westminster John Knox, 1990).

[12] Ibid. See also Stolz, *Das erste und zweite Buch Samuel*; Robert Alter, *The David Story* (New York, NY: Norton, 1999); David H. Jensen, *1 & 2 Samuel*, Belief: A Theological Commentary on the Bible (Louisville, KY: Westminster John Knox, 2015), 210. Alden L. Thompson and George R. Knight, *Samuel*, The Abundant Life Bible Amplifier (Boise, ID: Pacific Press, 1995), 222.

[13] Brueggemann, *First and Second Samuel*, 267, states: "No doubt he [Mephibosheth] is also useful to David, rather like a White House Media event with a poor family, to show that the government has not forgotten the politically powerless."

[14] A. A. Anderson, *2 Samuel*, Word Biblical Commentary (Waco, TX: Word Books, 1989), 143, argues that "it is impossible to say whether or not David was guided by any ulterior motives."

mostly from political or common sense considerations and draw their conclusions accordingly. Conclusions drawn from a carefully conducted close reading of the passage seem to be rare.

The following study therefore offers findings of a close canonical reading of 2 Sam 9 that do not seem to be overtly present in general publications on this chapter.[15] These findings will be presented in descriptions of the narrative's characters, their background and relations, and the narrative strands coming together in this story. A discussion of whether these elements entail any (implied) information on David's intentions, and how the narrative reflects back on the *kindness of God* will conclude the study's results.[16] That the narrative was intentionally written and elaborately crafted is as much a premise of this study, as well as an undisputable conclusion to be drawn after closely observing literary, linguistic, and contextual features of the passage. In focus will be composition, characterizations, contextual connections, contrasts, repetitions, and typological allusions.[17] "It is by such means that a story succeeds in characterizing people."[18]

Composition

Various structures have been proposed for the narrative in question, though some of them differ from each other only slightly.[19]

At first glance the narrative is composed of a prologue, three interactions and dialogues, and an epilogue. The interaction between David and Mephibosheth is framed by the interactions between

---

[15] Fokkelman's *King David*, Morrison's *2 Samuel*, and Borgman's *David, Saul, and God* are examples of close readings in an otherwise mostly text-insensitive landscape of commentaries and studies on the David narrative as presented in the books of Samuel.

[16] Aspects regarding textual history and placement of this and other connected narratives in the books of Samuel and their chronology play a minor role for this narrative analysis and will therefore not be addressed.

[17] Repetitions are a major literary device in the Hebrew Bible, as well as context and contrasts, and they play such an essential part in the shaping of this narrative that they will be organically included into the distinct observations without occupying separate sections.

[18] Fokkelman, *King David*, 29.

[19] See Morrison, *2 Samuel*, 120, for a proposal of a topical chiasm.

David and Ziba and thus is in the center of the narrative, with v. 7 as the focal point.[20]

Prologue (v. 1)

Ziba and his dialogue with the king (vv. 2-4)

Mephibosheth and his dialogue with David (vv. 5-8)

Ziba and his instructions from the king (vv. 9-12)

Epilogue (v. 13)

Slightly different, however, is an equally possible proposal for a two-panel structure (sections A and B) with respect to the way that David is referred to by the narrator (underlined below). Several observations in this study as perceived in the text are reflected in this structure.

Prologue (v. 1-2c "David")

Section A

1. The King and Ziba (vv. 2d-4, "the king")
a. Name-asking (v. 2d)
b. "I am your servant" (v. 2g)
c. Desire to show "the kindness of God to him" [remnant of Saul's house] (v. 3)

2. David and Mephibosheth (vv. 5-8, "King David" and "David")[21]
a. Name exclamation (v. 6e)

[20] See Fokkelman for details on the structural analysis of 2 Sam 9. Fokkelman's analysis of this narrative extends to the following two appearances of Mephibosheth and Ziba, in chs. 16 and 19 respectively, and the exact correspondence in speaker changes in these two chapters, according to the speaker changes in ch. 9 (Fokkelman, *King David*, 25).

[21] The usage of "King David" in the description of the very formal sending and bringing of "him" (i.e., Mephibosheth, v. 5) is kept as official as the arrival of Mephibosheth (v. 6a); after these very formal/ceremonial remarks, the naming switches immediately to the more personal "David." See also Fokkelman, *King David*, 29.

b. "I am your servant" (v. 6g)
c. Desire to show "kindness for the sake of your father Jonathan" (v. 7)

Section B

1. *The King and Ziba (vv. 9-11d, "the king")*
   a. "Mephibosheth your master's [the former king's] grandson shall always eat at my table" (v. 10e)
   b. "Ziba had fifteen sons" (v. 10f)
   c. "and twenty servants" (v. 10f)

2. *David and Mephibosheth (vv. 11e-12, "David")*
   a. "Mephibosheth ate at David's table, like one of the king's sons" (v. 11e)
   b. "Mephibosheth had a young son" (v. 12a)
   c. "All who lived in Ziba's house became Mephibosheth's servants" (v. 12c)

Epilogue (v. 13, "the king")

Characterizations

The characters carrying the narrative are King David, Ziba, and Mephibosheth.

In the background, Jonathan and King Saul are essential figures that not only provide and deepen the illustration of the background story, but also serve as crucial elements of the narrative and David's actions. We will dedicate a section to each of these characters, examining how the text introduces and characterizes them.

Characterization of David

The narrative begins with David's question for any remaining Saulide to which he may show kindness for Jonathan's sake (2 Sam 9:1). This question is repeated in verse 3, albeit with slight variation. Instead of *ḥesed* "for Jonathan's sake" (חֶסֶד בַּעֲבוּר יְהוֹנָתָן), David expresses to Ziba that he wants to show God's *ḥesed* (חֶסֶד אֱלֹהִים) to any remaining descendant of Saul's house. This change grabs the reader's attention because it is not only a variation from an expression just mentioned before, but it also invokes a standard that is bound up with the Most High, the one on whose anointing the whole kingship of David was based (1 Sam 16). The question for the nature of this *ḥesed* is posed at the beginning of the narrative; the specification of it as *God's ḥesed* starts David's personal interaction in this passage. It thus serves as a point for David's agenda and for the purpose of this narrative: Does David indeed show the *ḥesed* of God to the remaining Saulide? And how is God's *ḥesed* described throughout this story?

Corresponding to the purpose of showing *ḥesed* are the narrative's thematic fields of family and hierarchical structures, which are expressed by the extensive repetitions of terms like house (בַּיִת), servant (עֶבֶד), king (מֶלֶךְ), son (בֵּן), and father (אָב). The arena in which God's *ḥesed* is demonstrated is clear—the closest human relationships. As our further study will show, the concepts of son and sonship are especially at play here. In fact, the metanarrative regarding Saul, Jonathan, and David is in many ways a tale of two sons: Saul's son Jonathan and "the son of Jesse," as David is repeatedly referred to by Saul with a clearly negative connotation.[22] In 2 Sam 9, a third son is added to these interlocked narratives: Mephibosheth, the son of Jonathan.

Since the narrative is carried by the direct interactions between the characters, the following characterization of David will feature portrayals of his relationships and/or interactions with the following people: the house of Saul and Jonathan, Ziba, and Mephibosheth.

David and Jonathan

No direct mention is made of David's experience with Saul or Saul's house. But the backstory of 2 Sam 9 is fresh in the reader's memory: David's close friendship with Jonathan,[23] David's treatment by Saul,[24] as well as his reaction to the deaths of Saul and Jonathan, Abner, and Ish-Bosheth.[25] It is all the more surprising to find commentators making remarks like "David fought against Mephibosheth's grandfather,"[26] thus brushing over details the text itself expresses clearly, such as David's very deliberate distancing

---

[22] See 1 Sam 20:27, 30, 31; 22:7–9, 13.

[23] For a chronological sketch of David and Jonathan's friendship, see Morrison, *2 Samuel*, 121–122.

[24] Saul's disposition toward David went sour early on (1 Sam 18:9) and became much worse as time went on (see 18:10–12, 20–25; 19:1–17; 23:26; 26:2).

[25] See David's lament over Saul and Jonathan (2 Sam 1:17–27), Abner (3:31–35), and Ishbosheth (4:9–12), and his dealings with their presumed/real murderers (1:2–16; 4:9–12).

[26] Jensen, *1 & 2 Samuel*, 210.

from and punishing those who killed the Saulides.[27] Admittedly, Mephibosheth was most likely not aware of these nuances and he certainly considered the new king responsible for many or all of the deaths in his (Mephibosheth's) family.[28] King David transporting him to the kingly court must have felt like an approaching death sentence. However, the attentive reader of 2 Sam 9 has a different picture of David, because the author of 2 Sam 9 seems to have intentionally built upon the knowledge about David through the string of previous narratives. For instance, the different names given to David by different conversation partners show different levels of closeness. David is referred to as "king" or "King David" when talking to Ziba (vv. 2–5, 9–11), whereas he is called by his first name "David" when talking to Mephibosheth (vv. 6–7, 11).

The friendship between David and Jonathan started in close proximity to Saul's jealousy and murder attempts against David (1 Sam 18:1–11) and it tragically "ended" against the backdrop of Saul's death threat against David in 1 Sam 20 (especially vv. 16 and 46). As friends unwilling to part ways, Jonathan desired to be co-regent with David. They had a hunch that this was a final goodbye yet hope for a reunion was still flickering. In light of Jonathan's words in 1 Sam 20:15, the timing of David remembering his covenant with Jonathan in 2 Sam 8:14 ("and the Lord gave victory to David wherever he went") is fitting. Already in 2 Sam 7:9, God himself said to David: "And I have been with you wherever you went and have cut off *all your enemies from before you* (וָאַכְרִתָה אֶת־כָּל־אֹיְבֶיךָ מִפָּנֶיךָ). And I will make for you a great name, like the name of the great ones of the earth," a clear correspondence to

27 Stolz, *Das erste und zweite Buch Samuel*, 230, considers a chronological misplacement of ch. 21 possible and argues "that this chapter [2 Sam 9] was preceded by a certain narrative context that is no longer extant."

28 The choice of words by various commentators seems either ambiguous or to indicate that David is seen as the one "who has eliminated the boy's family!" Brueggemann, *First and Second Samuel*, 268; Keith Bodner, *David Observed*, Hebrew Bible Monographs 5 (Sheffield: Sheffield Phoenix, 2005), 77. Bodner is forthright about the 'fact' that David "has reduced the rival house of Saul to the lowly Mephibosheth, a crippled subaltern who becomes dependent on the royal house for his daily bread," ignoring several aspects that the David narrative is quite clear about.

Jonathan's words: "and do not cut off your steadfast love from my house forever, *when the LORD cuts off every one of the enemies of David from the face of the earth*" (בְּהַכְרִת יְהוָה אֶת־אֹיְבֵי דָוִד אִישׁ מֵעַל פְּנֵי הָאֲדָמָה; 1 Sam 20:15).[29] The text underlines David's proactivity in fulfilling his covenant with Jonathan, at the right time.

After the covenant description in 1 Sam 20:14–17, the testing moment came for Jonathan to learn about his father's true attitude toward David. This attitude led Jonathan to rise "from the table in fierce anger. . . for he was grieved for David, because his father had disgraced him" (1 Sam 20:34). The author's strong intentionality to draw connections between the stories of 1 Sam 20 and 2 Sam 9 is also elaborately shown in the unique use of the word "table" (שֻׁלְחָן; 2 Sam 9:7, 10, 11, 13) in the books of Samuel. It is only used in connection with Jonathan and Mephibosheth. Only two other narratives in the entire books of Samuel feature that word: 1 Sam 20:5, 29, 34 and 2 Sam 19:28.[30] Whereas Jonathan rose from "the king's table" in anger because of his father's corrupt standing toward the Lord's anointed (1 Sam 20:34), his son Mephibosheth can now sit down again at "the king's table" exactly because of Jonathan's good standing toward the Lord's anointed (2 Sam 9:7, 10–13). The word *table* is not mentioned in the books of Samuel between the rising of Jonathan and Mephibosheth's sitting down. Due to the new king's understanding of God's *ḥesed*, Jonathan's house (in the form of his son) was finally able to sit down again at the king's table. Fokkelman summarizes that

> we can see how David, once a fugitive, now a king, mirrors as well as inverts this situation. He sends men to bring him the son of Jonathan [. . .], but this [Mephibosheth] is not at all doomed to die. David's lovingkindness takes him out of the anonymous and fearful existence of–as it seems–a refugee and gives him and his family a proper life. Thus the love between David and Jonathan attains a new stature.[31]

---

[29] Emphasis supplied.

[30] "For all my father's house were but men doomed to death before my lord the king, but you set your servant among those who eat at your table. What further right have I, then, to cry to the king?" (2 Sam 19:28).

[31] Fokkelman, *King David*, 30.

The King and Ziba

The interaction between David and Ziba spans over a third of the narrative of 2 Sam 9 (five and a half verses) and functions as a frame for the focal encounter between David and Mephibosheth (vv. 6–8). After somebody at David's court ("they") called Ziba to king David, the king asks "Are you Ziba?" (v. 2), to which the former servant of Saul replies: "[I am] your servant." David poses his modified initial question to him (v. 3), to which Ziba briefly replies in a way that was probably surprising for the king. David's initial question regarding remaining members of Saul's house was indeed asked with Jonathan in mind, yet the wording indicated that David's kindness was supposed to be extended to include *all* possible descendants of Saul. The text shows that David had no awareness of his initial question actually being relevant for a direct son of his close friend Jonathan. How much bigger the emotional response from him upon learning that his kindness would immediately benefit somebody closest to Jonathan: his own son. David's eager, cut-to-the-chase questions and actions regarding Mephibosheth in vv. 4–6 testify to his willingness to meet this son of Jonathan and his desire to waste no time talking about that person, but to gain enough information to actually send for him. David asks for the location of Jonathan's son (v. 4) and lets him be brought to the court right away (v. 5). The seemingly unnecessary repetition of Mephibosheth's location in v. 5 seems to indicate the target-focus of David in getting exactly this man from exactly this location.

After David's dialogue with Mephibosheth, the king turns to Ziba again and arranges for the items of his plan to be put into action (vv. 9–10). Ziba is David's informant in their first interaction; his obedient executor in their second.[32]

David fully acknowledges Ziba's master as being Saul (vv. 9–10: "your master's [grand]son," בֶּן־אֲדֹנֶיךָ), while Ziba confirms that he understands himself now as servant of "my lord the king" (אֲדֹנִי הַמֶּלֶךְ).[33] The unpretentious, calm demeanor emanating from David's choice of words regarding Ziba's loyalty to the Saulide family is again a contrast to the jealousy-driven behavior of the former king, who still needed the acknowledgment of his royal

[32] Ibid., 25.

[33] See also his verbal forms of deference (*your/the king's servant*) in vv. 2 and 11.

position even when he knew that his kingship had been taken from him (starting in 1 Sam 15).

Another significant characteristic of the portrayal of David in this narrative is the fact that David does not react to or even mention Mephibosheth's crippledness. Ziba considered it of such an importance that he mentions it as the very second piece of information (2 Sam 9:3), right after saying that this person is a son of Jonathan.[34] The narrator brings it up again at the end of the story (v. 13), as the last piece of information, redirecting the reader's attention back to this lamentable physical condition of Mephibosheth. Whether this is done in order to highlight the immense value of David's action toward the disabled Mephibosheth on a purely human level, or for other reasons, remains unclear. What the text does communicate though, is that Mephibosheth's crippledness is neither an impediment to, nor a catalyst for, David's covenantal faithfulness. It seems that it simply did not matter to him.

David and Mephibosheth

David's interaction with Mephibosheth (vv. 6-7) is framed by his interaction with Ziba and forms the center of the chiasm in 2 Sam 9.

Upon Mephibosheth's arrival and prostration before David, David calls his name, "Mephibosheth" (2 Sam 9:6). This is not a request to Mephibosheth to identify himself, as was the case with Ziba (v. 2),[35] but rather an exclamation: "Mephibosheth!" Like Saul, who knew David's name without being told (1 Sam 16:19), now David mentions Mephibosheth's name without any record of being told.[36] This parallel to Saul is one of many that invite the active contrast between both kings and their characters. Though naming can

---

[34] Whether Ziba mentions Mephibosheth's physical condition out of care for him, in order to emphasize that he poses no threat to David's royal standing, or whether he does so out of derogatory motives, remains unclear in 2 Sam 9.

[35] The personal pronoun (2nd person singular, *you*) in combination with the interrogative particle (הַאַתָּה, are you. . . ?) preceding Ziba's name (v. 2) is missing in front of Mephibosheth's name (v. 6), and thus shows that the mention of his name is not a request for identification or identity affirmation, as has been argued, like the case of Saul's former servant (v. 2), but rather an exclamation.

[36] Brueggemann, *First and Second Samuel*, 268.

be an act of expressing dominion over the one named,[37] yet there is no real necessity to do that here. David's kingly role has been established by now and is in no way challenged by Ziba, nor by Mephibosheth, in subsequent verses.

Three further aspects underline this reading as David's emotional exclamation. First, a clear indication is how David is called. The portrait of King David in 2 Sam 9 is painted with various colors and components. A very obvious one is the way he is called throughout the passage, as mentioned earlier.[38] As he wonders about a Saulide remnant in v. 1, the text introduces him as "David." As soon as Ziba enters the narration, however, David is referred to as "the king" (vv. 2b–4, 9–11a). In select moments of executing kingly authority and demonstrating royal privileges, he is called "King David," as is the case in v. 5a, where he sent to have Jonathan's son brought to the court, as well as in v. 11 ("like one of the king's sons") and v. 13 ("ate always at the king's table"). However, in the beginning of the narrative, where he states his plan, and throughout his interaction with Mephibosheth, he is exclusively referred to by first name only (vv. 1, 2a, 6, 7, 11b). This feature not only does not confirm the hypothesis that the narrative needs to emphasize David's controlling power over Mephibosheth, but rather undermines it. David is the *human David*, the private person, when he's interacting with Mephibosheth.[39] The difference in closeness is seen in contrast to the way he is called when talking to Ziba—to Ziba he is *the king*.

Second, a simple comparison with king Saul suffices to see that David's exclamation of Mephibosheth's name is more than just pronouncing this person's name. Saul and others oftentimes called David "son of Jesse;" all of these instances, as already mentioned, are negatively connotated.[40] Saul's demonstration of increased

[37] Ibid.

[38] Morrison, *2 Samuel*, 120, notices the different uses of David's name/title but limits it to the fact that "the narrator is attentive to the proper use of David's royal title."

[39] See also 1 Sam 20:5–6, where David is presented just as the *human David* in the presence of Jonathan, complete with fears and hunches, when he asked Jonathan to lie to his father Saul in the plan to have the jealous king show his true colors regarding David (1 Sam 20:5–6).

[40] See also 1 Sam 25:10 and Nabal, who is likened to Saul in his *kingly demeanor* (25:36) and antagonism toward David ("Who is the son of Jesse?").

closeness is expressed by phrases like "my son David" (1 Sam 26:17, 21, 25; 24:16), an expression that involves David's first name. Thus, the naming instances, when Ziba says that "a son of Jonathan" is left (2 Sam 9:3) without mentioning his name, while David only mentions his first name ("Mephibosheth!"), are not detached from the context and earlier experiences of David, and therefore seem to be very intentionally crafted into the narrative of 2 Sam 9.

Third, context also provides the key to this moment of connecting between David and Mephibosheth, and thus a re-connecting between David and Jonathan. David's close affectionate friendship with Jonathan is the main backdrop against which we need to look at 2 Sam 9.[41] Seeing for the first time the son of his most intimate, now deceased, friend was not a moment void of intense emotions for David. To the contrary, in a very condensed, economic form, the author presents this moment as one of high emotional involvement. David is calling out the name of someone he never met, yet who is very dear to him.[42] It is no stretch of the imagination to picture David as observing facial and bodily features in Mephibosheth that remind him of Jonathan; maybe the sound of his voice, and certain types of movements or gestures make him think of Jonathan.

To imagine this scene of David meeting Mephibosheth (especially vv. 6–8) as a matter-of-fact sober declaration of covenant benefits, misses David's intimate bond to Jonathan and David's righteous character and humanness, all aspects that previous narratives portray very carefully and repeatedly. David's warm emotional engagement in his interaction with Mephibosheth can be safely concluded from these first verses seen against the backdrop of David's love for Jonathan. Regarding 2 Sam 1 and other texts, Borgman is correct when he objects to notions of

> the hiddenness of David, including his emotional responses. . . to the point of denying any insight given by the text into David's heart. [. . .] Such a judgment is problematic on several counts.

---

[41] For a succinct summary of David's bond and attachment to Jonathan, see Paul Borgman, *David, Saul, and God* (New York, NY: Oxford University Press, 2008), 155–56.

[42] Fokkelman, *King David*, 29, notices the name-mentioning parallel to Ziba's in v. 2, yet still considers it a question, albeit truncated, and not an exclamation.

> There is David's confessed love for Jonathan, difficult to simply dismiss (presumably on the grounds that the entire eulogy is purely political, designed to rally Saul's house behind him).[43]

What was hinted at when they parted ways in 1 Sam 21:41 ("And as soon as the boy had gone, David rose from beside the stone heap and fell on his face to the ground and bowed three times. And they kissed one another and wept with one another, David weeping the most") may be seen especially in David's reaction to the death notice of Saul and Jonathan (2 Sam 1). This is particularly and intensely clear in his eulogy for them (vv. 19–27)—the text is clear that his reaction was genuine, his love authentic. "I am distressed for you, my brother Jonathan; very pleasant have you been to me; your love to me was extraordinary, surpassing the love of women" (v. 26).

David and the Killings of the Saulides

Commentators have argued that David's complicity in the death of Saul's descendants excludes a mere benevolence toward Mephibosheth or makes it at least seem ironic.[44] After all, what is this individual kindness toward Saul's grandson worth when many of the former king's progeny have been ruthlessly handed over to be impaled, such as the seven male descendants in 2 Sam 21:1–14?

The arguments for the hypothesis that the events of 2 Sam 21 occurred chronologically prior to 2 Sam 9 and therefore triggered David's serious questioning as to whether anybody is "still left" from the house of Saul are not conclusive.[45] As has been pointed out

---

[43] Borgman, *David, Saul, and God*, 291, fn. 2, replies to Marti Steussy's argument for David's hiddenness by noting that, among other reasons, "with the possible exception of 2 Sam 13:21 [. . .] David is never said to love either God or another human person. Love for Jonathan may (or may not) underlie David's sparing of Mephibosheth in 2 Sam 21:7." Cf. Marti J. Steussy, *David*, Studies on Personalities of the Old Testament (Columbia, SC: University of South Carolina Press, 1999), 70.

[44] Robert Polzin, *David and the Deuteronomist*, A Literary Study of the Deuteronomic History pt. 3 (Bloomington, IN: Indiana University Press, 1993), 95, notes that "By the time David comes to question whether there is anyone left [. . .] in Saul's house, the reader cannot help but wonder whether David's loyalty (*ḥesed*) for the sake of Jonathan counts for anything."

[45] Fokkelman, *King David*, 26, points to the terms "still" (עוֹד) and "left" (נוֹתַר) in 2 Sam 9:1b, and their triple appearance in the chapter that

above, David knew about Mephibosheth in 2 Sam 21:1–14 (especially v. 7) but he was not yet aware of him in 2 Sam 9:1.[46]

Apart from the discussion on whether 2 Sam 21 chronologically preceded 2 Sam 9, the narrative is clear that the handing over of the seven Saulides in ch. 21 cannot simply be seen in the category of removing potential rivals for the throne. Second Samuel 21 presents a three-year famine in Israel, brought on by the Lord because of "the bloodguilt on Saul and on his house, because he put the Gibeonites to death" (v. 1b).[47] The context is thus one of gross covenant breaking by Saul, who tried to exterminate the Gibeonites from Israel. This constituted a literal breach of Joshua's covenant with the Gibeonites (Josh 9). The narrator presents a proactive David, inquiring of the Lord (2 Sam 21:1) and then inquiring of the Gibeonites with the expressed intent to "make atonement" (v. 2). What follows is a quasi quid-pro-quo request for a symbolic number of Saul's descendants (seven!) as an atoning act for the attempted annihilation of the to-be-protected Gibeonites. To consider David's obliging in this as an act of proactive or complicit extermination of Saulides, in an attempt to secure his own power, grossly misreads the severity of the famine, the genuine reaction he showed to the deaths/killings of previous Saulides,[48] the seriousness of Israel's collective *ḥesed*-duty within its covenants with others—as deceitfully as these may have been obtained, as in the case of the Gibeonites (Josh 9)—as well as the weight of bloodguilt on individuals and families, which required atoning.[49] David took covenantal faithfulness very seriously.

---

show "David in search, remedying his lack of information through Ziba," as enough evidence that "we need not waste any energy on the . . . question as to whether 2 Sam 9 presumes ch. 21." However, it is also well thinkable that David became more aware of remaining members of Saul's family as he got more acquainted with Mephibosheth and as the remaining Saulides gained trust in David's non-threatening standing towards them.

[46] Morrison, *2 Samuel,* 121. See also David G. Firth, *1–2 Samuel,* Apollos Old Testament Commentary 8 (Downers Grove, IL: InterVarsity, 2009), 32.

[47] Saul's crime against the Gibeonites is referred to only in 2 Sam 21:1.

[48] Saul and Jonathan (2 Sam 1:1–27); Abner (3:28–39); Ishbaal (4:5–12). Borgman, *David, Saul, and God,* 151–175, offers an insightful portrayal of David when confronted with "News of Death."

[49] Gen 9:4–6; Deut 19:10; 21:12–14.

Furthermore, he not only promised protection of descendants to Jonathan (1 Sam 20), but also to Saul (1 Sam 24: 21-22). Similarly, the hasty conclusion that David proactively or complicitly supported the killing of Saul's descendants needs to be reconsidered carefully. Thus, the contradiction, or maybe even irony, in David's kindness toward Mephibosheth as contrasted with other Saulides is not warranted.

Characterization of Ziba

Ziba's Submission

The reference to Ziba comes unannounced. Somebody must have known about this former servant of Saul and "called him to David" (2 Sam 9:2). He has not been mentioned previously,[50] but he will reappear in 16:1–4 and 19:25–31. Upon arrival he is asked by David "Are you Ziba?" to which he replies "[I am] your servant." This is the first time in the David narrative that David is addressed in this respectful way, marking his completed transition to the kingship: "the shepherd who long ago referred to himself as 'your servant' before King Saul has become head of state in Jerusalem (8:15–18) and thus merits the deference worthy of a king."[51]

In contrast to Mephibosheth, however, Ziba's sign of deference is incomplete: while the crippled royal descendant, the former king's grandson, prostrates himself,[52] the servant did not manifest a similar behavior. This contrast inspires doubt about Ziba's verbally expressed loyalty to David. His verbal expression of identifying himself as a servant (v. 2) is repeated by his confirmation in v. 11: "According to all that my lord the king commands his servant, so will your servant do." However, Ziba's expression of loyalty is further complicated by the fact that his words in v. 11 come in reply to David's remarks in v. 10, where David announced to Ziba that he

---

[50] One can assume that Ziba was among the crowd of servants mentioned as standing around Saul when the king uttered his invectives in 1 Sam 22:6–10. If that is the case, Ziba was there when Saul began to chase after David, which, peculiarly enough, started with the annihilation of priests.

[51] See Morrison, *2 Samuel*, 123, for a brief summary of David's deference toward Saul, starting with 1 Sam 17:32, where David called himself for the first time "your servant."

[52] The difficulty of bowing down as a lame/crippled person is apparent and has widely been noted.

will be a servant again, a servant of Mephibosheth. This fact is stated six times in vv. 10–12, yet Ziba does not seem to confirm himself as being willing to be a servant to Mephibosheth. Together with Ziba's words in v. 11, which sound like an expression of loyalty, the reader is left once again with an ambivalent feeling about the trustworthiness of his words, since he underlines that he considers David his master. This breathes a certain duplicity that will become apparent in chs. 16 and 19—if one is to believe Mephibosheth's version of what took place during David's flight from Absalom.[53] In that case, Ziba appears outright deceptive and opportunistic, a servant who is more loyal to himself than to his master's grandson.[54] This impression is confirmed especially in comparison with Mephibosheth's reaction to David's return to Jerusalem (19:24–30). Having neglected personal body care as a sign for inner turmoil and sorrow for David's absence, Mephibosheth's words to David even more underline the dedication this son of Jonathan had for his new lord and friend. Ziba's behavior toward David lacks the genuineness that exudes through the actions and words of Mephibosheth as portrayed in these respective narratives.[55]

Ziba and Mephibosheth

The information Ziba provides to King David about potential royal descendants is limited according to the narrative: a son of Jonathan, crippled in his feet (2 Sam 9:3). And upon David's inquiry for this descendant's location, he adds "the house of Machir, the son of Ammiel, at Lo-debar" (v. 4). Why he mentioned the man's lameness is not explained in the text.[56]

In vv. 9 and 10, David instructs Ziba on how to manage the family land for Mephibosheth, and confirms to Ziba that Mephibosheth would be integrated into the royal household. David's

---

[53] Stolz, *Das erste und zweite Buch Samuel*, 230. See Fokkelman, *King David*, 30–40, for an analysis of both texts, 16:1–4 and 19:25–31.

[54] Morrison, *2 Samuel*, 123.

[55] Fokkelman, *King David*, 28-29.

[56] He may have wanted to present him to the king as not being a threat to the throne, due to his physical impairment (Brueggemann, *First and Second Samuel*, 267). Another interpretation could be that Ziba subtly expressed a form of repugnance at Mephibosheth, not only for being the descendant of a disgraced king but also for being immensely impaired on an individual level. Both interpretations seem vague.

restoration of Saul's family land to Mephibosheth goes hand in hand with the restoration of authority and rulership structures: as Ziba served Saul, he now serves Saul's grandson. Ziba's new master is Mephibosheth.[57]

The prior fate of Saul's lands remains unaddressed in this narrative.[58] We could imagine a previous dispossession at some earlier point, which would partially explain Mephibosheth's need to stay at somebody else's house.[59] In any case, "Ziba's large work force of sons and servants" were charged with its maintenance.[60]

Ziba as informant and executor of David's plans for Mephibosheth does not receive further attention in this chapter. His alluded duplicity is picked up on and fleshed out in chapters 16 and 19, where his unethical, ingratiating dealing with David ultimately gains him half of the property David had restored to Mephibosheth in ch. 9.

Characterization of Mephibosheth

It is in this narrative that David seems to hear of Mephibosheth for the first time (2 Sam 9:3b). Ziba informs him that "there is still a son of Jonathan; he is crippled in his feet." David's sending for him, the repeated mentioning of Mephibosheth's exact location (twice in vv. 4–5), as well as his act of deference upon meeting David (v. 6) are detailed descriptions that culminate in the meeting of these two men. They are in vastly different circumstances of physical

[57] Klaus vom Orde, *Das zweite Buch Samuel* (Wuppertal: Brockhaus, 2002), 129. However, Ziba still calls David "my lord the king" (v. 11). In v. 9, Ziba is called *Saul's naar (lad/young man/servant*; נַעַר שָׁאוּל) while he was previously called *eved* (*servant*; עֶבֶד). See Anderson, *2 Samuel*, 142, for details.

[58] Stolz, *Das erste und zweite Buch Samuel*, 230, argues that Ziba still lived in Gibeah in Benjamin, where Saul once lived, and that he probably managed Saul's former estates but on his own account. Anderson, *2 Samuel*, 141, wonders whether Saul's estates had become crown property and thus David had the right to restore them.

[59] Vom Orde, *Das zweite Buch Samuel*, 128.

[60] See Brueggemann, *First and Second Samuel*, 268–269, who also points to the very scarce information regarding Saul's property.

condition, societal standing, and political power, yet they share a deep bond with the same person: Jonathan.[61]

Mephibosheth and Jonathan

The information regarding Mephibosheth[62] provided in the narrative portrays the identity of the recipient of David's benevolence in an interesting order. The seemingly most important piece of information is the first one: he is a son of Jonathan, most likely his only one.[63] On this issue of his descent from Saul hinges his qualification for David's *ḥesed.* But he not only fulfills the condition for David's targeted kindness in his chapter ("anyone left of the house of Saul," v. 1) but furthermore is he the *son* of Jonathan himself, for whose sake David asks this question in the first place (v. 1). To nobody of the house of Saul could the bond of David be stronger than to Mephibosheth, Jonathan's own son.

Mephibosheth's Lameness

The sad fate of Mephibosheth has already been described in 2 Sam 4:4, detailing the accident he suffered, dropped by his nurse while she was fleeing with the five-year-old after the news broke of the army's loss at Jezreel, where Saul and Jonathan died.[64] That day marked a tragedy for both men, David and Mephibosheth, in the loss of Jonathan. The child lost his father that day and also his mobility.[65] Ironically, this same day signaled an increase in mobility for David because his persecutor Saul was no longer alive. At the time of 2 Sam 9:1, approximately twenty years later, Mephibosheth was most likely in his twenties and had a son of his own (v. 12). Alter points to two possible reasons for the narrator's repetition of Mephibosheth's lameness. It may have been stated for underscoring the fact that he

[61] For the question as to whether Mephibosheth was rather Saul's son because of Saul's son by Rizpah with very same name (2 Sam 21:8), see Anderson, *2 Samuel*, 141. Jonathan's descendants are listed in 1 Chr 8:35–40; 9:41–44.

[62] 1 Chr 8:34 has him as Merib-baal.

[63] Stolz, *Das erste und zweite Buch Samuel*, 230, points out that Mephibosheth seems to be the only offspring of Jonathan, Saul's oldest son.

[64] Ibid., 230.

[65] Ibid. Mephibosheth's lameness was first mentioned in 2 Sam 4:4, is mentioned twice in 9:3, 13, and plays a role in David's encounters with Ziba and Mephibosheth in 16:1–4 and 19:25–31.

could not easily travel between Jerusalem and his now restored estates and thus naturally needed a retainer for his possessions. Another potential reason has to do with the contrast this information opens up "between the fates of the house of Saul and the house of David: King David came into Jerusalem whirling and dancing before the LORD; the surviving Saulide limps into Jerusalem, crippled in both legs."[66] As noted before, though, the narrative seems to suggest that, to David, Mephibosheth's lameness didn't seem to matter–neither as a hindrance for covenantal care and relationship, nor as a reason for the same.

Mephibosheth's Location

As Ziba draws attention to Mephibosheth's physical condition rather than mentioning his name (v. 3), he presents Mephibosheth as a no-name.[67] This, in turn, corresponds with the name of the place where he resides, or rather hides: Lo-debar, which means literally *no-word* (vv. 4–5). A no-name living in no-word.

The location of Mephibosheth is given in exact terms: Lo-debar, the house of Machir (a wealthy man, 2 Sam 17:27–29), son of Ammiel.[68] This northern Transjordanian town was close to a traditional Saulide area (Jabesh-Gilead), and also close to Mahanaim, where Saul's son Ish-Bosheth had set up his residence (2 Sam 2:8). The twofold mentioning of the location's name Lo-debar (vv. 4–5) underlines the character of this place as being somewhat of a hiding place for Saul's grandson. Living in *no-word* (we might say 'no man's land' today) corresponds to the submissive and fearful demeanor of Mephibosheth as it is revealed in the narrative. The narrative indicates the possibility that David and Mephibosheth had not met before. Not knowing David personally but knowing only *about* the new king, who, doubtlessly, was rumored to have actively eradicated most of Mephibosheth's family, most certainly instilled enough fear into the direct heir of Saul's throne that we can define

---

[66] Robert C. Alter, *The Hebrew Bible* (New York, NY: Norton, 2019), 342.

[67] Brueggemann, *First and Second Samuel*, 267.

[68] Morrison, *2 Samuel*, 123–124, suggests that Machir had been a member of Saul's court and would become a member of David's court as well, providing for David and his entourage during their flight from Absalom (17:27). See also Bodner, *David Observed*, 43.

his location as a hiding place. Considering the custom of new kings to annihilate all potential throne competitors, the name of Mephibosheth's place of residence suggests a rather bleak existence for a family's remnant member, living in fearful hiding.[69]

Mephibosheth's Submission

Mephibosheth's actions in this narrative are expressions of submission, most likely out of fear and deference. He not only "fell on his face and paid homage" twice (vv. 6 and 8)—once before David said anything and once after David announced his plans—but he did so while being crippled. And he accompanied his prostration with the expression "Behold, [I am] your servant" (v. 6).[70]

In v. 7, David reveals the reason for having brought Mephibosheth to the court: "Do not fear, for I will show you kindness for the sake of your father Jonathan, and I will restore to you all the land of Saul your father, and you shall eat at my table always." What starts as a classic salvation oracle ("Do not fear!") could also just be seen as a regular expression of encouragement.[71] After all, David was, undoubtedly, aware of Mephibosheth's fears. And these fears were legitimate, considering the situation Mephibosheth was in and the (probably incomplete/incorrect) information he had about this new king. The reader knows, but Mephibosheth did not, that David also heard these words once before, from Jonathan while he, David, was in hiding at a place unknown to the then-king Saul. The last time these exact words ("Do not fear" אַל־תִּירָא) were spoken in the David narrative was by Jonathan who "rose and went to David at Horesh, and strengthened his hand in God. And he said to him, 'Do not fear, for the hand of

---

[69] Anderson, *2 Samuel*, 141. On the treatment of members of an overthrown kingly family, see 1 Kgs 15:29; 16:11; 2 Kgs 10:6–7. Mephibosheth's words in 2 Sam 19:27–28 highlight this point even more expressly: "He [Ziba] has slandered your servant to my lord the king. But my lord the king is like the angel of God; do therefore what seems good to you. For all my father's house were but men doomed to death before my lord the king, but you set your servant among those who eat at your table."

[70] Jensen, *1 & 2 Samuel*, 230, notes that even if Mephibosheth had/felt any claim left to be heir to the throne, by repeatedly proclaiming himself to be David's servant, "he effectively relinquishes that claim."

[71] Other examples of salvation oracles may be found in Gen 35:17; 50:19, 21; Exod 20:20. See Firth, *1–2 Samuel*, 404.

Saul my father shall not find you. You shall be king over Israel, and I shall be next to you. Saul my father also knows this.' And the two of them made a covenant before the LORD.[72] David remained at Horesh, and Jonathan went home" (1 Sam 23:16–18). While Jonathan spoke these words during the last time the two friends met, David speaks these words at the first time he meets Mephibosheth.[73] This additional strong connection to the David-Jonathan story in the context of David's flight from Saul, strengthens the impression that we have a story of fulfillment on several levels in 2 Sam 9. Not only is the fulfillment described, but in several aspects seemingly prophetic allusions by Jonathan are also fulfilled.[74] Mephibosheth may not be co-regent, yet he is very close to the king, as close as the king's own sons.

Mephibosheth was the only son of the former king's oldest son, Jonathan. Thus, Saul's hereditary line goes straight through Mephibosheth. And since family property was, according to Israelite law, unalienable (Lev 25), this right is now fulfilled by David in handing the Saulide estates back to the last known descendant of Saul. In light of Lev 25:23, David's land restoration to Mephibosheth also signals the acknowledgment of a higher reality, since the LORD states, "The land shall not be sold in perpetuity, for the land is mine. For you are strangers and sojourners with me." The acknowledgment of God as the rightful landowner and the Israelites as His tenants was supposed to safeguard the land, and thus the people, against multiple abuses.[75] David proves himself to be a keeper of this divinely ordained principle. In the text's density, these four aspects (Fear not!, kindness for Jonathan's sake, land restoration, adoption into the royal

---

[72] This covenant may indeed have stipulated that David, once king, will appoint Jonathan as a kind of co-regent or significant official in his kingdom.

[73] Robert B. Chisholm Jr., *1 & 2 Samuel*, Teach the Text Commentary Series (Grand Rapids, MI: Baker, 2013), 229.

[74] The timing of David's remembrance of the house of Saul and the fulfillment of his covenant with Jonathan is another example of this feature: following the new king's military successes described in 2 Sam 8 (and 2 Sam 7:8), the timing of him thinking of any remaining Saulide corresponds to Jonathan's words in 1 Sam 20:15.

[75] The confiscation or shady annexing of land during monarchical times was harshly rebuked by the prophets (e.g., Amos 5).

family) move worlds for Mephibosheth. Nothing is the same anymore after he hears those words.

After learning about this new future of his, Mephibosheth prostrates himself again and says: "What is your servant, that you should show regard for a dead dog such as I?" (v. 8).[76] While the first expression of deference was probably in line with common court protocol, the second one is loaded. Not only is the dog metaphor (and *dead* dog even more) an expression of utter self-deprecation,[77] but moreover it carries biographical connotations for David. While in hiding for fear of Saul, David spared Saul's life and only cut off a corner of Saul's robe (1 Sam 24:4), an act for which David's sensitive conscience suffered remorse afterwards (v. 5). When he presented the shred to Saul after the king left the cave, David tried to reason with Saul (vv. 8–15), appealing to his heart, mind, and fear of God, trying to convince the king that he, David, posed no threat to Saul's kingship nor his descendants (vv. 21–22).[78] Before invoking the LORD to be judge between them (v. 15), David asked: "After whom has the king of Israel come out? After whom do you pursue? After a dead dog! After a flea" (v. 14). Over twenty years later, the roles have been switched. It is a descendant of Saul who now considers himself a "dead dog" in front of king David, with the difference being that he says it in the presence of favor and not in the presence of disfavor. Mephibosheth can let go of his fears at this point. David, at least, just gave him every good reason to do so.

The impression of Mephibosheth submitting more genuinely to David than Ziba is confirmed some years later, especially in comparison to Mephibosheth's reaction to David when the latter returns to Jerusalem (19:24–30). Not only does Mephibosheth explain why he did not join David on his flight from Absalom (vv. 24–28; Ziba deceived him and exploited his lameness), but he underlines his affectionate loyalty to David by his statement in vv. 27–28 and particularly v. 30: "Oh, let him [Ziba] take it all [the

[76] Anderson, *2 Samuel*, 142, and Kyu N. Jung, "Court Etiquette in the Old Testament" (Ph.D. diss., Drew University, 1979), 32–38.

[77] The "dead dog" metaphor links his current state of helplessness and low worth to that of David in 1 Sam 24:14 (cf. 1 Sam 17:43).

[78] A close reading of David's speech presents a goldmine for connections to 2 Sam 9 and the overall relations between Saul and David. See Chisholm, Jr., *1 & 2 Samuel*, 228.

Saulide land], since my lord the king has come safely home." This is the language of somebody who knows himself safe at the table of and in dialogue with the king.

Mephibosheth's Future

After describing the putting in place of arrangements for Mephibosheth's restoration as landowner and part of the royal household (vv. 9–11),[79] the text gives a further glimpse into Mephibosheth's future in mentioning his "young son" (בֵּן־קָטָן) Mica.[80]

Quasi overnight, Mephibosheth's life was moved from *no-word* to the capitol Jerusalem, with the allusion to peace (שָׁלוֹם) that the city's name brings. From hiding to the king's table. From lack of means to wealth. But, most importantly, from fear to calm. He was a free man now with his own, considerably large, estate.[81]

Contrasting Ziba and Mephibosheth

Several aspects in the narrative invite a contrast between Ziba and Mephibosheth. Both are called or brought to the king; both are closely connected to the former king Saul; both express signs of deference towards David, the new king; and both are given pronouncements by David that will significantly impact their lives and loyalties. One question that arises when contrasting these two: Is there a difference in their behavior when confronted with this new king in town?

As already mentioned above, the difference in deference is an obvious disparity: the servant merely states his servanthood whereas the royal offspring states *and* shows it. In later chapters, where they are mentioned again (2 Sam 16 and 19), aspects of their standing toward David and toward each other are further illuminated.

---

[79] Anderson, *2 Samuel*, 142, discusses the question as to whether Mephibosheth ate at David's personal table or received his own establishment.

[80] Stolz, *Das erste und zweite Buch Samuel*, 231, and Anderson, *2 Samuel*, 142, observe that the mentioning of Mica may indicate not only that David's arrangements were also valid for Mephibosheth's own family/descendants, but also that this was a point of interest for the author of 2 Samuel and the David narrative in general. For the impressive list of Mica's descendants, see 1 Chr 8:35–40; 9:41–44.

[81] Stolz, *Das erste und zweite Buch Samuel*, 230.

Characterization of God's *ḥesed*

God/Yahweh is not directly mentioned as an acting character in this narrative. He appears in 2 Sam 9:3 as the source of the kindness David intends to show to any remaining Saulide (חֶסֶד אֱלֹהִים; *the kindness of God*). By repeating his initial question ("kindness for Jonathan's sake," v. 1) with the variation "kindness of God" (v. 3), David brings his "words into closer conformity with Jonathan's appeal in 1 Sam 20:14: 'show me the steadfast love [*ḥesed*] of the LORD.'"[82] Yet through this attributive function, God's character becomes the standard by which the reader may legitimately assess whether the kindness David shows to Mephibosheth in this story is worthy to be called the *kindness of God.* As Fokkelman keenly observes:

> The protector of their covenant, and thus the standard for their relationship, which is described as *ḥesed*, is God himself. The expression in v. 3c, 'the lovingkindness of God,' (i.e. *ḥesed* which is pleasing to God and for which he sets the standard) is therefore the exact echo of *ḥesed YHWH* in 1 Sam 20:14. Only at this point does the story explicitly reach a conceptual level, the stratum of moral and religious values; other metaphysical data or ideological abstractions do not occur in these three scenes.[83]

A word study shows the construct phrase "the kindness of God" (חֶסֶד אֱלֹהִים) appears only in two texts: 2 Sam 9:3 and Ps 52:1. The latter is a psalm by David, "when Doeg the Edomite came and told Saul and said to him, 'David has come to the house of Ahimelech.'"[84] This psalm was thus written at the occasion of Doeg reporting on David's visit to the priest Ahimelech, David's first reported stop on his years-long flight from Saul (1 Sam 21:1–10). After that stop at Ahimelech's place, chs. 21–22 report four places David subsequently went to before the focus shifts to Saul and his

[82] Morrison, *2 Samuel*, 123.

[83] Fokkelman, *King David*, 26. See also 1 Sam 20:23: "And as for the matter of which you and I have spoken, behold, the LORD is between you and me forever," and 1 Sam 20:42.

[84] Alter, *The Hebrew Bible*, 135.

reaction to David's disappearance.[85] Starting in 22:6, the reader sees a furious king, spear in hand, reminiscent of the scene when he hurled it at his own son in 20:33 because of Jonathan's bond with David. With detailed information, these verses picture the fallen king, surrounded by "all his servants" (v. 6), lamenting about their faithlessness because "no one discloses to me when my son makes a covenant with the son of Jesse" (v. 8a).

What follows is the dialogue between Saul and Ahimelech the priest (22:11–16) as well as Saul's massacre of the priestly town of Nob (vv. 17–19). It is significant that both 2 Sam 9:3 and Ps 52:1 contain the phrase "the kindness of God" (חֶסֶד אֱלֹהִים) because both passages have close connections to David's deep bond with Jonathan. In regard to Psalm 52, this bond became the direct reason for Saul's fury that led to the massacre in Nob. Concerning 2 Sam 9, this bond became the direct reason for David's kindness that led to the full restoration and quasi-adoption of Mephibosheth. One response brought death, the other brought life. The textual context of 2 Sam 9 begs the question: How is the relationship of the fallen king and his house to the anointed of the LORD? Jonathan's early siding with David (1 Sam 18:1, "the soul of Jonathan was knit to the soul of David, and Jonathan loved him as his own soul"), and the covenant arising from that bond, ultimately provided a future for Jonathan's house.

The similar phrase "the kindness of the LORD" (חֶסֶד יְהוָה), which Jonathan first mentions in 1 Sam 20:14 (Jonathan asking David: "If I am still alive, show me the חֶסֶד יְהוָה, that I may not die"), is mentioned in only two more texts in the entire Tanakh: Pss 33:5 and 103:17, both psalms authored by David.[86] This phrase ("the kindness of the LORD" [חֶסֶד יְהוָה]) occurs only three times and the previously considered phrase only twice in the Hebrew Bible, all of them either

[85] These four stops were Gath's king Achish (1 Sam 21:10–15), the cave of Adullam (22:1–2), Moab's king at Mizpeh (22:3–4), and the forest of Hereth in Judah (22:5).

[86] While there is some uncertainty about the writer of this untitled psalm, there are several reasons why it is quite likely to have been David. For one, Ps 33 is attributed to David in the LXX. Furthermore, this psalm has a long history of being included in Book I of the psalms, the one dedicated to the Davidic psalms. Coffman discusses these and two more reasons in James B. Coffman and Thelma B. Coffman, *Commentary on Psalms* (Austin, TX: ACU Press, 1992), on Ps 33:1.

in the David narrative or directly from the pen of David himself. Thus, the impression is quickly born that this phrase, which originated with Jonathan (1 Sam 20), got picked up (Pss 33 and 103) and modified by David (2 Sam 9:3; Ps 52:1). The son of Saul became a shaper of David's view of *ḥesed*, a coiner of his language, and an influence on his own son's future.

As has been shown above, it is the connections to previous texts that build a rich tapestry of lived experiences and inform the reader of 2 Sam 9 of the background of David's interaction with Saul and his house. These textual connections, however, not only serve as mere information, but show by means of contrast what is possible in another person's life; through David's behavior in 2 Sam 9, as well as the transformation the persona of the king has undergone by comparing Saul to David. The contrast is emphasized by showing how David was treated when Saul was king and how David treats the last Saulide now that he himself is king.[87] The two following and last sections, however, will address implications that go beyond the mere interactions between David and the house of Saul, by reflecting on the picture of God's kindness that is evoked by what David did.

Discussion

Fully determining the motivation(s) of any person is an impossible and, more often than not, futile endeavor. The complex entanglement of human intentions and motives evades an exact explanation by outsiders. Only the One who can read the human heart can judge any inner motivations.[88] However, the biblical text intentionally communicates information that allows readers to view a story, a certain character, a dynamic, or a relationship, in a text-informed way. A close reading can bring these informative hints and clues to the attention of anyone willing to suspend judgment, disregard hasty twenty-first century common sense, and instead be led by text-inherent features.[89] The result will not be a resounding *We now know the exact motives of David's behavior here!*, but a humble yet confident *The author of this narrative suggests that the*

---

[87] Fokkelman, *King David*, 30.

[88] See, e.g., 1 Sam 16:7; 1 Chr 28:9; Pss 38:9; 44:21; 139:2–23; Jer 20:12; Ezek 11:5.

[89] See Fokkelman, *King David*, 1–18, for foundational remarks on his close reading approach.

reader understand David's behavior in the following way. Ultimately, it is mostly the faith-shaped understanding of the *believing* Bible reader that perceives the historical reality in the narrative. However, believer or not, anybody who respects and expects the sophisticated intentionality and beautiful complexity of biblical texts can observe what the stories themselves say.

As expressed in the text, David's kindness towards Mephibosheth happens on the grounds of his covenant with Jonathan. Among the possible motivations for David's kindness, especially in the adoption of Mephibosheth,[90] the most commonly concluded motive is that of keeping Mephibosheth "close at hand" in "a kind of luxurious house arrest."[91] And, judging from common sense and from political customs in antiquity, the slogan "Keep your friends close, but your enemies closer"[92] sounds plausible and could apply here.[93] However, judging from several aspects in the narrative itself, this option for David's motive does not bear weight. The emotional attachment David had with Jonathan is too large;[94] the entire package of privileges Mephibosheth was granted is too generous;[95] and the narratival evidence that David was nervous about potential throne rivals at this point is too scarce.[96] Thus "it [the narrative] can be used to portray David as a king who remained faithful to his covenant with Jonathan—the king's first order of

---

[90] Alter, *The David Story*, 243.

[91] Ibid. See also Jensen, *1 & 2 Samuel*, 210.

[92] This quote is attributed to the Chinese general Sun Tzu (6th century BC), the assumed author of *The Art of War*, certainly a man affiliated with friendships and enemies.

[93] Stolz, *Das erste und zweite Buch Samuel*, 230, suggests that he "was constantly under control and therefore had no opportunity to plan a coup d'état."

[94] Borgman, *David, Saul, and God*, 155–156.

[95] Acknowledging Mephibosheth's existence and letting him go back to Lo-Debar in peace would have been enough from a common-sense point of view, considering political customs of rival-annihilations at that time. David went far beyond that by lavishing other benefits on Mephibosheth that the latter surely did not expect.

[96] If Mephibosheth was ever perceived as a threat to the throne, it was no longer the case by the end of David's kingship, as 1 Kgs 2:5–9 implies, when David warns his son Solomon about possible dangers to the throne but Mephibosheth is not mentioned as one of them. Morrison, *2 Samuel*, 121.

business after establishing his government."[97] There is no direct nor subtle hint in this story, nor in previous or subsequent narratives involving Mephibosheth, that suggests that Mephibosheth was included into David's household for royal safety reasons. Nor does the text imply that David kept his covenant with Jonathan to demonstrate his covenantal faithfulness to the public. In fact, nothing in this text, nor in previous texts, implies that the friends' covenant was public knowledge.

A closer reading of the passage in question and its contextual allusions, however, not only excludes political and safety strategies as potential motivations, but also illuminates David's covenant fulfillment in colorful ways. Contrary to common, rather lifeless interpretations and depictions of David's interaction with Mephibosheth in this narrative,[98] the text in 2 Sam 9 alludes to a highly emotionally involved king who makes the cup of his friend's son run over, even by adopting him as his own son. As Leithart observes, the kindness David shows to Mephibosheth is indeed a "kindness of God," because "just as the Lord had shown Himself faithful to David by doing far more than David asked or imagined, so David was going to do the same for Mephibosheth."[99]

Another analogy to the kindness of God is created by an association that is opened up in 2 Sam 8:18 by the clause "and David's sons were priests," the last statement before the Mephibosheth narrative. Interpretation issues regarding this clause aside,[100] the clause connects to "the king's sons" in 9:11 ("Mephibosheth ate at David's table, like one of the king's sons") and corresponds (as the last statement in ch. 8) to the last statement

---

[97] Ibid.

[98] The portrayal of vv. 7–8 in Brueggemann, *First and Second Samuel*, 268, for example, shows a rather bloodless, detached king, implementing his "oath to Jonathan [which] is operative" as he makes Mephibosheth a part of the royal table-fellowship. This is not remedied by Brueggemann's seemingly passing remark that the text's "accent is on generosity and the honoring of Mephibosheth."

[99] Peter J. Leithart, *A Son to Me* (Moscow, ID: Canon Press, 2003), 230.

[100] This expression is hard to interpret because of the strong unlikelihood of David committing such a violation as to appoint his sons (non-Levites!) as priests (כֹּהֲנִים) without it being described as an issue in the Davidic narratives.

in ch. 9 ("Now he [Mephibosheth] was lame in both his feet" [v. 13]). The term *priests,* and the concepts of sonship, eating at the king's table, and lameness create an association that convincingly alludes to Lev 21:16–24. There, Aaron's physically impaired descendants are excluded from serving in the tabernacle, yet they can participate in eating from the portions of the sacrifices allotted to the priests (v. 22). Thus God provided also for those that were not customarily employed in the official sanctuary service because of their physical deformities. David fulfilled this principle from Lev 21:22 by providing for Mephibosheth in multiple ways (e.g. land restoration), but especially by letting him join his sons at the royal table, despite the lack of Mephibosheth's usefulness to him. "If a lame man was allowed to feed on Yahweh's bread, he should be permitted to feed on the king's bread."[101]

Furthermore, the typological link to God's ultimate Anointed One and his pursuit, restoration, and adoption of the descendants of the fallen human king (Adam) is very strong in 2 Sam 9, which presents the narrative as a prime story to show David being a type of the ultimate divine king. Multiple biblical texts prior to the Mephibosheth story hint at David previously being promised an unending dynasty.[102]

These characteristics of God's kindness (חֶסֶד אֱלֹהִים *ḥesed Elohim* and חֶסֶד יְהוָה *ḥesed YHWH*), as demonstrated in and connected to the narrative in 2 Sam 9, thus show not only a high point of David's kingship, character, and leadership but, to a greater degree, they portray the kindness God showed to David, and through David to others.[103]

Typological Echoes

David's *declaration of kindness* towards Mephibosheth (vv. 6–7) serves as the focal point of the narrative. It follows and reflects the *kindness of God/Yahweh*, his covenantal faithfulness, befitting the

[101] Peter J. Leithart, *A Son to Me*, 230.

[102] See 2 Sam 7:16, and confirmed in Isa 9:6–7; Ezek 34:1–24; and Heb 1:5, the latter text tying Jesus to the promise in 2 Sam 7:14.

[103] The following chapter (2 Sam 10) reports the kindness (*ḥesed*) David showed to the son of Nahash, the king of the Ammonites, paying back the *ḥesed* he received from Nahash. See Leithart, *A Son to Me*, 231, for a comparative study of chs. 9 and 10.

Anointed of the Lord. Moreover, in its brevity, the description of David's treatment of Mephibosheth comprises all the essentials that truly reflect *God's ḥesed* toward humanity as expressed through the biblical canon. In 2 Sam 9, we see that David called Mephibosheth by name; assured him not to fear; announced kindness and on whose behalf it was bestowed; and declared the restoration of previously owned land and the integration into the king's family. Beyond these actions, there are also the king's dealings with him that are not placed into the David-Mephibosheth dialogue itself (vv. 1–5, 9–13), i.e., the proactive seeking out of Mephibosheth (v. 5), and the effectuation of the promises to him (vv. 9–13). In light of the biblical macro-narrative, the typological echoes for God's own *ḥesed* are compelling:

2 Samuel 9		**Biblical Macro-Narrative**
David took initiative to seek out anyone who might be left of the house of Saul (vv. 1, 3) and sent to bring Mephibosheth to him (v. 5)	**1**	God is the One taking the initiative to seek out the fallen king's (Adam's) offspring[104]
David called Mephibosheth by his name (v. 6)	**2**	God calls them by their name[105]
David told Mephibosheth not to fear (v. 7)	**3**	God tells them not to fear[106]

[104] On God taking the initiative for connection to fallen humanity and bestowing His restoring care and salvation, see Gen 3:9; John 6:44; 15:16; Rom 5:8; 8:3; Eph 2:4–6; 1 John 4:19.

[105] See also Gen 22:11–13 (Abraham); 46:1–4 (Jacob); Exod 3:1–10 (Moses); 1 Sam 3:1–10 (Samuel); Isa 43:1 (people of Israel); Lk 10:38–42 (Martha); 22:31–32 (God); Acts 9:1–10 (Saul and Ananias).

[106] Throughout the Hebrew Bible, as well as the New Testament, God and angels are depicted as assuring humans they approach (often for the first time) to not fear. For these and other examples, see Gen 15:1; 26:24; 46:3; Deut 1:21; Isa 10:24; 41:10; Ezek 2:6; Dan 10:12; 1 Chr 28:20; Matt 14:27; 28:5; Mark 5:36; Luke 1:13, 30; 2:10; Rev 1:17.

David declared (v. 7) and implemented covenantal *ḥesed* (vv. 12–13) and he did not cut off his *ḥesed* from Saul's house (see covenant in 1 Sam 20:15) (vv. 7, 12–13)	**4**	God declares affectionate covenant-faithfulness and implements it[107]
David told others and Mephibosheth for whose sake he wants to show *ḥesed:* Jonathan (vv. 1, 7)	**5**	God communicates on behalf of whom the covenant-faithfulness was bestowed (Christ)[108]
David restored the lost land to Mephibosheth and cares for his subsistence (vv. 7, 9–13)	**6**	God restores the lost land and cares for subsistence[109]
David included the offspring of the fallen king into the royal family and table fellowship with him (vv. 7, 10, 11, 13)	**7**	God includes the offspring of the fallen king into the ultimate royal family and table fellowship with himself[110]

[107] See Acts 4:12; Rom 5:1–2; 8:38-39; Eph 2:4–10.

[108] On salvation and restoration on behalf of Christ, see, e.g., John 14:6; Rom 5:10; 8:34; 1 Tim 2:5; Heb 7:25; 9:24; 1 John 2:1.

[109] See Isa 65:17; Acts 3:21; 2 Pet 3:10–13; Rev 21:1–2; 22:3.

[110] The aspect of table fellowship/banqueting with God is widespread in Scripture, e.g., Ps 23:5; Matt 8:11; 22:2–14; Luke 12:37; 13:29; 22:29–30; Rev 19:9. On the aspect of adoption, see Ps 27:10; John 1:12; Rom 8:15; 9:8; Gal 3:26; 4:5–7; Eph 1:5; 1 John 3:2.

These typological echoes taken together do not create a simple chorus of merely technical fulfillment of duty, let alone a cacophony of mixed intentions. This text taken in its literary beauty and canonical context rather suggests a magnificent symphony on the theme of covenantal faithfulness, an uplifting composition of generous benevolence born of genuine interest, affection, and emotional involvement. David moved people, fates, and entities. Yet he also was moved himself. Moved by God's *ḥesed* for him, as can be seen in his psalms, and moved by the ones to whom he himself showed *ḥesed.* He was a moved mover. David's was not a dry fulfillment of a covenantal treaty. Rather, he lavished care, safety, and provisions on Mephibosheth, not *besides* being moved by love, but exactly *because* he, David himself, had been deeply moved by love. Just as David's covenant with Jonathan was born of the highest level of affection from the anointed one toward another human being, it also was fulfilled with the most intense possible outflow of generous affection, paved with "warmth and care for Mephibosheth."[111] And in that, David truly showed *God's* kindness. A kindness that is proactive, reassuring, future-giving, generous in every way, and based on a previous relationship–a covenant past leading to a future of love.

Considering the typological allusions, this story of three sons points to the ultimate son: Jesus, the Son of David. True kindness, true *ḥesed* for humanity, will be achieved on behalf of and through Him. And again, it is the honoring of a past covenant (Gen 3:15) that leads to a future of love. And in that Son of David, who is also the Son of God and the Son of Man, God showed himself as moved: moved by love and pity for His fallen human children. He is not the *unmoved mover* of Aristotle and Aquinas. From the beginning, He was deeply moved by the actions of humankind. In order to show the most affectionate, emotionally involved covenantal faithfulness to the fearful descendants of earth's fallen king, God in the Son of David moved heaven and earth–by moving himself.

[111] Fokkelman, *King David*, 28.

Divine Speeches in the Book of Psalms: Their Role, Placement and Implications for the Message and Structure of Selected Psalms

Dragoslava Santrac

Abstract

A major change in approaching the theology of the Psalms in modern psalmic scholarship came with the hermeneutical shift from viewing the Psalms solely as a random anthology of prayers and praises to viewing the Psalms as an intentional collection or a "book" with a clear purpose and a unified message. This approach has opened new avenues to recovering a theological emphasis in which individual psalms continue to speak in their canonical context, i.e., in connection to the other psalms in the present Psalter. This essay focuses on the direct citations of divine words in the Psalms in order to explore the artistry and complexity behind the message and structure of the individual psalms and of the book of Psalms as a whole. The divine speeches in our selected examples (Pss 75:2-3, 10; 81:6-16; 89:3-4, 19-37; 95:8-11) not only create a sense of God's immediate reply and presence but also appear to play a pivotal role in creating psalm groups or blocks and advancing the dialogue between the people and God in the book of Psalms. The psalm blocks share common themes, keywords, literary structure, and placement in the Psalter. The divine speeches elucidate, advance and/or complete the message of the connected psalms and of the entire block.

Introduction

I find exploring the Psalms in honor of the life of scholarship and service of Dr. Jo Ann Davidson entirely fitting. First, a literary masterpiece such as the book of Psalms provides endless avenues to gratify Jo Ann's great love for aesthetics in the Bible. Second, the psalmists were unrelenting and daring as light bearers and trailblazers for generations of believers. I believe it took Jo Ann a lot of work, faith, and courage to be the first Adventist woman to earn a Ph.D. in theology and to teach theology for the Adventist church, inspiring many other women after her, including me. Finally, I appreciate Jo Ann's piety reflected in her speeches and publications, and I cannot think of a superior text on piety than the Psalms.

The Psalms assume the dynamics of vivid interactions with God. The psalmists do not perceive God as a passive recipient of worship but expect Him to respond. They often implore God to "give ear" (listen),[1] "hear my prayer,"[2] "look,"[3] "answer me,"[4] "come to me,"[5] "make haste to (help) me,"[6] and "deliver me,"[7] and ask questions such as "Why?"[8] and "How long?"[9] God's response is usually indirect, conveyed in the inspired words of the psalm, or delayed and anticipated in the future, whether through God's intervention in granting the suppliant's plea or by some other means. However, in some psalms God is portrayed as speaking in first person and His words are quoted in the psalm.[10] Apart from the obvious effect of creating a sense of God's immediate reply, and thus of God's closeness and perhaps more direct involvement in people's worship than in some other psalms, the divine speeches (direct quotations of God's words) in the Psalms seem to have other roles as well.

I address two interrelated questions in this chapter: 1) Why are the divine speeches introduced in the Psalms? and 2) Does their placement in the Psalms indicate any specific purpose or intended design?

Consideration of place precludes a discussion of each instance of divine speech in the book of Psalms. For the purpose of this essay, we will examine four examples (Pss 75:2-3, 10; 81:6-16; 89:3-4, 19-37; 95:8-11) to demonstrate the important function of the divine speeches for the message and structure not only of individual psalms but also of larger units where they play a pivotal role in connecting the surrounding psalms. I shall suggest some preliminary

---

[1] Pss 5:1; 17:1; 39:12; 54:2; 55:1.

[2] Pss 39:12; 54:2; 84:8; 143:1.

[3] Pss 11:2; 25:18; 80:14; 84:9; 119:132; 142:4.

[4] Pss 27:7; 102:2; 143:1, 7.

[5] Pss 101:2; 119:77.

[6] Pss 38:22; 40:13; 70:1, 5; 71:12; 141:1.

[7] Pss 6:4; 7:1; 22:20; 25:20; 31:1-2, 15.

[8] Pss 10:1; 22:1; 42:9; 43:2; 44:23–24; 74:1, 11; 80:12; 88:14.

[9] Pss 6:3; 13:1–2; 35:17; 74:10; 79:5; 80:4; 89:46; 94:3.

[10] Pss 2:6, 7–9; 12:5; 46:10; 50:7–23; 60:6–8; 75:4–5; 81:6–16; 82:2–7; 91:14–16; 95:8–11; 105:11, 15; 110:1, 4; 132:11–12, 14–18.

observations about how the divine speeches function in the selected psalms and their role in the formation of larger blocs in the book of Psalms. However, first I will give some general remarks about the divine speeches and the literary features, which show that certain passages function in a paired relationship with each other.[11]

I. Discerning the Divine Speeches

A. God's Word and Human Response

Divine speeches are by no means to be viewed as "God's Word" on a greater level than the rest of the Psalms, because the Psalms are not solely human prayers directed to God, but the Word of God directed to His people on the same level as the rest of the Scriptures (Mark 12:36; Acts 4:24, 25). In other words, the Psalms are the *inspired* prayers and praises of Israel, and so in the Psalms the voice is that of God with an echo of His people's voice responding to God's revelation with praise and lament. The remarkable beauty and appeal of the Psalms as prayers and praises lie in the fact that the Psalms are concurrently the pious prayers and praises of believers and God's inspired word.[12] This view, however, does not explain the mystery of the Psalms that Bonhoeffer succinctly captured: "The Holy Scripture is the Word of God to us. But prayers are the words of men. How do prayers then get into the Bible? Let us make no mistake about it, the Bible is the Word of God even in the Psalms. Then are these prayers to God also God's own words? That seems

---

[11] I acknowledge the contribution of Lawrence Boadt's research presented in his article "The Use of 'Panels' in the Structure of Psalms 73-78," *The Catholic Biblical Quarterly* 66 (2004): 533-550. Although Boadt's research does not pertain to divine speeches in the Psalms, it provides an insight into the use of large blocks or panels in the construction of the Psalms and suggests a useful methodology for studying possible structural interrelatedness of certain Psalms. I also draw on my research in *Psalm 76-150*, Seventh-day Adventist International Bible Commentary (Nampa, ID: Pacific Press, 2022).

[12] The history of interpretation of the Psalms ranges from the traditional Jewish and Christian historical and theological interpretations of the Psalms as God's inspired Word, to the post-enlightenment approaches to the Psalms as solely human responses to God's words and actions. For a survey of the history of interpretation of the book of Psalms, see Bruce K. Waltke and James M. Houston, *The Psalms as Christian Worship: A Historical Commentary* (Grand Rapids, MI: Eerdmans, 2010), 19–112.

rather difficult to understand."[13] Bonhoeffer points out that we can grasp the mystery of the Psalms only when we learn to pray them in the name of Jesus Christ. The Psalms thus provide the people of God with moments of intimacy with God when they can experience what the apostle Paul describes in Rom 8:26–27: "Likewise the Spirit also helps in our weaknesses. For we do not know what we should pray for as we ought, but the Spirit Himself makes intercession for us with groanings which cannot be uttered. Now He who searches the hearts knows what the mind of the Spirit is, because He makes intercession for the saints according to the will of God."[14]

As the Creator and Savior, God initiates and sustains the dialogue with His people. Kraus effectively captures the "dialogical principle" of the Psalms as "an answer inasmuch as it is a reaction to what Yahweh has previously said and done."[15] He rightly maintains that it is wrong to deduce from the "dialogical principle" that "the two partners [i.e., God and the people] are equal to each other and stand on the same level, and that a 'dialogical principle' could plumb the mystery of this correspondence."[16] The wonder of God's revelation and hiddenness feeds the unfathomable and surprising manner of the dialogue in the Psalms.

B. Locating Them in the Text

The most obvious way to recognize the divine speeches is through announcements such as "says the Lord" and "the Lord said" (e.g., Pss 12:5; 68:22; 110:1). These announcements are reminiscent of the formulas used by the prophets (e.g., 2 Kgs 7:1; 20:1; Jer 2:5), pointing to the role of divine speeches in the Psalms as poetic-prophetic expressions. In other instances, the psalmist introduces the divine oracle by clearly identifying the Lord as the one speaking (e.g., Pss 2:4-9; 50:3-23; 60:6-8; 89:19; 95:7).

Some divine speeches interrupt the usual pattern in the form of announcement, and the Lord is not openly mentioned as the speaker

---

[13] Dietrich Bonhoeffer, *Psalms: The Prayer Book of the Bible* (Minneapolis, MN: Augsburg, 1970), 13.

[14] Unless noted otherwise, all biblical quotations are from the New King James Version.

[15] Hans-Joachim Kraus, *Theology of the Psalms* (Minneapolis, MN: Fortress, 1992), 12.

[16] Ibid.

(e.g., Pss 46:10; 75:2-3, 10; 89:3-4; 91:14-16). In these cases, the audience has to deduce from the context that the words are God's words.[17] Some English versions add "You say/said" or "Thou hast said," which is not present in the Hebrew, in order to make it clear that the first person speaker is God (e.g., Pss 75:2, NIV; 89:3, NIV, RSV).

Booij correctly argues that the citations of the Lord's words in the Psalms are not "Fremdkörper" ("strange bodies," i.e., insertions), but represent an integral part of the psalms in which they occur and are sometimes marked by special metrical patterns, different forms of parallelism, and unique positions in the poems.[18]

II. Literary Features Pointing to Paired Texts

A. Acrostics

In a Hebrew acrostic poem, the verses of each stanza begin with the same letter of the Hebrew alphabet. The acrostic gives the impression of comprehensiveness and order to the poem, and implies that the subject matter of the poem is given full treatment. Acrostics are probably the most obvious literary feature that unmistakably point to connected psalms (e.g., Pss 9 and 10; 111 and 112).

B. Parallelism

The recurring juxtaposition of symmetrically constructed thoughts, sentences, phrases, and words can be used to tie parts of individual psalms or even whole psalms together. The parallelism of meaning registers more clearly to the English reader. Far more complex is parallelism made with grammar and syntax. Parallelism serves to stress balance and show development of thought, additional quality or contrast.[19]

Chiastic parallelism and chiasms focus attention on the two ends of comparison or to the middle term, creating the effect of a mirror

---

[17] Beth Tanner, "Psalm 75: An Answer to Where God Has Gone," NICOT (Grand Rapids, MI: Eerdmans, 2014), 604, 606.

[18] Th. Booij, *Godswoorden in de Psalmen: Hun Funktie en Achtergronden*, Th.D. Thesis (Amsterdam: Editions Rodopi, 1978), 31-33, quoted in Carl J. Bosma, "Discerning the Voices in the Psalms: A Discussion of Two Problems in Psalm Interpretation," part 2, *Calvin Theological Journal* 44 (2009): 132.

[19] Robert Alter, *The Art of Biblical Poetry* (New York, NY: Basic Books, 1985), 3-26.

image. Chiastic structures are important because they suggest an intentional pattern created by the author, and thus direct us to interpret the different sequences of the text in the light of their parallel counterparts. In the book of Psalms, examples of chiastic structures can be seen in the structures of entire psalms (e.g., Pss 86; 92; 115) or of smaller parts of psalms (e.g., Ps 141:1).

C. Repetition

Repetition of the same words or roots in key positions can be used effectively to tie smaller parts or entire psalms together. Refrains and the *inclusio* are common examples of neatly organized repetitions.[20] Repetition of words or concepts can be used with a greater degree of flexibility and with no schematic regularity. Likewise, the repetition of a word in a psalm or several psalms does not always mean the mechanical repetition of a concept. More often, repetition points to a more complex, albeit unified, context, like in the instance of emphatic repetition where each new repetition heightens the meaning or urgency of the original term (e.g., the repetition of "How long" in Ps 94:3).[21] In addition, repetition of thought concepts within an individual psalm or more seemingly unrelated psalms may indicate an intentional emphasis and deserve special attention.

D. Canonical Context

The canonical context is another indicator pointing to possible purposeful grouping of psalms. The canonical context of a psalm refers to the literary context of the whole book of Psalms in its present canonical form. In other words, the Psalms are not seen as a random anthology of prayers and praises but as an intentional collection with a clear purpose and a unified message, as with other biblical books.[22] "Looking for interaction between psalms within a context means that the contemporary reader can seek out themes and emphases or look for threads running through pairs or groups of

---

[20] Boadt, "The Use of 'Panels' in the Structure of Psalms 73-78," 536.

[21] Alter, *The Art of Biblical* Poetry, 64, 65, 188, 189.

[22] M. D. Futato, *Interpreting the Psalms: An Exegetical Handbook* (Grand Rapids, MI: Kregel, 2007), 57.

psalms which point to topics that editors of the final form of the Psalter wished to emphasize."[23]

Canonical approaches can be seen as a positive tool in that they focus on the unity of the book of Psalms.[24] The belief is that the Holy Spirit inspired and guided not only the writers of the Psalms, but also the editors who collected, arranged, and preserved the Psalms. The present shape of the book of Psalms is clearly not the work of King David, but of later (most likely postexilic) editors.[25] The question arises: Do the divine speeches play any role in the arrangement of certain psalms? I will try to answer this question in the following study of the divine speeches in four selected psalms.

III. Examples of Divine Speeches and Their Role in the Psalms

In order to determine whether the divine speeches might have significant function for the structure and development of thought

---

[23] J. A. Grant, "The Psalms and the King," in *Interpreting the Psalms: Issues and Approaches*, ed. D. Firth & P. S. Johnston (Downers Grove, IL: IVP Academic, 2005), 107.

[24] Whereas canonical approaches can be used as positive tools for the study of the psalms, a danger exists in the tendencies of certain canonical scholars to undermine the historical reliability and divine inspiration of the biblical text and to study it primarily as sacred literature. However, most weaknesses are not intrinsic to the method of canonical approach but relate to the critical tendencies and presuppositions of certain scholars.

[25] For example, Ps 72:20 suggests that David's psalms end with Book II, but is most likely the ending of an earlier collection of psalms, because the psalms of David appear in the remainder of the Psalter (Pss 86; 101; 103; 108–110; 122; 124; 131; 133; 138–145). The postexilic date of the present shape of the book of Psalms can be deduced from the presence of a number of postexilic psalms. These psalms reflect the challenges of the Jewish people in postexilic times when the main pillars that represented their national and religious identity (the temple, the king, and the land) seemed to have collapsed (e.g., Pss 74; 79; 89). The pathos of these psalms concurs with the postexilic laments (Jer 51:51; Lam 1:7, 8; 2:6, 7; 3:56–64; 4:14–19; 5:1–3, 20–22; Zech 7:1-3; 8:18, 19). For more information, see, for example, Gerald H. Wilson, "The Use of the Royal Psalms at the 'Seams' of the Hebrew Psalter," *Journal for the Study of the Old Testament* 35 (1986): 85–94; James L. Mays, *The Lord Reigns: A Theological Handbook to the Psalms* (Louisville, KY: Westminster John Knox, 1994), 99–107; Santrac, *Psalms 76-150*, 340, 392-394.

within the Psalter, two lines of analysis will be pursued. The first will be an internal study of the selected individual psalms that include divine speeches. The second will be investigating whether these psalms are related to their surrounding psalms in order to create structural and thought pairs. The psalms that form pairs or blocks share several common elements (e.g., themes, keywords, literary structure, and placement in the Psalter). Each psalm in the block elucidates, advances, and/or completes the message of the other psalm(s), and by doing so contributes to unveiling the message of the entire block.

A. *Psalm 75:2-3, 10*

Psalm 75 praises God for His deliverance through His judgments. The previous two psalms deal with the problem of the prosperity of evil. Psalm 73 deals with this as a personal dilemma, as suggested by the use of the first person singular (e.g., vv. 2, 13, 17, 22). Psalm 74 deals with evil as a national dilemma, supported by the use of the plural to denote those in whose name the psalm has been composed (e.g., vv. 1, 4, 8). The possible thematic and structural links between Pss 74 and 75 suggest that Ps 75 furthers the conversation and brings the resolution to the problem of God's absence that is notably lacking at the end of Ps 74. The following table illustrates some structural and thematic parallels between Pss 74 and 75.

Psalm 74	Psalm 75
Lamenting plea that God has cast off His people (is far from them) and exhortation to God to act (74:1-3)	Praise to God whose works declare He is near and God's reply (75:1-3)
The boastful confidence of the wicked in their actions and speech (74:3-10)	The futility of the boastful confidence of the wicked in their actions and speech (75:4-16)
Invoking God's sovereign power and judgment (74:11-20)	Confirming God's sovereign power and judgment (75:7-8)
Praise of God is a hopeful desire in the future (74:21)	Praise of God is offered and lasts forever (75:9)
Final exhortation to God to deliver (74:22-23)	God's final confirmation of deliverance (75:10)

God's speech in Ps 75:2-3 abruptly interrupts the psalm, and the lack of introduction for the divine oracle obliges the audience to deduce from the context that these are the words of God, for the speaker is identified only as "I" (also in v. 10).[26] This pattern expressively reinforces God's declaration in v. 2 to speak and act according to His own timetable and not on a schedule.[27] The divine oracle announces God's judgment, and also initiates a series of reversals of the circumstances lamented in Ps 74, thus serving as the pivotal point of the argument about God's absence. The fact that divine judgment is proclaimed in the first person, i.e. in God's own voice, signifies that God chooses to break His own silence and subsequently silence the arrogant speech of the wicked in Ps 74. Interestingly, God does not directly answer the question "Why?" in the opening verse of Ps 74. He rather addresses the perhaps more urgent question in v. 10: "O God, *how long* will the adversary reproach?" (emphasis supplied). To this question, God gives an appropriate answer: "When I choose the proper time, I will judge uprightly" (Ps 75:2). The "proper time" (Heb. *mo'ed* "appointed time, appointed meeting place") in Ps 75 matches its homonym in Ps 74 that describes the meeting places destroyed by the enemies (Ps 74:4, 8).

---

[26] Psalm 75:2 could be understood as either God or a human judge or king speaking, because all of them have the responsibility of judging Israel. However, v. 3 clarifies that it is God speaking, for no mortal could manage to secure the pillars of the earth. Likewise, it is most likely God who speaks in v. 10. It does not seem that the psalmist would speak so boldly, especially since previously it is noted that only God has the prerogative to raise and lower humans (v. 7) (Beth Tanner, "Psalm 75: An Answer to Where God Has Gone," 604, 606). Introducing the divine oracle in Ps 75:2-3, the NIV adds "You say," which is not present in the Hebrew, in order to make it clear that the first person speaker is none other than God Himself (Tremper Longman III, *Psalms*, Tyndale Old Testament Commentaries 15-16 [Downers Grove, IL: IVP Academic, 2014], 282). See also, for example, Robert Alter, *The Book of Psalms: A Translation with Commentary* (New York, NY: W.W. Norton & Company, 2007), 264; Marvin E. Tate, *Psalms 51-100*, Word Biblical Commentary 20 (Grand Rapids, MI: Zondervan, 2015).

[27] Hans-Joachim Krause, *Psalms 60-150* (Minneapolis, MN: Augsburg, 1989), 104.

In Psalm 74 the sanctuary lies in ruins, symbolic of Israel's utter defeat (vv. 3-8). For biblical Israel, the sanctuary represents more than a place of worship. It is the symbol of the stability and strength of God's people (Ps 2:6) as well as of the whole earth (Ps 93:1-2). It represents the heights or heavens and points to the heavenly sanctuary where God resides (Pss 78:68-69; 99:2, 5; 125:1). The ruined sanctuary thus signals that the survival, not only of God's people, but of the entire world, is threatened. The divine speech in Ps 75:3 fittingly responds to the concerns of Ps 74: "When the earth and all its people quake, it is I who hold its pillars firm" (NIV). God's speech juxtaposes divine judgment with the stable pillars of the earth, i.e. the creation theme (Ps 75:2-3), similarly to Ps 74:12-17. Injustice and lawlessness cause "shaking of the earth's foundations" (1 Sam 2:8; cf. Pss 11:3; 82:5), and consequently the undoing of God's creation. God's judgment will restore justice in the world, and then the foundations of the earth will be stable again (Ps 82:8).

God's sovereign judgments in Ps 75 also reverse the boastful confidence of the enemies in Ps 74. The emphasis of Ps 75 on the arrogant speech of the wicked and not just their evil actions (vv. 4-5) matches the prominence that is given to the blasphemous speech of the enemies in Ps 74 (vv. 8, 10, 18, 22, 23). The speech of the wicked dominates Ps 74, and the unhindered praise of God's people is only a hopeful desire in the future (v. 21). Psalm 74 ends with the uproar of the wicked that "increases continually" (v. 23). Psalm 75 breaks that pattern. It opens with Israel's increasing praises of God (v. 1) and God's speech announcing the judgment of the wicked (vv. 2-3), counteracting the clamor of the enemies in Ps 74.[28] God's intervention reverses the perception of what can last forever. In Ps 74, God's apparent rejection of His people and the triumph of the wicked seem to last forever (vv. 1, 10, 19), but Ps 75 brings reassurance that it is only the praise of God that will remain forever (v. 9). The final scenes in Ps 75, portraying the psalmist's praise of God and the wicked being brought low as their horns are cut off (75:9-10), reverse the final scenes in Ps 74, depicting the enemies' reproach of God and the tumult of those who rise up against God (74:22-23). While it is the wicked who have the last word in Ps 74,

[28] The sense of increasing praise in Ps 75:1 is created with the emphatic repetition of "we give praise" that culminates in God's wondrous works, i.e., the whole creation joins Israel's praise of God.

God's final oracle in Ps 75:10 reverses that situation. God has the last word, confirming His judgment of the wicked and deliverance of the oppressed. God's final oracle in Ps 75 also reverses the opening address of God's people in Ps 74:1; it is not God's people whom God will utterly cast off, but He will cut off the oppressors.

The reversal between the two psalms and the climax in the form of a divine oracle can be presented as the following chiastic structure:

A Lament over the persecution of the wicked (Ps 74)
B God's response of a promised judgment (Ps 75:2-3)
A' Divine reversal of the circumstances in Ps 74 (Ps 75:4-10)

The thematic and linguistic links between Pss 74 and 75 discussed here seem to indicate a larger series of related psalms. Boadt recognizes the use of "panels" in constructing Pss 73-78 together as a group.[29] He argues that Pss 73-78 follow the same "panelling" or structure, having two major contrasting panels and the same number of subpanels that serve as explanation of the major panels in the psalm. Each psalm also sets the stage for the psalms that follow. For example, Pss 73 and 74 both relate to the sanctuary and the prosperity of God's enemies. Psalms 75 and 76 continue with the cosmic victory of God over his enemies; the specific reference to the exodus at the end of Ps 77 sets the stage for Ps 78.[30] Boadt concludes that "Psalms 73 and 78 fittingly serve as bookends to this series of proclamations of God's cosmic rule over all nations, which ensures that divine justice will triumph."[31] He observes that "[t]he movement from liturgical praise of God's maintenance of the divine order in the universe to the hope for a new exodus to rescue the nation from exile explains the progression of Psalms 73-78."[32]

The significance of the divine speech in Ps 75 is twofold: 1) it is the only divine oracle in the Pss 73-78 series; and 2) it confirms divine judgment in God's own voice and initiates a series of reassurances and examples in the rest of Ps 75 and Pss 76-78 that demonstrate that God can save and maintain justice in the world and

[29] Boadt, "The Use of 'Panels' in the Structure of Psalms 73-78," 534.
[30] Ibid., 541-546.
[31] Ibid., 548.
[32] Ibid., 546.

so remove any possible doubts that were raised in Pss 73 and 74. The possible parallels between Pss 73-78 certainly deserve further study. However, the discussed parallels between Pss 74 and 75 seem to be sufficient to suggest that the divine oracle in Ps 75:2-3 plays a significant role in replying to the concerns of Ps 74 regarding the prosperity of the wicked and the destruction of the sanctuary. The effect of the divine speech is to emphatically announce the reversal of the people's circumstances and highlight the certainty of divine judgment, as well as the fact that God takes the suffering of His people with utmost seriousness.

B. Psalm 81:6-16

Psalm 81 calls Israel to praise God during His festivals.[33] To the solemn and even joyous atmosphere depicted in the first part of Ps 81 (vv. 1-5), God responds in the first person, and recalls the time of the Exodus and of Israel's wandering in the desert. This psalm of Asaph emphasizes the episode in Meribah, which epitomizes Israel's rebellion (cf. Exod 17:1–7; Num 20:13). The people are admonished not to repeat the mistakes of past generations, but to trust God and follow His path, causing God to act on their behalf and bless them.

Psalm 81 combines the elements of hymn and divine oracle. These are reflected in the psalm's twofold literary structure:

1. A Call to Praise God at the Time of Festivals (81:1–5)
2. The Divine Oracle (81:6–16)

Although they have the common thread of the Exodus experience, the two parts of the psalm seem to fit somewhat oddly.[34] First, the shift from vv. 1-5 to the divine oracle is abrupt and unclear. Verse 5 ends with a difficult line ("where I heard a language I did not understand") because the psalm changes to the first person without

---

[33] The psalm's references to the trumpets and the New Moon (v. 3) refer to the Feast of Trumpets (Lev 23:23–25; Num 29:1). "Our solemn feast day" (Ps 81:3) is the Feast of Tabernacles (Lev 23:33–34), also called *the* Feast (cf. 1 Kgs 8:2; Neh 8:14; John 7:37).

[34] For a brief summary of some views that treat the two sections in Ps 81 (vv. 1-5b and vv. 5c-16) as two unrelated parts and an explanation as to why such a hypothesis is not necessary, see Tate, *Psalms 51-100*, 322-323.

clearly indicating the speaker.[35] The line is possibly "a kind of interjection on the part of a speaker who is a representative Israelite, recalling 'his' time of enslavement in Egypt when his taskmasters spoke an alien tongue."[36] Second, the divine oracle (vv. 6–16), with its reproachful tone, clashes with the joyous sentiments in the first part of the psalm and is an unexpected response to the people's worship of God. The divine oracle probably serves as a reminder to the people that worship includes more than praise and music. Obedience and faithfulness to God's word are essential for the worship of the Lord (cf. Ps 95). However, when Ps 81 is read in its canonical context, the purpose and placement of the divine oracle become more evident. The following parallels between Pss 80 and 81 seem to suggest that the divine oracle represents a divine reply to the people's petitions and accusations in Ps 80, also a psalm of Asaph.[37]

---

[35] The LXX reads "he" (Joseph, that is, the people of Israel) instead of "I." The NEB omits the line as a later marginal note.

[36] Alter, *The Art of Biblical Poetry*, 289. It is widely assumed today, however, that the change of speaker at v. 5c announces the divine oracle in v. 6 by the speaker who claims to be the mouthpiece of God and testifies to his inspiration (Tate, *Psalms 51-100*, 323; Derek Kidner, *Psalms 73–150*, KCC [London: InterVarsity, 1975; repr. Downers Grove, IL: IVP Academic, 2008], 325; Robert Davidson, *The Vitality of Worship: A Commentary on the Book of Psalms* [Grand Rapids, MI: Eerdmans, 1998], 268; Longman, *Psalms,* 302–303). Tate suggests that "a language I did not understand" (v. 5c) refers to God's voice that the speaker did not understand at first or "a message previously unknown, probably in the sense of not understanding its full meaning" (Tate, *Psalms 51-100*, 3, 23). However, the divine oracle in this psalm is clear. It tells about the divine deliverance from Egypt at the time of the exodus and calls the people to heed God's voice. It would be very unusual if the poet depicted the well-known founding history of Israel as "unknown language." Tanner argues that "a language I did not know" depicts God's hearing the groaning of the Israelites in Egypt that motivated God to act in Exod 2:24 (Beth Tanner, "Psalm 81: God's Side of Story," 639). Yet it remains unclear how the people's cries for help that God supposedly did not understand could motivate Him to act on behalf of the people. To conclude, the view that v. 5c depicts the language of Egypt and the poet's identification with his ancestors seems to fit the context best.

[37] Psalm 81 is generally considered to be closely related to Pss 50 and 95, all three having a sermonic style or edifying purpose. For example, Tate, *Psalms 51-100*, 321; James L. Mays, *Psalms*, Interpretation: A Bible

Both Pss 80 and 81 use "Israel" and "Joseph" to designate God's people (Pss 80:1; 81:4, 5). They both abound in imperatives. Psalm 80 entreats God to listen to what Israel says (v. 1), followed by a series of other imperatives that implore God to act on the people's behalf (vv. 2, 3, 7, 14, 19). Psalm 81 implores God's people to listen to what God says (v. 8), combining this exhortation with other imperatives that ask God's people to act according to God's will.[38] In both Psalms the relationship between God and His people is disturbed and in need of renewal.[39]

Both Psalms recall Israel's history, particularly the time of the Exodus (Pss 80:8; 81:10). Psalm 80 does that from the people's perspective, stressing the fact that both the past prosperity and the present misery of the nation are the result of God's sovereign actions (vv. 5–16). Psalm 81 recounts Israel's history from God's perspective, stressing the episode in Meribah (vv. 7-9). In biblical narrative, Meribah is known as the place where Israel tested God by challenging His faithfulness and power to provide for their needs (cf. Ps 95:8, 9). Psalm 81 makes an intriguing reversal and interprets the same event as the time when God tested Israel (v. 7). The people failed God's test because they challenged God by their disobedience and lack of trust (v. 11).

The event demonstrates that God's judgment is righteous and follows the people's actions. The following parallels between Pss 80 and 81 further endorse that conclusion. The depiction of God's judgment in Ps 81:12 as God's giving over (Heb. *shalakh*) of His people to their stubborn heart corresponds to the depiction of Israel's growth in Ps 80:11 as Israel sending out (Heb. *shalakh*) her boughs

---

Commentary for Teaching and Preaching (Louisville, KY: John Knox), 266.

[38] For example, the people of God are called to "sing aloud" (v. 1), "make a joyful shout" (v. 1), "raise (a song)" (v. 2), "strike (the timbrel)" (v. 2), "blow (the trumpet)" (v. 3), "open (your mouth)" (v. 10).

[39] Although in Ps 81 God does not charge the people with any particular sin, He admonishes them to obey Him (v. 8). The term "admonish" is the translation of the hiphil (causative) form of the verb *'ud*. This Hebrew term "marks the address as a warning witness that calls on those to whom it is addressed to right a relationship that has gone wrong (see the use of the term in 2 Kgs 17:13, 15; Jer. 11:7–8; Neh. 9:29, 30, 34; compare the prose of Jer 7:16–29, where the crucial motifs of Psalm 81 also appear) (Mays, *Psalms*, 266). The NIV states "I will warn you."

to the Sea and her branches to the River. When read with Ps 80, Ps 81 seems to imply that Israel's geographical advancement was not followed by the nation's spiritual progress. On the contrary, Israel "walked in their own counsels" (Ps 81:12), away from God. The people's failure to acknowledge their own apostasy in Ps 80 can be credited to the people's "stubborn heart" (Ps 81:12), namely their vain confidence in the virtue of their own argument that God had abandoned His people for no apparent reason (Ps 80:4-18). The Hebrew word for "stubborn" (*sherirut*) depicts "self-reliance, doing one's own will, and idolatry."[40] The term is found only in Ps 81 in the Psalms, but many times in the book of Jeremiah where it is often translated as "imagination" (KJV), pointing to the deceitful and futile nature of human self-containment (e.g., Jer 3:17; 7:24; 9:14).

The other parallels between Pss 80 and 81 further illustrate the dialogical tension between the two sides. Psalm 80 asks God how long He will be angry with His people, allowing the enemies to mock them (vv. 4, 6). Psalm 81 seemingly provides the answer: "I would *soon* (*me'at* "as a little," "shortly") subdue their enemies, and turn My hand against their adversaries" (v. 14; emphasis supplied). However, a condition is attached to this promise–Israel's obedience to God (v. 13). The parable of the vineyard in Ps 80 does not relate the people's present misery to their disobedience to God (contra Isa 5:1–7). The people's voice in Ps 80 identifies God as the primary source of their misfortunes: "*You* have fed them with the bread of tears; *You* have made them drink tears" (v. 5; emphasis supplied). Psalm 81 portrays God as "defending" Himself by stating that He will feed them "with the finest of wheat; and with honey from the rock" (v. 16), so fulfilling His covenantal promises (cf. Deut 8:8). The diet of the finest wheat and honey in Ps 81 represents a remarkable reversal of the bread of tears in Ps 80:5.

Psalm 81 reverses numerous other things found in Ps 80. For example, Ps 80 implies that the divine Shepherd is not listening to His flock and so is implored to listen, look down, and see (vv. 1, 14). By contrast, Ps 81 states that Israel does not listen to God (v. 8, 11). Psalm 80 beseeches God to save His people. Psalm 81 is a reminder that God has always saved them in the past (vv. 6, 7), implying that this will also be the case in the future. In Ps 80, Israel's enemies prosper (vv. 6, 13), but in Ps 81, God judges Israel's enemies for

[40] Tate, *Psalms 51-100*, 320 n. 13b.

their wickedness (vv. 14, 15). These reversals in Ps 81 not only provide an explanation of the people's state in Ps 80, but also defend God from their accusations and demonstrate His faithfulness and love for them.

The notion of divine faithfulness and love is reinforced in Ps 81:10: "Open your mouth wide, and I will fill (Heb. *mala'*) it." This image recalls a mother bird filling the widely opened beaks of her young with food. It also corresponds to the depiction of divine blessing in Ps 80:9: "You prepared room for it, and caused it to take deep root, and it filled (Heb. *mala'*) the land." The source of the people's misery is not God's neglect, but the people's apostasy. Both Psalms look to God's *hand* as the agent of deliverance and prosperity (Pss 80:17; 81:14). However, their emphasis is different. Psalm 80 repeatedly stresses that God is expected to deliver His people first in order for the people to be able to respond with praises and faithfulness (Ps 80:2, 3, 7, 18, 19). Psalm 81 calls the people to return to God and walk in His ways, and He will deliver them (vv. 13, 14).

Psalm 81 must not be seen as the counterargument to Ps 80. The fact that both psalms stand together strongly argues that "[b]oth judgments are biblical, and both need to be heard"[41] in order to understand the biblical message. The covenantal relationship between God and His people is always evolving and cannot be confined to a mathematical formula. God's grace both precedes and follows the people's responses of trust and obedience. Likewise, the promise of immediate salvation for those who submit to the Lord (Ps 81:13, 14) is paired with another promise that concerns those who persist in their rebellion against God: their punishment (*'et*, "fate," "doom") will last forever (v. 15).

The literary and theological interrelatedness of Pss 80 and 81 is reflected in their matching structures.

[41] Brueggemann, *The Message of the Psalms: A Theological Commentary* (Minneapolis, MN: Augsburg, 1984), 94.

Themes	Psalm 80	Psalm 81	Parallels
Exhortations	vv. 1-7	vv. 1-5	- Joseph (Pss 80:1; 81:5) - Abound in imperatives: Ps 80: *ha'azinah* "give ear," *hofi'ah* "shine forth," v. 1; *'orrah* "stir up," *lekah* "come," v. 2; *hashibenu* "restore us" [2x], *haer* "cause to shine" [2x], vv. 3, 7. Ps 81: *harninu* "sing," *hari'u* "make a joyful shout," v. 1; *se'u* "raise," *tenu* "strike," v. 2; *tiq'u* "blow," v. 3.
Exodus	vv. 8-11	vv. 6-10	- Ps 80: God caused Israel, His vine, to fill (*mala'*) the land; "deep root" (v. 9). - Ps 81: God fills (*mala'*) the mouth of His people; "mouth wide" (v. 10)
Judgment	vv. 12-16	vv. 11-12	- Ps 80: The people say that God has turned against His people and implore God to return to them. - Ps 81: God says that Israel has turned against Him and implores them to return to His ways.
Ways to Reconcilia-tion	vv. 17-18	vv. 13-14	Chiasm: A Let Your hand be Upon the man of Your right Hand (Ps 80:17) — B' That Israel would walk in My ways (Ps 81:13) X B Then we will not turn back from You (Ps 80:18) — A' My hand against their adversaries (Ps 81:14)
Deliverance	v. 19	vv. 15-16	- Ps 80: God is implored to save - Ps 81: God promises salvation to the faithful, but the fate of the haters of the Lord and of the pretenders is eternal condemnation

The theological assumption of Pss 80 and 81 is that of the Mosaic covenant (Exod 19:5; Deut 11:26–28). When Pss 80 and 81 are read together, the divine speech in Ps 81 highlights the notion of salvation by God's grace; when the covenant is broken by disobedience, it can be renewed only by the grace of God, so that the people can enjoy its blessings anew. Most Psalms typically end with praise, promise, or in a poetic manner, imparting a sense of completeness and closure to the poem. However, Ps 80 ends with expectation of God's intervention that will renew Israel's good fortune and will then lead to renewed praise to God (vv. 17-19). Psalm 81 ends abruptly, with a sudden switch from the third to first person (v. 16),[42] leaving the reader with the impression that God rashly stopped in the middle of His speech ("I sated you with honey from the rock," v. 16b). This switch could poetically imply that God decided to refrain from further speech, for it is now time for Him to act.

C. *Psalm 89:3-4, 19-37*

Psalm 89 is a communal lament for the restoration of the Davidic dynasty. It engages two themes: the sovereignty of God as the Creator, and the faithfulness of God in establishing the everlasting covenant with David. The psalm laments over the harsh reality that seems to oppose them. Ethan the Ezrahite, the psalm's author, was most likely a temple musician (1 Chron 15:17, 19).

God's promise to David in 2 Sam 7:10–16 is delivered in Ps 89 in the first person singular, as if God is speaking, most likely to deem it more authentic (vv. 3–4; 19–37). God's speech is marked with key words such as mercy (*khesed* "lovingkindness," "grace" in vv. 24, 28, 33), faithfulness (*'emunah* "firmness" in vv. 24, 33, 37), and forever (*'olam* "everlasting," "evermore" in vv. 28, 29, 36, 37), unmistakably underlining God's irrevocable choice of the Davidic dynasty. The creation theme strengthens the certainty of God's covenant with David and offers the context for everlasting praise of the Lord's covenantal faithfulness (vv. 1, 2, 5-8, 36–37). Some scholars observe that vv. 1–4 in reworked form reappear again in vv. 28–29 and 36–37 to reinforce the glorious promise that the Davidic line can indeed suffer punishment, but never outright rejection (vv. 30–34).[43] Certain key words and themes in Ps 89 echo the concern in the previous Psalm that the Lord has abandoned His servant. The

---

[42] The switch from third to first person is not preserved in some English versions (e.g., NASB, NIV, NLT, RSV), but the meaning of verse 16 in Hebrew is: "He fed him (Israel) the finest wheat; I sated you with honey from the rock."

[43] Richard J. Clifford, "Psalm 89: A Lament over the Davidic Ruler's Continued Failure," *Harvard Theological Review* 73 (1980): 35–47.

divine speech in Ps 89 appears to serve as a divine reply to the concerns expressed in two adjacent laments, namely in Ps 88 (a psalm written by another Ezrahite[44]) and Ps 89:38-52.

The structure showing the close linkage between Pss 88 and 89 with the divine oracles at the center can be outlined as follows.

Introduction: Acknowledgment of the Lord's salvation (88:1)
I Lament due to God's apparent abandonment (Ps 88:2-37)
A The psalmist's deadly affliction (88:2–5)
  B God as the source of the psalmist's troubles (88:6–8)
    C Reasoning with God (88:9–14)
A' The psalmist's deadly affliction (88:15)
  B' God as the source of the psalmist's troubles (88:16–18)

II Acknowledgment of God's faithfulness and the Divine speeches (Ps 89:1-37)
A The psalmist's praise of the Lord for His faithfulness and love (89:1–2)
B Divine speech: God's covenantal faithfulness (89:3–4)
A' The creation's praise of the Lord for His faithfulness and love (89:5–18)
B' Divine speech: God's covenantal faithfulness (89:19–37)

I' Lament due to God's apparent abandonment (Ps 89:38-51)
A God as the source of the king's troubles (89:38–40)
  B The king's deadly affliction and God as the source of his troubles (89:41–45)
    C Reasoning with God (89:46–49)
A' God as the source of the king's troubles (89:50a)
  B' The king's deadly affliction (89:50b–51)
Conclusion: Acknowledgment of the Lord's praise (89:52)

The two laments (Pss 88:1-18; 89:38-52) have a similar structure. The structure of Ps 88 turns twice from describing the

[44] Herman the Ezrahite, a temple musician (1 Chr 25:5, 6). "The Ezrahite" may be a familiar designation derived from "Zerah" in 1 Chr 2:6 (Alter, *Psalms*, 308)."

psalmist's affliction (A, A') to finding God's actions as the source of the affliction (B, B'). The psalmist's reasoning with God appears to put these two themes in theological perspective at the center of the psalm (C). Likewise, but in reverse order, the structure of Ps 89 turns twice from finding God as the source of the affliction (A, A') to describing the people's affliction (B, B'), and places the reasoning with God at the center (C).

The divine speeches (section II in the outline above) are placed between the two laments (sections I and I'). Section II contains a balanced structure as well: each divine speech (B, B') is introduced with praise for the Lord's faithfulness and love (A, A').

God's servants in both laments (sections I and I') face deadly afflictions. The affliction is so great that nothing the people have done seem to merit it. The suffering remains inexplicable and therefore must be due to God's sovereign and unfathomable wrath (Pss 88:6–8, 16–18; 89:38–40, 41–45, 50a). Nevertheless, the sufferers turn to God, and try to remonstrate with Him. The Psalms are a reminder to never cease speaking to God, even at death's door. The reasoning with God in both laments centers around the theme of praising God and the inability of the dead to worship God (Pss 88:9–14; 89:46–49). In other words, the reason why God should save His servants is that they may praise and worship Him. God is questioned as to why He hid Himself (Pss 88:14; 89:46), and the afflicted feel God has forgotten them (Pss 88:5; 89:50). Mortals can do nothing to escape God's wrath and the power of the grave, and only God's faithfulness and love can save them (Pss 88:11; 89:48, 49).

The placement of the two divine speeches in Ps 89 at the center of the crisis, namely between the two laments where God is named as the cause of His people's misfortunes and of being aloof from their cries, renders the divine speeches as a debate about theodicy. Is God indifferent and did He cause His people's suffering? Do the wicked prosper more than those who obey God? The fact that God delivers His "defense" in person, directly and powerfully breaks His perceived silence and brings reassurance of His loyalty to His covenant with Israel. Each divine speech is introduced with praise, matching the concern for praise in the two laments and showing that the praise of God is inexhaustible and can and should be offered in all circumstances.

The divine oracles do not seek so much to reverse or openly refute the people's charges against God in the adjacent laments, but rather offer a fresh reminder of God's loyalty and the unchanging character of His love in the context of creation that attests to God's sovereignty and goodness (Ps 89:1, 2, 8–16). Knowing that God is in control should inspire hope even when God's people go through inexplicable individual and communal suffering and spiritual crisis. When the suffering servants of God feel they bear the terrible burden of God's indignation (Pss 88:15; 89:50), the Lord promises to strengthen and exalt them with His hand (Ps 89:20-22). Although the laments give the impression that God's wrath is never ending (Pss 88:7, 16; 89:46), only God's love and faithfulness are repeatedly highlighted and said to endure forever (Ps 89:4, 28, 29, 33, 36, 37). Even when circumstances necessitate it, God's wrath is only for a time and does not extinguish God's love and faithfulness. The acknowledgment of God's salvation in the opening of Ps 88 and the acknowledgement of God's praise in the conclusion of Ps 89 could be seen as an *inclusio* that ties all that is spoken and experienced in Pss 88 and 89 within the context of God's grace.

Further linkage between Pss 88 and 89 can be found in their both being understood as Messianic psalms.[45] Although the human component of the covenant failed, the people could rest in the assurance of the unchanging purposes of God through the Davidic King, the Messiah, who embodies all righteousness and is the salvation of Israel and of the whole world (Ps 89:28–37, 49).

D. Psalm 95:8-11

Psalm 95 is a call to worship the Lord who is the great God and King above all others. The Lord deserves ceaseless praises as the Creator and Sustainer of His people Israel and of all creation.

Psalm 95 contains three exhortations followed by reasons for the exhortation:

---

[45] Psalm 88 is not directly quoted by Christ in the Gospels or by the apostles in connection to Christ, as are some other Psalms (e.g., Pss 2, 16, 22, 110, 118). Yet the tremendous suffering that is voiced in this Psalm strongly reflects Christ's agony, particularly at the close of His earthly ministry (e.g., Matt 14:32–41). The Psalm's theme is strongly reminiscent of certain Messianic psalms (e.g., Ps 22).

A. First exhortation:
- a. Call to worship the Lord (95:1–2)
- b. Reasons for the exhortation (95:3–5)

B. Second exhortation:
- a. Call to worship the Lord (95:6)
- b. Reasons for the exhortation (95:7a)

C. Third exhortation:
- a. Call to obey and trust the Lord (95:7b–9)
- b. Reasons for the exhortation (95:10–11)

The first two exhortations are jubilant calls for the worship of the Lord. They are reinforced by giving the true motivation for praise. Israel belongs to God for two unbreakable reasons, namely creation (vv. 2–4) and salvation/covenant (vv. 1–3, 7). The third and final exhortation in the Psalm is the strongest. The psalmist's words suddenly give way to a divine oracle that admonishes the people to understand that worship does not involve only music, songs, and prostration (vv. 1, 2, 6), but also obeying and trusting God's voice (vv. 7–10). The divine oracle reminds the people that special covenantal privileges come with covenantal responsibilities.

Psalm 95 is rightly regarded by some as a royal psalm because its themes harmonize with the spirit of the surrounding royal Psalms (Pss 93–100).[46] Following the same line of analysis as in our previous examples, we find a number of thematic and lexical parallels between Ps 95 and the previous psalm (Ps 94). They are presented in the following table.

Psalm 94	**Psalm 95**
Judgment is Invoked (94:1-11)	**Praise is Invoked (95:1-7)**
- Covenant motif (vv. 1-7) - Creation motif (vv. 8-11)	- Creation motif - (vv. 4-6) - Covenant motif (vv. 1-3, 7)

[46] For example, Mays, *The Lord Reigns* (Louisville, KY: Westminster John Knox, 1994), 12–15; McCann, *A Theological Introduction to the Book of Psalms: The Psalms as Torah* (Nashville, TN: Abingdon, 1993), 41–48.

The Righteous and Their Outcome (94:12-22)	The Apostate and Their Outcome (95:8-11)
- Know God's ways (v. 12) - Have upright heart (v. 15) - God gives them rest (v. 13)	- Do not know God's ways (v. 10) - Go astray in their heart (v. 10) - God will not give them rest (v. 11)
Judgment of the wicked reinforced – repetition of "cut them off" (v. 23)	**Judgment of the wicked reinforced – God's oath (v. 11)**

When Pss 94 and 95 are read in their canonical order, one finishes reading Ps 94 with the image of the Lord as the "rock of my refuge" (v. 22), and finds the same description of the Lord in the opening of Ps 95 as "the Rock of our salvation" (v. 1). Those who are causing distress and are thus recipients of divine judgment in both Psalms are the wicked among God's people.[47] In Ps 94, they test God's forbearance by arrogantly claiming that God does not see or pay heed to their evil actions (v. 7), foolishly ignoring the abundance of evidence demonstrating God's sovereignty and power (vv. 8-10). Similarly, in Ps 95 the apostate people test God's longsuffering, defiantly disregarding His mighty works that they have witnessed (v. 9). The direct speech of the wicked in Ps 94:7 is refuted by God's direct speech in Ps 95:8-11. While the solemn warning tone of the divine oracle seems not to be completely in tune with the jubilant

[47] That Ps 94 raises voice against the corrupt leaders of Israel seems to be the case for several reasons. If the oppressor here is the foreign nation, would not the pagan tyrant oppress the entire company of Israel and not merely "the widows, the aliens and the fatherless" (Ps 94:6)? Israel's judges were instructed specially to care for these categories of people who represented the weakest in Israel (Deut 10:18; 14:29; Ps 82:2–4). The wicked are also notably emboldened to continue in their wickedness because they think that *the Lord* does not see nor care for the things occurring on earth in v. 7 (cf. Pss 10:11; 73:11). A foreign tyrant would certainly give no importance to what the Lord sees or does not see. Therefore, the psalmist laments the arrogance and wickedness of the local oppressors.

feelings expressed in the first part of Ps 95, it duly relates to the urgency felt in Ps 94 (e.g., vv. 1-7, 16, 21).[48]

There is widespread consensus among biblical scholars that Ps 94 severs the compact sequencing of the surrounding psalms celebrating the Lord's kingship (Pss 93, 95–99). This psalm is typically not considered a royal psalm because it does not explicitly address the Lord's kingship, like the surrounding Psalms.[49] However, Ps 94 engages in certain themes that are closely related to God's kingship. For example, the image of God as Judge (v. 2) is common in the royal psalms, highlighting the sovereignty of the divine King over all nations and kings (cf. Pss 96:10, 13; 97:8, 10; 98:9; 99:4). The mention of a corrupt human throne (v. 20) may also serve to contrast with the Lord's everlasting throne that is based on righteousness and justice (Pss 93:2; 97:2). In addition to this, it is possible that the thematic and lexical parallels between Pss 94 and 95 have led the editors of the Psalter to place Ps 94 next to Ps 95 in the sequence of the Psalms on the Lord's kingship.[50] The divine speech in Ps 95 not only provides the reasons for the third exhortation in the Psalm, but seems to serve as a direct divine confirmation and reinforcement of the divine judgment upon the apostate among God's people announced in Ps 94.

IV. Conclusion

Our study of the divine speeches in the Psalms reveals just a tiny fragment of the excellent artistry and amazing complexity behind the message and structure of the individual psalms and of the book of Psalms as a whole. The direct citations of divine words in the Psalms not only create a sense of God's immediate reply and presence but also play a pivotal role in creating psalm pairs or groups and advancing the dialogue between the people and God.

---

[48] Psalm 94 opens with a sense of urgency. God is invoked personally over and over again: O LORD God, O God, O Judge, LORD, O LORD. The psalmist appeals to God's vengeance, which is God's just punishment of the evil ones (vv. 1-5).

[49] See the examples mentioned in Tanner, "Psalm 94: God Will Judge the World," 709. For a different view see Tate, *Psalms 51-100*, 488-490.

[50] Tate suggests that Ps 91:14-16 and Ps 95:8-11, being the only two divine oracles in Pss 90-100, form an inclusio around Pss 92-94 (Tate, *Psalms 51-100*, 450).

The following points sum up the ways the divine speeches are used to advance the message of some Psalms.

Statements of divine theodicy. The divine speeches in our four examples as well as in some other psalms[51] are closely tied to laments where God is charged with being the cause of the people's trials, being silent to their cries, and/or is mocked by the enemies. The occurrence of the divine oracles in these contexts shows that there is more than the human voice, whether that of God's people or of the wicked, in the midst of suffering and injustice in the world. The divine oracles stress God's immanent presence among His people and signal God's special care and immediate response to the people's prayers. The artist portrays God as revealing Himself anew and addressing His people's most distressing concerns and complaints. When people put God on trial (e.g., Pss 74:1, 10, 11; 80:4-17; 88), it is God's desire to utterly vindicate His people, and not Himself, that compels God to respond. James A. Wharton rightly points out that the anticipated or received answer from God invariably comes in the form of vindication or deliverance.[52] The fact that God speaks at all reveals something about His character: the Lord is a deity who answers mere mortals. In other words, the very presence of the divine speech implies God's concern for His people and serves to vindicate them, and by extension clears the Lord of the people's accusations.

Prophetic judgment texts. The prophetic character of divine oracles is observed in their dramatic proclamation of the imminent divine judgment as God's response to the problem of evil, akin to the prophets' declarations in the Bible (e.g., Ps 75:2–3 and Isa 49:8; Ps 81:13–14 and Jer 15:19; Ps 89:3–4 and Jer 33:17). Some divine oracles are introduced with an announcement that is reminiscent of the prophets' statement "thus says the Lord" (Pss 12:5; 68:22). An additional argument in support of the close connection between psalmody and prophecy can be found in the fact that the Old Testament composition of many hymns of praise is closely related to prophecy (e.g., Exod 15:20, 21; Judg 4:4; 5:1–31; 1 Sam 5:9).[53] Being pronounced in first person as if God is speaking directly, the

---

[51] E.g., Pss 2:6, 7–9; 12:5; 46:10; 82:2–7; 91:14–16.

[52] James A. Wharton, *Job*, Westminster Bible Companion (Louisville, KY: Westminster John Knox, 1999), 165, 169.

[53] Bosma, "Discerning the Voices in the Psalms," 146.

divine speeches stress the imminence of God's judgment and acts of salvation.

Heralds of reconciliation. There is an important dialogical element in the Psalms, especially the psalms of lament, in which the reader encounters a dramatic interplay between human words addressed to the Lord (including a quotation of the boastful words of the adversaries) and words from the Lord to the petitioner.[54] As in the book of Job, the divine oracle breaks God's perceived silence and does not let the sufferer become or remain an opponent of God but pursues his reorientation.[55] In His mercy, God responds to His people's pleas and complaints until their trust is fully restored and culminates in praise. This shows that the role of divine speeches is not just to correct the people but also rebuild their relationship with God as part of the reconciliation process.

Stylistic devices. The divine oracle "constitutes an essential part of the poet's dramatic scene."[56] God's speeches proclaim in a striking manner the divine intervention as they abruptly interrupt the Psalm by either not being announced (e.g., Ps 75:2–3) or drastically changing the tone of the Psalm (e.g., Pss 81:6–16; 95:8–11). In their final canonical placement in the Psalter, the divine oracles connect adjacent and seemingly unrelated Psalms, serving as the pivotal point of the discussion and of the literary structure. As Bosma has correctly observed, "the newer canonical reading strategy in the exegesis of the Psalter alerted us to another important expression of the word of God in the Psalter, in addition to the quotations of God speaking directly (e.g. Pss. 2:7–9; 12:5) or indirectly through his official ministrants in the cult (e.g. Pss. 20:6; 28:5), namely, the 'voice' of the canon conscious editors of the final shape of the Psalter."[57] In our examples, the reversal that the divine speeches announce for the fortunes of God's suffering people is reflected in the literary structure, with the divine speech as the peak or turning point.

---

[54] Ibid., 142.

[55] See Daniel Timmer, "God's Speeches, Job's Responses, and the Problem of Coherence in the Book of Job: Sapiential Pedagogy Revisited," *The Catholic Biblical Quarterly* 71 (2009), 297–298, 303.

[56] Booij, *Godswoorden in de Psalmen*, 31-33, quoted in Bosma, 132.

[57] Bosma, "Discerning the Voices in the Psalms," 167.

Citations of past divine announcements. The poetic interpretation in Ps 89 of God's promise to David in 2 Sam 7:10–16 is delivered in the first person singular, as if God is speaking, most likely to deem it more authentic, urgent and personal in the time of Israel's great crisis (vv. 3–4; 19–37). In this way, the poet confirms the validity of God's word given to Israel in the past and points to it as the foundation of Israel's hope at all times. By delivering the past divine announcement in the form of divine oracle, the poet also effectively conveys that God's word is fresh and living among the current generation of God's people (cf. Pss 2; 110).

Some scholars point to the use of direct quotes of divine speeches as oracles within a cultic situation.[58] The possible cultic situations and the use of the Psalms in Israel's worship have been the subject of much reflection, research, and speculations that could not be addressed in this essay.[59] One could imagine, however, that divine oracles were recited by a worship leader or priest in the worship service in the Temple.

The questions that remain after examining the examples of direct quotations of divine speech are whether the poets intended the discussed Psalms to be harmonized the way proposed here, and whether the pairing of these Psalms was envisioned by the editors of the final canonical shape of the Psalter. While I doubt anyone can determine the answers with certainty, the inner-biblical parallels

---

[58] The cultic approach to the Psalms has focused on attempts to reconstruct from the Psalms the liturgy in which they were used. See, for example, a proposal of the enthronement festival of Yahweh in Sigmund Mowinckel, *The Psalms in Israel's Worship* (Grand Rapids, MI: Eerdmans, 2004), 1:106–192. Hans-Joachim Kraus proposed the annual celebration of the royal Zion festival (Hans-Joachim Kraus, *Theology of the Psalms* [Minneapolis, MN: Fortress, 1992], 107–123). Artur Weiser suggested the covenant festival as the real original setting in life of the Psalms (Artur Weiser, *The Psalms: A Commentary* [London: SCM, 1962], 27–52).

[59] Many cultic reconstructions of the Psalms have been renounced by numerous scholars as highly speculative. See, for example, Helmer Ringgren, *Faith of the Psalmists* (Philadelphia, PA: Fortress, 1963), 93; Claus Westermann, *The Psalms: Structure, Content & Message* (Minneapolis, MN: Augsburg, 1980), 109; Walter Brueggemann, *Israel's Praise: Doxology against Idolatry and Ideology* (Philadelphia, PA: Fortress, 1988), 4; Longman, *Psalms*, 334; B. Tanner, "Psalm 93: God is King," 706.

seem to strongly suggest a purposeful design behind the placement of the divine speeches in some psalms and of the placement of these psalms in the book of Psalms. In my view, the voices of the poets and the editors are intimately intertwined because they inherently resound God's voice. Moreover, the existence elsewhere in Scripture of the divine speeches responding to the human subject's situation and concerns (e.g., the book of Job), similar to that in the discussed Psalms, merits notice as a significant argument in favor of similar arrangement in the Psalms.

The Cup at Crossroads: A Narrative Analysis of Jesus' Struggle in Matthew 26:36-46

C. Adelina Alexe

Abstract

The Matthean depiction of Jesus' struggle in Gethsemane is rich in literary features revealing this crucial episode in Jesus' ministry. Through the joint effect of the use of temporal and spatial markers, characterization, actions, props, tempo, and literary structure, Matthew gives the reader a glimpse into the depth of the cost of salvation. Situated between the Last Supper and Jesus' arrest, Matt 26:36-46 is a turning point in the story of Jesus. And since Jesus' choice in Gethsemane has an everlasting effect on us, this episode also represents a turning point in the life of the faithful reader. This chapter is an invitation to a deeper look into the experience of Jesus during the tensest moments of his life on earth, and to a renewed appreciation for God's immeasurable love, which is as costly as it is infinite.[1]

---

[1] I am much indebted to Dr. Jo Ann Davidson for broadening my spiritual and intellectual horizon with valuable insights into biblical narrative analysis. Her contribution to my development as a Christian and as a scholar has irreversibly changed the way I read the Bible. Once one's mind is trained to see narrative details, it is impossible to "unsee" them. This process has brought me closer to the Bible and to God. It has also enabled me, in turn, to empower others to seek the beauty of God through literary depth. I cannot think of a more profound impact on people than forming helpful new paths into their brain. When so much goes wrong in the world, acquiring such patterns through committed mentorship stands as a testimony of God's goodness to both the messenger and the recipient. Therefore, may my lasting conversion from dry exegete into lover of narrative beauty be for God's glory–a divine goodness unmistakably manifested in the work God has accomplished through the dedicated ministry of Dr. Davidson.

Introduction

The scene of Jesus' agony in Gethsemane, recorded in Matt 26:36-46, marks a pivotal point in the story of the atonement, as several features of the narrative suggest. The passage is nestled between the Last Supper and the arrest of Jesus, and thus the tense prayer in the garden is the last action Jesus performs in freedom. This halt in the timeline of Jesus' ministry indicates that the passage marks a turning point in Jesus' progression toward the cross. The spatial location where the events occur suggests a crossroads as well. Jesus comes to pray in "an enclosed open-air structure," a "protective or safe space,"[2] but by the end of the passage, a transition is indicated in Jesus' words *Get up, let us be going; behold, the one who betrays Me is at hand!* [3] (v. 46). Furthermore, the depiction of Jesus' turmoil though characterization, actions, and the literary structure, also suggests that Jesus is now at a turning point in his ministry. Lastly, the slowing of narrative time with reference to hours and multiple prayers indicates that important events are happening in the garden. Thus, in the Matthean portrayal of Jesus' struggle, settings, characterization, actions, literary structure, and tempo all converge to reveal the significance of the passage not only in Matthew's Passion narrative, but also in the entire Gospel. This chapter offers an analysis of several narrative characteristics that demonstrate the intensity of Jesus' struggle at this key turning point in his ministry, which deepens our understanding of the great cost of salvation.

Settings

Both the spatial and the temporal settings emphasize Jesus' struggle. The spatial markers suggest a great deal of movement taking place in Gethsemane from the moment Jesus freely enters the garden until he leaves arrested. Two patterns can be noted.

In the first part of the story we see Jesus progressively distancing himself from the disciples. The progression *here* (v. 36), *there* (v. 36), *here* (v. 38), *a little further* (v. 39), *on his face* (v. 39), are markers of this distancing. In accordance with the Matthean theology

---

[2] James L. Resseguie, *Narrative Criticism of the New Testament: An Introduction* (Grand Rapids, MI: Baker, 2005), 101.

[3] In this chapter, the italic font indicates quotations from the Bible.

of prayer (Matt 6:5-15), Jesus seeks out solitude in order to commune with his Father (cf. 6:6; 14:23).

In the second part of the story, the movement pattern changes into a back-and-forth motion. From his place of prayer, he goes back to the disciples (v. 40), then away (v. 42), back again (v. 43), away again (v. 44), and finally back to them (v. 45). James Resseguie suggests that Pilate's going in and out of the building during Jesus' trial, his "shuttling back and forth," indicates indecisiveness as a key motif in the story.[4] In a similar way, the back-and-forth movement in Matt 26:36-46 may be indicative of wavering, tension, distress, and uncertainty for Jesus, particularly since this movement is interwoven with the three prayers which reveal the same motifs of wavering, tension, and distress. He prays, goes back to the disciples, prays again, goes back to them again, prays the third time, and returns to the disciples (vv. 36, 40, 42, 43, 44, 45). However, even though both Jesus and Pilate are characterized through a similar spatial pattern of movement which bespeaks wavering, Pilate's decision reflects the will of the crowd, while Jesus' choice reflects the will of the Father.

The repetition of *again* (vv. 42-44) intensifies the portrayal of Jesus' struggle, and Matthew's inclusion of the numerals *a second time* (v. 42) and *a third time* (v. 44) strengthens the tension. The mention of *one hour* in verse 40 suggests a prayer length indicative of intensity.

In the last part of the story the repetition of *at hand* (vv. 45-46) suggests the urgency of the time. The concentration of temporal markers on the nearness of the betrayal is conveyed through a progressive revelation of this impending immediacy: *Behold, the hour is at hand and the Son of Man is being betrayed into the hands of sinners. Get up, let us be going; behold, the one who betrays Me is at hand!* (vv. 45-46). First, Jesus makes a rather ambiguous statement that indicates nearness: *The hour is at hand.* Then, he introduces the reality of the betrayal—*The Son of Man is being betrayed*. And finally, he couples the concept of betrayal with its immediacy, in the complete revelation that *The one who betrays Me is at hand.* The space of protection, a garden that was "likely fenced or walled and had an entrance, perhaps even a gate,"[5] is about to be

[4] Resseguie, *Narrative Criticism*, 45.

[5] John MacArthur, *Matthew 24-28*, The MacArthur New Testament Commentary (Chicago, IL: Moody Press, 1089), 168.

left behind as Jesus moves forward towards the cross. Thus, both the temporal and spatial data emphasize the loss of liberty Jesus will experience: from this place and time onward, he will be bound, powerless in the hands of sinners until his mission is complete in his death and resurrection.

Props

The entire passage is a spiral of actions revolving around the only metaphorical prop present in the story: the cup. This singularity, connected with the agony of prayer in which it is mentioned, illustrates the centrality of the concepts linked to it. The cup is mentioned once explicitly (v. 39) and twice implicitly (vv. 42 and 44), each time in the context of Jesus' communication with his Father.

Commentators generally agree that this metaphoric use of *potérion* (meaning "a wine cup") deals with Jesus' suffering. David Hagner writes that "this cup is a metaphor for the suffering and death that he was soon to face."[6] Similarly, Mark Nolland suggests that the cup in Matt 26 is the same cup Jesus drank with his disciples at the Passover supper recounted in the previous chapter, and argues that the cup "probably refers to his coming death with a conscious link to the Last Supper imagery."[7] R. T. France ties the idea to the Old Testament usage of the cup of God's wrath and judgment. Jesus' death is a result of this cup of wrath. France notes "it was this aspect of his suffering, not merely the physical pain and death in themselves, that most distressed him."[8]

Since the suffering–symbolized here by the drinking of the cup–is the reason for Jesus' crisis, its presence and function in the development of the narrative is crucial, and an analysis of the characters, actions and narrative structure shows the ripple effects this prop creates in Matt 26:36-46.

---

[6] Donald A. Hagner, *Matthew 14-28*, Word Biblical Commentary 33B (Dallas, TX: Word Books, 1995), 783.

[7] Mark Nolland, *The Gospel of Matthew*, The New International Greek Testament Commentary (Grand Rapids, MI: Eerdmans, 2005), 1099.

[8] R. T. France, *The Gospel of Matthew* (Grand Rapids, MI: Eerdmans, 2007), 1005.

Characters

Jesus is the main character of the story. The characterization of Jesus is first done directly, through telling. Thus, in verse 37, Matthew discloses that Jesus *began to be grieved and distressed.* Repetition of words and actions suggest significance. The reiteration of Jesus' distress in the following verse (v. 38), this time revealed in his own words, *My soul is deeply grieved, to the point of death*, has the effect of amplifying the struggle. This disclosure is indeed remarkable, since "apart from the reference to Jesus' compassion (e.g. 9:36) Matthew has virtually no reference to Jesus' emotions prior to this point."[9] As R. T. France put it, the narrator's double reference (vv. 37-38) to Jesus' distress makes the passage stand out even more and reinforces the motif of struggle through "extravagantly expressed emotions."[10] Even though Jesus had predicted his death many times before, he is now forced to mentally and emotionally face up to what atonement meant in practice.

Beyond telling, the narrative is also rich in indirect markers showing the same motif of distress. Most of the showing consists of Jesus' actions and words: he feels the need for companions (took with him three disciples, v. 36), for spiritual and emotional support (asked the disciples to watch and pray with him, v. 38). Yet he chooses to be alone (*went a little farther*, v. 39) in order to talk to his Father (prays to God three times, vv. 39, 42, 44). The passage also reveals him supplicating (*fell on his face*, v. 39), disappointed, and frustrated (*So, you men could not keep watch with Me for one hour?* v. 40). His persistence (prayed three times, vv. 39, 42, 44) and determination (*get up, let us get going,* v. 46) change the tone of the story at the end, when his distress has been overcome.

The other characters present in the story are: the Father, the disciples, the betrayer, and the sinners. While Jesus is the central character, all others are displayed by the narrator in a manner that reflects their physical, emotional and spiritual closeness or distance from him. The following diagram illustrates this:

[9] Nolland, *Matthew*, 1097.
[10] France, *Matthew*, 1002.

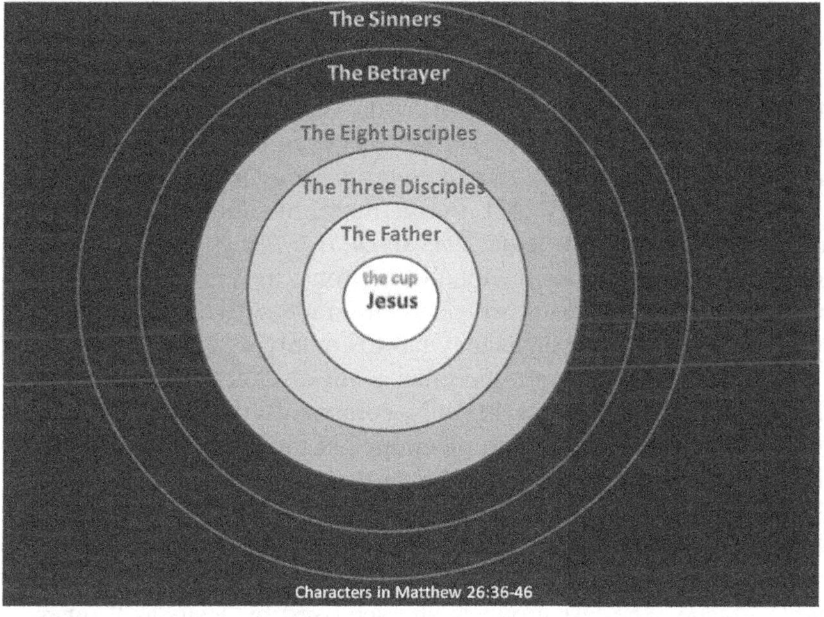

Chart 1

Closest to Jesus is the Father, who is addressed three times and with whom Jesus shares his inmost struggle. This indicates profound intimacy with the Father, who alone in this story knows the inner life of Jesus. Also suggestive of intimacy is the use of the personal pronoun *My*, prefacing each prayer we hear, and implicit in the third (*saying the same words again,* v. 44). This intense intimacy multiplies the dramatic effect of the cup of wrath.

The next proximate characters are the three disciples to whom Jesus discloses that he is in distress, though they are not the reason for it (*My soul is deeply grieved, to the point of death,* v. 38), and to whom he commands something (*remain here and keep watch with Me*, v. 38). Gethsemane provides a context where the disciples can prove their commitment. In an ironic twist, however, their opportunity becomes the occasion for Jesus challenging "the discipleship not only of the sons of Zebedee, who brazenly avowed that they could drink the cup of suffering that Jesus was going to drink (Matt 20:22), but also of Peter, the one who boldly protested to

Jesus that even if all the disciples fall away because of him, he would not."[11] In verses 40-41 we see Jesus' attempt to invoke the disciples' cooperation as he addresses them with words that indicate disappointment, possibly even irritation: *So, you men could not keep watch with Me for one hour?* (v. 41). Yet even in his disappointment, he pleads with them to *keep watching and praying that you may not enter into temptation* (v. 41). Furthermore, his ability to understand and articulate their struggle (*the spirit is willing, but the flesh is weak*, v. 41) ameliorates the tonality of irony, as it is balanced by His compassion. While Jesus struggles, his redemptive work for them remains unremitting even as they fail to comply.

Farther from Jesus are the other eight disciples, who are also in the garden, but to whom he only commands that they stay there while he prays. The betrayer, mentioned at the end of the passage, is the human agent that begins the process leading to Jesus' death. Emotional distance between the betrayed and betrayer is implicit in the very concept of betrayal, though it is also displayed by Judas coming from outside into the garden, and by the ironic kiss in the next passage. The last group is characterized by Jesus as "sinners." The betrayer will hand him over to them. The Father and the three disciples, as well as the other eight, are all linked in the narrative to the enclosed, protective space of the garden where Jesus prays. The betrayer and the sinners are outside, yet about to invade the space of safety.

Actions

Jesus is the agent of most of the active voice indicative Greek verbs in the passage. He *came* to Gethsemane. He *spoke* to his disciples, *took* the three and *began to be distressed.* He *told* the disciples he was in distress, *went* farther, *fell* on his face, and *prayed.* He *came* to the disciples, *found* them sleeping, and *spoke* to Peter. He *went away* again and *prayed*, then he *came* to the disciples again and *found* them sleeping. He *left* them, *went away*, *prayed*, *came* to the disciples and told them that he *is being betrayed*. Finally, he *told* them to rise and go.

In stark contrast with Jesus' movement, the strong imagery of a cup that remains unmoved through the entire story deepens the

[11] Paul Heil, *The Death and Resurrection of Jesus: A Narrative-Critical Reading of Matthew 26-28* (Minneapolis, MN: Fortress, 1991), 43-44.

overtones of anxiety and bespeaks the unmoved determination of God to save the human race, even if the ransom demands the turmoil and death of his own Son.

The intense movement of Jesus is also underscored by the lack of activity on the part of the disciples, who function as a foil. Jesus moves, talks, prays, and stays awake, while the disciples are mute, sleeping, deaf, and unresponsive. They are at peace and asleep as he struggles. While he finds victory in going through the struggle, they are in a calm before the storm breaks when they will flee their master. The contrast between what they are asked to do and what they do is striking. On the one hand we see Jesus pleading with them to watch and pray. On the other hand, we see the disciples sleeping and failing to pray. Their actions, rendered in Greek by present participle, indicate a persistent, continuous state from which they do not emerge until the end of the story. It is also notable that the only explanation the narrator inserts in the narrative is his editorial comment regarding the disciples' sleep: *for their eyes were heavy* (v. 43), which can also be interpreted symbolically as a sign of their spiritual blindness.

Once Jesus enters the garden with the disciples, the entire action occurs within the first three circles of figure 1, with Jesus going back and forth between the Father and the three disciples. The going back-and-forth between the Father and the disciples suggests the tension that Jesus experiences as He faces the heart-wrenching choice between separation from the Father or separation from the disciples. As Matt 27:46 indicates, His death on the cross means separation from his Father: *My God, My God, why have You forsaken Me?* This separation seems to be linked with the Gethsemane story where he prays that the cup would pass away. Thus, the suffering that the cup stands for is not only the suffering of Jesus' passion and death, but also the suffering of separation from his Father. On the other hand, since the cup also represents the wrath of God, Jesus' drinking of the cup signifies that he bears the sins of the world to the cross. As Matthew writes earlier, the Son of Man came to give His life as a ransom for many (Matt 20:28). The implicit conclusion is that if in Gethsemane Jesus had chosen not to drink the cup, the wrath of God would have been poured on humans for their sins instead of on Jesus. The separation from the Father that Jesus suffered as he faced the judgment of God in our place would have become separation between God and us. Thus, this movement back and forth between the Father and the disciples may echo Jesus' inner struggle as He chooses one separation over another.

Literary Structure

The literary structure of the narrative supports the same motifs of struggle and distress, and further emphasizes the contrast between Jesus and the disciples. Structurally, the narrative seems to be built in two patterns: a chiasm and a panel structure. As the chart below shows, the chiasm is displayed as the outer layer of the story and frames the three prayers of Jesus, while the panel structure includes the three prayers and could be described as the inner layer of the story.

A Jesus and the disciples ***come*** to Gethsemane. (v. 36)

B Jesus asks the disciples to ***sit*** there while he goes and prays. (v. 36)

C Jesus ***discloses*** his turmoil. (vv. 37-38)

Jesus	**The Three Disciples**
Jesus <u>goes</u> farther, falls on his face, and *prays*. (v. 39)	Jesus <u>returns</u> to the disciples and finds them *sleeping*. (v. 40)

Jesus <u>addresses</u> the disciples. (vv. 40-41)

Jesus <u>goes</u> and *prays* a second time. (v. 42)	Jesus <u>returns</u> to the disciples and finds them *sleeping*. (v. 43)

Jesus <u>leaves</u> the disciples. (v. 44)

Jesus <u>goes</u> and *prays* a third time. (v. 44)	Jesus <u>returns</u> to the disciples and finds them *sleeping*. (v. 45)

Jesus <u>awakens</u> the disciples. (v. 45)

C' Jesus ***discloses*** the near and impending betrayal. (v. 45)

B' Jesus asks the disciples to ***rise***. (v. 46)

A' Jesus tells the disciples to ***get going***. (v. 46)

Chart 2

The chiasm has three levels of correspondence (A, B, C, C′, B′, A′). In the beginning, Jesus and the disciples come into the garden. Then, he asks the disciples to sit. Next, Jesus takes three disciples farther with him and discloses to them his distress. At the end of the story, Jesus discloses his impending betrayal, asks them to rise, and they leave the garden.

In between the two parts of the chiastic structure, the panel structure presents the repetitive act of Jesus' prayer and return to the three disciples. The parallelism between Jesus and the disciples underscores the contrast between them in two ways. First, the narrative portrays Jesus as consistently praying, while the disciples are consistently sleeping. Second, the panel also illustrates a motif of struggle. While Jesus' struggle is depicted both directly, via telling, and indirectly, as shown in his words and actions, the disciples are also struggling, even though the text does not give any indication that they are aware of their struggle. Jesus' address to them in verse 41, however, implies a struggle on their part: *Watch and pray so that you will not fall into temptation. The spirit is willing, but the flesh is weak.* Thus, while Jesus is well aware of his struggle and prays about it, the disciples are blind to their own as they sleep through the entire episode.

Another pattern that emerges from the panel arrangement is a double motif of resignation. On the one hand, Jesus gradually resigns to the will of his Father and eventually accepts it. On the other hand, he progressively resigns to the lack of support from the disciples in response to his requests.

The wording of the prayers reveals progression in Jesus' yielding to the Father's will, as displayed in Table 1 (below). While in his first prayer Jesus asks that the cup be taken away *if it is possible,* in his second prayer the possibility is phrased negatively: *if it is not possible for this cup to be taken away,*[12] suggesting "a deeper resignation to the Father's will. There is no request for the cup to pass away, only agreement with the Father that the cup can pass away only if Jesus drinks it."[13] Moreover, Jesus' added words *unless I drink it*, reveal a growing acceptance of a negative outcome to his

[12] Rudolf Schnackenburg, *The Gospel of Matthew* (Grand Rapids, MI: Eerdmans, 2002), 271.

[13] David L. Turner, *Matthew*, Baker Exegetical Commentary on the New Testament (Grand Rapids, MI: Baker, 2008), 632.

plea. Thus, while in his first prayer Jesus "left open the possibility that his Father's will might correspond to his own will not to drink the cup . . . in the second prayer he realizes that it is not possible for him to escape drinking the cup and without any further mention of his own will totally resigns himself to the will of God."[14] The cup cannot pass away unless it is consumed by Jesus.

Ref.	Subject	Condition	Petition	Exception	Commitment
v. 39	*My Father,*	*If it is possible*	*May this cup be taken from me*		*Yet not as I will, but as you will.*
v. 42	*My Father,*	*If it is* **not** *possible*	*For this cup to be taken away*	***Unless I drink it***	*May your will be done.*

Table 1

His growing acceptance of the Father's will is paralleled by a growing resignation to the failure of his disciples. When he first finds the disciples asleep, he awakens and addresses them. The second time he finds the disciples asleep, he leaves them. The third time he finds them asleep, Jesus awakens them with a dry remark about their sleep and a command to get up and leave. Thus, there is present in the passage a sense of Jesus' amplifying isolation. It is in this utter aloneness that Matthew presents Jesus making the crucial decision to proceed to the cross as a ransom for many (Matt 20:28).

The narrative records Jesus' and the disciples' actions as triads of events: three times Jesus prays (vv. 38, 40, 42), three times the disciples are reported as sleeping (vv. 40, 43, 45), and three times Jesus returns to the disciples (vv. 40, 43, 45). This may suggest a sense of completeness or fulfillment.[15] Accordingly, the triads point to a progressive settling of Jesus in his decision to obey God, as well as a settling of the disciples in their slumber, while Jesus' return to the disciples three times suggests redemptive persistence.

---

[14] Heil, *The Death and Resurrection*, 47-48.

[15] Resseguie, *Narrative Criticism*, 49.

The threefold repetition of Jesus' struggle in prayer also recalls the three temptations of Jesus at the beginning of his ministry recorded in Matt 4:11-17, when the devil offered him a different way, one that evaded the cross. Jesus withstood it then, yet in Matt 26:36-46 the author informs us that the possibility of a different way also arises from within. Thus, Jesus' ministry is bracketed by these two critical instances where, in a sequence of three actions, Jesus overcomes both external and internal temptation, and his victory is complete each time.

The narrative begins and ends with a very different tone. In the beginning, Jesus is deeply distressed, seeks support, and is struggling. In the end, he is calm and resolute. There is a clear progression from inner struggle to inner peace, from distress to composure, from sorrow to acceptance. Having overcome his anxiety, Jesus displays hero-like characteristics when he rises and goes to meet his betrayer. Thus, framed between Jesus and the disciples sitting and Jesus and the disciples rising, the story gains the overtone of a way station, a stopping point on the way to fulfilling his mission, which underscores its significance as a crossroad and pivotal point in the story of atonement.

The prayers of Jesus seem to be carefully timed so that, by the moment the betrayer enters the scene, Jesus has finished saying the last and decisive prayer. This juncture creates a paradox for the reader who is following Matthew's story of the redeeming Messiah. On the one hand, Jesus' submission to the will of God generates a sense of relief, for this submission is crucial to the fulfillment of atonement, which brings salvation. On the other hand, Jesus' submission to God's will involves submission to his betrayer, and the binding of Jesus instills in the reader a sentiment of grief that persists through the entire passion of Jesus, even while remaining aware that his sacrifice is the means for atonement. That the suffering of Jesus brings joy, and that the consummation of the cup of suffering and death brings life is a real paradox in the story of atonement.

The Cup: An Inexorable Road to Redemption

In the narrative of Jesus' three prayers in Gethsemane, Matthew offers us a unique facet of the story of atonement. It is in Gethsemane that "the die has been cast,"[16] or, as Karl Barth put it,

[16] France, *Matthew*, 1006.

"only in Gethsemane does Jesus' staurological future take on a categorical, as opposed to hypothetical, standing."[17] In between Jesus' many predictions of his passion and death and the completion of atonement in his actual crucifixion, is this story in Gethsemane, a story that makes clear to the reader that the fulfillment of the will of God in atonement requires the free choice of the Son of God. He could have chosen differently than he did, yet he decided to obey the Father's will to drink the cup of wrath, suffering, and death.

Furthermore, Jesus makes the decision to drink the cup in full awareness of both the cost and the reward this act entails. He is not blindly taking the road to the cross, and even while he submits to his Father's will, the sacrifice is made with Jesus' full consent. The next passage reveals that Jesus has divine power available to him at any moment, and his words in verse 53–*Or do you think that I cannot appeal to My Father, and He will at once put at My disposal more than twelve legions of angels?*–leave no doubt in the reader's mind that the betrayer's actions could be overturned at his wish. However, overturning the betrayal would be synonymous with the refusal to drink the cup, which in turn would be a refusal to do God's will.

The Gethsemane narrative also bears witness to the fact that Jesus' death was inevitable for the salvation of humankind. The cup cannot be removed unless it is drunk by Jesus. Jesus' words, *Let your will be done*, echoing the prayer he taught the disciples to pray (Matt 6:9-15), show that all throughout his struggle he only looked for "what is 'possible' within his Father's will,"[18] and the progression of the story in the following chapters reveals clearly that the Father's will was Jesus' sacrificial death. God's implicit negative answer to Jesus' prayer for another way reinforces the inevitability of Jesus' death as the cost of redemption.

The intensity of Jesus' struggle, as shown through this narrative analysis, informs us that, even though Jesus chose to fulfill his mission, the carrying through of the plan to its completion was not effortless. Matthew 26:36-46 offers the reader remarkable insight into Jesus' internal life regarding the sacrifice he made. Because of this glimpse that the narrative gives us into the deep distress of Jesus, we are "enabled to grasp the seriousness of the settled purpose of

---

[17] Paul Dafydd Jones, "Karl Barth on Gethsemane," *International Journal of Systematic Theology* 9 (2007): 159.

[18] France, *Matthew*, 1002.

God which calls for his Son to be rejected and killed in Jerusalem."[19] Our appreciation for his sacrifice becomes deeper as we see more clearly the difficulty Jesus overcame in making this momentous decision.

[19] France, *Matthew*, 1002.

Part 2:
Beauty in Archaeology and Culture

Beauty and Complexity: Esther's Night with the King in Biblical and Cultural Context

Sarah Gane Burton and Constance Clark Gane

Introduction

The story of Esther illustrates the life of a person of God in an alien world. The beauty of the narrative, and in Esther as the protagonist, lies in Esther's ability to navigate the complex and often dangerous Persian court while maintaining a character that causes her to "win favor" in the eyes of those around her (Esth 2:15, ESV here and following).

However, Esth 2 presents the reader with a variety of dilemmas relating to Esther's morality, specifically her willingness, or unwillingness, to go to the palace and become the wife of a Gentile. Commentators and preachers have speculated about her behavior, alternately placing her on a pedestal as an example of a faithful, beautiful woman in a position of authority or casting her as an immoral and worldly woman who used her sexuality to get what she wanted. Feminist commentators hold up Vashti as a paragon of the strong female and accuse Esther of passivity while others assert that Esther was the victim of kidnapping, sexual objectification, and rape.[1]

In popular publications, opinions about Esther are just as broad. Evangelical author Lisa Ryan upholds Esther as a model for the purity

---

[1] See discussion of various authors in J'annine Jobling and Alan Roughley, "The Right to Write: Power, Irony, and Identity in the Book of Esther," in *Sacred Tropes: Tanakh, New Testament, and Qu'ran as Literature and Culture,* ed. Roberta Sabbath, Biblical Interpretation Series 98 (Boston, MA: Brill, 2009), 318; Nicole Duran, "Who Wants to Marry a Persian King? Gender Games and Wars and the Book of Esther," in *Pregnant Passion: Gender, Sex, and Violence in the Bible*, ed. Cheryl A. Kirk-Duggan (Atlanta, GA: Society of Biblical Literature, 2004), 77; Ericka S. Dunbar, "For Such a Time as This? #UsToo: Representations of Sexual Trafficking, Collective Trauma, and Horror in the Book of Esther," *The Bible & Critical Theory* 15, no. 2 (2019): 29–48.

movement,[2] while Carolyn Custis James makes the disturbing claim that:

> [Esther] didn't display the same passionate loyalty to God or to his people that drove the actions and flooded the prayers of [Joseph and Daniel]. Instead, she shed her Jewish name, concealed her true identity, and morphed into the surrounding culture . . . She didn't simply survive her abduction into Xerxes' harem. She made the most of it. She auditioned for the queen's crown by having sex with a man who was not her husband. Then, after winning the tiara, she joined herself in marriage to a pagan man.[3]

Was Esther an exemplary virgin who waited to have sex until her wedding night, a seductress who engaged in premarital sex, or a victim of kidnapping and rape? Do modern concepts of marriage even apply to the Persian harem? This article attempts to situate Esther's "night with the king" in its biblical and Persian context.

Many of the challenges raised regarding Esther's morality lie in assumptions about what the text says or does not say about Esther and presuppositions about the nature of marriage (especially royal marriage) in the Old Testament and Persian empire. We will address some of these challenges through a review of scholarly literature on Esth 2, dealing specifically with Esther's sexual relationship with the king. This will be followed by our own analysis of the narrative. We will then discuss Old Testament descriptions of marriage, paying particular attention to royal marriages and harems. Next, we will investigate Persian and Greek texts regarding Persian courts and harems. Finally, we will argue that Esther is an example of a woman living in the "thick of it." She is not a role model in the sense that we should copy her actions, which occurred in a particular historical context, rather we should be inspired by and emulate her attitude of grace and courage.[4] The book of Esther is a beautiful redemption story that demonstrates God's faithfulness in the most complex of situations.

---

[2] Lisa Ryan, *For Such a Time as This: Your Identity, Purpose and Passion* (Sisters, OR: Multnomah Publishers, 2001), 23, 33.

[3] Carolyn Custis James, *Lost Women of the Bible: Finding Strength & Significance through Their Stories* (Grand Rapids, MI: Zondervan, 2005), 148.

[4] Karen Jobes, *Esther,* The NIV Application Commentary (Grand Rapids, MI: Zondervan, 1999), 113.

Literature Review

We begin our literature review with the Jewish commentators, for whom the text of Esther holds more than just theological import but also describes the salvation of their nation and the establishment of a national holiday. According to the early rabbis, Esther sleeping with a man was not a legal problem: by having sex with him, she becomes either his concubine or wife. However, sleeping with a non-Jew is forbidden (Exod 34:12-16; Deut 7:3, 4; Lev 21:14; Ezra 10; and Neh 13; however, note Deut 21:10 where the captive woman can be taken as a wife/concubine). This is the conspicuous legal issue of the book of Esther and—along with the fact that God is never mentioned—is the reason why Esther was the last book added to the canon of the Hebrew Bible.[5]

The Talmud (Gemara) raises the issue of Esther's "cohabitation" as "a public sin," questioning "why then did Esther not surrender her life rather than engage in intercourse?"[6] The Gemara then answers as follows:

> Abaye says: Esther was merely like natural ground, i.e., she was a passive participant. The obligation to surrender one's life rather than engage in forbidden sexual intercourse applies only to a man who transgresses the prohibition in an active manner. A woman who is passive and merely submits is not required to give up her life so that she not sin. Rava says that there is another justification for Esther's behavior: When gentiles order the transgression of a prohibition not in order to persecute the Jews or to make them abandon their religion, but for their own personal pleasure, it is different. In such a situation there is no obligation to sacrifice one's life, even when the sin is committed in public.[7]

Thus Esther is seen as a passive victim and as such not an accomplice to the violation of the law. The sin is that of the intention of the active player, in this case, Xerxes. For some commentators, this was not satisfactory. Instead, God sent a female spirit to become Esther "for

---

[5] Aaron Koller, *Esther in Ancient Jewish Thought* (Cambridge: Cambridge University Press, 2014), 215–16.

[6] bSanhedrin 74b. See also Koller, *Esther in Ancient Jewish Thought*, 216.

[7] bSanhedrin 74b.

the purposes of sex."[8] According to Leonard Greenspoon, "such a substitution, well known in other circumstances from many ancient sources, would satisfy the needs of both the pious reader and the voracious Jewish woman that the midrashim construct."[9]

Moving to modern commentators (Jewish and non-Jewish), Ronald Pierce is more critical of Esther, asserting that she "participates in the contest with no evident reluctance" when "there is no hint that Ahasuerus would have killed Esther for simply revealing her Jewishness, and perhaps not even for refusing to participate in his contest."[10] He views Esther as a secular character who hides her identity for no reason except to have a better chance at winning the king's favor. Rather than her passivity being a reflection of her status as a displaced orphan girl in the harem of an often-drunk and sometimes vindictive emperor, he sees her as a woman of ambition who sells her virginity and Jewish identity in order to marry a benevolent Gentile monarch. "Lest one attempt to justify the actions of the beautiful young Jewess by citing her bravery to deliver her people, it must be kept in mind that there was no threat facing the people when Esther sold herself to a gentile for the price of the crown."[11] It is people like Esther, Pierce asserts, who are responsible for the exile: "Indeed, Esther's marriage to Ahasuerus tragically mimics one of the key failures of the Jewish people that resulted in her family being brought to Susa."[12] For Pierce, the heroism Esther and Mordecai display later in the story is necessitated, not aided, by their assimilation into Persian court and culture.

Where Pierce sees Esther's actions as a betrayal of her Jewish heritage, Jon Berquist reads her behavior throughout the book as being directly tied to her loyalty to the Jewish people. She "expended her virginity"—for the sake of ethnic loyalty—in order to become queen and exploited her sexual relationship with the king to save the Jews

---

[8] Leonard Greenspoon, "The Taming of the Two: Queen Esther and Queen Vashti in Midrash," in *Women, Gender, and Religion*, ed. Susan Calef and Ronald A. Simkins, Journal of Religion & Society Supplement Series 5 (Omaha, NE: Creighton University Kripke Center, 2009), 161.

[9] Greenspoon, "The Taming of the Two," 161.

[10] Ronald W. Pierce, "The Politics of Esther and Mordecai: Courage or Compromise?" *Bulletin for Biblical Research* 2 (1992): 83–84.

[11] Ibid., 83.

[12] Ibid., 84.

from destruction: "Thus Esther's sexuality became an important ingredient in the salvation of the Jews."[13]

Adele Berlin deemphasizes the sexual nature of Esther's encounter with the king. She takes the reference to the king's royal palace (*bet malkut*) in 2:16 as an indication that Esther is entering the space once occupied by Vashti (1:9) and does not see the term as a reference to the king's private quarters. Although she acknowledges that previous virgins spent a night with the king, she seems to suggest that Esther's selection as queen may have preceded a shared bed.[14]

Similarly, Angel Manuel Rodriguez disputes what he sees as scholars' overemphasis on Esther's sexuality, declaring it a reflection of "our modern Western understanding of beauty in terms of sex appeal."[15] While he does not explicitly rule out a sexual encounter, he maintains that "Esther's visit with the king does not have the purpose to determine sexual compatibility or to persuade the king to choose her as queen because of her sexual charms . . . He evaluates her beauty from a broad perspective: her physical appearance as well as her style, personality, and demeanor."[16]

Rodriguez does not comment directly on the morality of Esther concealing her ethnicity, but he praises her respect for and obedience to Mordecai.[17] Similarly, Jon Levenson comments that "neither before nor after her elevation to the queenship did Esther break faith with her foster father."[18] Indeed, "Esther's hiding her Jewishness and her connection to Mordecai is a narrative necessity. Without it, Haman's genocidal plot could never have been launched. With it, her foiling of the plot becomes vastly more powerful, for it coincides with the disclosure of her Jewishness (7:4), so that as in the cases of Joseph and Moses, the national and personal stories intersect and reinforce each other."[19]

---

[13] Jon Berquist, *Judaism in Persian's Shadow: A Social and Historical Approach* (Minneapolis, MN: Fortress, 1995), 228–29.

[14] Adele Berlin, *Esther*, JPS Bible Commentary (Philadelphia, PA: Jewish Publication Society, 2001), 28–29.

[15] Angel Manuel Rodriguez, *Esther: A Theological Approach* (Berrien Springs, MI: Andrews University Press, 1995), 67.

[16] Ibid., 68.

[17] Ibid., 66.

[18] Jon D. Levenson, *Esther* (Louisville, KY: Westminster John Knox, 1997), 61.

[19] Levenson, *Esther*, 61.

Karen Jobes strikes a more nuanced tone, noting that the passive voice is used when the Jews were "carried" into exile (2:6) and later when Esther "was taken" (2:8).[20] However, she observes that the text gives no indication of Esther's response toward being taken, nor does the author pass judgment on Esther's union with a Gentile king. The question arises: should we as readers, pass judgment? Perhaps, as Jobes suggests, "the author does not intend to hold up Esther as a moral example to be followed."[21] Instead, "the author is skillfully describing a morally ambiguous and complex situation because that is the way real life often is in this fallen world."[22]

Michael V. Fox points out that the use of the word *dat* ("law") in 2:8 "reminds us of the unalterable law of the Persians and suggests that Esther's induction into the harem was an ineluctable fate, which neither Mordecai nor Esther could withstand."[23] Women were not the only ones taken involuntarily to the court. According to Herodotus, boys were also taken from Babylonia and Assyria every year to become eunuchs for the court in Persia.[24] "The brutality of the system in this regard was thus not what we recognize as sexism."[25]

Nicole Duran views the taking of Esther as a "kind of kidnapping."[26] Thus "if Esther takes advantage of the situation to gain some privilege, it is for the same reasons that Joseph rises to be head slave and head prisoner—because a survivor is defined by his or her ability to succeed in any circumstance."[27] Despite portraying Esther as victim, Duran finds her success with the king unsavory compared to Vashti's refusal to compromise and concludes, like Berquist, that Esther "sell[s] her womanhood" for the sake of her people.[28]

Pushing the concept of kidnapping a step farther, Ericka S. Dunbar argues that the book of Esther presents us with an ancient equivalent to a massive sex-trafficking ring. Dunbar contends that the book describes a similar organizational pattern to sex-trafficking rings in which there

---

[20] Jobes, *Esther*, 99.

[21] Ibid., 113.

[22] Ibid., 114.

[23] Michael V. Fox, *Character and Ideology in the Book of Esther*, 2nd ed. (Eugene, OR: Wipf & Stock, 2010), 31.

[24] Herodotus, *Hist.* 3.92.

[25] Fox, *Character and Ideology*, 34.

[26] Duran, "Who Wants to Marry a Persian King," 77.

[27] Ibid., 77.

[28] Ibid., 78.

are "four key roles": that of perpetrator (Ahasuerus), vendor (king's servants and eunuchs), facilitator (officers sent to gather the women), and victim (virgin girls).[29] As often occurs in modern sex-trafficking, Hegai, the eunuch tasked with grooming the captive women for their encounter with the king, is also a victim of sexual violence.

Dunbar's reading situates the narrative of Esther in the broader context of imperial politics, power, and abuse. The sexual victimization and commodification of women within an imperial setting is ancient and enduring. Viewing the experience of the young girls as a "beauty competition"[30] akin to a modern romantic reality TV show or a "rags-to-royal-riches" fairytale[31] (for Esther) disregards the terror and heartbreak these young women suffered. Dunbar warns that "this type of silencing and invisibility enables sexual trafficking to survive and thrive, both in the biblical narrative and within contemporary contexts."[32]

Summary of Literature Review

The literature reviewed here offers a brief glimpse into the broad spectrum of interpretation regarding Esther's night with the king. Without providing a full analysis of each commentator's presuppositions toward the text, we can observe that a negative view of Esther's behavior derives from the belief that she was in control of her situation in the harem. This view is often held in tandem with the perception that her hidden Jewishness is further evidence of her betrayal of Jewish faith and values. At issue, then, is not only her union with a Gentile, but also her silence regarding her people and faith. However, as we will demonstrate in the sections that follow, the author of Esther does not seem to share the same concerns as modern commentators. Indeed, Esther is described with positive phrases reserved for some of the most important and noble characters in Jewish history (Joseph, Daniel, even Jesus). We would argue, with Fox, that negative commentary on Esther's conduct is "indifferent to the severity of the crisis that stands at the story's heart: the mortal danger to the

---

[29] Dunbar, "For Such a Time as This? #UsToo," 34.

[30] See Vanessa L. Ochs, *Sarah Laughed: Modern Lessons from the Wisdom & Stories of Biblical Women* (Philadelphia, PA: Jewish Publication Society, 2011), 63.

[31] Greenspoon, "The Taming of the Two," 159.

[32] Dunbar, "For Such a Time as This? #UsToo," 36.

Jewish people."[33] It forces modern Western concerns on the text and "in effect it blames the author for not dealing with other, supposedly more important issues, such as the dignity and independence of women in the Persian court."[34]

Dunbar's reading is informative and complex, but we must question whether using modern terminology such as "sex-trafficking" is compatible with biblical thought. Robert S. Kawashima argues persuasively that biblical literature does not perceive sexual violence in the same way as the modern mind, although the lived reality of ancient victims may have been identical to modern victims.[35] This makes it difficult to accurately ascertain how the author of Esther would have viewed the gathering of the virgins, or how Esther and the other harem women would have viewed their situation.

Immediate Context: Esther 2

Following the banishment of Vashti in chapter 1, Ahasuerus takes the advice of his attendants for a kingdom-wide search of beautiful women (2:2–4). The women are to be gathered (*qabats*) to the harem and the one who "pleases" the king will be queen. While one can imagine that some ambitious parents may have volunteered their daughters to the officials/overseers who sought out beautiful virgins or that some girls would have regarded this as an honor, it is also not hard to imagine that others may have protested or hidden their daughters, albeit in vain.

Esther's introduction to the narrative occurs parenthetically between the king's decision and its implementation.[36] We are given both her Hebrew and Persian names, which alerts the reader to a tension in her identity and aligns her with other Israelites in foreign courts who possessed Israelite and Gentile names, such as Joseph and Daniel.[37] Esther comes from a line of exiles who were carried away from Jerusalem, and in her own short life experiences dramatic transitions or

---

[33] Fox, *Character and Ideology*, 208.

[34] Ibid., 208.

[35] Robert S. Kawashima, "Could a Woman Say 'No' in Biblical Israel? On the Genealogy of Legal Status in Biblical Law and Literature," *Association for Jewish Studies Review* 35, no. 1 (2011): 4; see also Joan Scurlock, "But Was She Raped?: A Verdict Through Comparison," *NIN Journal of Gender Studies in Antiquity* 4, no. 1 (2006): 61–103.

[36] Jean-Daniel Macchi, *Esther* (Stuttgart: W. Kohlhammer, 2018), 118.

[37] Ibid., 123.

"takings": from her parents to Mordecai, from Mordecai to the harem, and from the harem to the king. Timothy Laniak notes that "Esther enters the story as an archetypal *dependent.*"[38] She belongs to a liminal class of persons recognized in Deut 10:18 as needing special protection and consideration.[39]

Esther 2 does not tell us much about the protagonist, except for her background and one key quality: her beauty. Jean-Daniel Macchi points out that her beauty is at the center of verse 7, sandwiched between statements about her parentage and adoption. This suggests that her beauty will play a key role in the story.[40] The phrase in 2:7 used to describe her attractiveness—"beautiful figure and lovely to look at" (*yepat-to'ar wetobat mar'eh*)—is almost identical to descriptions of Rachel and Joseph (*yepat-to'ar wipat mar'eh*; Gen 29:17; 39:6). Similar wording is used for the "good" or "pleasant" appearance of Daniel and his Jewish companions in Dan 1:15.

The king's command to gather beautiful young women is issued as an order (*debar*) and law (*dat*). Both terms appeared earlier in Esth 1: Vashti refused the command (*debar*) to come before the king (1:12) and was subsequently banished by royal order (*debar*), which was written in the law (*dat*) of the Persians and Medes (1:19). With this legal background, we have no reason to believe Esther could avoid being taken even if she had no desire to go the palace.[41]

Once in the harem, Esther wins the favor (*khesed*)[42] of Hegai (2:9) and later the favor (*khen*) of all who saw her (2:15). Both words are used to denote a (divinely given) positive attitude in other stories of Jews in court situations: Joseph found favor (*khen*) in the sight of Potiphar (Gen 39:4), and God "showed him steadfast love (*khesed*) and gave him favor (*khen*) in the sight of the keeper of the prison" (Gen 39:21); God "gave Daniel favor (*khesed*) and compassion in the sight of the chief of the eunuchs" (Dan. 1:9); and Ezra attributed his success to the steadfast love (*khesed*) that God extended to him "before the king and his counselors, and before all the king's mighty officers" (Ezra

[38] Timothy S. Laniak, *Shame and Honor in the Book of Esther* (Atlanta, GA: Scholars Press, 1998), 61.

[39] Ibid., 61.

[40] Macchi, *Esther*, 124–25.

[41] Fox, *Character and Ideology*, 31.

[42] The word *khesed* can also be translated as lovingkindness or steadfast love and is often associated with God (Ex 20:6, 34:6–7).

7:28). The Greek equivalent, *charis*, is used in Luke 2:52 in reference to Jesus: "And Jesus increased in wisdom and in stature and in favor (*charis*) with God and man."

Although God is not mentioned, given the similar wording in other narratives it is likely that the reader would have credited the deity for Esther's success.[43] The usage of these terms for favor is important because it reflects a widespread positive attitude toward Esther and, importantly, implies that the sentiment is shared by the author. If Esther was viewed as a backslidden Jew during her time in the harem and the king's bedchamber, as some commentators suggest, it would be strange for her to be the recipient of such praise during the very occasions commentators view as being morally questionable. Instead, she is portrayed as the female counterpart to Joseph and Daniel.[44]

Esther plays an active role in "winning" (*qal* form of *nasa'*) favor and kindness, although we are not told how she achieved this.[45] One indicator may be the wisdom she displays in deferring to Hegai's advice in 2:15, which is immediately followed by the assertion that she "was winning favor in the eyes of all who saw her." As with Joseph and Daniel, the "favor" she receives from Hegai "is more than a positive feeling; it is concrete support" demonstrated through the preferential treatment she is given.[46]

The author's comment regarding Esther's silence about her Jewish heritage (2:10) comes directly after a description of the tangible results of Hegai's favor and before the statement that Mordecai walked daily in front of the court to ascertain Esther's wellbeing. The silence of the text does not provide us with either approval or judgment of her actions. There is no indication that she conceals her Jewishness for the purpose of ambition, rather, she is described as obeying a command from Mordecai that appears to have been given out of concern for her safety. This is supported by his obvious care for her wellbeing (2:11) and later developments that affirm the presence of anti-Semitic sentiments within the court.[47] It is worth noting that Esther is not described as actively

[43] Laniak, *Shame and Honor*, 64.

[44] Koller, *Esther in Ancient Jewish Thought*, 77–78.

[45] Laniak, *Shame and Honor*, 64; Macchi, *Esther*, 126–27.

[46] Ibid., 64. For more on winning favor, see Charles D. Harvey, *Finding Morality in the Diaspora?: Moral Ambiguity and Transformed Morality in the Books of Esther* (Berlin: de Gruyter, 2003), 24–25.

[47] Fox, *Character and Ideology*, 32–33.

deceiving others—she simply refrains from making her identity known. As Charles D. Harvey points out, "the manner in which Esther went about her concealment appear[s] not to be a great point of interest for the author," nor does the author deem it important for the audience to know exactly *why*.[48] What is important is that she was successful in her silence, giving her leverage in the narrative's climax.[49]

A parenthetical description of the procedure for the virgins prepares the reader for what will happen to Esther. In Esth 2:12, the phrase "go in to" (*labo' 'el*) contains "sexual overtones."[50] That coitus took place between the young virgins and the king is emphasized by their transferal to the second house of women the morning after their encounter. Rather than being an example of pre-marital sex, this initiated the "marriage" of the young girl to the king, changing her status to that of a concubine (see discussion below). Nothing in the text supports a reading of this nocturnal visit being non-sexual. The evidence is clear: beauty preparations, consisting of various oils and aromatics[51]; the length of stay from evening to morning; the movement from one harem to another; and the change in authority from Hegai to Shaashgaz, who oversaw the concubines, clearly refer to this being a sexual encounter.[52]

Esther's encounter with the king is preceded by her deference to Hegai's advice and the statement that she "was winning favor in the eyes of all who saw her" (2:15). The author thus sets her up for this event in positive terms. Rather than seeking to shock the audience by her union with the king, the author encourages the reader to favor Esther for her beauty and wisdom. The king responds to Esther with an intensified version of the favor she has already received: "the king

---

[48] Harvey, *Finding Morality in the Diaspora*, 24.

[49] Ibid., 24.

[50] Berlin, *Esther*, 27. See also Gen 16:4 where Abraham *wayyabo'* ("went in to") Hagar and she conceived. Other texts include Gen 29:21; 30:4; 38:18; 39:14; 2 Sam 11:4; 12:24; 16:21; Ruth 4:13; 1 Chron 7:23; and others. Macchi, *Esther*, 128, especially nt 55.

[51] Myrrh is mentioned repeatedly, though not exclusively, in connection with love making in the biblical text: Prov 7:17; Song 1:13; 3:6; 4:6; 4:14; 5:1; 5:5; 5:13.

[52] On Persian harems and the status of concubines, see A. Shapur Shahbazi, "Harem in Ancient Iran," *Encyclopaedia Iranica* 11, fasc. 6: 671–72 and 12, fasc. 1:1–3. Cited 22 March 2022. Online: https://www.iranicaonline.org/articles/harem-i.

loved Esther more than all the women, and she won grace (*khen*) and favor (*khesed*) in his sight more than all the virgins" (2:17). The use of both *khen* and *khesed* together "suggests that the king is doubly impressed with Esther's charm."[53] Adele Berlin takes this as an indication of the king's genuine admiration for and attraction to Esther, which includes, but is not limited to, sexual attraction.[54]

That Esther's charm results in her becoming queen does not negate its use as a survival tactic. We should not view her as a power-hungry seductress. Rather, like many women before her (Tamar, Jael, Abigail), she uses what resources and agency she possesses as a female in a patricentric world. In light of Vashti's exile, the king desired a beautiful woman to take her place "who would . . . be prepared to be what Vashti was not: the consummate Other, a wife prepared to surrender entirely her own subjectivity and will. The passivity discerned in Esther's behavior reflects an adaption strategy fitted to the realities of her situatedness."[55] It appears that the king has found such a queen in Esther, but the reader will discover that Esther is a woman of great intelligence and courage who, rather than being Vashti's opposite, is a heroine in her own right.

Chapter 2 concludes with Esther's coronation and a feast held in her honor. The feast is held following her coronation, which seems to indicate that its purpose is to celebrate the new queen. Does this also function as a marriage ceremony? It certainly elevates her status from harem girl to queen and publicly proclaims her as his wife. However, it's placement after Esther's night with the king should not lead readers to conclude that 1) she was not sexually involved with the king prior to the feast or 2) that such involvement constituted premarital sex because a formal event had not yet taken place.

Josephus clearly views the events of 2:18 as a wedding feast and describes it taking place in the twelfth month, two months after Esther's introduction to the king (2:16).[56] Whatever his sources, whether

---

[53] Berlin, *Esther*, 29.

[54] Ibid., 29.

[55] Joshua Berman, "*Hadassah Bat Abihail*: The Evolution from Object to Subject in the Character of Esther," *Journal of Biblical Literature* 120, no. 4 (2001): 649.

[56] "But, when Esther came to him, he was pleased with her and then, having fallen in love with her, made her his lawful wife and held their wedding in the twelfth month, called *Adar*, in the seventh year of his reign. He also sent *Angari*, as they are called, or messengers unto every nation; and gave

tradition or some record no longer extant, the biblical text does not explicitly use wedding terminology or provide us with a date for the feast. Levenson suggests that the author of Esther may have intentionally "avoided marital terminology in order to play down the violation of Jewish law involved in Esther's matrimony with a non-Jew."[57] It is more likely, in our opinion, that the author of Esther did not include an explicit reference to a wedding because it was not deemed necessary. The most important facts were included: that Esther was crowned queen in place of Vashti. The fact that the author does not describe a wedding service in modern, western terms should not disturb or surprise the reader. As will be shown in the next sections, Esther's union with the king generally followed the cultural norms of the ancient Near East.[58]

Esther rises from orphan to queen through a complex set of circumstances outside of her control. She does so apparently without avarice and maintains an outer and inner beauty—from her entrance to the harem until her selection as queen—that attracts everyone around her.

Old Testament Context

To strengthen our analysis of Esth 2, we will examine the understanding of betrothal and marriage in biblical narratives with the assumption that these narratives provide a foundation for interpreting the story of Esther in a manner consistent with the ancient Jewish social context.

As in much of the ancient Near East, biblical marriages were established through a two-step process: betrothal (after which the woman was called "wife") followed by—sometimes several years later—the woman being taken by the man into his home, at which point

---

orders that they should keep a feast for his marriage: while he himself treated the Persians, and the Medes, and the principal men of the nations, for a whole month; on account of this his marriage. Accordingly Esther came to his royal palace; and he set a diadem on her head. . ." (Josephus, *Ant.* 11.199–203, italics supplied).

[57] Levenson, *Esther*, 62.

[58] As will be discussed later, the king's marriage to Esther deviated somewhat from the Persian custom of choosing a wife from one of the seven noble families. However, he was not the only Persian king to do so.

they were deemed "married."[59] In one of the more elaborate descriptions of betrothal and marriage in the Old Testament, Jacob and Rachel are betrothed for seven years while Jacob works for Laban for the right to marry her (Gen 29:18, 20). At the end of the seven years, Jacob tells Laban to give him his "wife." Laban holds a feast for the couple and, in the evening, takes Leah (not Rachel) to Jacob, at which time their marriage is consummated (Gen 29:22–23).

Most accounts of biblical marriages provide only a few (if any) details about the betrothal followed by marital union (usually without mentioning a marriage feast).[60] This is important because it signals that a feast or ceremony prior to a couple's cohabitation need not be explicitly noted, or perhaps even required, for their union to be understood as a marriage.[61] This is true not just of Israelite society, but the ancient Near East in general, as will be discussed below.[62] The consent of the female party is rarely mentioned in biblical marriages: most women are "given" in marriage by their fathers.[63] A few narratives provide examples of female volition: Rebekah and Abigail express

---

[59] Annalisa Azzoni, *The Private Lives of Women in Persian Egypt* (Winona Lake, IN: Eisenbrauns, 2013), 14. Raymond Westbrook and Bruce Wells divide this process into four stages rather than two, see Raymond Westbrook and Bruce Wells, *Everyday Law in Biblical Israel: An Introduction* (Louisville: Westminster John Knox, 2009), 56–60; Victor H. Matthews and Don C. Benjamin, *Social World of Ancient Israel 1250–587 BCE* (Peabody, MA: Hendrickson, 1993), 13–15.

[60] For example, Isaac and Rebekah (Gen 24:22–67), Ruth and Boaz (Ruth 4:10, 13), and David and Michal (1 Sam 18:20–27).

[61] Biblical authors include only the information they deem necessary to the communication of their story or message. Thus the lack of information about marriage rituals means that: either the author assumes that the audience knows there is a ceremony and so does not mention it, much like a modern author might say "and they got married," which most would assume involves a wedding ceremony even though it is not stated; or it means that formal public ceremonies did not always take place. Certainly, status seems to play a role in whether a ceremony is described (or performed). There is no indication, for example, that concubines, captive wives, and women taken for a royal harem would have had formal ceremonies.

[62] Westbrook and Wells, *Everyday Law in Biblical Israel*, 56–57.

[63] Daniel I. Block, "Marriage and Family in Ancient Israel," in *Marriage and Family in the Biblical World* (ed. Ken M. Campbell; Downers Grove, IL: Intervarsity, 2003), 54–57; Westbrook and Wells, *Everyday Law in Biblical Israel*, 58.

some measure of consent to marriage (Gen 24:57; 1 Sam 25:39–42) and Ruth initiates a discussion of marriage with Boaz (Ruth 3:9).[64]

Descriptions of royal marriages are strikingly sparse (apart from Song 3). Negotiations, agreements, or local ceremonies are usually not mentioned.[65] When details are provided, they usually involve the marriage of two royals (e.g., the marriage alliance between Pharoah and Solomon, 1 Kgs 3:1; 9:16). Evidence suggests that women taken to the royal house for the king's pleasure automatically assume the status of wife or concubine.[66]

A striking parallel to Esther appears in 1 Kgs 1:1–4: The aged king David is unable to keep warm and his advisors recommend—as the advisors of Ahasuerus recommend—that "a young woman be sought for my lord the king" (1:2). A nationwide search ensues "for a beautiful young woman" and ends with the finding of Abishag the Shunammite, who is described as being "very beautiful" (1:4).[67] Although David does not have a sexual relationship with Abishag, her status appears to be equivalent to a wife or concubine. At the very least, she is uniquely connected to the reigning king, so that Solomon views Adonijah's request for Abishag as wife as tantamount to a bid for the throne (1 Kgs 2:23–24).

This suggests that a woman brought permanently into the harem of Israelite royalty, whether she remained a virgin or not, was legally bound to the king. Whether or not he chose to engage in sexual activity

---

[64] It should be noted that Rebekah's father and brother give permission to Abraham's servant to take her, effectively betrothing her to Isaac, in Gen 24:51. Her verbal consent comes later, when Abraham's servant urges an immediate return to Abraham and Isaac (24:57). Abigail and Ruth were previously married, which changes the betrothal process and seems to allow them more volition.

[65] This is also the case with captive wives, see Deut 21:10–14 and Judg 21. Westbrook and Wells, *Everyday Law in Biblical Israel*, 64.

[66] Bathsheba is an exception, as she was married to Uriah when David first took her. She does not become David's wife until Uriah is killed and David brings her to the royal house the second time (2 Sam 11:27).

[67] See Macchi for a more detailed discussion of possible parallels between the Esther narrative and the succession narrative of 1 Kgs 1–2. Macchi, *Esther*, 121.

with her did not lessen his responsibility toward her or the fact that she was the sexual property of the king.[68]

In sum, biblical literature informs us that most marriages followed a process of betrothal and union that did not require a formal public ceremony for them to be legal and binding.

Case Studies: Sarah and Bathsheba

A few biblical narratives warrant special mention for the way they might illuminate the ethical challenges of Esther's presence in the harem. In these narratives, women are noted for their beauty and taken to the royal house.[69] The key difference is that these women—Sarah and Bathsheba—are married, which makes it a clear sin for the respective monarchs to take them. In the case of Sarah, Abraham's wife, the kings are unaware of her marital status and sin unintentionally (Gen 12:18; 20:4–6), but David is fully cognizant that Bathsheba is married (2 Sam 11:3).

Sarah, Abraham's wife, is taken not once but twice by two different foreign monarchs (Gen 12:15; 20:2). Both times, Abraham advises her to hide her marital relationship to him (Gen 12:11–12; 20:5).[70] Although Sarah never sleeps with them, there is no evidence that she protests being taken to the royal dwelling(s). Bathsheba, wife of Uriah the Hittite, is taken by King David and he engages in intercourse with her (2 Sam 11:4). The text does not record any protest from Bathsheba either, although she does hold David accountable for her pregnancy

[68] Nathan's condemnation of David's behavior toward Bathsheba includes an interesting statement about Saul's wives: "I gave you your master's house and your master's wives into your arms and gave you the house of Israel and of Judah" (2 Sam 12:8). This accords with the broader ancient Near Eastern custom of a royal successor inheriting or taking possession of the previous king's wives. See Marten Stol, *Women in the Ancient Near East* (trans. H. Richardson and M. Richardson; Berlin: de Gruyter, 2016), 106, 491. This text does not necessarily mean that David slept with these women, but it does indicate that they were considered his responsibility. Richard M. Davidson, "Polygamy in the Old Testament," in *Pathology of Polygamy: Cross-Cultural Mission on a Biblical Basis*, ed. Ron du Preez (Berrien Springs, MI: Omega Media, 2007), 35.

[69] Macchi, *Esther*, 125. On the similarities between Esth 2 and Gen 12 see Koller, *Esther in Ancient Jewish Thought*, 143–45.

[70] Harvey, *Finding Morality in the Diaspora*, 22.

(11:5). The important point is that the women are not condemned.[71] Instead, God places the onus on the kings: Both the court of the Pharoah and that of the king of Gerar are afflicted with a plague (Gen 12:17) or infertility (Gen 20:17) until Sarah is returned to Abraham. For killing Uriah and taking Bathsheba, David suffers the loss of his son and the rest of his reign is beset with familial discord and violence (2 Sam 11:10, 14).

Interestingly, Abraham's deception is rebuked both times by the monarchs and the inclusion of their speeches to Abraham in the narrative suggests that the author shares their displeasure with Abraham's willingness to allow his own wife to be taken. Abraham, not Sarah, is held responsible for the deception.

These examples offer a number of insights into the story of Esther. There is precedence, as early as the patriarchal period, for a beautiful woman who attracted the attention of a king to be taken to the royal house to become his wife. This action was only explicitly condemned by the author if the woman was already married, in which case it was an act of adultery and punishable by God. In such situations, the monarch bore the responsibility for taking a married woman, and the husband (in Abraham's case) for allowing his wife to be taken by another man. The woman was not considered at fault. Given these observations, it is reasonable to assume that the author of Esther: 1) would not have held her morally culpable for being "taken" or spending the night with the king, and 2) would not have viewed the gathering of the beautiful virgins as particularly extraordinary, except, perhaps, for the scale on which it was carried out.

Persian Period Context

Having examined the biblical context, we now turn to extrabiblical evidence during the Persian period. In the multi-cultural Persian satrapy of Elephantine, a betrothal agreement and "documents of wifehood" or marriage agreements have been found.[72] The latter bear certain similarities to each other, including the date, introduction of concerned

---

[71] Interestingly, both women go on to play important roles in the history of Israel: Sarah as the matriarch of Israel and Bathsheba as the matriarch of the Davidic dynasty. On David and Bathsheba, see Richard M. Davidson, "Did King David Rape Bathsheba?: A Case Study in Narrative Theology," *Journal of the Adventist Theological Society* 17, no. 2 (2006): 95.

[72] Azzoni, *The Private Lives of Women in Persian Egypt*, 5.

parties (groom and bride's guardian), and verbal formularies that mark the "transition of bride and groom to wife and husband, respectively."[73] Given the presence of various peculiarities in each of the Elephantine documents and that the betrothal agreement is not accompanied by a later written marriage agreement, it is plausible that "at Elephantine . . . a written marriage document was only implemented in atypical situations."[74]

There are few extant indigenous records of marriage practices during the Persian period. Much of what we know comes from non-royal documents and the later Greek writers, whose views of the Persians complicate the historical narrative.[75] Persian nobility often formed political alliances through marriage to strengthen loyalty between military and administrative leadership and the throne, and between the Persian kings and non-Persian rulers.[76] This practice, which was not original to the Persians, was carried on by the Macedonian Alexander the Great and used as a means for legitimizing "his right to the Persian throne."[77] Arrian of Nicomedia, in his *Anabasis of Alexander*, provides a brief description of the Persian wedding customs observed in the mass wedding hosted by Alexander the Great in Susa. The wedding, which included the marriage of some ninety Macedonian men to Persian and Median noblewomen, also included the marriage of Alexander and Barsine, daughter of Darius III. According to Arrian, "These weddings were solemnized in the Persian style; chairs were placed for the bride-grooms [*sic*] in order, then, after the healths had been drunk, the brides came in and each sat down by the side of her bridegroom, and the men took them by the hand and kissed them, the king setting the example, for all the weddings took place together . . . After receiving his bride each bridegroom led her home."[78] In a similar

---

[73] Ibid., 15, 21, 26.

[74] Azzoni, *The Private Lives of Women in Persian Egypt*, 20. Azzoni cites Martha Roth who, in examining Babylonian marriage agreements, states that "marriage documents normally were concluded orally, probably before witnesses, and perhaps were accompanied by ceremonies or rites of which we remain ignorant." Martha T. Roth, *Babylonian Marriage Agreements: 7th–3rd Centuries B.C.*, AOAT 222 (Kevelaer: Butzon & Bercker, 1989), 28.

[75] Azzoni, *The Private Lives of Women in Persian Egypt*, 1–3.

[76] Maria Brosius, *Women in Ancient Persia (559–331 BC)* (Oxford: Clarendon, 2002), 40, 45, 47, 70.

[77] Ibid., 38, 77.

[78] Arrian, *Anab.* 7.4.4–8.

spirit to Ahasuerus' actions following the feast of Esther, Alexander gave gifts to the newly married couples and forgave the debts of his soldiers.[79]

The Persian royal harem was comprised of women with a variety of backgrounds and roles, including the queen mother, royal princesses (daughters of the king), royal wives, and royal concubines.[80] Scholars believe that the wives of Persian kings were usually Persian. This is supported by Herodotus, who recounts that Cambyses, a predecessor to Ahasuerus, demanded the daughter of Amasis, king of Egypt, and instead was given another noblewoman because Amasis was afraid his daughter would be treated as a concubine.[81] The Queen Consort or primary wife was typically "the daughter of a Persian prince and the mother of the heir to the throne."[82] There were exceptions: Ochus, who assumed the name Darius II and took the throne from Sogdianus after the death of Xerxes II, was the son of Artaxerxes I and a Babylonian woman.[83]

Royal women were not confined to their living quarters, as some modern representations suggest. The king and his harem were less visible to the public than modern royalty; however, as Lloyd Llewellyn-Jones argues, this should be viewed as intentional *separation* as opposed to *seclusion*. This "ideology of royal separation" did not "exclude royal women from active participation in the affairs of the dynasty, or from economic transactions, or from independent travel, or even from the owning or maintenance of personal estates of land."[84]

The Persepolis tablets document that several royal women owned palace estates and villages across the empire, employed large work groups, and utilized personal seals in directing officials under their control. They also traveled both privately and for official purposes, often accompanying the king during military campaigns and court

---

[79] Arrian, *Anab.* 7.5.

[80] Lloyd Llewellyn-Jones, *King and Court in Ancient Persia* (Edinburgh: Edinburgh University Press, 2013), 110–11.

[81] Herodotus, *Hist.* 3.1.2.

[82] Shahbazi, "Harem in Ancient Iran"; also Brosius, *Women in Ancient Persia*, 32.

[83] Brosius, *Women in Ancient Persia*, 33; Heleen Sanchisi-Weerdenburg, "Darius iv. Darius II," *Encyclopaedia Iranica* VII, fasc. 1: 50–51. Cited 22 March 2022. Online: http://www.iranicaonline.org/articles/darius-iv.

[84] Llewellyn-Jones, *King and Court in Ancient Persia*, 98.

travels, and received travel rations.[85] Xenophon records that Parysatis—mother of Cyrus the younger and Darius II—owned villages along the Chalos (modern Queiq or Aleppo river) and Tigris rivers and property in Nippur, in Babylonia. The income from these estates appears to have belonged to Parysatis, as she had in her employment an account administrator.[86] The queen and queen mother were particularly independent and were the only women who regularly dined with the king.[87] According to A. Shapur Shahbazi, the queen was "subject only to the king . . . had her own living quarter, her own revenue and estates and a large number of servants, which included harem eunuchs and concubines."[88] Royal or noble women sometimes played an intercessory role before the king on behalf of family members, such as convincing the king to transmute a sentence from death to exile.[89]

While concubines were inferior to wives, they were not considered mere mistresses or prostitutes and could achieve a higher status if favored by the king.[90] Concubines were bought, captured, given as tribute, or gathered to the harem from across the empire (as in Esth 2).[91] It was not uncommon for Persian kings to take by force young boys and girls for the service of the royal court. Some of the girls became concubines while others became palace slaves. After the Ionian uprising, Persian commanders under Darius I "chose out the most handsome boys and castrated them, making them eunuchs instead of men, and they carried the fairest maidens away to the king."[92] The Chronicle of Artaxerxes III describes the capture of women from Sidon in 345 BC, "which the king sent to Babylon, that day they entered the palace of the king."[93]

---

[85] Brosius, *Women in Ancient Persia,* 25, 28, 87–93, 180–81. Irdabama, of the court of Darius I, was one such woman. Maria Brosius, "Women in Pre-Islamic Persia," *Encyclopaedia Iranica*, n.p. [cited 22 March 2022]. Online: https://iranicaonline.org/articles/women-i.

[86] Xenophon, *Anab.* 1.4.9; 2.4.27. Stol; *Women in the Ancient Near East*, 552–53.

[87] Brosius, "Women in Pre-Islamic Persia"; see also Plutarch, *Art.* 5.3.

[88] Shahbazi, "Harem in Ancient Iran."

[89] Brosius, *Women in Ancient Persia*, 118–19.

[90] Llewellyn-Jones, *King and Court in Ancient Persia*, 118.

[91] Shahbazi, "Harem in Ancient Iran."

[92] Herodotus, *Hist.* 6.32.

[93] ABC, Chronicle 9.

The writings of the Roman historian Aelian provide a "highly romanticized" view of women taken to the Persian court.[94] Although the events in this narrative took place over a hundred years after the setting of the book of Esther (and Aelian wrote some five hundred years after the events he narrates), interesting similarities can be seen between the stories. Aelian describes how a young woman named Aspasia was taken by an officer of Cyrus the Younger (d. 401 BC), "against her will, and her father had not wished to let her go; but she was compelled, as often happens when cities are captured or tyrants and satraps insist."[95] She was brought before Cyrus along with three other women, who were evidently wealthier than Aspasia and eager to be displayed before Cyrus. The three others had been accompanied by maids who styled their hair and probably applied the makeup the women are reported as wearing. These women had been groomed "by their tutors on how to win Cyrus' favour, how to flatter him—not to turn away at his approach, not to be annoyed by his petting, to accept his kisses, all the tricks that are taught to courtesans and women who trade in beauty."[96] According to Aelian and Plutarch, Aspasia shunned Cyrus's advances and consequently he loved her more than any of the other women.[97]

Several of the dynamics explored above are paralleled in the book of Esther: Women, such as Esther and Aspasia, were taken for the harem during conquest, for tribute, as gifts, or in a special gathering (as in Esth 2). The imperial nature of the gathering cut out an important party generally present in biblical and ancient Near Eastern marriage customs, namely the father or male guardian of the woman given in marriage. The giving of a so-called "brideprice" is also notably absent.

It is probable that Esther was groomed in a manner similar to the women presented before Cyrus the Younger. The twelve months of preparation provided ample time for beautification as well as education on the graces of being a royal woman and the laws governing the Persian court (2:12).

---

[94] Llewellyn-Jones, *King and Court in Ancient Persia*, 119. As Llewellyn-Jones notes, Greek authors were obsessed with the "sex life of the Persian monarch," rendering their descriptions of harem life less than reliable. Despite the eroticization of Aspasia, the basic elements of the story can be reasonably compared to that of Esther (*King and Court in Ancient Persia*, 118).

[95] Aelian, *Var. hist.* 12.1.

[96] Aelian, *Var. hist.* 12.1.

[97] Aelian, *Var. hist.* 12.1; Plutarch, *Art.* 26.4.

In light of our discussion of the Persian context, we can better understand Esther's situation and the scope of her agency in the palace, and find parallels between her story and those of other royal women. She achieved a higher status in the harem when favored by Hegai and later by Ahasuerus (2:9, 17). Prior to becoming queen, her autonomy was limited to her deportment and the articles she chose to take with her during her night with the king (2:9, 15). After her coronation, she interceded on behalf of her people (7:3–4; 8:3, 5–6), took ownership of the estate of Haman (8:1), aided in the formulation of laws to reverse Haman's edict (9:13–14), and authorized the establishment of Purim (9:29).

Conclusion: The Beauty of Esther

The book of Esther is full of aesthetic details, such as the extravagant and ornate decorations of the palace (1:6) and the beautifying cosmetics and oils for the young virgins (2:12). The women are extraordinarily beautiful: Queen Vashti, the gathered virgins, and Esther. But when we are invited by the author to gaze at Esther, the author does not offer a view like the one Ahasuerus' desired of Vashti (which he wanted to share with his guests, and which Vashti refused to offer)—a gaze on external beauty. Instead, we see Esther as a young woman who is winning favor and grace, like other faithful heroes of Jewish history. The text makes clear that she is beautiful (2:7). This is a vital detail that explains her presence in the harem and links her to other women in Jewish history who were taken for their beauty. However, in choosing to repeat the theme of winning favor and grace, the author shifts our gaze from Esther's surface beauty to the beauty of her character.

The vast collection of so many beautiful women attests to the rapacious desires of both king and court (it was the attendants who suggested the gathering) and is also an indication of the king's dominance "not simply of man over women or of master over slaves, but of monarch over Empire."[98] Indeed, collected women, at any time in the empire's history, "were physical manifestations of the Persian realm itself."[99] Within the context of imperial grasping for beauty and pleasure, Esther makes no special requests for herself (2:15). Perhaps, when reading Esther in our twenty-first century context, we should

[98] Llewellyn-Jones, *King and Court in Ancient Persia*, 119.

[99] Ibid., 119.

extend to her the golden scepter and allow her to find grace and favor in our eyes.

The story of Esther is beautiful from the broader perspective of identity and redemption. Esther's was a multi-faceted identity—what Beal terms "an aggregate of selves"—Jewish exile, orphan girl, and Persian queen.[100] This complexity requires the reader to hold these identities in relation to each other, illuminating the tension in her lived experience. Rather than providing concrete answers on how to behave in a particular situation, the book of Esther presents us with an almost impossible scenario that forces us to ask questions about our own identities and social agency. The dramatic reversal that resolves the crisis at the heart of the book is a testament to "subtle divine oversight" and the "great personal courage" of a woman who used her beauty, favor, position, and Jewish identity to save her people.[101]

This essay is dedicated to our friend and colleague, Jo Ann Davidson, whose love of beauty and biblical aesthetics has deepened our appreciation of the complexity and beauty found in the story of Esther. She has eloquently summarized and applied the message of Esther as follows:

> The Book of Esther contains an impressive narrative of a miraculous deliverance of the Hebrew people—a narrative of divine grace! Esther was not only an exile, but also an orphan and a person who had to hide her ethnicity. Yet through subtle divine oversight, through her obedience to her foster parent and great personal courage, she rose to royal heights and worked for the deliverance of her threatened people. A woman leader, representing a hated minority, Esther responded to God's call, risking her life to stand against an evil abuse of power. In the Persian patriarchal culture, God chose a woman as a deliverer. The life of Esther can help us, often more subtly than we might yet recognize, to acknowledge the power and grace of the God of Israel. What a narrative of the gospel![102]

God continues to raise up women to lead amid the complexities of our current age—women whose inward beauty surpasses all superficial

[100] Timothy K. Beal, *The Book of Hiding: Gender, Ethnicity, Annihilation, and Esther* (New York, NY: Routledge, 1997), 47.

[101] Jo Ann Davidson, "The Gospel and a Queen," *Perspective Digest* 26, no. 2 (April 2021): n.p. [cited 22 March 2022]. Online: https://www.perspectivedigest.org/archive/26-2/the-gospel-and-a-queen.

[102] Davidson, "The Gospel and a Queen."

beauty standards and inspires us to turn our gaze to the ultimate Source of beauty: God Himself.

Women Leaders in the Greco-Roman World: Lydia and the Women at Philippi

Carina Prestes

Abstract

In the last few decades, a number of Christian denominations have been discussing the participation of women in the church as ordained ministers. Much of the conversation is based on the exegesis of selected passages from 1 Corinthians and 1Timothy. However, little attention has been given to the finds of archaeological work and the broad study of the Greco-Roman world. Therefore, in this chapter I first analyze the Greco-Roman background. With this understanding, then, I look at the account of Lydia in Acts 16 and the other women who came after her in Philippi. After that, I turn my attention to the archaeological remains and literary references in order to build a more balanced and hopefully more precise account of the active participation of women in Philippi in the first centuries of Christianity.

Introduction

In the first semester of my master's degree at the Seventh-day Adventist Theological Seminary at Andrews University, I had the privilege of taking a class with Dr. Jo Ann Davidson. In that class, she lectured on the theology of beauty and its connections with the construction of the Israelite tabernacle. I really appreciated her lecture. On that occasion, I learned that Bezalel is the first person that the Bible describes God filling with his Spirit, in order to qualify him for the construction of the temple (Exod 35:30–33). As an architect, I was profoundly affected by this insight. Since then, I have seen art and architecture through a different lens. Now, many years later, my specialization is in Early Christian archaeology, which is a rich field for the study of art, architecture, and beauty.

One of the beautiful things in archaeological studies is their potential to inform and nuance our current understanding of the past, especially of biblical periods, which can lead to different and more accurate interpretations of the biblical texts, hopefully inspiring people with a better vision of life. The stories people accept become part of their worldview, guiding the way they interpret the world.

A large part of the Christian worldview is made up of biblical stories. That is, Christians are greatly influenced by their understanding and interpretations of the biblical narratives. Archaeology, then, is quite helpful by informing the background of the stories of the Bible, and contextualizing them, making them multi-dimensional.[1] Thus, when archaeological work nuances some aspects of biblical history, it can bring more accurate interpretations. This potential in archaeological studies can be seen in the study of women in Early Christianity.

Although there are currently different beliefs regarding the participation of women in the Early Christian church, the common element is that women had a very limited role in society during the New Testament period. It is believed that women stayed at the house and could not be seen in public, did not own property and wealth in their own name, and were subject to a male figure during all stages of their lives. In other words, women were almost invisible in ancient societies.[2] This position often comes from the writings of ancient

---

[1] By multi-dimensional, I mean that archaeology brings color, taste, smell, texture, topography, climate, and other elements to the biblical narratives.

[2] Among the scholars that believe that women had quite a restricted life are Everett Ferguson, *Backgrounds of Early Christianity* (Grand Rapids, MI: Eerdmans, 2003), 78; Risto Saarinen, *The Pastoral Epistles with Philemon & Jude*, Brazos Theological Commentary of the Bible (Grand Rapids, MI: Baker, 2008), 67; Craig S. Keener, *Paul, Women, and Wives: Marriages and Women's Ministry in the Letters of Paul* (Peabody, MA: Hendrickson, 1995), 165. Other authors acknowledge that some women had more freedom, but most of them lived restricted lives. Among them are: Karen J. Torjesen, *When Women Were Priests: Women's Leadership in the Early Church & the Scandal of Their Subordination in the Rise of Christianity* (San Francisco, CA: Harper San Francisco, 1993); Ross S. Kraemer, "Jewish Women and Women's Judaism(s) at the Beginning of Christianity," in *Women & Christian Origins*, ed. Ross S. Kraemer and Mary R. D'Angelo (Oxford: Oxford University Press, 1999), 72; Beth A. Barr, *The Making of Biblical Womanhood: How the Subjugation of Women Became Gospel Truth* (Grand Rapids, MI: Brazos, 2021), 46.

authors such as Livy, Plutarch, and Philo.[3] However, these authors represent a very limited part of the first-century population around the Mediterranean basin.

Because of these beliefs regarding the limited role of women in Greco-Roman societies, some affirm that women did not speak in public or teach a man in the first century, and therefore women could not have been church ministers and leaders in Early Christianity. Others affirm that, while in the broader society women had more limitations, Christian circles allowed more prominent roles for women and that is partly why Christianity attracted large numbers of women.[4]

The belief that women had a limited role in society during the first century deeply influences the interpretation of critical passages in the New Testament regarding women's silence in the church and their unquestioned submission to males. Furthermore, current Christian practices regarding the leadership of women in the church[5] tend to be based on biblical passages from 1 Corinthians and 1 Timothy that are interpreted through the traditional assumptions regarding women in the period of the New Testament. However, these assumptions about women in antiquity are rarely questioned when dealing with modern ecclesial praxis. Some of the questions that need to be asked are: What is the basis for these common beliefs? Are they accurate? Were women really that restricted in the

---

[3] Livy: "What sort of practice is this, of running out into the streets and blocking the roads and speaking to other women's husbands? Could you not have made the same requests, each of your own husband, at home?" (*Hist.* 34.2.8; Sage, LCL). Plutarch: "womankind is typified by 'keeping silent'" (*Moralia*, 142c–d). Philo: "a woman, then, should not be a busybody, meddling with matters outside her household concerns, but should seek a life of seclusion" (*The Special Laws*, 3.169ff.).

[4] Rodney Stark (*Rise of Christianity: How the Obscure, Marginal Jesus Movement Became the Dominant Religious Force in the Western World in a Few Centuries* [New York, NY: Harper One, 1996], 128) suggests that because of women's greater numbers in Christian communities they enjoyed a higher status, attracting even more women. See also Ben Witherington, "Women in the New Testament," *Anchor Bible Dictionary* 6:957–61.

[5] Different Christian churches do not give women the opportunity to be ordained ministers and participate in church leadership because of their interpretation of these biblical passages.

first centuries of the common era? What information do the archaeological remains give about societal roles of women?

In order to address these questions, in this article I will first look at the relevant historical background of the New Testament, specifically addressing the role of women in society in light of the archaeological and literary evidence. This will include exploring the Greco-Roman historical background, along with the topic of patronesses and women as religious leaders in the Roman world. Based on those findings, I will address the participation of women in the early churches. Then I will highlight one particular passage of the New Testament that mentions a woman living in Philippi engaged in Christian leadership, Lydia in Acts 16, focusing on her role as servant and hostess in light of the historical and archaeological background. Lastly, I will look at other Christian women that were leaders at Philippi according to the New Testament and the later archaeological and literary evidence.

Women in the Greco-Roman World

Early Christian communities extended through three continents—North Africa, Asia, and Europe—with people of varied backgrounds. Furthermore, Christian communities were an interesting mix of these local peoples with the Greek, Roman, and Jewish cultures.[6] The Greek culture remained dominant in the Mediterranean in the first couple centuries of the common era, even after the ascension of the Roman empire.[7] This is so because Alexander the Great created an efficient system of acculturation of conquered peoples, which preserved the Greek culture for centuries. This system was mainly based on the construction of Greek cities (*poleis*), which facilitated the conquered peoples to assimilate the

---

[6] In this chapter there is not a full section for Jewish women. Nevertheless, the chapter mentions different Jewish women. To talk about the role of Jewish women in the first century can be a little misleading since there were Jewish women spread all around the Mediterranean. Thus, there was a large variety in regard to the status of women within first century Judaism, even within the Jewish women of Jerusalem. For more information on Jewish women in the Greco-Roman world, see Tal Ilan, *Jewish Women in Greco-Roman Palestine* (Peabody, MS: Hendrickson, 1996).

[7] David A. deSilva, *Honor, Patronage, Kinship & Purity: Unlocking New Testament Culture* (Downers Grove, IL: IVP Academic, 2000), 36.

Greek culture.[8] Later, when the Roman empire rose to power, it added more diversity to the communities. However, it was not a simple task to switch from one culture to another and completely rebuild numerous cities. Some places were more open to cultural transitions than others. In addition, because of the strategic location of some cities, Roman authorities had closer control over them, resulting in greater assimilation of the Roman culture in some locations than in others. All of these elements brought a large cultural variety to the Christian communities in the first centuries. Considering such multiplicity of cultural backgrounds within Christian communities, it seems somewhat reductionist to affirm that women had a limited role in all societies across the entire Mediterranean basin during the first century. Such affirmation does not consider the nuances present in such broad territory. Can almost half of the entire population—women—in such a wide territory be described that simply? The following sections on Greco-Roman women will show that this is not the case.

Greek Priestesses

Recent scholarship has analyzed the archaeological remains of women who served as Greek priestesses.[9] The results were illuminating. They found that the "equality of men and women as priests and priestesses in ancient Greece was nothing short of remarkable."[10] Joan B. Connelly in her ground-breaking book *Portrait of a Priestess* revealed that priestesses had quite a prominent position in society. I will summarize here some of her findings. She shows that priestesses led public processions; oversaw *polis* festivals; were publicly honored with portrait statues; had reserved theater seats; signed and used their own seals on documents; went before the city council and the assembly to argue cases of temple law; selected sacred officials; gave guidance to distinct men; and

---

[8] Eric M. Meyers and Mark A. Chancey, *Alexander to Constantine: Archaeology of the Land of the Bible* (New Haven, CT: Yale University Press, 2012), 13.

[9] Joan B. Connelly, *Portrait of a Priestess: Women and Ritual in Ancient Greece* (Princeton, NJ: Princeton University Press, 2007).

[10] Simon Price, "Religious Personnel: Greece," in *Religions of the Ancient World*, ed. S. I. Johnston (Cambridge, MA: Harvard University Press, 2004), 303.

prescribed the regulations of the temple they served.[11] Their office was a public one with broad civic engagement. The cultic leadership of priestesses was in effect also political—meetings of the citizen assembly at Athens first discussed religious matters followed by secular issues. Furthermore, temples also functioned as financial institutions. Thus, priestesses were also leaders in those institutions. Some of these temples were quite large, like the temple of Artemis in Ephesus. Furthermore, priestesses were expected to financially support the religious demands of the cult, like festivals and building maintenance.[12] Hence, their office involved priesthood and patronage.

Priestesses were also respected by distinguished men for their wisdom. We are told by Aristoxenos that a Delphic priestess called Themistokleia taught philosophy to Pythagoras.[13] In addition, in Plato's *Symposium*, we are told that Socrates consulted Diotima, a religious expert, on the subject of love.[14] The fact that philosophers like Pythagoras and Socrates were intellectually helped by priestesses suggests that these women were perceived as wise persons that were able to help even these important men.

Thus, Greek priestesses occupied religious, political, social, and economic positions. They were responsible for making the cult a success.[15] The tradition of such priestesses was present in many areas around the Mediterranean where Greek culture and language was dominant at the start of Christianity. That was the case in Asia Minor, Macedonia, Greece, Syria, South Italy, and Sicily.[16]

A common belief regarding Greek priestesses that must be addressed is the practice of sacred prostitution. This practice is believed to have existed mainly in Corinth, Ephesus, and Paphos. These three cities were visited by the apostle Paul during his ministry. These cities also had in common the fact that they were

---

[11] Connelly, *Portrait of a Priestess*, 197–221.

[12] Connelly, *Portrait of a Priestess*, 44.

[13] Diogenes, *Laertius* 8.8, 21 (frag. 15 Wehrli); found in Connelly, *Portrait of a Priestess*, 220.

[14] Plato, *Symposium* 201d1.

[15] Connelly, *Portrait of a Priestess*, 20.

[16] See, for instance, inscriptions of priestesses around the Mediterranean in Mary R. Lefkowitz and Maureen B. Fant, *Women's Life in Greece and Rome: A Source Book in Translation* (Baltimore, MD: Johns Hopkins University Press, 2016).

port cities with large numbers of transient visitors and sailors that used the services of prostitutes.[17] This was and still is a normal practice in port cities. However, to connect this practice with sacred prostitution is a large stretch.[18] There is no material evidence supporting this position; it is an argument from silence. In Corinth, for example, where prostitution quarters were found, they were close to the port, whereas the temple of Aphrodite (where it is usually believed that sacred prostitution took place) was on the summit of the Acropolis. These two places were miles away from each other, and archaeological evidence suggests that instead of serving as prostitutes, priestesses acted in and around the temple in a way that was similar to caring for households, an activity very familiar to these well-educated and wealthy women.[19]

Women in the First Centuries CE

A great amount of our current knowledge of daily life in the Mediterranean during the first century comes from Pompeii and Herculaneum, cities buried by the eruption of Mount Vesuvius in 79 CE. In these cities one can find the remains of Roman cities not disturbed by later human activities, such as wars and building constructions. These cities are among the most studied and known ancient cities in the world. One can learn a lot about the ancient world and the participation of women in society in the first century by studying these cities.

One of the most enlightening sources of information from these two cities is their wall frescoes. In those paintings one can see women working in shops, and interacting with customers. These snapshots of ancient life challenge the common assumptions that women were circumscribed to the domestic environment. Furthermore, other remains (stone and terracotta reliefs) with visual portrayals of women working outside the house were also found in Rome and Ostia, portraying similar realities. In addition to this visual

[17] Connelly, *Portrait of a Priestess*, 19.

[18] For a larger discussion on sacred prostitution see John McRay, *Archaeology and the New Testament* (Grand Rapids, MI: Baker, 2003), 315.

[19] Connelly, *Portrait of a Priestess*, 5.

evidence, numerous inscriptions have been found attesting to the work of women outside the house.[20]

A woman working at the Verecundus Shop in Pompeii, first century CE.

[20] Evidence of the following female workers have been found: skilled workers of gold (*CIL* VI 9214); players of musical instruments; singers; readers; farm managers (Cato, *On Agriculture*, 142–3); shepherdesses (*BGU* VI 129.11, *PMich.* Iv. 23. G); doctors (*CIL* VI 9614, 9615, 9617, 6851); midwives; physicians (*CGF* 45 = Plesket 1. G); entrepreneurs; and businesswomen (*CIL* I2. 3011a). For a more detailed list of women's occupations in the Greco-Roman world, see Lefkowitz and Fant, *Women's Life in Greece and Rome*.

Poultry dealer – in Museo Torlonia, Rome, first century BCE.

A woman selling chickens and eggs in a terracotta relief from Ostia, second century CE.

This phenomenon of women working outside the house might be the result of the massive military campaigns of the Roman army in the first century BCE. Because a large part of the male population was gone either for training or battle, and many men died in the process, the male population decreased substantially.[21] Such a scenario forced women to step up and take positions in society that were previously occupied by men, in order to keep society functioning. In addition, the men who died in these military campaigns left their widows in control of their wealth.[22]

Patronesses

The excavations of Pompeii and Herculaneum have also revealed statues and statue bases of patronesses and priestesses. Eumachia, from Pompeii, is of special importance. This woman made a generous donation for the construction of a building and a colonnade in the forum of the city. A large inscription on top of the colonnade of the forum attests her donation; and another inscription at the base of her statue mentions her as a priestess. One of these inscriptions reads: "Eumachia, daughter of Lucius, *public priestess*, in her *own* name and that of her son, Marcus Numistrius Fronto, built with her *own* funds the porch, covered passage, and dedicated them to Concordia Augusta and to Pietas."[23]

---

[21] Emily A. Hemelrijk, *Women and Society in the Roman World: A Source Book of Inscriptions from the Roman West* (Cambridge, MA: Cambridge University Press, 2021), 68; Susan Treggiari, "Women in Roman Society" in *I Claudia*, 120.

[22] This phenomenon of wealthy widows can be observed in the writings declaring the fear of women's wealth and independence (e.g., Elder Cato) at the same time (Treggiari, "Women in Roman Society," 120).

[23] Translation from Lefkowitz and Fant, *Women's Life in Greece and Rome*, 191; emphasis added.

Inscription at the architrave in the building of Eumachia at the Pompeii forum.

It is significant that the inscription affirms that Eumachia funded the construction out of her own resources and did it in her own name and the name of her son. It seems to indicate that she wanted to make sure that people knew that she was the person paying for the benefactions, not her husband; she was the person that should be honored and respected as a patroness. When the inscription mentions that she herself funded these constructions, it also implies that she had wealth in her name and that she had some freedom to manage it.

The fact that Eumachia received an honorary statue is also relevant. Statues of women were a rare honor in Roman society before the first century BCE. Cleopatra in the first century BCE started a tradition of women being portrayed in artistic works.[24] This tradition was followed by empress Livia (wife of Augustus and

[24] Before Cleopatra, only one woman had received an honorary statue: Cornelia, the mother of Gracchi. Diana E. Kleiner, "Imperial Women as Patrons of the Arts in the Early Empire," in *I Claudia. Women in Ancient Rome*, ed. Diana E. Kleiner and Susan B. Matheson (New Haven, CT: Yale University Art Gallery, 1996), 36.

mother of Tiberius) and later by other women.[25] So, the statue of Eumachia in the first century CE was probably among the first ones of women outside the imperial family, and therefore a great honor given to her. Eumachia received a statue because she was a patroness and a priestess, probably of Venus. In her statue she is portrayed with her head covered by a veil, a Roman priestly indicator,[26] similar to that of Empress Livia at the Ara Pacis in Rome.

Eumachia is not an isolated phenomenon of female patronage or priesthood in Roman society. In Herculaneum, 40% of the dedicatory statues are of women,[27] which suggests a certain normality in regards to female patronage. The Roman society was composed of 60% men and 40% women,[28] which agrees with the number of female dedicatory statues in Herculaneum. This indicates that men and women could serve as patrons, no matter their gender. As such, these women received honor, respect, and authority. In addition, in Asia Minor more than 160 benefactresses have been found and almost half of them mention only a woman as the donor.[29]

As seen in Eumachia's example, patronage and priesthood were often complementary roles. In Pompeii seven inscriptions of patronesses were found; five of which mention that the women were priestesses as well.[30] There are several other inscriptions of women who were patronesses and priestesses.[31] That is the case with the empress Livia. She was actively managing her assets and offering public patronage, and her benefactions inspired other wealthy

---

[25] Ibid.

[26] Lefkowitz and Fant, *Women's Life in Greece and Rome*, 191.

[27] Giuseppina C. Irelli, "Archaeological Research in the Area of Vesuvius: Portraits from Herculaneum," in *Pompeii and the Vesuvian Landscape: Papers of a Symposium Sponsored by the Archaeological Institute of America, Washington Society and the Smithsonian Institution* (Washington, DC: Smithsonian Institution and Archaeological Institute of America, 1979), 20.

[28] Stark, *Rise of Christianity*, 97.

[29] Connelly, *Portrait of a Priestess*, 194.

[30] Brenda Longfellow, "Female Patrons and Honorific Statues in Pompeii," in *Memoirs of the American Academy of Rome* 59/60 (2014–2015): 82–83.

[31] For more on Roman inscriptions of patronesses and priestesses, see Lefkowitz and Fant, *Women's Life in Greece and Rome* and Hemelrijk, *Women and Society in the Roman World*.

women of the empire, like Eumachia, to also fund benefactions.[32] Just like Eumachia, Livia was a priestess too, but she was the priestess of the cult of the emperor Augustus (her husband). According to David A. deSilva, patrons received so much honor that in some cases they were even worshipped by their clients.[33] That is the case with the empress Livia; after her death she was deified and received religious devotion and worship from some of her subjects.[34] Thus, priesthood and patronage were often connected in antiquity.

Empress Livia took a leading role in the empire after her son, Emperor Tiberius, retired to Capri. On that occasion the emperor did not closely attend to the matters of the empire, leaving his mother to do most of the work. According to Dio Cassius, Empress Livia "undertook to manage everything as if she were sole ruler."[35] Livia was perceived as a monarch with state authority.[36] Considering that she managed the empire, it would be fair to assume that she was involved in the politics of the empire. Furthermore, women outside of the imperial family seem to have been somewhat involved in politics as well. Archaeological work in Pompeii has revealed around fifty posters of women using their influence to support political candidates.[37] Thus, to say that women were excluded from politics is not accurate in light of the evidence.

Livia's involvement in politics and art likely resulted from Cleopatra's visit to Rome in the first century BCE. As the queen of Egypt, Cleopatra was the political and military leader who was the recipient of artistic portrayals. Before the first century, it seems that Roman women had not explored political and military activities. Cleopatra was the living proof that women could step into those areas. Her visit to Rome created a ripple effect on the behavior of women in society, starting with the people who were closer to her, like senatorial families, and eventually reaching the communities of the common people. This can be seen in the public portrayals of

---

[32] Kleiner, "Imperial Women as Patrons," 33.

[33] deSilva, *Honor, Patronage, Kinship and Purity: Unlocking the New Testament Culture*, 102.

[34] Emily A. Helmerijk, "Local Empresses: Priestesses of the Imperial Cult in the Cities of the Latin West," *Phoenix* 61 (2007): 320.

[35] Cassius Dio, *Roman History* 57.12.

[36] Kleiner, "Imperial Women as Patrons," 30.

[37] Hemelrijk, *Women and Society in the Roman World*, 297.

women after the first century BCE,[38] in the influx of obelisks from Egypt to Rome after her death at the battle of Actium (31 BC), and in the frescoes portraying Egyptian scenes in Roman houses.[39]

Women as Religious Leaders

In Roman cults women commonly acted as priestesses, such as Eumachia and Livia mentioned above. At Pompeii, for instance, there are eleven other women who were honored as priestesses.[40] In other words, Eumachia was not an isolated case in Pompeii. There are numerous other inscriptions coming from various places that indicate that women were priestesses.[41]

An additional element that contributed to the participation of women as priestesses was the rise of the Emperor Cult in the first century.[42] Evidence has been found of priestesses of other deities besides the emperor, such as Cybele, Cerres, Tellus, Juno, Vesta, Isis, and Venus (one of the most popular deities of the Roman empire).[43] Thus, women were commonly found serving as priestesses when Christianity began to spread around the Mediterranean.

Women were not only religious leaders in pagan cults. Inscriptions have been found of women as leaders of synagogues as well. These women are called "head of synagogue," "elder," "leader," "mother of synagogue," and "priest."[44] According to Kraemer, "In diverse Jewish communities in the Greco-Roman diaspora, Jewish women were active participants in communal life, contributing financial resources and serving as synagogue officers and benefactors."[45] The inscription of Rufina, a female leader of a

---

[38] Kleiner, "Imperial Women as Patrons," 39.

[39] Ibid., 35.

[40] Longfellow, "Female Patrons and Honorific Statues in Pompeii," 84.

[41] For more inscriptions of Roman priestesses see Lefkowitz and Fant, *Women's Life in Greece and Rome*; and Hemelrijk, *Women and Society in the Roman World.*

[42] Emperors were deified and received worship. Livia was the first priestess of her deceased husband, Augustus. Helmerijk, "Local Empresses," 319.

[43] Hemelrijk, *Women and Society in the Roman World*, 221.

[44] Bernadette J. Brooten, *Women Leaders in the Ancient Synagogues*, Brown Judaic Studies 36 (Chico, CA: Scholars Press, 1982).

[45] Kraemer, "Jewish Women and Women's Judaism(s) at the Beginning of Christianity," 72.

synagogue in the second century CE, reads: "Rufina, a Jewess, head of synagogue, built this tomb for her freed slaves and the slaves raised in her house. No one else has the right to bury anyone (here). If someone should dare to do, he or she will pay 1500 denars to the sacred treasury and 1000 denars to the Jewish people. A copy of this inscription has been placed in the (public) archives."[46]

From this inscription one can learn that Rufina, a Jewess, owned slaves and a tomb. She probably owned property in her own name because no man is mentioned in connection with her in the inscription. The inscription also indicates that she was the leader of a synagogue. According to Brooten, the title "head of synagogue" meant that the individual who held this title was the leading official in the ancient synagogue, acting in administration, teaching, and exhorting.[47] This inscription was found in Smyrna and is dated to the second century CE. Thus, Rufina was a Jewess, living in a Hellenized city of Asia Minor (Smyrna), but certainly was somehow influenced by Roman culture because her name was a Roman name. Rufina's inscription exemplifies the mix of Greek, Roman, Jewish, and local cultures mentioned above. Now I will analyze the archaeological remains of some Early Christian communities in light of the historical background mentioned above, namely, that women had prominent roles in the Greco-Roman world.

Women in Early Christianity

It is widely accepted that the earliest Christian churches met in houses. This consensus is mostly based on the New Testament[48] and on the remains of two early Christian structures, a house church and a meeting hall.[49] The house church in Dura Europos (200 CE), Syria, was basically a large house that was modified to accommodate the meetings of a Christian group. The other structure is the rectangular hall found at Kefar 'Othany, near Tell Megiddo, Israel. It is

---

[46] *CIL* 741; *IGR* IV 1452, found in Brooten, *Women Leaders in the Ancient Synagogues*, 5.

[47] Brooten, *Women Leaders in the Ancient Synagogues*, 15–32.

[48] Luke 4:38–41; 10:38; Acts 2:2; 5:42; 8:3; 12:12; 16:15; Col 4:15; 1 Cor 16:19; Rom 16:5; 2 John 10.

[49] Charles A. Stewart, "Churches," in *The Oxford Handbook of Early Christian Archaeology*, ed. David K. Pettegrew, William R. Caraher, and Thomas W. Davis (New York, NY: Oxford University Press, 2019), 129–130.

commonly known as the Megiddo Hall. According to excavators, this hall looked like a house from the outside.[50] Thus, these two earliest known and undisputed Christian meeting places allude to domestic structures. The New Testament also mentions other meeting places such as synagogues, halls (like the hall of Tyrannus in Acts 19:9), and gardens.[51] But the most frequent meeting place described in the New Testament is the house.

The accounts of Christian meetings in houses are so numerous in the New Testament that most scholars agree that houses were the most common place of Christian meetings and worship. Many of these New Testament references to house churches are connected with women as hostesses. Being a hostess carried with it the idea of serving the guests, especially the meal, which was the central part of worship.[52] The Greek word normally used for "servant" in the New Testament is *diakonos*, from which comes the English word "deacon."[53] The root of this word is also used as a verb (*diakonein*) meaning "to serve" or "to minister," and is used frequently in the New Testament for both men and women.[54]

---

[50] Yotam Tepper and Le'ah Di Segni, *A Christian Prayer Hall of the Third Century CE at Kefar 'Othany (Legio): Excavations at the Megiddo Prison 2005* (Jerusalem: Israel Antiquities Authority, 2006), 54.

[51] Stewart, "Churches," 128.

[52] Richard Krautheimer, *The Early Christian and Byzantine Architecture* (New Haven, CT: Yale University Press, 1986), 24.

[53] F. W. Dunker, ed., *Greek-English Lexicon of the New Testament and Other Early Christian Literature*, 3rd edition (Chicago, IL: University of Chicago Press, 2000), 230–231.

[54] Cf. BDAG, 229. In Acts 6:2–6 seven men are called to serve (*diakonein*) tables. This passage mentions that the apostles laid their hands on the seven men and prayed for them. A couple of verses down, the same verb (to serve) is used for the ministry of the apostles (Acts 6:4). But they served/ministered the word to the crowds, while the seven men served/ministered the tables. Thus, Acts 6 portrays two kinds of ministry: the ministry of tables and the ministry of the word. The same Greek verb (*diakonein*) is also used in Luke 4:39 for the mother-in-law of Peter. After she was healed by Jesus, she got up and served (*diakonein*) the guests. The same verb is used in Luke 8:3 for the women who were accompanying Jesus and the twelve apostles. These women were, out of their own means, supporting/ministering (*diakonein*) to Jesus and his disciples. The verb is also used in Luke 10:40 in the story of Martha and Mary, where Martha is serving (*diakonein*) alone while Mary is at the feet of Jesus. The verb is

The liturgy developed by early Christians was a good fit for domestic buildings. That is so because the shared meal was the most important part of the early Christian meeting.[55] The other parts of the liturgy (prayer, preaching, and reading) were planned around or during the meal.[56] Organizing meals and hosting guests was the responsibility of the women. Houses were the female domain, since they managed the household in the Roman society. Andrews Wallace-Hadrill explains, "The ideology of the Roman family secured respect for the *materfamilias* [the married woman in the house], present at the heart of the house and in all its areas, a position of authority over children, slaves, or outsiders who were her social inferiors; but that position of respect is bought at the price of explicit subjection to the *paterfamilias*."[57] Nevertheless, as mentioned above, a large number of men were frequently absent from the house in the first century because of the military. Thus, women were quite frequently alone managing the household.

Women managing the household was a deep tradition in Mediterranean cultures. A much earlier account of a similar dynamic can be seen in the woman described in Prov 31.[58] In this proverb, the woman is in charge of managing the household. She does that with excellence and for that she is publicly praised. Additionally, she performs many activities that include and go beyond the domestic boundaries, challenging our ideas about women's roles in antiquity.

---

used numerous times in the Bible. Remarkably, Jesus described his own ministry with the idea of serving: the Son of Man came not to be served (*diakonein*) but to serve (*diakonein*) (Matt 20:28).

[55] Krautheimer, *The Early Christian and Byzantine Architecture,* 24.

[56] Andrew McGowan, *Ancient Christian Worship: Early Church Practices in Social, Historical, and Theological Perspective* (Grand Rapids, MI: Baker Academic, 2014), 20.

[57] Andrew Wallace-Hadrill, "Engendering the Roman House," in Kleiner and Matheson, *I Claudia. Women in Ancient Rome*, 114.

[58] Carolyn Osiek, Margaret Y. MacDonald, and Janet H. Tulloch, *A Woman's Place: House Churches in Earliest Christianity* (Minneapolis, MN: Fortress, 2006), 151.

Proverbs 31: 10–31
10 A wife of noble character [a "valiant" or "courageous" woman][59] who can find?
She is worth far more than rubies.
11 Her husband has full confidence in her
and lacks nothing of value.
12 She brings him good, not harm,
all the days of her life.
13 She *selects wool* and flax
and works with eager hands.
14 She *is like the merchant ships*,
bringing her food from afar.
15 She gets up while it is still night;
she provides food for her family
and portions for her female servants.
16 She *considers a field and buys it*;
out of her earnings she plants a vineyard.
17 She sets about her work vigorously;
her arms are strong for her tasks.
18 She *sees that her trading is profitable*,
and her lamp does not go out at night.
19 In her hand she holds the distaff
and grasps the *spindle* with her fingers.
20 She *opens her arms to the poor*
and extends her hands to the needy.
21 When it snows, she has no fear for her household;
for all of them are clothed in scarlet.
22 *She makes coverings for her bed;*
she is clothed in fine linen and purple.
23 Her *husband* is respected at the *city gate*,
where he takes his seat among the elders of the land.

---

[59] The Douay-Rheims version reads "a valiant woman" and NETS reads "a courageous wife." The Hebrew word for noble character is חַיִל (*hayil*). This word is generally translated as strength, might, efficiency, wealth, and army. It is mostly used in the Hebrew Bible in the context of war and many times it is translated as "valiant" or "valiantly." However, in Prov 31:10 most translations do not express this idea. The only named woman called חַיִל in the Old Testament is Ruth, but while she was single (Ruth 3:11).

[24] She makes linen garments *and sells them,*
and supplies the merchants with sashes.
[25] She is clothed with strength and dignity;
she can laugh at the days to come.
[26] *She speaks with wisdom,*
and faithful instruction is on her tongue.
[27] *She watches over the affairs of her household*
and does not eat the bread of idleness.
[28] Her children arise and call her blessed;
her husband also, and he praises her:
[29] "Many women do noble things,
but you surpass them all."
[30] Charm is deceptive, and beauty is fleeting;
but a woman who fears the LORD is to be praised.
[31] *Honor* her for all that her hands have done,
and let her works bring her praise at the city gate. (NIV; emphasis added)

The woman described in this passage is in charge of agricultural activities and commercial enterprises that go beyond the physical boundaries of the house, but are considered within the female domain. She brings food from afar; assesses, buys, and plants a field; manages her assets; opens her arms for the poor; and supplies merchants with sashes. The text also mentions that her works were praised in the city gate, where economic, legal, and civic activities were conducted. While all of these activities were perceived as good management of the household, she and her works were clearly not confined to the domestic environment. The archaeological remains together with some literary sources point to women continuing to manage the household until the first century.[60]

---

[60] There are a couple of similarities between the woman of Prov 31 and women in the Greco-Roman world. One of them can be seen in both textual and archaeological remains, namely, women working with wool. It was an activity performed by the wise woman described in this proverb nearly 1000 years before Christ, and it remained a marker of a woman of valor through the Greek period until the time of the New Testament. Numerous funerary inscriptions praise deceased women stating that they worked with wool. Here are some examples: ". . . loved her husband with all her heart. She bore children, one of whom she left on earth, the other beneath it. She had a pleasing way of talking and walking. She tended the house and *worked*

Similar to the woman of Prov 31, the women of the first century had a more prominent role in antiquity than what is commonly assumed nowadays. For example, the women who hosted and financially supported the early Christian meetings were often remembered in the decoration of church buildings. That seems to be the case with the two earliest Christian meeting places: the house-church at Dura Europos and the hall at Megiddo. Both buildings honored women in their decoration. Dura Europos had the frescos of women in its baptistry walls, with around ten women in procession dressed in white and carrying in one hand a torch and in the other hand a bowl. These women portrayed in the procession are depicted much taller than the other figures in the frescos, suggesting the importance of women for the community. In a similar way, the hall of Megiddo displayed the names of female donors in its mosaic floor close to the central table or altar.[61]

The women represented in these early Christian buildings were a reflection of the large number of women in early Christian communities, which were probably 60% women and 40% men,

---

wool. . ." (*CIL* 6.15346); emphasis added. "My dearest mother merited the greater praise for that, because she was the equal and match of other women of upright character in her modesty, probity, chastity, obedience, *wool working*, diligence, and fidelity" (*CIL* VI, 10230); emphasis added. Even women from the family of Augustus worked with wool in order to demonstrate their feminine qualities. Suetonius says that Augustus almost always wore the tunics made by the women of his household ("On all but special occasions he [Augustus] wore house clothes produced for him by his sister, wife, daughter and grand-daughters." Suetonius, *Augustus* 73). The women from the imperial family modeled the behavior of good women for the empire. Their wool working inspired other women in the empire to follow their example. Comparing the Roman inscriptions with the description of the woman in Prov 31, it is possible to see that wool work remained a sign of a virtuous woman. Just like wool work, women's management of the household also remained a characteristic of the Mediterranean cultures for centuries.

[61] See Stewart, "Churches," 128–130; Joan E. Taylor, "Christian Archaeology in Palestine: The Roman and Byzantine Periods," in *The Oxford Handbook of Early Christian Archaeology*, ed. David K. Pettegrew, William R. Caraher, and Thomas W. Davis (New York, NY: Oxford University Press, 2019), 369–373; and Tepper and Di Segni, *A Christian Prayer Hall of the Third Century CE at Kefar 'Othany (Legio)*, 54.

roughly the opposite of the ratio in pagan society.[62] The strong participation of women in the early Christian movement can also be seen in the female conversions mentioned in the book of Acts.[63] The decoration of these early Christian buildings seems to portray a certain continuation of female leadership roles, as seen in Rom 16. In this chapter Paul portrays women in active ministerial leadership: Phoebe was a deacon and a patroness (vv. 1–2), Prisca was a hostess and fellow worker of Paul (vv. 3–5), Mary worked hard for the Romans (v. 6), Junia was an apostle (v. 7), and Tryphaena and Tryphosa (v. 12) were workers in the Lord. Besides Rom 16, the New Testament mentions other women serving Christian communities, according to Jesus's example of ministry. Among them are the women who opened their houses to host Christian meetings, like Lydia (Acts 16:12–40), Mary, the mother of John Mark (Acts 12:12), Nympha (Col 4:15), and Apphia (Phlm 2).

Lydia and the Women of Philippi

With this updated knowledge about the role of women in the Greco-Roman society, I will take a closer look at one hostess mentioned in Acts 16: Lydia, the first convert to Christianity in Europe. According to Peterson, Lydia along with her household "frame the rest of the material" in chapter 16, particularly "drawing

---

[62] Rodney Stark, *The Rise of Christianity* (San Francisco: Harper San Francisco, 1997) and Carina O. Prestes, "A Portrait of the Leadership of Women in Early Christianity: An Archaeological Study in Light of the Historical and Socio-Cultural Contexts" (PhD diss., Andrews University, forthcoming).

[63] The book of Acts describes important women receiving Paul's missionary efforts: Lydia (16:12–40), the prominent women in Thessalonica (17:4) and Berea (17:12), Damaris at Athens (17:34), and Priscilla in Corinth (18:2). The author of Acts made sure to include prominent women accepting Paul's message. These women in Acts 16–18 were all in Macedonia and Greece, areas that experienced women in leadership. Wiseman gathered evidence that some important Macedonian families retained prominent roles in Philippian society, among others. These prominent roles were occupied by men and women. It was money and social status that qualified men and women for important roles in religious settings (James Wiseman, "A Distinguished Macedonian Family of the Roman Imperial Period," *American Journal of Archaeology* 88, no. 4 [1984]: 567–582).

attention to her significance as a patroness of the community and hostess for the missionaries."[64] The text mentions that Lydia was from Thyatira, a city in Asia Minor. The city of Thyatira was formerly in the kingdom of Lydia before it was incorporated by the Romans to the province of Asia.[65] Thus, the name Lydia may point to her background. She is portrayed as a dealer of purple. Thyatira was known for purple dye. The purple dye was made from the juice of madder root, typical from that region. The mention of her business might indicate that she was a person of means.[66] Purple products were expensive and often associated with royalty, which likely made the purple dye business lucrative.[67] The account of Lydia and Paul's encounter narrated in Acts 16 exemplifies a number of elements described in the previous section. Acts 16:12–40 reads:

> **12** From there we traveled to Philippi, a Roman colony and
> the leading city of that district of Macedonia. And we
> stayed there several days. **13** On the Sabbath we went
> outside the city gate to the river, where we expected to
> find a place of prayer. We sat down and began to speak to
> the women who had gathered there. **14** One of those
> listening was a woman from the city of Thyatira named
> Lydia, a dealer in purple cloth. She was a worshiper of
> God. The Lord opened her heart to respond to Paul's
> message. **15** When she and the members of her
> household were baptized, she invited us to her home. "If
> you consider me a believer in the Lord," she said, "come
> and stay at my house." And she persuaded us . . . **40** After
> Paul and Silas came out of the prison, they went to
> Lydia's house, where they met with the brothers and
> sisters and encouraged them. Then they left (NIV).

This passage demonstrates well the blend between Greco-Roman, Jewish, and local cultures seen in the Christian communities

---

[64] David G. Peterson, *The Acts of the Apostles*, Pillar New Testament Commentary (Grand Rapids, MI: Eerdmans, 2009).

[65] Clyde E. Fant and Mitchell G. Reddish, *A Guide to Biblical Sites in Greece and Turkey* (Oxford: Oxford University Press, 2003), 328–331.

[66] John B. Polhill, *Acts*, NAC 26 (Nashville, TN: B&H, 1992), 349.

[67] She was probably a person of means but of low status. Mikeal C. Parsons, *Acts*, Paideia Commentaries on the New Testament (Grand Rapids, MI: Baker Academic, 2008), 230.

of the first century. Paul met Lydia in Philippi, a Greek city, which was a Roman colony, on a Sabbath at a place of prayer, which implies a Jewish gathering. Even though the text does not state clearly that it was a Jewish meeting, this is possible in light of the writings of the first-century (CE) Jewish historian Flavius Josephus. Josephus uses the Greek word (*proseuchē*) to refer to large Jewish meeting places, which is the same word used in Acts 16:13.[68] According to Josephus, these meeting places should be located by sources of fresh water for Jewish purity rituals.[69] Thus, the place of prayer (*proseuchē*) was a place where Jews met on Sabbath and went through purity rituals with fresh water. This description of activities fits well with the description of activities that happened at first-century synagogues.

Lydia is characterized as a "worshiper" of God in Acts 16:14. The Greek word used here for "worshiper" (participle of *sebo*) is used elsewhere in Acts to designate Gentile converts to Judaism (see Acts 13:43, 50; 17:4, 17; 18:7). Hence, Lydia was likely a Gentile woman who converted to Judaism and for this reason was meeting with other Jews on Sabbath. This reinforces the idea that she was attending synagogue or a Jewish meeting place on Sabbath.

The story of Lydia informs us of Lydia's hospitality, which is another deep tradition of Mediterranean cultures. Because of hostile climate conditions, Mediterranean travelers had to rely on the hospitality of strangers to survive. This attitude is portrayed in the biblical text multiple times, including this famous one: "Do not forget to show hospitality to strangers, for by so doing some people have shown hospitality to angels without knowing it" (Heb 13:2, NIV). Other passages that portray hospitality in the Bible are Gen 18:1–8; Rom 12:13; 1 Tim 5:10; 1 Pet 4:9; and 3 John 1:8. In the case of Lydia, she showed hospitality to Paul and his companions. After Paul and Lydia had met by the river, Lydia offered her house for Paul and his companions to stay in, and they agreed.

The theme of hospitality is deeply connected with the house, the common gathering place in Early Christianity. The owners of the houses where Christians met had to show hospitality to attendees. Interestingly, Acts 16 states that when Paul and Silas got out of prison a couple of days later, they went back to Lydia's house and

[68] Cf. Josephus, *Life,* 277, 280.
[69] Cf. Josephus, *Jewish Antiquities,* 14:258.

met with the brothers and sisters. In other words, the text indicates that the people who accepted the message of Paul continued to meet in Lydia's house, which seems to suggest that a house church formed at Lydia's house and that she became the hostess and therefore patroness of this group.

In addition, this account portrays Lydia in charge of a house and a business without a male figure attached to her. The text does not mention a husband or a male figure. Thus, she was in charge of her business (purple cloth) and probably owned the house and household in her own name, which gave her the freedom to manage them. In the first century, women could manage their own businesses. Augustus made a law (*ius liberorum*) exempting mothers of three or more kids from being required to have a legal guardian, which allowed them freedom to manage their own assets. This law was probably a result of the reduction of the male population because of the first century BCE wars.[70] Even for the women who still had a male guardian, these men were more likely a formality to fulfill a legal requirement, or a benefit to help them if needed, not necessarily a restraint.[71]

Lydia was originally from Thyatira (Asia Minor) and was living in Philippi (Macedonia). In both regions—Asia Minor and Macedonia—there is much evidence of women in religious and civic leadership.[72] These areas were heavily influenced by Hellenism, where women were commonly leaders. Since that was Lydia's background, she was likely used to women in leadership positions. Lydia was the leader of her household and her business, and acted as such by hosting the group of travelers. Lydia's hosting also fits well with the dynamic of patronage. By hosting meetings, as the hostess or patroness, Lydia likely was organizing the gatherings and serving food, while the guests (Paul and companions) would be the ones offering a speech to the people present at the occasion.

---

[70] Hemelrijk, *Women and Society in the Roman World*, 68.

[71] Susan Treggiari, "Women in Roman Society," 119.

[72] In Asia Minor, there is some evidence of women holding high public offices. Inscriptions call women *asiarch*, or *archiereiai*. The role of these offices is still controversial, but they were public offices attained by election. Steven J. Friesen, "High Priests of Asia and Asiarchs: Farewell to the Identification Theory," in *Steine and Wege. Festschrift für Dieter Knibbe zum 65. Geburtstag* (Austria: Österreichisches Archäologisches Institut, 1999), 303–07.

This account of Lydia has some elements in common with the case of Rufina mentioned above. Both seem to own property in their own name, are not connected to a male figure, are in a Jewish setting, come from Hellenized cities (Rufina from Smyrna and Lydia from Thyatira), and have some kind of leadership role. Based on Rufina's inscription and the other evidence shared above, it seems that women in leadership roles like Lydia were common in the first century.

Moreover, sometime later Paul sent a letter to the Christian community which had started in this city, the letter to the Philippians. In chapter 4 of this letter, Paul mentions two women by name who worked by his side in the cause of the Gospel: Euodia and Syntyche (Phil 4:2). This mention of women seems to suggest that women continued to hold religious leadership in the Philippian community after Paul left the city.

Archaeological finds seem to further indicate that it was customary for women to have religious leadership in Philippi. Excavations at Philippi revealed over two hundred stone reliefs that either depicted or were dedicated to the goddess Diana.[73] This large number of reliefs demonstrates the devotion of the Philippians to Diana and shows how important her cult was in that city. Considering that the female goddess Diana had only women as cult personnel, the large number of stone reliefs found of her indicates both this city's adherence to this goddess and acceptance of women's religious leadership, even though it was a Roman military colony.[74] In addition, at the Antonine forum of the second century in Philippi, a temple dedicated to the empress Livia was found. Excavators also found a temple of Isis. These three cults—Diana, Livia, and Isis—had women officiating as priestesses.[75] Thus, archaeological remains strengthen the idea that women commonly had prominent religious roles in Philippi.

---

[73] Laura S. Nasrallah, *Archaeology and the Letters of Paul* (Oxford: Oxford University Press, 2019), 117.

[74] Philippi was a Roman military colony of veterans, of which Antony was the primary founder. Octavian and Antony had previously won the battle against the other members of the triumvirate (Cassius and Brutus) on the low plains southwest of Philippi (Ibid., 120).

[75] Ibid., 117.

Moreover, remains of the fourth and fifth century attest to the presence of women in leadership roles in the Christian churches of Philippi, which seems to be a continuation of the religious practices of the first century in the area. These remains come from a period when Christian artistic manifestations were allowed and started to become popular. The most informative remains are the inscriptions, two of which mention female deacons (*diakonos*) named Agatha and Posidonia. Another inscription notes a canoness named Pancharia, and still another mentions a "servant of Christ" named Theodora.[76] Some might be inclined to interpret Theodora's service as a slave or a virgin, not a minister. However, Theodora was married to a centurion, with quite a high position in society, so she was not a slave or a virgin.[77] The deacon Agatha was married to John, who was a cashier and a linen weaver.[78] There are other inscriptions of women that were deacons in Macedonia,[79] indicating that this phenomenon was not an exception in Philippi, but a common practice. Further archaeological evidence for women as leaders in Christian communities can be found around the Mediterranean basin.[80]

Hence, the available evidence indicates that women were religious leaders at Philippi before Christianity reached the city. It is also possible to see that women became leaders of the Christian community when it started, as a natural development from the Greco-Roman culture in the first-century. The archaeological

---

[76] Valerie Abrahamsen, "Women at Philippi: The Pagan and Christian Evidence," *Journal of Feminist Studies in Religion* 3.2 (1987): 17–30.

[77] Julien M. Ogereau, "The Social Constituency and Membership of the First Christian Groups at Philippi: A Literary and Epigraphic Survey," in *The First Urban Churches 4: Philippi*, ed. James R. Harrison and L. L. Welborn, Writings from the Greco-Roman World Supplement Series (Atlanta, GA: SBL Press, 2018), 109.

[78] Ute E. Eisen, *Women Office Holders in Early Christianity: Epigraphical and Literary Studies* (Collegeville, MN: The Liturgical Press, 2000), 180.

[79] They include Agatholkleia, Matrona of Stobi, Theodosia, and Theoprepeia. Kevin Madigan and Carolyn Osiek, *Ordained Women in the Early Church: A Documentary History* (Baltimore, MD: Johns Hopkins University Press, 2005), 207.

[80] For more examples of women as ministers see Eisen, *Women Office Holders in Early Christianity* and Madigan and Osiek, *Ordained Women in the Early Church.*

remains also show that women continued to hold ministerial roles during the next few centuries, similar to other communities around the Mediterranean in that time period.

Interestingly, the literary evidence also suggests female Christian leadership in the same time period of the inscriptions from Philippi above-mentioned. In particular, a letter that pope Gelasius I sent to South Italy and Sicily at the end of the fifth century (495) forbids women to participate at the altar: "To all episcopates established in Lucania, Brutium, and Sicilia: '. . . we have heard to our annoyance that divine affairs have come to such a low state that women are encouraged to officiate at the sacred altars, and to take part in all matters imputed to the offices of the male sex, to which they do not belong.'"[81] Even though this letter was not sent to Macedonia, it attests to the practice of women acting as ministers in the fifth century, the same time period that the inscriptions of Philippi are dated. Additionally, Sicily and South Italy were heavily influenced by Greek culture, like Macedonia.[82]

Conclusion

In this article I collected data from multiple sources about women in the Greco-Roman world. I covered a variety of sources (literary, epigraphical, and archaeological) in order to help minimize biases of specific media. While this position has not been often contemplated, the data raised in this study indicate that women held quite a prominent role in the Greco-Roman society during the first centuries of the Christian era. Women were educated and trained in philosophy, religious rites, and community leadership. And yet, they also continued to manage the household, since it was their domain. The changing role of women in the Greco-Roman society in the first century, combined with the house being the common place of

---

[81] Gelasius I, *Ep.* 14, 26; quoted in Eisen, *Women Office Holders in Early Christianity*, 129.

[82] This letter was written in a period when the church was turning more hierarchical and authoritarian. It was during the fifth century that the Roman church established its structures of ecclesiology, canon, and architecture through the popes Celestine I (422–432), Leo I (440–461), and Gelasius I (492–495). Thus, as the church became more structured and authoritarian, it tended to push women away from ministry leadership. Mary M. Schaefer, *Women in Pastoral Office: The Story of Santa Prassede, Rome* (Oxford: Oxford University Press, 2013), 321.

Christian worship, created the perfect circumstance for the participation and leadership of women in Early Christianity.

This study also points to what can be considered a good example of the leadership of women in the early church, that is, the account of Lydia in Acts 16. She is a biblical example of a woman who was influential beyond the domestic environment, who owned property in her own name, and still managed her household. Lydia's account seems to agree with the archaeological and historical evidence shared in this chapter that shows that women could have a prominent role in society and be leaders during the New Testament period.

Since the idea of women in prominent roles in society and religious leadership has not been commonly entertained in New Testament scholarship, I suggest that the data presented in this chapter regarding women in the Greco-Roman world and the evidence of their ministry in the early Christian church should be carefully considered whenever interpreting the New Testament. Moreover, based on said data, it would be beneficial to return to the passages of the New Testament which mention women working in the church and reevaluate common interpretations.

Eshet Hayil: A Study on the Role of Women in Ancient Israel's Society

Christie G. Chadwick

Abstract

The Bible is often considered to be a patriarchal document that presents women from a biased perspective. This article asks the question, how many have been reading what the Bible says about women correctly? Are we reading through the "lens of modern culture" or through a biblical lens? Both the Bible and archaeological discoveries show the role of women in a light very different than this "patriarchal" reading, and should draw the reader's attention to how to read the Bible without bringing our own perspectives and culture into it.

Introduction

There seems to be in contemporary society a general perception of the Bible as a patriarchal document that presents women from a biased perspective. Beth Allison Barr traces the historical trajectory of this construction of a "patriarchal"[1] Bible, arguing that this view is not the biblical view. She asks her readers a very relevant question, "What if evangelicals have been understanding Paul through the lens of modern culture instead of the way Paul intended to be understood?"[2] Although Barr is specifically addressing her evangelical context, her question can be broadly applied to other faith communities that have fallen into similar misunderstandings. This article asks a similar question, how many have been reading what the Bible says about women correctly? Are we reading through the "lens of modern culture" or through a biblical lens?

---

[1] Barr uses the following definition of the word "patriarchal": "A Society that promotes male authority and female submission," extracted from historian Judith Bennet's work *History Matters: Patriarchy and the Challenge of Feminism* (Philadelphia, PA: University of Philadelphia Press, 2006).

[2] Beth Allison Barr, *The Making of Biblical Womanhood: How the Subjugation of Women Became a Gospel Truth* (Grand Rapids, MI: Brazos, 2021), 41.

There are two main sources for the study of ancient Israelite women, the Hebrew Bible and archaeological evidence. The Hebrew Bible was originally written by those who lived in ancient Israel's society, and carries not only their view, but that of God through the process of inspiration. Archaeology has provided useful evidence for the study of ancient Israel both in the form of artifacts, and in ancient written texts. This study will draw information from these sources, comparing them and using them in a complementary fashion, to form a picture of the role of women in ancient Israelite society. Both sources show the role of women in a light very different from this "patriarchal" reading, and should draw the reader's attention to how to read the Bible without bringing our own perspectives and culture into it.

Women in the Household

There seems to be a general expectation nowadays that women in ancient Israelite society were mostly limited to the domestic spheres of society, being almost physically limited to the house. It must be understood however that ancient Israelite society was quite different from modern western societies. Understanding the work of a woman inside the household in ancient Israel requires setting aside the modern-day view of work inside the house as being of no economic value.[3] According to Meyers the household in Iron Age Israel was "the central institution for most economic, social, educative, political, and religious aspects of life."[4] In a society in which the household was the main independent economic unit, any work connected with the household had great economic value, such as processing the grain for eating or fibers for weaving. Moreover, ethnographic studies of pre-modern societies have shown that even though responsibilities and activities could be divided according to gender, the division was not necessarily hierarchical, but much more complex.[5]

---

[3] Carole R. Fontaine, "Wife," in *Women in Scripture*, eds. Carol Meyers, Toni Craven, Ross S. Kraeme (Grand Rapids, MI: Eerdmans, 2000), 303.

[4] Carol Meyers, *Rediscovering Eve: Ancient Israelite Women in Context* (New York, NY: Oxford University Press, 2013), 125.

[5] Meyers, *Rediscovering Eve,* 196-99; C. Meyers, "Material Remains and Social Relations: Women's Culture in Agrarian Households of the Iron

While there is indication in the Bible that a few roles were not shared, many roles were.

Shepherds

Men and women could be shepherds. Prominent female shepherds include Rachel (Gen 29:6, 9); and the seven daughters of Reuel (Exod 2:16). Shepherding in the Bronze and Iron ages required great independence. Shepherds had to walk their sheep great distances in order to find appropriate food and water. Shepherds migrated through different routes at different seasons and were often many days away from home and in the wilderness (Gen 37:12, 17; 1 Sam 16:11). They also had to be ready to defend the flock from the wild animals roaming the landscape (1 Sam 17:34-35).

Reapers, Planters, and Harvesters

As preserved in the book of Ruth, Boaz had hired men and women to reap in his field. It may be presumed that if women could reap, they would also have planted, therefore both could work the land planting and harvesting (Ruth 2:8). Of the few that are not shared, shearing and military roles seem to have been exclusive to men. For instance, in the book of Ruth, guarding the grain was a task relegated to men only (Ruth 3:14). Whenever shearing is mentioned in the text it is usually associated with men. Absalom only invited the king's sons, not his daughters, to his shearing banquet (2 Sam 13:23-24).

Bakers

Women are commonly portrayed as baking in the Hebrew Bible. Sarah is asked to bake bread for Abraham's guests herself, even though there were many servants in her household (Gen 18:6). The witch of Endor baked bread and prepared a meal for Saul (1 Sam 28:24). Tamar was called specifically to bake cakes for her brother Amnon (2 Sam 13:8); and the widow of Zarephath was about to bake her last bit of bread when Elijah found her (1 Kgs 17:12-13).

Age," in *Symbiosis, Symbolism and the Power of the Past: Canaan, Ancient Israel, and their Neighbors from the Late Bronze Age through Roman Palaestina: Proceedings of the Centennial Symposium*, eds. W. G. Dever and S. Gitin (Winona Lake, IN: Eisenbrauns, 2003), 434-35, 437.

Baking is only one step in the complex process of producing bread, one of the main staples of the ancient Israelite diet. Bread provided most of the caloric intake and was the most common source of both protein and carbohydrates for centuries. Grain was also very expensive to export/import, and therefore was mainly produced locally.[6] Famine was largely related to a lack of grain (Gen 41:54-57).

While the Hebrew Bible attests that the sowing and harvesting steps of the process were shared between genders, ethnographic studies have shown that the processing of the grain into edible products was done mainly by women[7]. After the harvest the grain was probably stored as whole kernels for better preservation. It was then ground into flour in small amounts at a time and stored in smaller jars (1 Kgs 17:12). The Hebrew term *raḥayim* (Jer 25:10) designates the grinding stones, and the dual form of this word indicates that the term includes both the quern and loaf-shaped grinders, that is, the lower and upper stones, respectively. These are commonly found in archaeological ruins of domestic settings. The presence of implements and installations for grinding and baking within each household demonstrates that the work was done within the household, and the presence of several sets of grinding stones indicates that women likely worked in groups.[8] Further archaeological evidence for women baking bread in groups comes from a communal dough-kneading trough found at Tel Dor,[9] and from the location and number of ovens in settlements, some located in between dwellings, which also points to shared use. There is also iconographic evidence that women were the ones to grind the grain and knead dough, such as a figurine from ez-Zib[10] along with tomb

---

[6] Stephen A. Reed, "Bread," in *The Anchor Bible Dictionary*, ed. D. N. Freedman. (New York, NY: Doubleday, 1992), 1:777-780.

[7] Meyers, *Rediscovering Eve*, 128.

[8] O. Borowski, *Agriculture in Iron Age Israel* (Boston, MA: American Schools of Oriental Society, 2002), 90; Meyers, *Rediscovering Eve*, 130.

[9] E. J. Stern, A. Berg, I. Gilboa, and J. Zorn, "Tel Dor, 1994–1995: Preliminary Stratigraphic Report," in *Israel Exploration Journal* 47, no. 1/2 (1997): 29-56.

[10] James B. Pritchard, *The Ancient Near East: An Anthology of Texts and Pictures* (Princeton, NJ: Princeton University Press, 2011), Fig 22. This archaeological site is known today as Ahziv and is located in Israel, on the Mediterranean coast, near the border with Lebanon.

paintings and models from Egypt, which portray women involved in bread-making.[11]

Weavers

Another activity often associated with women was weaving, such as the women weaving for Asherah in the Temple (2 Kgs 23:7). Even though this reference is related to worship, the fact that women were weaving outside the household implies that within the household that activity was also one of their tasks. The plural form is also notable, implying that several women shared that task and perhaps worked together. Weaving instruments, such as spindle whorls, loom-weights, and needles, are ubiquitous in domestic contexts of Iron Age Israel. The presence of several sets of implements indicates that women worked in groups, as with grinding and bread-making. Making garments in the Ancient Near East was considerably more complex than making one's own garments in the 21st century, or even in the Middle Ages, when at least textiles were available for purchase. During the Biblical period it was necessary to first spin the wool, then weave it into textile fabrics, then make it into a garment. Ethnography has estimated that it would take 100 hours of spinning wool to make one simple garment.[12] A special garment, such as one gifted to Joseph by his father (Genesis 37:3), described as having many colors and possibly also long sleeves, would have meant weeks of labor and several women working on it. Its economic value highlights Jacob's special love and his brothers' particular jealousy.

Because of the large amount of work that goes into weaving and producing textiles and clothes, this activity was of considerable economic value within the household. Notice that one of the treasure pieces stolen by Achan during the Israelite conquest was a "beautiful Babylonian garment" (Josh 7:21).

Both weaving and baking are activities of high economic value for the household, because of the large amount of work that goes into preparing bread, and producing textiles and clothes.[13] In ancient Israel it was women who literally provided the family's bread and clothing on a daily basis. Women's tasks inside the household often

---

[11] Meyers, "Material Remains," 432.

[12] Meyers, *Rediscovering Eve*, 133.

[13] Meyers, "Material Remains," 435.

extended outside as well, through the informal networks between neighbors as women got together to grind, bake, spin or weave. According to Meyers, these informal associations were essential to maintaining community life and "had ramifications for the sociopolitical dynamics of their communities"[14] Ethnographic data suggest that women could even influence the outcome of legal or political decisions.[15]

Authority Figures (and Educators)

There is biblical evidence that women were respected as authority figures in the dealings of the household. Abigail, the wife of Nabal, is a prime example of a wife's authority within the household. In 1 Sam 25, Abigail's servant reported to her and trusted her judgment in order to correct the situation with David (1 Sam 25:14). Her servants also obeyed her in all her arrangements to appease David, even though she was going against her husband's own orders and without his knowledge (1 Sam 25:18-19). Abigail demonstrated complete authority over servants and property in this passage, without question from those in the household.

Women were also responsible for the education of children in their early years, as seen in the example of Hannah and Samuel. The vow of Hannah is not questioned or cancelled by the father, and the decision of how long to keep the child at home and when to wean him were also left to the mother in this case (1 Sam 1:22-23). Women named their children in 62% of the instances, and that does not include the instances where both parents chose the name.[16] This is significant when taking into account that naming is an important gesture in the Hebrew Bible. God named humanity–Adam (Gen 1:26-28); and named "woman"–'ishah (Gen 2:23).[17] The man named the animals brought to him before the creation of woman (Gen 2:20), and he named the woman "Eve" after sin (Gen 3:20). All these seem to have hierarchical implications, which means women and men

---

[14] Meyers, *Rediscovering Eve,* 139.

[15] Ibid., 144.

[16] C. Meyers, *Households and Holiness: The Religious Culture of Israelite Women* (Minneapolis, MN: Fortress, 2005), 42.

[17] This naming is implied in the Hebrew by the use of the Divine passive form of the verb.

together had authority over their children from the moment they were born.

Hired Servants

The work women did within their homes could also be done as a hired servant. It seems that at least some chores had gender preferences, as implied by the list in 1 Sam 8:11-13, where activities are divided by gender. According to this list female hired servants were responsible for baking, cooking and making perfume, while male hired servants were involved in plowing and reaping, making weapons and chariots, and commanding army units. This division allows for different occupations, but it does not exclude women from working outside of the house. This evidence strengthens the view that women were not limited to the household, and were active figures beyond what we deem today the "domestic sphere."

Women Beyond the Household

Seals also contribute to our understanding of women's roles in society and their work outside of the household. Seals are small inscriptions, often made of stone. Most seals found in the region of ancient Israel were shaped as stamps. They were used to impress the inscription into clumps of clay–called bullae–that in turn were used to seal or sign a document. They could contain a symbol, a single name, a name and a patronymic ("name son of name" formula), or a name followed by the owner's profession or title. Bullae and seals bearing women's names account for approximately 3% of the currently known seals and impressions.[18] Most related the name of a woman to that of her father or husband, such as "X daughter of Y" or "X wife of Y."[19] Since seals were used in legal or economic documents, this indicates that women were active and participated in the community in both legal and economic matters. Additional evidence comes from ostraca containing women's names, evidence that women could take part in economic transactions.[20] Ostraca were ancient inscriptions written in ink on pottery fragments and include a wide variety of styles and uses.

---

[18] Ibid., 173.

[19] Meyers, *Households and Holiness*, 42.

[20] Meyers, *Rediscovering Eve,* 173.

Professional Mourners

It is also possible that women worked as professional mourners. David summoned the "daughters of Israel" to weep over Saul and Jonathan, which may be a reference to the active participation of women in mourning (2 Sam 1:24). In Jer 9:17-18 [Heb 9:16-17], there is mention of wise or skilled mourners among the women of Israel. According to Meyers, iconographic and archaeological sources demonstrate that mourners were exclusively women in Egypt, and mainly women in other ancient Near Eastern contexts.[21]

Wise Women

Women are often portrayed as wise, such as Abigail the widow of Nabal (1 Sam 25:3), the wise woman of Tekoa (2 Sam 14:2), the woman who hid David's messengers from Absalom (2 Sam 17:19-20), and many others. The word itself in Hebrew is in the grammatical feminine, and wisdom is personified as a woman in Proverbs. The wisdom of the wisest man mentioned in the Hebrew Bible, King Solomon, is demonstrated in comparison to the wisdom of women. First, two harlots come to him for judgment regarding their sons, one dead and one alive, both claiming the one alive as their own. Solomon outsmarts them with his suggestion of splitting the alive babe between them (1 Kgs 3:16-27). Second, the queen of Sheba came to "test him with difficult questions" and was deeply impressed by his wisdom (1 Kgs 10:1, 6-7, NASB).

Ethnographic studies seem to indicate that older women were responsible for imparting knowledge to the younger generation, a tradition that gave rise to the term "old wives' tales."[22] In Hittite rituals the "old woman" is an expert ritual practitioner and often the officiant, such as in the Ambazzi ritual, the Tunnawi ritual, and the Malli ritual, among others.[23]

---

[21] Ibid., 175.

[22] Meyers, *Rediscovering Eve,* 137.

[23] D. P. Wright, *The Disposal of Impurity in the Priestly Writings of the Bible with Reference to Similar Phenomena in Hittite and Mesopotamian Cultures* (Berkeley, CA: University of California Press, 1984), 36-38, 102, 346.

Political Authorities

There is an unnamed wise woman from a town in the north of Israel, Abel Beth-maacah, who negotiated a peace treaty between her city and Joab, demonstrating her influence with the people and elders of her community (2 Sam 20:22) and with the commander of the king's army, who believed she had the authority to negotiate on the town's behalf (2 Sam 20:17). Her actions and influence indicate that she functioned as an elder in that town, and as such acted with political and military authority in that situation, given to her by her community and accepted by the royal army's commander.

There are a few other women in the Bible who have shown political authority. Maacah, mother of King Asa, had to be deposed by her son because of the political and religious power she held as queen mother (1 Kgs 15:13). Athaliah, the mother of Ahaziah, took the throne of Judah upon the death of her son. She murdered all but one of her grandchildren in order to make herself queen of Judah and reigned for 7 years (2 Kgs 11:1-20). Her political power was such that the plans to reseat the surviving king Joash included calling all the guards of the temple to duty at the same time. The guards at the temple served in three units, one on duty and the other two free. But in order to succeed, Jehoiada the priest made sure his entire body of soldiers was available when proclaiming Joash king. His admonition, "whoever comes within the ranks shall be put to death" (2 Kgs 11:8), points to the support the queen might have had within the city of Jerusalem. One must not exclude the infamous queen Jezebel, whose royal seal has been recently identified.[24] Two of the queens mentioned above, Maacah and Athaliah, were "Queen Mother," a possible title within the kingdom of Judah.[25] These women received the title (*gebirah* in Hebrew) after their sons became kings. Jezebel however, had considerable influence and power during the reign of her husband, even though he probably had other wives and concubines (2 Kgs 10:1).

---

[24] Marjo Korpel, "Fit for a Queen: Jezebel's Royal Seal," *Biblical Archaeology Review* 34/2 (2008): 32-37.

[25] Linda S. Schearing, "Queen," in *The Anchor Bible Dictionary*, ed. D. N. Freedman (New York, NY: Doubleday, 1992), 5:583-586.

Religious Leaders

Women are not directly linked with worship in the texts of the monarchic period, but there are indications that they were not excluded. According to 1 Sam 1:24-25, Hannah (the mother) was the one who brought Samuel to the temple and performed the dedication rites and the Nazirite vow with the priest. Earlier in the text, Hannah came to the tabernacle alone to petition before God, indicating that women were allowed in the public areas of the tabernacle (1 Sam 1:9-12).[26] Later, women are again portrayed within the temple precinct, indicating that women were probably allowed in the temple area throughout the First Temple period (2 Kgs 23:7). Women worked at the entrance of the tent of meeting (1 Sam 2:22), perhaps in some cult-related capacity or, as suggested by Bird, preparing the sacrificial meals that were to be eaten in the sanctuary. Ethnographic evidence suggests that since women were responsible for food preparation in the household, they are likely to have been involved in food preparation for religious purposes as well, such as preparing sacrificial meals and food for the religious festivals.[27]

The Hebrew verb used in 1 Sam 2:22, *tzovot*, is only otherwise used in relation to work in the Temple by the Levites (Num 4:23, 8:24). It is first used to indicate the work of the women at the entrance of the Tent of Meeting in Exod 38:8. There are also references to women partaking in sacrificial meals (1 Sam 1:4-5; 2 Sam 6:19). Second Kings 22:23 implies the presence and participation of women in cultic activities and festivals, since the husband of the Shunammite expected her to go see the man of God on a new moon or a Sabbath. There are instances of a woman consulting a prophet for an oracle or for a miracle (1 Kgs 14:2-3; 2 Kgs 4:22-23). Female prophets, such as Miriam (Exod 15:20), Deborah (Judg 4:4), and Huldah (2 Kgs 22:14-20), are also known in the Bible.

[26] See also Mayer I. Gruber's discussion of Hannah's participation in the rites according to prescriptions in the Pentateuch ("Women in the Cult According to the Priestly Code," in *Judaic Perspectives on Ancient Israel*, eds. J. Neusner, B. A. Levine, and E. S. Frerichs [Philadelphia, PA: Fortress: 1987], 35-48).

[27] Bird, "The Place of Women in the Israelite Cultus," in *Ancient Israelite Religion*, eds. J. Patrick D. Miller, P. D. Hanson, and S. D. McBride (Philadelphia, PA: Fortress: 1987), 406.

However, one of the most interesting texts relating to the religious participation of women in cultic practice is the Nazirite vow in Num 6. The Bible states that both men and women could take that vow. The Nazirite vow brought a common Israelite person as close to holiness as the high priest. Only the high priest and the Nazirites were completely banned from touching corpses, even of those people closest to them. As Roy Gane puts it, "Although the Lord has set up a closed priestly circle to do special sacred tasks in intimate proximity to himself, he allows any member of his 'Kingdom of priests and a holy nation' (Ex. 19:6) to reach a high level of holiness as a Nazirite."[28]

Conclusion: Who Can Find a Virtuous Woman?

The Hebrew expression behind the "virtuous woman" translation of Prov 31:10 is *eshet hayil.* The description of the *eshet hayil* in Prov 31:10-31 has been generally understood as the ideal biblical woman. Indeed, the woman portrayed here is in full accordance with the portraits of women detailed throughout this article. She provides food for her household (v. 14-15), as we have seen in the archaeological evidence, not only participating in the planting and harvesting, but also processing the grains into bread. She invests and brings economic gain to her household (v. 16, 18, 24), using her seal to buy and sell land, and produces textiles for the home and for commerce (v. 13, 19, 21, 22, 24), which was an activity of high economic value, as seen above. She also acts as an administrator of the household (v. 15, 21, 27), cares for the community (v. 20, 31), similar to the example of the woman elder from Abel Beth-maacah, and is wise and strong (v. 17, 25, 26), such as Abigail and Ruth. Proverbs culminates with the religious characteristics of this woman. "She fears the Lord" and this is the foundation for all the other things. *Eshet hayil*, the Hebrew expression in Prov 31:10, is often translated as "virtuous woman." However, the original implies more than the translation of "virtuous" can convey, and instead indicates a woman of power and valor.[29]

There is always the danger of reading into the biblical text aspects from our own times and cultures. In fact, it is unavoidable.

---

[28] Roy Gane, *Leviticus, Numbers*, The NIV Application Commentary (Grand Rapids, MI: Zondervan, 2011), 533.

[29] Fontaine, "Wife," 303.

Awareness of what we bring into the text is just as important as the awareness that the Bible has much more to give to us than we do to give back. The Bible should be approached with the humility of a true learner, one willing to give up their own presuppositions in exchange for true knowledge and wisdom.

The Bible portrays women as strong, brave, wise, and confident. I see JoAnn Davidson as such a woman. She is, in my humble opinion, an *eshet hayil*. I have had the opportunity to see and admire her wisdom, courage, kindness and strength in practice. But above all, her "fear of the LORD" shines through her everyday life. She inspires me to say, "strong is the new beautiful."

The Concept of Clothes in Jewish Culture, Old and New Testaments: A Tribute to the Glitz and Glam of Adventist Fashionistas

Hyveth Williams

Abstract

This chapter considers the biblical treatment of clothes and adornment. I examine the many biblical references in Scripture that portray clothes in different ways, from outer and inner garments, to clothes serving as illustrations for deeper spiritual states or reality. Many references to clothes are linked to adornment, including cosmetics, jewelry, masks or veils, head coverings, and even footwear. Adventist perspectives on adornment are complex and have not always taken into account a holistic view of the various perspectives and nuances found in the Old and New Testaments. Scripture does not directly condemn the use of adornment, but does teach a balanced, godly perspective on its use. The clearest application of this study is the divine gift of choice that allows us to choose our own garments as a fundamental part of embracing our own identity and individuality.

Introduction

Let's talk about a favorite subject—clothes. This plural of cloth includes outer garments, under garments, head coverings, adornments, shoes and facial coverings such as veils or masks popularized since the COVID-19 pandemic began in 2020. Clothes—"love 'em or hate 'em, we must have 'em," should be our national motto. They are so significant that we quickly wrap babies in them after birth. And as children grow, we teach them tricks of the human trade such as how to use clothes to conceal sin or reveal shamelessness. So important are clothes to humans, the world's economy depends on the making, selling and buying of them. Nations and religions have laws restricting the design and wearing of clothes, but regrettably, these are primarily for women. Clothes represent more than superficial coverings that adorn and enhance the image of persons wearing them. Every day we put them on and take them off without realizing that they reveal or conceal our identity and reflect our attitude toward ourselves and value placed on those with whom we associate. It is therefore no secret or breaking news that we judge ourselves based on our concept of glitz and glam, or lack thereof, and evaluate the significance of others based on their choice or lack of clothing, especially in the first few minutes of meeting. Many today tend to affirm this both materially and emotionally.[1]

In fact, from the beginning of creation to the present day, the covering provided by clothes, more than fashion which exploits our weakness for this commodity, has been very important to both God and human beings. The psalmist declared: "The Lord is clothed with majesty; The Lord has clothed and girded Himself with strength" (Ps 93:1).[2] Many stories in the Bible confirm that clothing can greatly influence first impressions and make lasting impact on anyone with whom one interacts. Additionally, in Scripture, our divine Creator has demonstrated a unique appreciation for clothes, especially the glitz and glam or splendor displayed in His affectionate use of them as metaphors for His spiritual and physical attributes. That being said, I want to explore some topics present in the Old Testament that can help us better understand the concept of clothes. I will survey several categories such as: biblical references to outer and inner garments, clothing as illustrations, God's garments, garments for

---

[1] Adam & Galinsky describe the effect clothing has on a person's mental process, feelings, and functioning in areas like attention, confidence, or abstract thinking (See "Enclothed Cognition," *Journal of Experimental* we want to appear as a big-ideas person at work, we wear a suit because it is believed that wearing formal business attire increases abstract thinking, long-term strategizing, creativity and feelings of power. If you have ever watched the rehearsal process of professional actors, you know just how powerful clothes are. Even in the very early stages of a project, they will practice in certain pieces of clothing that make them feel more like their character and invoke the right swagger, grace, or edge. A few weeks later, when they are closer to opening the show, they will wear the real costumes in a "dress" rehearsal. The right clothes bring the performances up to a whole new level and transform the actor into the character. There is power in clothing.

[2] All Scriptures are taken from the New American Standard Bible version, unless otherwise identified.

overcoming guilt and shame, adornments, cosmetics, jewelry, masks or veils, head coverings, and footwear. I will also provide some reflections based on those findings that speak specifically to the context of Adventist fashionistas.

Biblical References to Outer and Inner Garments

In the Old Testament, there are several specific articles of clothing every adult, male Jew was required to wear. This included a mantle, a girdle, an inner tunic also called an undergarment, and an outer coat sometimes referred to as a robe.

The mantle (Hebrew *addereth*), a large cover-garment (e.g., 1 Kgs 19:13, 19) or large shawl also known as a prayer shawl, was first mentioned by Moses (Num 15:38–41). It has tassels, described as "edges," on a distinctively Jewish tallit or fringed garment traditionally worn as a prayer shawl. The tallit had special twined and knotted fringes (Hebrew *tzitzit*) attached to its four corners as a permanent reminder of the Ten Commandments (Deut 22:12).[3] Originally divinely designed with five cords or threads in a blue color obtained from the glands of a small sea urchin, these tassels also represented God's presence and covenant with His people. In the New Testament, tassels were referred to as hems or fringes on coats worn by rabbis (and Jesus in Mark 6:56), which people, like the woman with the issue of blood, touched for healing. Usually made of wool, a mantle could be large or small, thick or fine, colored or natural, but men preferred undyed types. Sometimes translated as "cloak" in English, the mantle was also worn by Old Testament prophets as a sign of their calling from God. Elijah wore it (1 Kgs 19:13; 2 Kgs 2:8, 13), and threw it around Elisha to symbolize the passing on of his ministry to his protégé. The prophet Samuel wore a mantle which Saul seized and tore when he was told of his disobedience resulting in his divine rejection as king (1 Sam 15:27). The prophet's mantle was therefore an indication of authority and responsibility, as God's chosen spokesperson with power to perform miracles (2 Kgs 2:8).

---

[3] A. Hooker, "What is a Prayer Shawl and Why it is Significant?" Retrieved July 2022, from https://www.crosswalk.com/faith/prayer/what-is-a-prayer-shawl-and-why-is-it-significant.html.

The girdle[4] or band of cloth, made of cord or leather and also known as a belt or sash, was often hollow and served as a purse.[5] It is described as part of the priestly garments God commanded Moses to put on Aaron to distinguish him as high priest (Lev 8:7). It was usually worn next to the skin by Jewish males after puberty, or by rich folks over long robes, in to which they were tucked when maximum freedom of movement was needed or to permit work and easy walking. The expression "to gird up the loins" signified that the person was ready for service and is equivalent to the modern saying, "roll up your sleeves" for work, fight or service. John the Baptist wore a leather girdle (Matt 3:4); the resurrected and ascended Jesus, dressed as a high priest in His mediatorial ministry, wore a golden sash (Rev 1:13); and a few men, especially soldiers, sometimes carried money in their girdle.

The tunic (Hebrew *kutonet*)[6] was a very significant inner vest or under garment (Lev 6:7). This undergarment, worn next to the skin, resembled a long, loose-fitting shirt and was made of white linen or soft wool, except when worn for penance. Then, it was woven with rough, prickly wool to make it uncomfortable next to the skin. Early in Israel's history, this was usually worn by people of rank and importance, for instance under the ephod by the high priest. It is the garment usually torn in times of distress, as Ezra did when he heard of intermarriages with pagans by the people left behind after the exile to Babylon. He wrote: "So when I heard this thing, I tore my garment and my robe, and plucked out some of my hair of my head and beard, and sat down astonished" (Ezra 9:3). David wore a tunic on the occasion of the transfer of the ark to Jerusalem (1 Chr 15:27).

The divine design of this undergarment was given to Moses by God (Exod 28:39–40), who told him it should be made seamless except for sleeves extended to the wrist. Later, God told Ezekiel it was to be worn by priests to prevent sweat while serving in His presence (Ezek 44:17–18), because sweat was part of the curse (Gen

---

[4] F. F. Bruce, ed., *Vine's Complete Expository Dictionary of Old and New Testament Words* (Iowa Falls, IA: World Bible Publishers, 1978), 147–148.

[5] Ibid.

[6] *Strong's Hebrew Dictionary of the Bible (English and Hebrew Edition)* (Hawthorne, CA: BN Publishing, 2012).

3:19). Although this undergarment originally reached only to the knees, later some reached the ankles. Jesus' tunic was likely knee-length and sleeveless, made without seams as God commanded (John 19:23). In the days of Saul, an adult wearing only this garment was said to be naked (1 Sam 19:24). Nothing was worn underneath this undergarment, and in first-century Judaea these were normally very thin when worn by children.

In the Old Testament the high priest wore over his tunic a long seamless robe (*me'il*), all of blue (Exod 28:31–35). Hannah "made a little robe" for Samuel every year and brought it to him when she came to the sanctuary with her sacrifice (1 Sam 2:19), and "David was clothed with a robe of fine linen with all the Levites who were carrying the ark" (1 Chr 15:27). The term *me'il* may also be used to refer to a mantle or cloak (e.g., 1 Sam 28:14; Ps 109:29). Another Hebrew word for "robe" or "mantle" is *'aderet*, also meaning "splendor," which is used for the robe of state of the king of Nineveh (Jonah 3:6) and other prominent persons (Josh 7:21), and the mantle of Elijah (1 Kgs 19:15, 19; 2 Kgs 2:8, 13–14).

In New Testament times, the robe (Greek *stolē*) was a long, stately garment reaching to the feet, sometimes with a train behind.[7] It was worn by the scribes, who "liked to walk about in long robes" (Mark 12:38; Luke 20:46), and was the "best robe" brought by the prodigal son's father to honor his long-lost son (Luke 15:23). Such a robe was also worn by the angel in Jesus' empty tomb after His resurrection (Mark 16:5) and will be the garments of the glorified believers in heaven (Rev 6:11; 7:9, 13–14).[8]

Clothing as Illustrations

Old Testament writers used images of clothes to illustrate their divinely directed visions and lessons. For instance, white robes and royal vestments are used to communicate holy and righteous acts or deeds (Job 29:14; Isa 11:5; 59:17; 61:10), while tattered, filthy clothing represents iniquity or sinfulness of individuals and nations

---

[7] F. F. Bruce, ed., *Vine's Complete Expository Dictionary of Old and New Testament Words* (Iowa Falls, IA: World Bible Publishers, 1978).

[8] The term *stolē* is also used in the LXX to refer to the royal robes of the Persian king which Haman was forced to place upon Mordecai to honor him (Esth 6:8). The Hebrew simply uses the general term *lebush* ("garment").

(Isa 58:6; Zech 3:3–4). The prophet Isaiah (Isa 50:9), railed against his opponents saying they will "wear out like a garment, the moth consuming them." Similarly, Jeremiah was divinely instructed to buy a beautiful linen loincloth and adorn himself with it (Jer 13:1–11). Then, he was instructed to take it off, bury it and dig it up later, but when he dug it up, it was ruined. God used this to illustrate that as the loincloth clung close to the prophet's body, so He brought Israel close to Himself, but they would not obey Him, preferring to serve other gods. Therefore, like the soiled loincloth, God buried the errant people of Israel and Judah in exile in Babylon as their land lay in ruins.

In Scripture, changes in the style or type of clothing can denote the different stages of an individual's life, whether ascending to greater heights with God or descending into the pits of iniquity. For instance, the removal of the High Priest's filthy garments symbolized forgiveness of sin and liberation from shame (Zech 3:3–5). But when Adam and Eve made for themselves and put on garments of fig leaves (Gen 3:7), their action represented attempts to conceal sin and cover their shame in the original, seminal act of autosoterism, which has infected the human family in every gender and generation.

God's Garments

The psalmist declared that God is clothed with splendor and majesty (Ps 104:1). Isaiah asserted that "He [God] puts on righteousness like a breastplate, a helmet of salvation on His head; garments of vengeance for clothing and wraps Himself with zeal as a mantle" (Isa 59:17). God is also portrayed as wearing several different garments (Isa 6:1), some spiritual and a few physical, from the creation of the world to this day. But in the last days He is pictured as a bridegroom adorned with a royal diadem (Isa 61:10), and His bride, the church, is decked in fine linen (Ezek 16:10).

Clothes were and are important to God, but for different reasons than humans. He is pictured in Scripture as clothing Himself with divine light when creating the world (Pss 93:1, 104:1–2). And only after He said, "Let there be light," which illuminated the world like a garment, perhaps from the luster of His majesty, did God actually begin to create the sun, moon and stars. Norman Cohen notes that in Jewish tradition:

> God is portrayed. . . as wearing seven different garments that would be worn successively from the creation of the world to the messianic era. These include garments of majesty, strength, vengeance, zeal, righteousness, compassion and purity. Many individual verses in the Bible describe God as "wearing" these and other qualities. Then, in the end of days, God is pictured as a bridegroom adorned with a royal diadem. Israel is described as a bride bedecked in her finery, and Messiah will be covered with the very same primordial garment of light whose splendor radiates from one end of the world to the other (Isaiah 61:10).[9]

In effect, the act of creation was God covering the entire world with a tent-like garment of light, including the first human beings whom He dressed in that divine radiance. Only after their fall did God clothe them in garments of animal skin (Gen 3:21).

Garments for Overcoming Guilt and Shame

The divine garment of light with which Adam and Eve were originally clothed[10] underscored the fact that they were the first and only "created" children of God. All other humans, thereafter, are made in His image, but are born of blood, the will of the flesh and the will of humans, unless or until they are born again as children (*tekna*), to whom God personally gave birth (John 1:12). Before Adam and Eve disobeyed God's specific command, they were both naked (*'erom*) and not ashamed (Gen 2:25).

However, the moment they transgressed God's command (Gen 3), to not eat from the tree of knowledge of good and evil, the protective covering or righteous robe of light disappeared, and immediately they began to see through a glass or lens darkly and became aware of their nakedness or faults. Their eyes were opened, and they saw each other, as if for the first time. This made them experience fear and shame, which were unknown to them up until that time. Suddenly, they became afraid of God and ashamed of each other, indicating their great loss of innocence, which they traded for

---

[9] Norman Cohen, *Masking and Unmasking Ourselves: Interpreting Biblical Texts on Clothing & Identity* (Woodstock, VT: Jewish Lights Publishing, 2012), Kindle loc 113.

[10] For the biblical evidence supporting this conclusion, see Richard M. Davidson, *Flame of Yahweh: Sexuality in the Old Testament* (Peabody: MA: Hendrickson, 2007), 56.

knowing and seeing good and evil. They lost their oneness with the Divine and, in the process, their own sense of unity, purity and beauty. They were forced to recognize their essential stark differences, and had to relate to each other in a different manner, for their loss caused each of them to feel embarrassed, vulnerable and ashamed (Gen 3:7).

On that tragic day, they exchanged the radiant garment God made for them, along with the wholeness it brought, for something they fashioned for themselves out of fig leaves and, for the very first time, as I imagine, they were astonished by the different shape of their bodies. Adam recognized his maleness and Eve, her femaleness and instinctively they felt ashamed and hid themselves from God (perhaps even each other), with coverings of fig leaves for protection. Instantly, to protect themselves, helping each other became a thing of the past as they literally "girded" their own loins or private parts, which are described in Scripture as being so delicate they are covered with two and three layers of clothing (see 1 Cor 12:23). From that day in Eden, when God confronted the couple with a harsh but just judgment, whenever humans are judged or criticized, we automatically feel uncomfortable, awkward, and vulnerable, deprived of our humanity, and almost as if we are naked and stripped of garments that cover or enhance our image.

It could be said that, even in recent history, evil men and women have used clothing deprivation to evoke similar deep raw feelings and therefore break the will or spirit of their captives. Such depravation occurred during the Holocaust when the Nazis forced Jews to strip naked in many public contexts, but especially in the concentration camps.[11] To enrich themselves, American slave traders travelled over land and sea to capture Africans, whom they stripped of all clothing, abused them in the most inhumane ways, and left them bereft of dignity. That treatment was more destructive and devastating than even stealing them from their families and native land because it permanently demoralized the captives,[12] making them lose their dignity and become easy to be ruled with fear and cruelty.

---

[11] See the *Holocaust Encyclopedia* at https://encyclopedia.ushmm.org/content/en/article/public-humiliation.

[12] Edward E. Baptist, *The Half Has Never Been Told: Slavery and the Making of American Capitalism* (New York, NY: Basic Books, 2014).

In the Old Testament, nakedness is also symbolic of sinfulness, and a myriad of prophetic texts utilize the image of the stripping of garments as a way of revealing a person's sinful and shameful acts. In fact, one of the most oft-used phrases by the prophets is the "uncovering of one's nakedness," which underscores the pernicious act. For example:

> Thus said the Lord God: Because of your brazen effrontery, offering your nakedness to your lovers for harlotry. . . I will expose your nakedness and all shall [see it]. . . .They shall strip you of your clothing and take away your dazzling jewelry, leaving you naked and bare (Ezek 16: 36–39).

The prophet Isaiah poetically captured the power of nakedness in the case of the daughters of Zion, of whom he wrote:

> In that day, Adonai will strip off the finery of the anklets, the skins, and the crescents; . . . the bracelets and the veils; the turbans, the armlets and the sashes; . . . the festive robes, the mantles and the shawls; . . . the lace gowns and the linen vests; and the kerchiefs and the capes. And then—instead of perfume, there shall be rot; and instead of an apron, a rope; instead of a diadem of beaten-work, a shorn head; instead of a rich robe, a girding of sackcloth; a burn instead of beauty (Isa 3:18–24).

Note how, without the use of a single verb, but with the stark repetition of the word "instead," the deprivation, loss of dignity, humiliating barrenness, sin, and shame of the once proud, wealthy, privileged and extravagantly dressed sinners are highlighted. There are also several examples in which individuals who felt vulnerable covered themselves as a means of protection. For instance, Rebecca did just that when she first laid eyes on Isaac (Gen 24:64).

However, God, the divine Tailor, has sewn some internal garments into the spiritual DNA of all who accept and believe in Jesus Christ as personal Savior. These include, but are not limited to, majesty, strength, righteousness, compassion, and purity of thought and action. The lack or loss of these garments, referred to as "fine linen, bright and pure, for the fine linen is the righteous acts of the saints" (Rev 19:7), will cause humans to embrace natural feelings of vulnerability.[13] It is time to put on the full garment of grace adorned with the impressive glitz and glam of heaven and be authentically vulnerable.

Adornments

Ornaments in the Bible, in general, include finely embroidered or decorated fabrics for pleasure (Exod 26:36; Ezek 16:10–13); for trade and spoils after winning a war (Ezek 27:16; Judg 5:30) and for punishment (Ezek 26:16). In Jer 2:32, the term "ornament" includes jeweled, embroidered clothing such as a richly woven veil, girdle and turban, worn by the high priest and patrons of the wealthier class in his day. Before the creation of the earth and the advent of sin, the Almighty created Lucifer with a magnificent array of adornment to enhance his appearance and beauty, which the Lord declared was perfect. He was adorned with at least nine precious stones including ruby, topaz, diamond, beryl, onyx, jasper, lapis lazuli, turquoise and emerald, not counting the pure gold in which they were set (Ezek 28:12–13). This means that since the angels seemingly were created sometime before the physical universe (Job 38:4–7), Lucifer was honored by being decorated with these ornaments or precious stones before they existed in the physical realm of earth. Wretched excesses created by the presence of sin have turned a divine gift for pleasure and beauty into corrupt usage.

Ornaments are also described in detail under their own titles, and fall under the category of glitz and glam eschewed by some. They are summarized as follows: finger-rings, particularly prized as seal or signet-rings (Gen 38:18, 25; Jer 2:24); arm-rings or bracelets and bangles (Gen 24:22; 2 Sam 1:10); earrings (Gen 35:4; Exod 32:2); nose-rings (Gen 24:47; Ezek 16:12); anklets or ankle-chains (Isa

[13] A defense against fear of being vulnerable, recommended in a *Psychology Today* article, includes: (a) bring shame into light by revealing its existence; (b) untangle what you are feeling; (c) unhitch what you do from who you are; (d) recognize your triggers; and (e) make connections, because the source of shame is fear of disconnection used by persecutors, predators and perpetrators of evil to hold a victim hostage (David Sack, "Embarrassment: 5 Ways to Silence Shame," *Psychology Today* 36, 2015), https://www.psychologytoday.com/us/blog/where-science-meets-the-steps/201501/5-ways-silence-shame.

3:16,18); head-bands and necklaces or neck-chains (Gen 41:42; Isa 3:18; Ezek 16:11). The high-priestly tunic, for example, was made of pure linen, covering his entire body from neck to feet, with embroidered sleeves reaching to the wrists. Over this was the ephod, an elaborate garment worn only by the high priest upon which the breastplate containing the Urim, meaning "lights," was on one side, and the Thummim, meaning "perfections," was on the other side. It was made of gold, purple and other fine threads embedded with twelve dazzling gemstones such as emerald and lapis lazuli (Exod 28:39). God also commanded the High Priest to wear these special ornate garments when performing his duties before Him (Exod 28).

Contrary to common, spoken, and graphic illustrations, Joseph's coat was not a patchwork of colorful cloth, but the Hebrew (*kutonet passim* in Gen 37:3) likely refers to a woolen cloth on which precious ornate stones were sewn to make it stand out and blaze with multi-colorful rays from every angle, like a prism.[14] It was also a sign of royalty and authority,[15] and the only other use of this phrase is in 2 Sam 13:18, where King Saul's daughter is described as wearing a similar ornamented tunic.

In common with all other ancient Near Eastern peoples, ancient Jews took pleasure in wearing ornaments, and God generously endowed them with many different types. However, as time passed, their tendency to extravagance produced pride, arrogance, selfishness and materialism, which were often met with stern, painful prophetic rebuke (Isa 3:16-24; Ezek 13:18-20). But God loved them so much He kept giving them adornments for their pleasure (Ezek 16:10–14). There are several events involving divine orders to wear adornments for pleasure, as well as to compensate for pain or suffering. For instance, God commanded Moses to have the women collect jewelry from their masters as payment for the many bitter years of labor as

---

[14] G. Hasan-Rokem, and I. Gruenwald, et al, *Louis Ginzberg's Legends of the Jews: Ancient Jewish Folk Literature Reconsidered* (Philadelphia, PA: Jewish Publication Society, 2014), 5:43.

[15] Roy Gane (Personal Commuinication, 2022), professor of Hebrew Bible and Ancient Near Eastern Languages, offers this commentary: Ellen G. White in *Patriarchs and Prophets*, 209, just refers to "a costly coat, or tunic, such as was usually worn by persons of distinction." Thus, she avoids the traditional rendering "of many colors," which comes from a guess by the Septuagint translation: Greek *poikílon* (lexical form *poikílos*), "many-colored."

slaves in Egypt (Exod 3:21–22; 11:2; 12:35). Such treasures included chains, earrings, nose and finger rings, trinkets and other ornamentation, which the Lord also commanded them to keep wearing and put on their children as they left Egypt (Exod 3:22). However, when Israel fell into idolatry in the worship of the golden calf at Mt. Sinai, God commanded them to "take off your ornaments, that I may know what to do with you." This was a time of investigative judgment, and "the people of Israel stripped themselves of their ornaments from Mount Horeb onward" (Exod 33:5–6, ESV).[16]

New Testament Considerations

While not as much is said about adornment in the New Testament, Jesus made vague references (Luke 7:25; 12:23), and James strongly rebukes those who judge others by their flashy ornaments instead of moral character (Jas 2:2). Many other examples of God's endorsement of the use of various materials to adorn a place, or honor and enhance the appearance of a person, exist in both Testaments. For instance, among these are the divinely designed priestly garments (Exod 28), and the New Jerusalem's twelve foundations made from various precious stones of pearl and streets of gold so pure it appears to be transparent (Rev 21:18–21).

Although in Scripture both men and women wear adornments, Christians (especially women) are taught that they should dress modestly and place a high priority on pursuing good works and a godly character in place of obsessing about adornments. Since the New Testament is considered commentary on the Old, we can study this admonition from the apostle Peter:

> Do not let your adornment be merely outward—arranging the hair, wearing gold, or putting on fine apparel, rather let it be the hidden person of the heart, with the incorruptible beauty of a gentle and quiet spirit, which is very precious in the sight of God. For in this way in former times the holy women also, who hoped in God, used

---

[16] Some English versions read "at/by Mount Horeb" (e.g., KJV, NKJV, NIV), but the preposition *min* "from" which precedes "Mount Horeb" does not mean "at/by" but "from," in this context referring to time and not location. This is correctly translated by most modern versions (e.g., ESV, NASB, NJSP, NLT, NRSV, NCSB, CJB, NAB, NJB, JPS, RSV).

> to adorn themselves, being submissive to their own husbands (1 Peter 3:3–5).

I believe that the word "merely" underscores Peter's point that outward adornment is not bad in and of itself (as is seen in the above passages), but should not be simply, merely or entirely the focus of outward appearance. The focus must be on winsome and noble traits of character flowing out of a gentle, quiet spirit in the sight of God, and the adornment an accessory to those attributes. In verse 6 Peter emphasized, "For in this manner, in former times, the holy women who trusted in God also adorned themselves, being submissive to their own husbands." Does this admonishment apply to only married women? Does it mean those holy women wore outward adornment, but didn't make it their obsession? Absolutely, their use is a vivid illustration of balance! Moreover, the original Greek text omits the word "fine" before "apparel" (verse 3), so that it really says a woman's beauty should not come from "putting on apparel." Taken in its most literal sense, this particular sentence seems to imply that the ancient apostle was encouraging women to go naked, confounding the most astute Christian. Therefore, Peter's point is not that Christian women should refrain from clothing or even from making an effort to beautify their outward appearance, but rather that such activity should come from possessing an inward beauty of spirit in Christ.

The apostle Paul does not mince words, but seems more emphatic in his reproof. For instance, he wrote: "I desire therefore that the men pray everywhere, lifting up holy hands, without wrath and doubting" (1 Tim 2:8–10). Note he begins his admonishment by addressing demeanor during worship, as he continues to say:

> In like manner also, that the women adorn themselves in modest apparel, with propriety and moderation, not with braided hair or gold or pearls or costly clothing but, which is proper for women professing godliness, with good works.

Paul also began with, "I desire" (in verse 8 and implied in verse 9), which is different than saying "God requires," to indicate he is recommending a standard based on the principle of modesty. A principle is a permanent divine command or rule which cannot be changed by human desires or endeavors, while a standard, even when based on principle, can be changed according to culture, customs and current conditions. Unfortunately, some people turn standards into policies and present them as principles, but what is reasonable in one city or culture may not be acceptable elsewhere or be made the rule everywhere. For instance, in Jamaica, where I was born and domiciled until I was thirteen, men are required to wear suits and women hats as part of Sabbath dress, and these are strictly enforced for worship. Yet, these requirements are not encouraged or acceptable in most American churches, even some of the most conservative ones. The problem exists if or when we make a standard a principle, or vice versa. When this happens, we often mistakenly treat it as a divine edict exercised without compassion, contextual consideration, or understanding, and instead exercise it with a judgmental, arbitrary or authoritarian policy.

Furthermore, the phrase "when they pray" (verse 8), implies the context is worship. Therefore Paul is not discussing the general dress women should wear in public, but only what he desires them to wear in public worship. Thus, what he presented is a standard of conduct he desired for a man's demeanor and a woman's dress in worship. His counsel is not against glitz or glam adornment, and is worthy of deep consideration as a standard which can be changed according to time and place, plus culture or custom, in order to uphold a desired public worship decorum. It is clear that modesty, propriety, and moderation in appearance during worship are Paul's key points, not the idea of eliminating outward adornment. For instance, like women today who braid, weave and color their hair, those ancient females plaited and pinned their hair high in elaborate designs. And, because they didn't attend parties or places where they could show off their beauty and hair, they turned the worship assemblies into fashion shows. Some even attempted to "one-up" their contemporaries with flashy, expensive clothes and costly jewelry. Thus, Paul denounced such gaudiness and disruptive behavior by urging that "which is proper for women professing godliness, with good works," not the latest glitz or glam.

Cosmetics

Direct references to the use of cosmetics, also known as makeup, are somewhat rare in the Old Testament, occurring only five times (2 Kgs 9:30; Esth 2:7–12; Isa 3:14–16; Jer 4:30; Ezek 23:40). The first reference is about Jezebel "painting her face" or applying makeup in order to influence and win favor with Jehu, king of Israel (2 Kgs 9:1–6, 30). Esther accepted “beauty treatments” or makeup to prepare her for the potential role as queen of the Persian Empire (Esth 2:9, 12). These treatments apparently included the use of “cosmetics,” or “different kinds of makeup.” To summarize, Scripture does NOT condemn the use of cosmetics as sin, but rather admonishes against immodesty, improper use and its priority in a person’s life. References to eye paint or “eye shadow” are also scarce, the most prominent being Jezebel’s use of it (2 Kgs 9). Another misconception or misinterpretation in many sermons, is using this story to prove wearing makeup is divinely despised. The fact is that Jezebel, who practiced sorcery and murder, was judged and killed for her wicked deeds, not the clothes, adornment or cosmetics she wore.

Since women are generally addressed or attacked in preaching and teaching by those who are opposed to the wearing of cosmetics, it is important to remember that faithful, godly women in the Bible adorned themselves, much more than we do today (Jer 4:30). It is also important to remember that, “man looks at the outward appearance, but the Lord looks at the heart” (1 Sam 16:7).

Jewelry

The wearing of jewelry is not condemned in the Old Testament, for when Rebekah married Isaac, one of the three patriarchs referred to as a friend of God, she wore a gold nose ring, gold bracelets, and other expensive jewelry she received as gifts from her future father-in-law (Gen 24:22, 30, 53). Jewelry is also used in favorable illustrations. For instance, a person who offers good advice is compared to “an earring of gold. . . to the receptive ear” (Prov 25:12). God Himself compared His treatment of the nation of Israel to that of a husband who adorns his bride with bracelets, a necklace, and earrings which made the nation “extremely beautiful” (Ezek 16:11–13). However, the value of inner beauty, in contrast to sacrificing it for outward appearance or adornment, is strongly expressed in Proverbs: “Charm is deceptive, and beauty is fleeting; but a woman who fears the Lord is to be praised. Honor her for all that her hands have done, and let her works bring her praise at the city gate” (Prov 31:30–31).

One of the biggest misinterpretations by anti-adornment Christians is regarding Isa 3:16–26, in which the women of Judah or "daughters of Zion," are divinely denounced for being "haughty" or full of pride. They lived in luxury, decked out in fine jewelry and other fancy adornments provided by husbands who were "crushing God's people and grinding the faces of the poor" (verses 14–15). Note that God didn't say, "I'm taking away your adornment and luxuries because you should never have them," but "I'm taking away these things to punish you for living aloof, without compassion while others are suffering." The fact is, jewelry is sometimes divinely despised (Ezek 7:20), but it is when used for idolatry, materialistic excesses, ill-treatment of others and, above all, rejection of God's commands to care for widows, orphans and the poor. Jewelry is more often used to describe the resplendent majesty of God (Exod 28:15), as reflected in creation.

Masks or Veils

Masks are more popular, plentiful, and controversial today than any other time in modern history. Although most people are unaware of their origin and the ways they have been worn since invented, masks have been present in nearly all cultures, for various reasons, since the first couple sewed fig leaf body masks in Eden. Facial masks have primarily been associated with ceremonies of religious and social significance such as funeral customs, fertility rites and the magical curing of diseases.[17] As time passed, masks were used on festive occasions or to portray characters in dramatic performances, especially in reenactments of mythological events. Others were used for warfare, and as protective devices in particular activities or during inclement weather. Ancient Greeks used masks in their theatrical performances on a regular basis as the *hypocriteis*[18] (origin of hypocrite) or actor pretended to be something or someone else. Full face masks were a uniquely effective way of establishing character or mood, often at a considerable distance, so that the wearer's facial features could be either exaggerated, simplified, or simultaneously convincingly human and yet unnervingly artificial. In our day, many memorable and iconic television and movie characters are identifiable purely by their masks, and one of the standard visual

[17] Paul S. Winger, "Mask Face Covering," *Encyclopedia Britannica* (2021). Retrieved from https://www.britannica.com/art/mask-face-covering.

[18] F. F. Bruce, ed., *Vine's Expository Dictionary of Old and New Testament Words* (Iowa Falls, IA: World Bible Publishers, 1981).

graphics of "drama" is a pair of masks with expressions representing "comedy" and "tragedy."

Some masks are necessary for health purposes and fit over the nose and mouth or as full-face coverings, particularly common during various pandemics, including influenza in 1918 and coronavirus in 2020. Otherwise, they are worn primarily by medical professionals. Not all masks are of the material kind, for the word "mask" is also used as a metaphor, indicating a change in appearance or behavior that misleads others. It can be a cloak that suggests hiding a movement or an intention, often by smiling to disguise discontent, to cover disgrace, or to hide true identity, feelings and mood.

There are many occasions in the Bible where characters disguised themselves and appeared totally different, usually to facilitate some significant purpose. For instance, the first face covering mentioned in the Old Testament occurred when Rebekah met Isaac, her future husband, and coyly covered her face with her veil (Gen 24:64–65). In the story of Esther and Haman, the servants covered his face when he fell or fainted upon hearing the king's accusation of his assault on Queen Esther (Esth 7:8). Upon his return from a face-to-face encounter with God where he received the Ten Commandments, Moses' face shone so brilliantly he had to wear a veil to protect the people (Exod 34:33–35). In a specific legislative act regarding contagious diseases such as leprosy, Moses ordered the wearing of masks and quarantine (Lev 13:45–46). When an Israelite prophet confronted King Ahab on the road, he was disguised as a bondman wearing a mask or "a bandage over his eyes" so he could gain access to the king and speak God's word of castigation (1 Kgs 20:38). While Judah wore a mask congenially to cover his deceitful behavior, Tamar's mask was used to reveal his true identity (Gen 38). But not every disguise back then was for a noble purpose, such as the mask worn by King Saul when he inquired of the witch of Endor (1 Sam 28:7–8).

There are many other examples, but more importantly, many Christians can be facile or glib when putting on masks of caring, sincerity, presence, worship and even love, which are learned, purposeful, pretentious, and studied attitudes.

Head Coverings

In Exod 28:4, Moses consecrated Aaron, the high priest, with a turban (*miẓnefet*), and the ordinary priests with a headband (*migba'at*), among their vestments (Exod 29:6). Later, he ordered the sons of Aaron to not let their "hair hang loose" while ministering in the sanctuary (Lev 10:6), and encouraged, if not required, the wearing of a turban, a type of headgear made by winding long lengths of cloth around the head (Ezek 24:17). Farmers are reported to have covered their heads in shame when the ground was dismayed by drought (Jer 14:4), and David praised the Lord for covering his head during battle (Ps 104:7). It was customary for women in the ancient Near East to cover their heads outside the home, but in case of adultery, they were punished by being forced to let their hair down in public (Num 5:18). For other transgressions, they would be divinely humiliated (Isa 3:17).

Footwear

Shoes are not just popular footwear, they are also used as a metaphor for life, social trends, protection or power. For example, as a metaphor, shoes can evoke tear-jerking responses to memorials of lives accidentally or brutally cut short. Whenever there is a disaster, photo journalists offer images of shoes forlornly scattered or discarded at the scene, often stained with blood, but always empty, poignantly separated from their owners. In 2020, during the first devastating year of the pandemic, 88 pairs of white shoes were placed in front of the White House to represent the number of nurses who had died in the fight against the coronavirus, and 164 pairs of nurses' shoes were placed on the U.S. Capitol lawn[19] to express anger and sadness over the increasing loss of nurses and emergency first responders that year. Thus, footwear has provided mournful, memorable, poignant, and powerful images of life.

Not everyone in ancient Israel had footwear (usually sandals, Hebrew *na'al*), for the poorest people and slaves often went barefoot. However, based on the accounts of Moses at the burning

[19] Caitlin O'Kane, "164 pairs of shoes placed on the lawn of the Capitol, representing nurses who died from coronavirus," *CBS News* (July 22, 2020). Retrieved from https://www.cbsnews.com/news/nurses-shoes-died-coronavirus-capitol-lawn-164-health-care-workers-pandemic/.

bush, and Ruth and Boaz, footwear has often been used in Scripture to symbolize earthly protection, divine power, and punishment for transgressions. For instance, removing the sandals signified putting off something profane, and was demanded of those approaching or serving the Holy God (Exod 3:5). Likewise, the commander of the Lord's army ordered Joshua to take off his sandals, for the place where he was standing was holy (Josh 5:15).

In Scripture, footwear is also given the same importance as feet, and together they become a symbol of supreme power or domination. The psalmist demonstrated this, saying: "You [God] have given him dominion over the works of your hands; you have put all things under his feet" (Ps 8:6). When alluding to victory over Edom, David declared "God has spoken in His holiness" saying, "I will throw My sandal over Edom" (Ps 108:7-10). According to ancient traditions, the victor put his feet, with sandals, on the vanquished to symbolize authority over them. The most powerful evidence is that Joshua commanded his victorious warriors to "put your feet on the necks of these kings" (Josh 10:24), to indicate that the enemy was defeated for all time to come.

Shoes (sandals) in the Bible also indicated the right of possession, so that a purchase became legal only when the seller took off his sandals and handed them to the buyer (Ruth 4:7–8).[20] This was so in all transactions, especially in the redemption of property by a *go'el* or relative. To loosen someone's shoestrings or carry their shoes was equivalent to subjugation, which showed the power and authority of the master over the servant. According to this practice, kings in ancient times sent their shoes as a sign of the subjugation of a vassal. Those shoes had to be carried by the inferior person on the shoulder as a mark of humility. But to cast a shoe at someone was considered a very high form of disrespect, which the strong committed against the weak (Ps 60:8). Being barefoot was utilized as a symbol of mourning (2 Sam 15:30), enslavement (2 Chr 28:15), and victory over an enemy (Isa 20:2). The terms sandal and shoestring were used on one occasion by Abram to express his independence in this response to the king of Sodom,

---

[20] John Hamlin, *Surely There Is a Future: A Commentary on the Book of Ruth*, International Theological Commentary (Grand Rapids, MI: Eerdmans, 1996), 59.

> I have raised my hand to the Lord God Most High, Creator of heaven and earth, that I will not accept even a thread, a shoestring or a strap of a sandal, or anything that belongs to you, lest you should say, "I have made Abram rich" (Gen 14:22–23).

Ancient shoes or footwear were also used as a symbol of power, for without them humans are powerless to move skillfully and easily. To deal with a particular issue of power that arose repeatedly among God's people as they traveled to the Promised Land, a divine law was given for levirate marriage (Deut 25:5–10). If a man refused to take his deceased brother's or next of kin's childless wife as his own and bear a child, the widow was to go to the city gate and call all the elders together for a meeting. She would then declare loudly that her husband's next of kin refused to take her as his wife and give her a child, and had therefore dishonored the name of his brother or next of kin. The elders would confer with the man and he was given another chance to either accept or refuse the request. If he accepted his duties as kinsman, plans were immediately made for the marriage and the matter was settled. It was then up to the Lord to provide a child. But if he did not take the woman as his wife, he had to state loudly so that everyone could hear, "I don't want to marry her." The widow would then pull off his sandal (usually the right sandal), spit in his face, hold the sandal high to publicly demonstrate his loss of respect and power, and shout: "His name shall be called the house of him whose sandal is removed" (Deut 25:10). The most familiar of these stories is in Ruth 4:1-13, where Ruth, a Moabite, whose nation was one of the bitter enemies of Israel, caused the kinsman of Naomi, who was supposed to marry her, to do so.

Perspective of an Adventist Fashionista

The subject of adornment is a misinterpreted, misused, misapplied and controversial doctrine in the Seventh-day Adventist Church. There exist strong positive and negative opinions regarding makeup, jewelry and accessories that are usually included in the word adornment. Some adherents were born into this conservative Christian faith and raised with anti-adornment views. Others joined by baptism or profession of faith and were taught to believe that wearing any type of adornment, even a colorful scarf, is a sin. And of course, there are those born and brought into the faith who believe there is nothing wrong with wearing adornment, and wear it even in worship. Regardless of all of these various opinions, our responsibility is to treat all with respect, even while asking: "Are these teachings and beliefs in harmony with Scripture? Is the wearing of makeup, jewelry, or other types of adornment condemned in the Bible?" Every generation of Adventists, and many other conservative believers, have wrestled with these questions in their quest to find the real truth. Because the answers are generally a mixture of misrepresentation and misinterpretation of Scripture, there is often no satisfaction or clear conclusion on this issue.

Ellen G. White has written volumes about the ill-effects of fashion and cosmetics, as well as the importance of dress reform for the health and spiritual wellbeing of women. Many of her warnings are specific standards for her time and cannot or should not be directly applied to nowadays. This is particularly the case given that contemporary developers, producers and distributors of fashion, cosmetics and other aspects of clothes or "dress"[21] must adhere to laws and the governance of a variety of federal agencies. However, this timeless caution should not be ignored:

> But what account can those who follow the fashions and follies of the present-day render to God for the use they have made of the time and abilities given them for wise improvement? Their minds, instead of being developed and strengthened by proper cultivation, have been dwarfed and crippled by being devoted almost entirely to the arrangement of the dress in accordance with the demands of fashion. This is the crying evil of our sex and lies at the bottom of many of the failures and miseries of life. Many women who profess to be followers of Jesus Christ are servants to the fashions of the world and delight to adopt new inventions in styles, constantly appearing out in new costumes and new deformities of dress.[22]

---

[21] Alison Lurie defines dress as involving symbolic power, including not only garments, but also hairstyles, makeup, body decorations, and jewelry (*The Language of Clothes*, [New York, NY: Random House, 1981], 4, 115, 212).

[22] Ellen G. White, *Letters and Manuscripts*, vol. 3 (Review and Herald, 1887), para. 9.

Therefore, close, careful examination of passages in which adornment is mentioned is warranted, while remembering that Ellen White also wrote:

> There is no excuse for anyone in taking the position that there is no more truth to be revealed and that all our expositions of Scripture are without error. The fact that certain doctrines have been held as truth for many years by our people is not proof that our ideas are infallible. Age will not make error into truth, and truth can afford to be fair. No doctrine will lose anything by close investigation. We are living in perilous times, and it does not become us to accept everything claimed to be truth without examining it thoroughly; neither can we afford to reject anything that bears the fruits of the Spirit of God; but we should be teachable, meek and lowly of heart. There are those who oppose everything that is not in accordance with their own ideas, and by so doing they endanger their eternal interest as verily as did the Jewish nation in their rejection of Christ. The Lord designs that our opinions shall be put to the test, that we may see the necessity of closely examining the living oracles to see whether or not we are in the faith.[23]

In order to broaden the understanding of those who support the wearing of makeup, jewelry and other types of adornment, as well as to develop more gracious attitudes toward those who oppose us on either side, it is crucial to examine various definitions, before taking a negative or positive stand or exercising a hard line. It is our privilege, in these days where knowledge has increased exponentially, to know the difference between divine endorsement and denouncement of adornment, whether it is jewelry, cosmetics or various accessories. Almost all dictionaries define adornment as accessories and jewelry is called ornaments, worn to embellish, distinguish or enhance the beauty of the wearer, as well as to define cultural, social, or religious status within a specific community. Ornaments are usually described as beautiful, often useful accessories or decorations made of gold, silver, brass, wood or stone. Cosmetics (or makeup) are most often defined as lipstick, mascara, and eye shadow used to color and beautify the face or apply to parts of the body, and include materials such as wigs, scarfs or special costuming.

---

[23] Ellen G. White, *Review & Herald* (Dec 20, 1892), para. 1.

However, the place from which we must draw our meaning and understanding is Scripture, to discover whether or not God assigns pleasure, abstinence or punishment to the use of adornment. Seventh-day Adventists have preached, taught and written extensively on this subject, mostly with denouncement, yet there is still no consensus of approval pertaining to its use. Braun suggested,

> The one consensus to this trend of denouncing the use of all jewelry and adornment is the series of studies in Spectrum in 1989 . . . One reason why Adventists are preoccupied with this matter can be found in our historical roots. . . This plain tradition had its roots in the Anabaptist fellowships spawned by the Protestant Reformation. . . A sizeable portion of the early Adventist pioneers originated from within the Methodist church. . . [which] "expected its clergy and laymen, whether rich or poor, to be dressed in plain garb without jewelry, ornamentation or frills."[24]

The writings of Ellen White, a former Methodist, on the matter of adornment are likely the greatest influence on Adventist attitude and policy. Quoting from a White Estate document "Preparation for Baptism," Braun notes that she says:

> Christians are not to decorate the person with costly array or expensive ornaments. All this display imparts no value to the character. The Lord desires every converted person to put away the idea that dressing as worldlings dress, will give value to his influence.[25]

Note the language used by Ellen White: "the Lord desires," not commands or requires. Ellen White's rationale for opposing the use of adornments was triggered by the urgency of the Second Coming of Christ, the significance of good stewardship, and her Methodist roots.[26] Consequently, as our prophet, it should be no surprise that her position on this subject has become the Adventist church's policy, particularly when she has written: "To dress plainly,

---

[24] D. H. Braun, *A Seminar on Adventists, Adornment and Jewelry* (DMin diss., Andrews University, 1996), 25–30.

[25] Braun, *Seminar*, 35. He is quoting from a White Estate document entitled "Preparation for Baptism."

[26] Braun, *Seminar*, 25–30.

abstaining from display of jewelry and ornaments of every kind, is in keeping with our faith."[27]

Conclusion

Many lessons can be learned from the study of the Biblical treatment of clothes. Perhaps among the most outstanding is the divine gift of choice that allows us to choose our own garments as a fundamental part of embracing our own identity and individuality. David demonstrated this when he wisely rejected Saul's armor, which was the strongest suit of armor available (1 Sam 17:38–39). About this, Norman Cohen commented:

> Scholars who study the nature of clothing and appearance vis-à-vis a person's identity speak of both role embracement and role distance. Role embracement refers to a close link between a particular role and the individual's identity. The role is likely to be integrated into one's self-concept. On the other hand, role distance relates to a lack of inner identification with a particular role.[28]

We have also discovered many biblical references in Scripture that portray clothes in different ways—from outer and inner garments, to clothes serving as illustrations for deeper spiritual states or reality. And from garments that tell us more about the person of God (literal or symbolic), to the relationship of clothes to guilt and shame and how to overcome them. Many other references to clothes are linked to the topic of adornment, including cosmetics, jewelry, masks or veils, head coverings, and even footwear. We have also seen how Adventist perspectives on adornment are complex and have not always taken into account a holistic view of the various perspectives and nuances found in the Old and New Testaments, as is clear from the examples previously offered.

In summary, Scripture does not condemn the use of adornment, but does teach a balanced, godly perspective on its use, which is endorsed by Ellen White, who presents a most balanced perspective as follows:

---

[27] Ellen G. White, *Testimonies for the Church,* vol. 3 (Review and Herald), 366.

[28] Cohen, *Masking and Unmasking,* Kindle loc 1811.

> There are many who try to correct the life of others by attacking what they consider are wrong habits. They go to those whom they think are in error, and point out their defects. They say, "You don't dress as you should." They try to pick off the ornaments, or whatever seems offensive, but they do not seek to fasten the mind to the truth. Those who seek to correct others should present the attractions of Jesus. They should talk of his love and compassion, present his example and sacrifice, reveal his Spirit, and they need not touch the subject of dress at all. There is no need to make the dress question the main point of your religion. There is something richer to speak of. Talk of Christ, and when the heart is converted, everything that is out of harmony with the word of God will drop off. It is only labor in vain to pick leaves off a living tree. The leaves will reappear. The ax must be laid at the root of the tree, and then the leaves will fall off, never to return.[29]

Finally, the seven garments of God—majesty, strength, vengeance, zeal, righteousness, compassion and purity, are the source of authentic identity and the reason for my tribute to Dr. Jo Ann Davidson. She is one of the first female professors at the Seventh-day Adventist Theological Seminary and an admired colleague who has blazed a trail of excellence in life, scholarship, and whatever to which she puts her hand and heart. She has not only blazed a trail of high spiritual and intellectual standards but has left a permanent model of dedication to the Word that is enhanced by her winsome personality. Dr. Jo Ann is an incredibly thoughtful and loving colleague and friend, who has inspired me to seek a biblical understanding of the importance of glitz and glam for godly Adventist fashionistas who daily wear Christ's robe of righteousness.

[29] Ellen G. White, *Signs of the Times* (July 1, 1889), para 7.

Part 3:
Beauty in Theology and the Character of God

The Imago Dei and the Beauty of God in the Eden Narrative

Marla A. Samaan Nedelcu

Abstract

The beauty of God and His Word shine brightly through the themes and linguistic devices of the creation narrative of Gen 1. In this narrative, the very language and syntax that are employed convey a sense of growing abundance and excitement as the days of creation progress towards day 6. Once the narrative of day 6 is reached, its climax is found in the chiasmus of Gen 1:26-28, which itself has the *imago Dei* as its apex (verse 27). The *imago Dei*, at the pinnacle of the six-day creation narrative, reveals the importance and beauty of the relationship God desires to have with His human creation.

This creation narrative additionally seems to indicate that the *imago Dei* relates to the human capacity to be more like God than any other created being can, in every aspect of humans' nature (biological/physical, relational, emotional/psychological, mental, volitional, and spiritual). However, in order to best comprehend what the image of God is, we must also delve into what the biblical Edenic narratives portray God to be like. Accordingly, the beauty of God as *Elohim* and *YHWH Elohim* in Gen 1-3 is explored, in order to give insight into what it means for humans to bear and reflect the glorious image of God.

Introduction

I have known Dr. Davidson almost my whole life—before she was Dr. Davidson and when she was just my best friend's mom.[1]

---

[1] Aside from my family, no one in my childhood made me feel as special as she did. From the time I was eight years old, I knew that she saw me and loved me, and I basked in the warmth of her beautiful gaze. I will always remember when I was eleven years old—wearing glasses for the first time, and feeling self-conscious about it. I don't know if she knew how I was feeling, but she made a point to emphasize to me how good I looked in those glasses, and her words helped me hold my head up high and regain my former carefree confidence. Fifteen years later, I had bought my wedding dress and she wanted to see it on me. When she did, she started crying because she said I was just so beautiful in it. At that time, her

When as a teenager I felt God calling me to study theology, I knew of no women in this field other than Dr. Davidson. Yet, this never intimidated me, because knowing her gave me the confident assurance that the path I had chosen was not a strange path. It was also not a path I ever felt I had to blaze for myself. I salute her as the pioneer whose sacrifice and steadfastness blazed the path that I could later walk down unencumbered. Dr. Davidson, it is my great honor to dedicate this chapter to you. As my professor, thank you for showing me the beauty of God's character revealed in the beauty of His Word. And as my friend and mentor, thank you for living out the beauty of God's love to me, thus helping me to live as one "accepted in the Beloved."

The Bible is a book of ravishing beauty—fully divine and fully human, awesome in its grandeur, its scope and its depth, exquisite in its ability to tug at the heartstrings and expand the intelligence.[2] Its first words—"In the beginning, God created the heavens and the earth"—bless humanity with a knowledge of the truth of a mighty Creator God, who created us and our world on purpose. The Bible, this theodrama of the ages, can be thought of as historical non-fiction.[3] Beginning with the creation of the heavens and the earth, and after documenting and foretelling thousands of years of tragedies, victories, plot developments, suspense, and a final glorious culmination, this saga promises a "happily-ever-after" ending with "a new heaven and a new earth" (Rev 21:1).

---

genuine reaction meant the world to me, and it is a gift that I will never forget.

[2] This is brought out masterfully in chapter 4 of Jo Ann Davidson, *Toward a Theology of Beauty: A Biblical Perspective* (Lanham, MD: University Press of America, 2008).

[3] "Genesis grounds the creation as the historical event that introduces and generates every other event in Scripture. It is the first event, the first genealogy without which all other events and genealogies could not have taken place. The fact that creation is the preamble of the history of Israel—and of the world—not only gives it a cosmic perspective, but also affirms and emphasizes its historical quality, which becomes the groundwork and foundation of all subsequent events. As such, to question the historicity of the creation story would be akin to doubting the historicity of all other accounts reported in the book of Genesis" (Jacques B. Doukhan, *Genesis*, Seventh-day Adventist International Bible Commentary [Nampa, ID: Pacific Press, 2016], 35).

The Eden narrative itself is a work of artistry, full of profound parallelism, chiastic structures, and elegant linguistic devices.[4] In fact, it lays the bedrock for all further theological development, and is alluded to throughout the whole of Scripture, its concepts forming the presuppositions that all future Bible writers adopt.[5] It begins, in Gen 1, by describing God's six-day creation. As this first week progresses, the accounts of the daily creations incrementally increase in verbiage—a stylistic tool which not only provides more detail to the narrative but which also mirrors the burgeoning abundance and variety which continue to build in God's created world.[6] This increasing proliferation of life and words propel the narrative on to day six, the final workday of creation week and the apex of the creation narrative up to this point.[7] The beauty of creation, of new life bursting on to a formless and void planet and of a home being crafted for this new life, is mirrored by the beautiful and grand linguistic devices the author employs to describe such an epic event.

---

[4] For a sampling of this, see Jacques Doukhan, *The Literary Structure of the Genesis Creation Story* (Andrews University Seminary Doctoral Dissertation Series 5; Berrien Springs, MI: Andrews University Press, 1978).

[5] See Richard M. Davidson, "Back to the Beginning: Genesis 1–3 and the Theological Center of Scripture," in *Christ, Salvation, and the Eschaton*, eds. Daniel Heinz, Jiří Moskala, and Peter M. van Bemmelen (Berrien Springs, MI: Old Testament Publications, 2009); Gerald A. Klingbeil, ed., *The Genesis Account of Creation and Its Reverberations in the Old Testament* (Berrien Springs, MI: Andrews University Press, 2015); Thomas L. Brodie, Dennis R. MacDonald, Stanley E. Porter, eds., *The Intertextuality of the Epistles: Explanations of Theory and Practice* (Sheffield: Sheffield Phoenix Press, 2006), especially 61-70.

[6] David A. Dorsey, *The Literary Structure of the Old Testament: A Commentary on Genesis—Malachi* (Grand Rapids, MI: Baker Academic, 1999), 49; Marla A. Samaan Nedelcu, "What Makes Humans Human? Personal Ontology in the Creation Narrative of Day Six (Gen 1:24-31)," in *Scripture and Philosophy: Essays Honoring the Work and Vision of Fernando Luis Canale* (Berrien Springs, MI: Adventist Theological Society Publications, 2016), 382-407.

[7] Of course, the seventh day of creation week remains "unique and unmatched" as the culmination of the whole creation week (Dorsey, *Literary Structure*, 49).

The Exegetical Import of the *Imago Dei*

Within the sixth day of the creation narrative itself, the concentric structure of Gen 1:24-30 draws attention to verse 27 as its midpoint.[8] Additionally, there is a chiasmus in verses 26-28 which highlights verse 27 as the climax of this structure:[9]

26 And God said: "Let Us make [נעשה] אדם in Our image, according to Our likeness, and let them rule over the fish of the sea and over the birds of the heavens and over the בהמה and over all the earth and over every creeper that creeps upon the earth."[10]

---

[8] Hajime Murai, "Literary structure (chiasm, chiasmus) of Book of Genesis," http://www.bible.literarystructure.info/bible/01_Genesis_e.html (accessed Mar 4, 2022). See also his "The Parallel Concentric Structures within Exodus," paper presented at the annual meeting of the SBL (Atlanta, GA), Nov 21, 2010. Luis Alonso Schökel, *A Manual of Hebrew Poetics* (Rome: Editrice Pontificio Istituto Biblico, 2000), 192.

[9] "All of these features of Genesis 1:27 indicate that it is the zone of maximum turbulence, the peak of the account" (C. John Collins, *Genesis 1-4: A Linguistic, Literary, and Theological Commentary* [Phillipsburg, NJ: P&R Publishing, 2006], ch. 4, D.). Scholars see this text not only as the high point of this pericope, but as a grounding text for Old Testament theology. For example, Theodorus C. Vriezen, who sees Gen 1:26, 27 as the "best synthesis of the whole Old Testament message" (according to Richard M. Davidson, "Biblical Anthropology and the Old Testament," paper presented at the Third International Bible Conference, Israel [June 16, 2012], 15; also see Vriezen's *An Outline of Old Testament Theology* [Oxford: Blackwell, 1970], 145).

[10] Translations of biblical texts are my own throughout. Some options for the translation of האדם are: humankind, humanity, humans, a human, man, mankind, Adam. I favor a translation that can refer both to the singular ("him") and the plural ("them"), as this word does in verse 27. The only option that seems to do this is "man," which can refer to Adam, to the collective Adam and Eve, and to humanity in general. However, inescapably "man" denotes "maleness," which is not the intended meaning of האדם in the Gen 1 narrative (although that is the intent of this word in Gen 2). Therefore, due to the lack of suitable alternatives, האדם will be referred to as האדם. If my usage of the personal pronoun "them" in conjunction with האדם feels awkward linguistically, please note that it is the same grammatical usage that is found in the original text.

The Hebrew word בהמה is translated and interpreted in many ways: cattle, livestock, domesticated animals, beasts of burden, animals in relationship with humans, higher-order animals, intelligent animals, animals

27 And God created [ברא] האדם in His image, in the image of God He created him, male and female He created them.

28 And God blessed them and said to them: "Be fruitful and become many and fill the earth and subdue and rule over the fish of the sea and over the birds of the heavens and over every living thing that creeps upon the earth."

In this, the Bible's first account of human creation, it is evident that verse 26 contains similar content to verse 28. Verse 26 recounts God's decision to make האדם and give them the function of rulership. Verse 28 comes after God has created האדם and recounts His blessing and commission to them to "be fruitful . . . and rule."[11] Sandwiched in between is the climax of this passage. Here the narrative breaks into poetry, as if prose is insufficient to express the grandeur of the event:[12]

---

capable of relationship with God, four-footed animals, high-carriage animals, wild animals. My study of biblical zoological taxonomy has not yet led me to be confident with one specific translation or interpretation, therefore here I use the original term, בהמה. For some of these usages, see the following: Collins, ch. 4; Daniel I. Block, "To Serve and To Keep: Toward a Biblical Understanding of Humanity's Responsibility in the Face of the Biodiversity Crisis," in *Keeping God's Earth: The Global Environment in Biblical Perspective*, eds. Noah J. Toly and Daniel I. Block (Downers Grove, IL: InterVarsity, 2010), ch. 5.

[11] It is possible that the blessing and the mandate to "be fruitful . . . and rule" applies not only to האדם but also to some land animals. Day five includes a blessing and a mandate to "be fruitful and become many and fill"; therefore, it seems reasonable that land animals would also receive some sort of divine blessing and mandate. Based on this and the difference between the listing of animals in verses 26 and 28, there is reason to believe that verse 26 applies specifically to האדם and that verse 28 could apply to האדם and some land animals. For a discussion of this, see A. Rahel Schafer's dissertation ("'You, YHWH, Save Humans and Animals': God's Response to the Vocalized Needs of Non-Human Animals as Portrayed in the Old Testament," PhD Diss., Wheaton College, 2016).

[12] Kenneth A. Mathews, *Genesis 1—11:26*, The New American Commentary 1A (Nashville, TN: Broadman and Holman, 1996), 172: "The construction of v. 27 is an embedded poem consisting of three lines."

27 And God created האדם in His image,	ויברא אלהים את־האדם בצלמו
in the image of God He created him,	בצלם אלהים ברא אתו
male and female He created them.	זכר ונקבה ברא אתם:

In this sole poem of chapter 1, the verb ברא ("created") is used three times, once in each colon. This repeated usage is intended to make a poetic impact, as neither this verb nor עשׂה ("made") was used more than once per creation day in the narrative that precedes day six.[13] Furthermore, the repeated usage of ברא ("created") here as opposed to עשׂה ("made") can connote a more personal, "'absolute' ex nihilo" creation by God.[14] In regard to the syntax of this poem, the first two lines are in chiastic structure, and the third line adds more detail to their meaning.[15] Some see the first two lines merely in

---

[13] After Gen 1:1 (בראשית ברא אלהים את השמים ואת הארץ), ברא is only used one other time before day six, and this is in day five (it is also used in 2:3 and 2:4a—the last two verses of this creation narrative—to refer to the totality and completion of God's creative activity). It is interesting how usage of ברא is reserved for the creation of the heavens and the earth (1:1; 2:3 [totality of creation]; 2:4a), water animals and winged animals (1:21), and humans (1:27), when the less personal עשׂה is the verb used for the rest of creation. It is possible that ברא is used in 1:21 specifically because of the inclusion of the "great sea creatures/monsters" (התנינם הגדלים) listed first in this verse, in order to indicate their subordinate and creaturely position in relation to God, as opposed to their position as divine monsters in certain ancient Near Eastern myths (see, for example, Doukhan, *Genesis*, 68; Mary K. Wakeman, *God's Battle with the Monster: A Study in Biblical Imagery* [Leiden: Brill, 1973], 79). God also highlights the special significance of His animal and human creation by specifically blessing only His fifth-day and sixth-day creatures: "Be fruitful and become many" (verses 22 and 28). Certainly between the longer narratives in days five and six, the usage of ברא in them, and the specific blessing given to animals and humans, it seems that the intensity of the creation narrative grows as it continues. Each aspect of creation is important, and God's planning is manifest as He creates each element in the necessary order, and builds up the whole ecosystem. But the literary elements of this narrative seem to suggest that creation week climaxes with the creation of האדם.

[14] Doukhan, *Literary Structure*, 62.

[15] For more on the chiastic arrangement, see Matthews, *Genesis*, 175. For the relationship between verse 27b and 27c, see Phyllis A. Bird, "Male

synonymous parallelism.[16] However, their inverted repetition shows that they indeed are in chiastic structure:[17]

A		And God created האדם	A		ויברא אלהים את־האדם
	B	in His image		B	בצלמו
	B`	in the image of God		B`	בצלם אלהים
A`		He created him	A`		ברא אתו

This structure of verse 27a-b is a tool the author uses to highlight the utmost importance given to the *imago Dei*, the element found at the heart of this structure. Verse 27c follows in synthetic parallelism to this structure, and explains how האדם can be both "him" of verse 27b and "them" of verse 27c.[18] How significant it is that in this first

---

and Female He Created Them: Gen. 1:27b in the Context of the Priestly Account of Creation," *Harvard Theological Review* 74/2 (1981): 149-50.

[16] See Paul K. Jewett, *Man as Male and Female: A Study of Sexual Relationships from a Theological Point of View* (Grand Rapids, MI: Eerdmans, 1975), 45; Willem A. M. Beuken, "The Human Person in the Vision of Genesis 1–3: A Synthesis of Contemporary Insights," *Louvain Studies* 24 (1999): 6–9.

[17] Matthews, *Genesis*, 175; Peter Mercer, *An Initiatory Catechism of Hebrew Grammar* (Melbourne: Walker, May & Co., 1876), 28. The first half of verse 27a (A above) uses proper nouns ("God" and "האדם"), and the second half of 27a (B) uses a personal (possessive) pronoun to refer to a proper noun ("His" refers to "God" found in the clauses after and before it); the first half of 27b (B`) uses a proper noun ("God"), and the second half of 27b (A`) uses personal pronouns to refer to proper nouns (both referents are in the first half of 27a, where "He" refers to "God" and "him" refers to "האדם").

[18] Bird, "Male and Female," 149, 150. See also Samaan Nedelcu, "What Makes Humans Human?" Because of semantic correspondence, some see a formal parallelism between "in the image of God" in verse 27b and "male and female" in 27c, which can lead to viewing God as bisexual. See Phyllis Trible, *God and the Rhetoric of Sexuality* (Philadelphia, PA: Fortress, 1978), 200. Karl Barth emphasizes the bisexuality of the *imago Dei* but does not go so far as to say God is bisexual (*The Doctrine of Creation*, vol. 3 of *Church Dogmatics*, ed. G.W. Bromiley and T. F. Torrance; trans. J. W. Edwards et al. [Edinburgh: T & T Clark, 1958], 2:236). Others see the correspondence between verse 27c and what precedes it as indicating an original androgynous האדם before the differentiation between male and female is introduced. See Judy Klitsner, *Subversive Sequels in the Bible: How Biblical Stories Mine and Undermine Each Other*

biblical reference to the creation of humans, and in this grand *imago Dei* text, the author makes a point to emphasize how God created in His image not just "him" but "male and female."[19] Here again, the beauty of the linguistic elements utilized reflects the beauty of God's creative work. As God is a God of beauty, so His creative work is a work of beauty, culminating in the creation of creatures who bear His very own image in every aspect of what it means to be human.

Theological Reflections on the *Imago Dei*

In considering the *imago Dei*, truly it is remarkable that the Creator would create creatures in His image. Because they are created in God's image, humans are endowed with a special worth, to an even greater extent than the rest of God's creation. This is seen in Gen 9:6—"'Whoever sheds man's blood, by man his blood shall be shed, for in the image of God He made man.'" Life created in God's image is of utmost value, and also may help explain why a loving Creator would later put aside heaven, put humanity upon Himself, and come to save those created in His image.

The *imago Dei* also provides the Eden narrative's best answer to why humans hold such a unique and special place in creation, even with their constitutional similarities to animals.[20] It is creation's

---

(New Milford, CT: Maggid Books, 2011), 112-14. In seeing verse 27c in synthetic parallelism to what precedes it, I am more in agreement with Bird: "The parallelism of the two cola is progressive, not synonymous. The second statement adds to the first; it does not explicate it" (149, 50). See also Richard M. Davidson, "Biblical Anthropology," 12.

[19] This will be explored further below. Gerhard von Rad states that this shows that the author's "idea of man . . . finds its full meaning not in the male alone but in man and woman" (*Genesis*, rev. ed. [Philadelphia: Westminster, 1973], 60). He continues by quoting Emil Brunner: "That is the immense double statement, of a lapidary simplicity, so simple indeed that we hardly realize that with it a vast world of myth and Gnostic speculation, of cynicism and asceticism, of the deification of sexuality and the fear of sex completely disappears" (*Man in Revolt: A Christian Anthropology* [Cambridge: The Lutterworth Press, 2002], 346).

[20] Samaan Nedelcu, "What Makes Humans Human?" 399: "Day six of the Creation narrative mentions *nepeš ḥayyāh* twice. In its first verse—'Let the earth bring forth *living creatures* according to their kind' (1:24), and at the end, where God gives 'every green plant for food' to every creature that has *nepeš ḥayyāh* (1:30). The next place *nepeš ḥayyāh* is found regards the creation of Adam: 'And the Lord God formed *hā'ādām* of the dust of the

"boldest affirmation of the remarkably unique relationship between humans and God—humans resemble God."[21] The *imago Dei* pronouncement in Gen 1 has been called "the outstanding feature of the conception of man in the Old Testament."[22] Indeed, as the linguistic and thematic climax of the whole creation narrative of Gen 1, it receives special attention, space, and even its own literary genre.[23] Because of the importance the text affords this concept, and because the text presents the *imago Dei* as a key factor in understanding what makes humans a special and unique creation of God, it is essential to study this concept and to explore how it relates to human ontology.[24] Would a study of the *imago Dei* indicate that an isolated part of a human being is constitutionally dissimilar from other creatures and thus the seat of the *imago Dei*? Would it show that the *imago Dei* is revealed in the various functions of human nature—biological/physical, relational, emotional/psychological, mental, volitional, and spiritual?

Indeed, according to the Eden narrative, the *imago Dei* is the greatest underlying distinction between humans and animals. But how exactly does the *imago Dei* make humans' constitution or nature different from that of animals? The Eden narrative does not give a precise definition of the *imago Dei*. But it does suggest that because

---

ground and breathed into his nostrils the breath of life and *hā'ādām* became a *living being*' (or *living creature*; Gen 2:7). There are three other occurrences of *nepeš ḥayyāh* in the creation narrative: Day five's 'swarms of *living creatures*' in the waters (Gen 1:20, 21), and Adam's naming of every living creature (Gen 2:19)." "It can seem surprising that after God's one-of-a-kind creation of *hā'ādām*, *hā'ādām* is given the same designation as all animals (*nepeš ḥayyāh*). Certainly it suggests that there is not a constitutional difference between animals and humans, by virtue of *nepeš ḥayyāh* being used of animals in the Gen 1 creation narrative, and of *hā'ādām* in the Gen 2 creation narrative."

[21] Doukhan, *Literary Structure,* 62.

[22] Vriezen, *Outline*, 144.

[23] See Samaan Nedelcu, "What Makes Humans Human?" 396-98.

[24] Human ontology or personal ontology is the study of human constitution (what humans are constituted of) and human nature (what makes humans unique from other creatures). See Marla A. Samaan Nedelcu, "Let Us Make אדם: An Edenic Model of Personal Ontology," PhD diss., Andrews University, 2019. Also Eric T. Olson, *What Are We?: A Study in Personal Ontology*, Philosophy of Mind Series (New York, NY: Oxford University Press, 2007).

of it, humans are endowed with the potential to be more like God (in comparison to the rest of creation), and to resemble Him more, in every aspect of who they are as humans.[25] Human nature is intimately tied to God's creation of humans in His image; human identity and uniqueness cannot be separated from that reality. As every aspect of human nature grows to image God, it becomes more akin to that of the Creator—God's children begin to resemble their Father.

Theologians through the ages have offered scores of answers to the question of what the *imago Dei* is. The quest to identify the *imago Dei*, and the debate surrounding that quest, has been nearly unceasing in the history of Christian theology. Perhaps a sole point of agreement may be summed up in the words of a Genesis commentator: "Although it is difficult to ascertain the meaning of the 'image,' it is closely associated with the uniqueness and distinctiveness of humans."[26] Nevertheless, here are some of the answers that have been offered: physical likeness, possession of mental and rational abilities, free will, emotional life, personhood and individuality, moral nature or a desire for holiness, spiritual nature or an openness to God, social and sexual natures which include marriage and family, the call to rule or care for creation, adoption and sonship, self-consciousness and identity, an innate sense of eternity, an immortal soul, or a combination of these.[27]

---

[25] Gulley, 86: "Herman Bavinck is right that the image of God in humans is not something they *bear* or *have*, but what they are. It is 'not *something in man* but *man himself*.' (I would add the image is not a soul, for the soul is the very person.)" Quote from Herman Bavinck, *God and Creation*, vol. 2, *Reformed Dogmatics*, ed. John Bolt (Grand Rapids, MI: Baker, 2004), 555, emphasis in original.

[26] James McKeown, *Genesis*, The Two Horizons Old Testament Commentary (Grand Rapids, MI: Eerdmans, 2008), 27.

[27] For a good survey of numerous answers, see Gunnlaugur A. Jónnson, *The Image of God: Genesis 1:26-28 in a Century of Old Testament Research*, Coniectanea Biblica, Old Testament Series 26, trans. Lorraine Svendsen (Lund, Sweden: Almqvist & Wiksell International, 1988). See also Collins, *Genesis*, ch. 4, C.6.; Frank M. Hasel, "The Nature of the Human Being in Christian Theology," in *"What Are Human Beings that You Remember Them?"* Proceedings of the Third International Bible Conference Nof Ginosar and Jerusalem, June 11-21, 2012, ed. Clinton Wahlen (Silver Spring, MD: Biblical Research Institute, 2015), 207-34.

Aside from the immortal soul alternative, none of the above options for the identification of the *imago Dei* are explicitly contradicted by the Eden narrative, although some do not appear obvious from the text.[28] Yet most of these options do not present answers that show how humans are truly unique. For while they speak to characteristics that humans certainly possess, humans generally do not possess these characteristics uniquely, but simply to a higher degree than do animals.[29] Is it possible, however, to ascertain what the Eden narrative itself might mean by the *imago Dei*, and what that might mean for human identity and uniqueness?[30]

---

[28] Those who believe that the image of God is an immortal soul would identify the immortal soul textually as נפש חיה ("living being/creature") or נשמת חיים ("breath of life"). But these terms in the Bible do not refer to an immortal soul or even to a part of the person identified as a soul; instead they refer to a unitary living, breathing human. See Samaan Nedelcu, "Let Us Make אדם," for a discussion on this; also footnote 20 above for how the same constitutional terminology is used of animals and humans at creation.

[29] I say "most" because we do not know enough about animals (from science or the Bible) to know exactly which of these characteristics they do possess, but we presume, for example, that they would not possess an innate sense of eternity or some of the other characteristics mentioned in the previous paragraph. However, evidence from science (and even from lay observation) now abundantly demonstrates how animals share many functions that were traditionally thought to be uniquely human qualities. There are even numerous biblical texts that point towards higher-order cognitive processing (for good or evil) in animals: Gen 9:5; Exod 21:28; Num 22:28-30; Job 38:41; Ps 103:22; 147:9; 150:6; Prov 6:6-8; 30:30; Jon 4:11; 2 Pet 2:16; Rev 5:13. Every year, increasingly more is discovered and published on animal behavior that reveals great similarities between humans and animals. For more on the relationship between God and animals, see Schafer, "You, YHWH, Save Humans and Animals."

[30] It must be stated that a more complete answer to the question of the *imago Dei* would be found in a study of the entire biblical canon, especially in looking at the life of Christ (Col 1:15; see Marc Cortez's *Christological Anthropology in Historical Perspective: Ancient and Contemporary Approaches to Theological Anthropology* [Grand Rapids, MI: Zondervan, 2016] for more on how Christ being incarnate helps us to know what it is to be human). However, we will focus merely on seeing what clues Gen 1-3 itself might have for understanding the *imago Dei* concept. Although this pericope is small, the insights found in it are expected to be valuable, considering that these chapters are foundational to the entire canon's teaching on personal ontology.

For once this is uncovered, there will be a better basis for evaluating the answers on the *imago Dei* that are found in Christian theology, and we will be better able to ascertain how God's beauty is reflected by humans, His image-bearers.

The *Imago Dei* and the Beauty of God[31]

When first turning to the Eden narrative to identify the image of God, we must ask ourselves not only what this pericope reveals the *image* to be, but who *God* is revealed to be from this text.[32] In fact, this should be the starting point of our study, for how can we really understand what the image is, without understanding who the text reveals the original of that image to be?[33] If we start by studying the

---

[31] For a discussion of the aesthetic nature of God, see Jo Ann Davidson, *Theology of Beauty*, chapter 2.

[32] Along this line, Collins mentions that: "In this pericope and the next, God displays features of his character: he shows intelligence in designing the world as a place for man to live; he uses language when he says things; he appreciates what is 'good' (morally and aesthetically); and he works and rests. He is also relational, in the way he establishes a connection with man that is governed by love and commitment (Gen. 2:15-17). In all of this God is a pattern for man" (*Genesis,* ch. 4, C.6.).

[33] God's transcendence and dissimilarity from earthly humans makes it nearly impossible for us to understand His essence or constitution. Thus the Eden narrative clearly reveals who God is on the level of nature, but not on the level of constitution. However, it is logical to assume some sort of *analogia entis* between God and humans, for how would a creation of a physical earth and physical humans take place if God were not able to relate to the physical realm? Additionally, the Eden narrative speaks of humans being created in the image of God, and shows this image to be on the level of nature. But in order for this image to be possible on the level of nature, there also should be some analogy between God and humans on the level of constitution—some image/likeness on the level of constitution that enables the potential for the image/likeness of God on the level of human nature. Yet, a careful exegesis of Genesis' human creation narrative reveals that humans are entirely physical on the level of constitution. So an *analogia entis* between God and humans on the level of constitution could then entail God's capacity to relate to human constitutional physicality as opposed to humans' capacity to relate to any divine constitutional non-physicality. Perhaps such ability of God to relate to human constitutional physicality is His ability to relate on the level of the basic characteristics of such physicality—space and time (see Canale, *A Criticism of Theological Reason*, 349-87).

image, and then work backwards to understand who the original is, we are in danger of seeing God as a grander version of who we are, of making Him into our human image. But if we begin with who the text reveals God to be, then we are on track to really understanding what it means for humans to be created in *His* image.

So who is God revealed to be in the Eden narrative? Does this pericope which introduces the *imago Dei* also reveal or define God? One of the first things noticed, when reading the passage with this question in mind, is that two different names for God are used. The creation narrative in Gen 1:1-2:4a uses *Elohim* (God, אלהים). And the creation narrative in Gen 2:4b-3:24 uses *YHWH Elohim* (Lord God, יהוה אלהים), with the exception of when the serpent and Eve are speaking about God in 3:1-5 (they use only *Elohim*, אלהים). What is the difference in meaning between these two appellations, and who do they reveal God to be in the Eden narrative?[34] Delving into this will reveal more of the beauty of God, as well as the high honor and calling He has entrusted humans with, as His vice-regents on earth.

The Image of *Elohim* in the Eden Narrative

Genesis' first creation narrative uses *Elohim* (אלהים), which signifies the text's focus on the "strength and preeminence" of God, "the great God who transcends the universe."[35] Fittingly, the immediate pericope in which it is found focuses on these aspects of God in creation. This first creation narrative highlights the grandeur of God and His creation, offering a large-scale portrayal of creation. In this narrative, the first image painted is of God as the maker of "the heavens and the earth"—everything that exists (Gen 1:1). He is "in the beginning," and nothing had its origin apart from His creating. His spirit is pervasive, and hovered over the chaotic void of this earth, incubating it or nurturing it before His words brought immediate order and plentitude to the earth (1:2; "and God said" is used at least once in each of Gen 1's six days of creation). What

[34] With the biblical exposition that follows, I have made the assumption that Gen 1-3 is able to inform our understanding of who God is in Himself. This is possible if God can operate in space and time, and thus the description of Him in this text can be taken as a direct description of His acts (which speak to His essence). This view of God arises from biblical evidence, as shown in Canale's *A Criticism of Theological Reason*.

[35] Doukhan, *Literary Structure*, 49.

power is in the words of *Elohim* that monumental things come into immediate being at the sound of His command—inanimate nature itself obeys Him (e.g., 1:11, 12)!

But not only does this narrative highlight the power of *Elohim*, it also highlights the order, wisdom, and strategy that are a part of His ability to design magnificently. God is strategic and methodical, He loves clarity, order, and organization, and He takes pleasure in evaluating the goodness of the created work that follows His design (e.g., 1:4, 5, 13, 18).[36] He knows how to make an ideal environment for life and living, even out of a void wasteland, and He executes His perfect plan one step upon another, each one building on what came before with increasing complexity (e.g., 1:2, 6, 7, 9, 19). He expertly manages His creation—calling it, identifying it, naming it, giving it its appointed place (1:8-10).

God is the ruler of His creation—and He is a good ruler who is intimately involved with it, speaking to and with it, caring for its welfare and prosperity, its nourishment, rest, and balance (e.g., 1:6, 8, 11, 15, 22, 29, 30; 2:2, 3). He puts rhythm and cycles in His creation, which display not only His wisdom in science, but also His artistic and even musical nature (1:14).[37] God loves life and activity, He creates His creatures to be and to do, and He designs His creation to be free and profuse within an ordered structure (e.g., 1:19-22).

He is not a creator God who hoards authority, although it is rightfully His alone. In the Godhead itself, there is a sharing of responsibilities and close relationship among the members (e.g., 1:1,

[36] "And God saw . . . that it was good" (or "very good") is recorded at least once in each of the six days of creation (except for day 2). God, who is a God of order, even introduces the first taxonomic system (especially evident with land animals—1:24, 25). In Moskala's words: "God sets the limits and gives boundaries, such as evenings and mornings (day one, two, three, etc.), reproduction by its kind, two special trees in the garden of Eden, time"—all this shows God as a God of order in the Genesis creation account (Jiří Moskala, "The Laws of Clean and Unclean Animals of Leviticus 11: Their Nature, Theology, and Rationale (an Intertextual Study)" [PhD diss., Andrews University, 1998], 284).

[37] See chapter 2 of Jo Ann Davidson's seminal work, and pages 17-18 for God's relationship to music. As she states it: "Concern for aesthetic value within Scripture is an essential element in a 'full-orbed' theology" (*Theology of Beauty,* 12).

2, 26, 2:4).[38] So with His human creation, He follows this pattern and desires to share a close relationship and the delegation of authority with them—and He even delegates some authority to His inanimate creation (1:16-18, 26-28). God appoints His human creation to be His vice-regents over all that He created on earth. They are to represent Him, to care for and lead and rule and reign as He does (1:26, 28, 29). Equipping them for this grand responsibility is the astonishing reality that God created humans in His image and likeness (1:26). That the God of all creation would craft creatures in His own image and likeness is a testament to His own humility and graciousness. Humans are dust (3:19), but are yet empowered by their Creator to rule over His own creation, even in its untainted pre-Fall perfection.

And at the end of creation week, in order to care for the wholistic health of His entire creation, God graciously rests on the Sabbath, blessing it and making it holy.[39] This blessed day highlights the importance God places on the relationship He desires to have with His creatures, and it also provides an example to Adam and Eve of God's way of rulership and creation care (1:28, 31; 2:1-3).[40] Yet the

---

[38] For more on the plurality of God in Gen 1, see Gerhard Hasel, "The Meaning of 'Let Us' in Gen 1:26," *Andrews University Seminary Studies* 13 (1975): 58-66; also Collins, *Genesis*, ch. 4, C.5. (see also footnote 47 below).

[39] Wholistic health is important to God, and certainly includes the spiritual. Here Moskala explains it in an insightful way: "In Hebrew thinking health expresses the totality of wellness of the human being. The physical, mental, spiritual, and social aspects are included. The psychosomatic approach can be discerned from the Hebrew Bible. In the words of Hasel: 'Health in the biblical view is not one particular quality among many that pertain to the human being; it is the wholeness and completeness of being in itself, and in relation to God, to fellow humans, and to the world.' Biblically speaking health is total well-being, a comprehensive wholeness" (*The Laws of Clean and Unclean Animals*, 233; quote is from Gerhard F. Hasel, "Health and Healing in the Old Testament," *Andrews University Seminary Studies* 21 [1983]: 191-202).

[40] Leon R. Kass, *The Beginning of Wisdom: Reading Genesis* (New York, NY: Free Press, 2003), quotes Umberto Cassuto: "Every seventh day, without intermission since the days of Creation, serves as a memorial to the idea of creation of the world by the word of God, and we must refrain from work thereon so that we may follow the Creator's example and cleave to his

beauty of God's strong desire for relationships is brought out even more in the narrative which uses His name *YHWH Elohim*.

The Image of *YHWH Elohim* in the Eden Narrative

The second creation narrative (2:4b-24) provides a more detailed and personal account of creation than does the first creation narrative (1:1-2:4a), and is also one that focuses primarily on the creation of human beings. In it, God's name *YHWH Elohim* (the Lord God, יהוה אלהים) is employed. *YHWH* is the personal, covenant name of God, and highlights the caring and intimate aspects of His nature.[41] *YHWH* and *Elohim* together provide to human understanding one of the fullest pictures of who God is, in His nature. The Lord God is at the same time infinite and intimate, powerful and caring. Just as the first creation narrative brought out the nature of *Elohim* as powerful Creator and masterful Designer, so the second creation narrative counterbalances that with the nature of *YHWH* that connotes tenderness, loyalty, love, and a desire for deep relationship.

So with whom does God have such relationships? With the members of the Godhead, with His human creation, and with the rest of His creation. The closest relationship of these is that of the Godhead, which can be characterized as oneness and unity (John 10:30).[42] It is interesting to note that the only place in the Eden

---

ways. Scripture wishes to emphasize that the sanctity of the Sabbath is older than Israel, and rests upon all mankind" (52, 53).

[41] Richard M. Davidson, "Back to the Beginning," 12.

[42] Even within the fullness or plurality of the Godhead, there is a oneness and unity, so much so that the singular and the plural are both used to reference God, in neighboring verses. Although the Godhead took on different functions in creation (and later, salvation), They seemingly conferenced together for Their decision on the creation of אדם: "Let Us make אדם in Our image, according to Our likeness" (Gen 1:26). These three plural usages in reference to God here are grammatically unambiguous in the Hebrew. However, it is noteworthy that when the author's narration resumes in verse 27, the singular for God is once again employed: "God created האדם in His own image, in the image of God He created him; male and female He created them." Here are the grammatical specifics: In Gen 1:26, "let Us make" is the first-person plural conjugation of the verb "make"; "in Our image" is the first-person plural pronominal suffix attached to the noun "image"; and "according to Our likeness" is the first-person plural pronominal suffix attached to the noun "likeness." In Gen 1:27, "in His own image" is the third-person singular pronominal suffix

narrative where a plural pronoun is used to reference God is in the keynote verse describing the creation of אדם in the image of God (1:26).[43] Perhaps this points to the potential that humans have to image God in the oneness that can exist within the plurality of their own relationships with God and with others.

In Genesis 2, *YHWH Elohim* is used most pointedly to highlight the unique relationship God has with His human creation. No verse in the Eden narrative brings this out more clearly than 2:7: "And *YHWH Elohim* formed/fashioned האדם from the dust of the ground and breathed into his nostrils the breath of life and האדם became a living being/creature." The all-powerful Creator, the genius Designer, is also the masterful Artist and Lover of humans. This divine Artist with His own hands sculpts Adam from the ground, because He loves His creation and desires to be intimately a part of this process.[44] This personal God then breathes His own life-giving breath into this sculpture of a human. Nowhere else in Scripture portrays such an intimate account of creation as is portrayed here with the creation of the first human. So the first human's first breath is God's breath, and *YHWH Elohim*, the God of intimate relationship, never turns away from pursuing this relationship with those He so deeply loves.[45]

---

attached to the noun "image," and the next two references to God are identical—"He created" is the third-person singular conjugation of the verb "create." See also footnote 35 above.

[43] See footnote 47.

[44] Of Adam, God formed/fashioned (יצר) him of the dust of the ground as a potter would a vessel. The choice of this verb highlights not only the artistic work of God, but also the total dependence of the created on the Creator. So explains Jacques Doukhan's commentary on Genesis (Nampa, ID: Pacific Press, 2016), 74. See also Jer 18:2-6; Ps 139:13-15; Job 10:8, 9.

[45] This verb יצר is also used in 1:25 in reference to the creation of the land animals, and so it is the second action of God in the creation of the first human that is the most unique. The second action of God here is to breathe (נפח). The animals also have God's breath, as shown in numerous texts including Gen 7:22 and Job 34:14, 15, but with the creation of Adam, we have the unique description of God breathing His life-giving breath into the first human (Gen 2:7). This is probably the most personal and intimate of any of God's creative acts, as it involves God's mouth breathing into Adam's nostrils. "*Breathed* is warmly personal, with the face-to-face intimacy of a kiss and the significance that this was giving as well as making, and self-giving at that" (Derek Kidner, *Genesis*, Tyndale Old

For His human creation, the creation which He gave His most intimate attention to, *YHWH Elohim* plants a garden (2:8). As the Creator of beauty, He makes the gift of this garden as marvelous as He can for His beloved creatures (2:9). It is a verdant place of abundant life, with rivers, glorious vegetation, and treasures of gold and precious stones (2:9-14). God gives each of the five senses exquisite stimulation and fulfillment through the delights of this Garden of Eden. He does not hold back good things from His human creatures, even sharing an ultimate gift of joy with them—access to eternal life through eating from the tree of life.

Into this environment, God put האדם—not for humans to selfishly enjoy or exploit their environment, nor to tyrannically dominate it, but to serve/cultivate (עבד) it and to keep/guard/preserve (שׁמר) it (2:15).[46] These God-given mandates bring a deeper understanding to the similar mandates in Gen 1:26 and 28 for האדם to rule over creation. All together, the mandates reflect the type of leadership God Himself displays.[47] Along with such servant (עבד) leadership there is no lack of authority, for God does not hesitate to

---

Testament Commentaries [Downers Grove, IL: InterVarsity, 1967], 60). Regarding Eve, God built/constructed (בנה) her of Adam's rib (צלע), as an architect and builder constructs an edifice. This is actually the only time in the Eden narrative that the verb בנה is used, indicating the special and personal importance of the creation of the woman here by God. Doukhan speaks to this importance by pointing out that these two words—בנה and צלע—are linked to the building of the sanctuary. Exploring this connection, he states that "this parallel of the rib-woman with the sanctuary is interesting as it suggests that the creation of the woman means more than the comfort of companionship to man; it may, in fact, have bearings on the salvation of humankind" (83).

[46] Philosophically speaking, this is the human as *Dasein*, being-in-the-world.

[47] Moskala perceptively elaborates on this further: "The Creation story is about the nurture of life, which is reflected in the Mosaic dietary laws, and is further recognized in the task of humans to rule and to govern the animal world, and to guard and preserve the creation order (compare Gen 1:28 with Gen 2:15). These two texts are not in contrast, but related to each other." Rolf Rendtorff put it this way: "Thus we learn that 'master' in Gen 1:28 does not mean 'subdue,' as is often rendered in English translations, but to work carefully and guard" (*The Laws of Clean and Unclean Animals*, 296; also quoted here is Rolf Rendtorff, "What We Miss by Taking the Bible Apart," *Bible Review* 14:1 [1998]: 44).

give האדם commands with severe consequences for disobedience (2:16, 17). The sight of the tree of the knowledge of good and evil itself was a perpetual reminder of God's authority and commands, and of האדם's position of being accountable and subject to Him (2:9). Yet God also always maintains and respects the free will of האדם (2:17); even the risk of האדם's rebellion does not prevent God from sharing His power and authority with האדם, His vice-regent on earth (2:19).

We also see that when God first speaks of the creation of האדם in His image (1:26-28), this האדם is explicitly stated to be male *and* female. Thus the text shows that both male and female together are created to image God and to make up the team that God designs to populate and rule the earth. Genesis 2, with its usage of *YHWH Elohim* revealing a God who desires intimate relationships, additionally gives a more detailed portrayal of this most intimate human relationship than what had been given previously.[48]

The use of the term עזר כנגדו (helper comparable/opposite) brings to light the honorable role of Adam's partner in the relationship, and how she is a God-designed match for him, both in her similarity and dissimilarity to him.[49] The nature of this relationship is not unlike that of the male/female partnerships that Adam observed the animals to have (an implication of 2:20 could be that animals also have their own עזר כנגדו relationship). However, the reality that humans are created in the image of God makes possible a greater communion and oneness, and thus, a greater team than might be possible with any other of God's earthly creatures.

---

[48] As God plans to create Eve and thus complete the human team He designed to image Him (which includes populating the earth and ruling His creation), He first allows Adam to miss the absence of a human partner in his life. Surrounded by a perfect world, with God conferring rulership on him through his naming of the animals (2:19, 20), Adam notices that he does not have a partner as the animals do. God wisely allows Adam to feel this need and longing before giving him this most-treasured gift. The Eden narrative does not say why this is. Perhaps it was so Adam would not take Eve for granted, and that he would appreciate his life with her, remembering what it felt like not to have her in it. "Then *YHWH Elohim* said, 'It is not good for האדם to be alone; I will make him a helper suitable for/comparable to/opposite (עזר כנגדו) him'" (2:18).

[49] See the section on "Functions," in chapter 3 of Samaan Nedelcu, "Let Us Make אדם," starting on page 117.

This special relationship began in a unique way, with God the Architect personally building (בנה) Adam's partner out of Adam's sleeping body (2:21, 22). When God brought her to him, in delight Adam exclaimed the miracle of her coming from his own flesh and bones. He then called her Woman (or recognized that as her name), the feminine version of his own designation, because she was taken out of Man (2:23).[50] Now Adam was lacking nothing. The partner he had longed for stood by him, as his second self—a miraculous creation that he had no part in, although she came out of his own body. This relationship was to be so close, reflecting the closeness of God's relationships, that even other human relationships must be loosened to accommodate the closeness of this one (2:24).

The perfect union, harmony, peace, security, love, intimacy, and devotion that God designed this marital relationship to have (2:25) mirror the way God is in relationships, shown here through this narrative that utilizes His *YHWH Elohim* name. It is significant then that *YHWH Elohim* is also the name that is used in the narrative of the Fall in Gen 3. The God who administers consequences for disobedience and offers hope to sinners is still the God of intimate relationship.[51] After the woman chooses to follow the serpent's deceptions and the man chooses to follow her, the narrative

---

[50] See Davidson, *Flame of Yahweh*, 32, 33, to explore the idea that in Gen 2:23, the man merely recognized the name that God had given her.

[51] However, there is an occasion in chapter 3 where *Elohim* instead of *YHWH Elohim* is used, and that is when the serpent speaks to the woman and she responds. How significant that the serpent chooses to use God's name that signifies His power and rulership, and specifically excludes His name that connotes His loving and intimate relationship with humans. And how interesting that the woman also follows suit, calling God *Elohim* in response to the serpent, even when in the rest of the chapter 3 pericope the narrator consistently uses the appellation *YHWH Elohim*. The serpent's disregard for *YHWH Elohim* in his references to God is strategic, for his purpose is to portray God as a jealous and mighty God who wants to keep all the power to Himself. The Eden narrative reveals the opposite to be true, however. God shares His power with His human creation, entrusting them with the perfect world He created, allowing them to rule it and taking the risk that they would rule it badly. He is *YHWH Elohim* who created humans in His own image, who molded them with His own hands, and who longs to share a deep relationship with them. And He is a God who allowed the serpent free speech, even when that speech was used to assassinate God's own character (3:1).

continues by pointing out the true character of *YHWH Elohim*. He is God of justice and faithfulness, who keeps His word and implements immediate consequences for the first humans' rebellion (3:7). Yet He is not only faithful to His word, He is also faithful to His relationship with them: He comes back to the garden and walks where He had habitually walked with them, tenderly calling out for them. He walks towards them in their sin, not away from them (3:8). He cares for their hearts as a kind and gentle parent, even patiently listening to their pointless blame games (3:9, 11, 13).

In grace and sympathy, He first offers the promise of His own sacrifice before He utters any judgments to the man and woman (3:15). And through it all, He is infinitely fair—dealing with the serpent first, the root of the problem (3:14), tailoring judgments to the specific sins of each of the players in this fall (3:16), and offering explanations for His judgments (3:17). *YHWH Elohim* met Adam and Eve where they were and offered help and salvific grace for their felt and real needs, clothing their shame and nakedness with animal skins (3:21). Previously, God had blessed Adam and Eve with the exalted position of ruling the world. Now any such leadership wisely also involved pain, sweat, and toil (3:19), helping them to become better and more sympathetic leaders of a sinful world. God's infinite wisdom in dealing with this fall was also manifested as He banished Adam and Eve from the garden as a consequence for their sin and as a realistic safeguard against eternal sin and misery (3:22-24).

The God of tender love and exquisite care, *YHWH Elohim* not only manifests such character with His relationships within the Godhead and with humans, but also with the rest of the created world. We have seen that the Garden of Eden was planted by God to be the idyllic environment for Adam and Eve. However, even outside of the garden, He designed the land and its natural components to be organized and beautiful (2:11). There was nothing harsh to be found in this perfect world that God had made, and even the water that sustained earthly life settled as a gentle mist on the earth, not a stout rainstorm or a chilly snowstorm (2:6).

God's character was also neither harsh nor coercive. He allowed a serpent to defy His authority and libel His name, granting free choice and free speech even to His animal creation (3:1). And He provided for the nourishment and proliferation of all His creatures great and small (1:24, 25, 30; 2:19, 20). The marvelous characteristics of God that are associated with His name *YHWH*

Elohim are just as important as the characteristics associated with His name *Elohim*. Humans imaging God will manifest the attributes that are connected to *Elohim* and the attributes that are connected to *YHWH Elohim*. We will see in this next section how both *Elohim* and *YHWH Elohim* are used purposefully in the Eden narrative to reveal a fuller picture of the beauty of who God is.

Imaging *Elohim* and *YHWH Elohim*

This is the God who is revealed through the Eden narrative. The usage of the title *Elohim* in Gen 1 shows the beauty of God as Ruler of all, omnipotent Creator, and masterful Designer. The usage of *YHWH Elohim* in Gen 2 and 3 reveals the beauty of God as a relational God who leads by tender love, detailed care, and through His example. Both *Elohim* and *YHWH Elohim* are integral to who God is—one is not more important than the other. God clearly states that האדם is created in the image of God (1:26, 27), and the previous pages have laid out who the Eden narrative describes God to be. So it is in this beautiful image of *Elohim* and *YHWH Elohim* that humans are created to be, and it is His design that this very image should characterize human nature.

When God planned on creating humans in the image of God as האדם, He first envisioned Adam and Eve functioning as rulers over His newly created world (1:26-28). He gave them this responsibility because they were best equipped for this task since they were created in His image. Following His example, they were to rule in a way that exhibited both the *Elohim* and the *YHWH Elohim* aspects of who God is. This meant that the power and authority they would have as rulers must always be mixed with wisdom and loving care.[52] God's example of rulership consisted of power and authority, wisdom and strategic planning, purposeful design and love for beauty, tender care

---

[52] One example: האדם should not be concerned merely with demonstrating authority over the animals through his naming of them (2:19, 20), but should also care for the alimentary provision of these animals as did God (1:30). Another example: the woman should have remembered her rightful place as ruler over the created world and should not have allowed an animal, the serpent, to usurp authority over her and beguile her into rupturing her intimate relationship with God and her husband (3:6, 7). But this rightful authority over the animals was not to be abused, and God never even gave provision for the animals to be used for food, providing for humans only plants as their alimentary provision (1:29).

and sympathetic regard, and a sharing of power and a loving sacrifice of self for those over whom He ruled. This is the example that God's vice-regents on earth, His image-bearers, were to emulate.

Moreover, just as the Eden narrative revealed God to be the God of relationships, humans created in His image were also made with the capacity and need for such relationships. In their relationships with God, with each other, and with the rest of the created world, they image God. That this relational aspect is tied to their being created in the image of God is evident from the Eden narrative's statement on the image of God: "Then God said, 'Let Us make man in Our image, according to Our likeness'. . . . God created האדם in His own image, in the image of God He created him; male and female He created them. God blessed them; and God said to them, 'Be fruitful and multiply, and fill the earth, and subdue it; and rule'" (1:26-28).[53]

Here also, more than anywhere else, Genesis brings to view both the oneness and the plurality that is inherent in the Godhead and in relationships. It is of vital importance that this description about divine relationship and human relationship is brought out in verses that neighbor each other, and center around the sole declaration of the *imago Dei* in the Eden narrative. It reveals that at least part of the image of God in humans has to do with their capacity to have intimate relationships (where oneness and plurality are both evident), mirroring the divine relationship within the Godhead.[54]

Obviously, this capacity for oneness and plurality in human-to-human relationships is clearly shown in the Eden narrative when describing the "one flesh" relationship of the first man and woman

---

[53] Verse 26 here in the Eden narrative is the only place where a plural pronoun is used (three times) to refer to God. In verse 27, the singular pronoun for God again becomes the one that is habitually used. Significantly however, in verse 26, where האדם is introduced for the first time, a plural pronoun is also used to reference האדם. This is followed in verse 27 by one usage of a singular pronoun to refer to האדם, followed by one usage of a plural pronoun to refer to האדם. In verses 28 and 29, multiple usages of a plural pronoun refer to האדם.

[54] See Jiří Moskala, "Toward Trinitarian Thinking in the Hebrew Scriptures," *Journal of the Adventist Theological Society* 21/1-2 (2010): 255-56. Hugh Ross speaks of these verses pointing towards "the uniplural God" (*The Genesis Question: Scientific Advances and the Accuracy of Genesis* [Colorado Springs, CO: NavPress, 2001], 54).

(2:23, 24). Although the first humans were similar enough to be called the same name (האדם—1:26, 27), they were at the same time dissimilar enough for the woman to be called and designed as עזר כנגדו, a helper comparable to—or more literally, in front of, or even opposite to, the man (2:20).[55] Even the oneness and interdependence of the Godhead is in a small way mirrored in the creation of two such humans in the beginning. The interdependent maleness and femaleness that is described at the creation of Adam and Eve is deeper and more complex than what is found in the animal kingdom, and it is an important factor in what it means to be created in God's image. "So God created האדם in His own image, in the image of God He created him; male and female He created them" (Gen 1:27).[56]

The creation in the beginning of an interdependent male and female also provides the basis for the social/relational function in human nature. The Eden narrative shows how humans are created for close relationships; this correlates with their being created in God's image.[57] Even God's relationships are not limited to the Godhead, but in the Eden narrative extend especially to humans (as those created in His image), and also to the rest of His created world. So likewise, human relationships in this narrative are not limited to the male-female relationship, but extend also to a relationship with God, any other human, and the created world (animals and environment). The relationship with God especially helps humans to reach their full potential in life and in every other relationship.

---

[55] Leon Kass uses the word "counterpart" (*The Beginning of Wisdom,* 73).

[56] That the man cherished this woman who was miraculously built from his own body is evidenced by the fact that he sadly chose loyalty to her over loyalty to God (3:6, 12). Although their relationship with each other changed after they rebelled against God (3:16), God still offered them salvation and restoration, and Adam recognized that God would use Eve as the "mother of all living" from which a savior would be born (3:15, 20). The level of closeness in this human relationship is made possible by the God of relationships creating האדם in His image.

[57] To be human is to be in relationships—with God, with fellow humans (personal, community, society), and with the environment around—where the closeness possible in these relationships is related to how much the relationships honor and mirror God.

The closeness of the relationship between God and humans is remarkable and unique in this world.[58] A main reason for the unique closeness of this particular relationship is the fact that God did create humans in His image. They are certainly not divine, and do not possess any divine traits inherently. But God designed them to image Him and to be closer to Him than any other earthly creature ever could be.[59] Even His whole self is involved in designing and fashioning man and woman, and this offers a glimpse of the hope He must have had for an ongoing intimate relationship with them (2:7, 20-22).[60]

In addition to humans' relationship with God and with each other, God also calls humans into relationship with His whole creation. Adam and Eve's relationship with the animals was meant to be one of blessing: they were to rule the animals as benevolently as God did, to serve them, to preserve food for them, to respect their worth, and to not allow them to usurp their authority (1:20-25, 28-30; 3:4-6). The beautiful world that God created, with all its abundance,

---

[58] See John 17:21.

[59] God created humans with the capacity for this intimate relationship, and He commissioned them to rule the world He created, and to procreate in their own image. The Eden narrative records that God habitually speaks to and with His human creation (1:28-31; 2:16, 17; 3:8-19), an indication of their close relationship.

[60] God also gives humans every gift so that nothing is lacking for their enjoyment or fulfillment. Especially for them, He designed a perfect garden home (the first earthly sanctuary where His presence dwelt with humans), and He blessed them with a unique one-flesh partnership (2:8, 9, 21-25). For more on this first earthly sanctuary, see Richard M. Davidson, "Earth's First Sanctuary: Genesis 1-3 and Parallel Creation Accounts," *Andrews University Seminary Studies* 53/1 (2015): 65-89, for over forty lines of evidence pointing to the Garden of Eden's status as the first sanctuary on earth.

Even after the first humans' rebellion, God still treats His relationship with them with care, honor, and respect. He comes to them gently, allowing them to state their own case, offering them the hope of salvation before ever pronouncing judgment on them, not berating them but offering them fair judgments that were consistent with His original command, and setting up safeguards that would make possible an eventual return to perfection (Gen 3). Certainly in treating humans the unique way He did, God saw that humans were capable of an unprecedentedly close relationship with Him, made possible by their being created in His own image.

Adam and Eve (and humans today) are called to preserve and develop.[61] As humans today fulfill this calling, they should ever remember that they as האדם are intimately tied to the ground, etymologically and constitutionally—the ground from which all earthly creation is constituted.[62] In summary, humans are fit for, and called to, this relational task of rulership because they are created in the very image of God. Thus, they are also expected to demonstrate the same characteristics of rulership that God did during His creation of the world.

Humans image God—as His representatives and rulers on this earth, and in relationship with Him, each other, and the whole creation. In fact, it is because they are created in the image of God that they have the capacity to reflect His beautiful character, to be His representatives, and to sustain such spiritually, emotionally, and physically intimate relationships. In living the life that God created them for, humans in their small way resemble God. When imaging God, they are also the most human (in the sense of how God originally created human nature to be); and through the beauty of their character and witness, they point the world to the beauty of their Father and Creator.

Sonship and the *Imago Dei*[63]

This resembling God is similar to the way that children often resemble their parents, both in outward appearance and in inner characteristics.[64] Textual evidence for connecting the *imago Dei* with

---

[61] This includes both plants and animals (see Richard M. Davidson, "Earth's First Sanctuary," 70, 71).

[62] Such intimate relationship with the ground brings pain and death, but also growth and life. Through this, humans remember their own mortality and at the same time the life-giving blessings of God. And as they toil to serve and preserve the land with care (2:15; 3:17-19), it blesses them reciprocally with abundant harvest and beauty.

[63] Note: I use "sonship" because I was unable to find a gender-inclusive alternative. In using it, I mean both son and daughter, and do not wish to prefer or exclude one gender.

[64] After all, it is האדם of all creation that the Bible calls a son of God (Luke 3:38). Adoption and how it relates to sonship is a theme brought up in the New Testament, so it will not receive focus here. But certainly adoption is a theological topic that has seeds in the creation and sonship of האדם in Gen 1. "This [Ps 8:5's] 'glory' (כבוד) bestowed exclusively upon

the notion of sonship comes most clearly from the very next occurrence of "image" (צלם) after Gen 1:26 and 27. It is found in Gen 5:3: "When Adam had lived 130 years, he fathered a son in his own likeness, after his image, and named him Seth." This text directly connects image and likeness with sonship, as is only implied in the Gen 1 creation narrative.[65] For Adam was created "in the image of God, according to His likeness" (1:26), and now he fathers a son "in his own likeness, according to his image" (5:3).

This notion of sonship could be a helpful addition to an interpretation of the *imago Dei* because it is more all-encompassing than the traditional alternatives.[66] It avoids the compartmentalization of "outward" (physical likeness) and "inward" (rational mind, spiritual soul, etc.) characteristics, and fits with a unitary view of humans, a view that is faithful to the Eden narrative that identifies humans as "living creatures" (or "living beings") not "souls" in bodies. Unfortunately, "most commentators have anatomized the individual person into material and spiritual properties, thus identifying the *imago Dei* as either physical or spiritual. This dichotomy, however, is at odds with Hebrew anthropology [where] . . . a person is viewed as a unified whole."[67]

---

human life, is distinguished in the Old Testament as the attribute of the Lord God. It is creation's 'glory,' indicating mankind's appointment as the Lord's ruling sonship, that is diminished through sin. Humanity's future 'glory' will be fully gained as adopted heirs through Christ his Son, who will 'bring many sons to glory' (Heb 2:10)" (Matthews, *Genesis,* 168, 169).

[65] "Image" and "likeness" are used in connection with each other, both in Gen 1:26 and 5:3. The connection between these terms and "sonship" is obvious in 5:3, and is implied in God's fashioning of האדם in chapter one's narrative. However, the solid confirmation of this "sonship" link to the Gen 1 creation narrative is found in Luke 3:38.

[66] Van Genderen and Velema also concur that sonship is an important element of the *imago Dei*: "We are of the opinion that God's image implies the relationship between Father and child. We posit this because we are obliged to do so on the basis of Ephesians 4:24 and Colossians 3:10" (321).

[67] Matthews, *Genesis*, 167. As Gerhard von Rad explains in his commentary on Genesis, "One will do well to split the physical from the spiritual as little as possible: the whole man is created in God's image" (*Genesis: A Commentary*, trans. John H. Marks (Philadelphia, PA: Westminster, 1961], 58). Also Collins brings out that "Genesis 5:1 looks back to Genesis 1:26-27, but it says that God made man in the *likeness* of

Throughout the Bible, humans are described with a variety of different anthropological terms. As a whole, the biblical usage of anthropological terms is more explanatory of the various expressions of what it means to be human, than it is a partitioning of specific anthropological parts over and against each other. This first chapter of the Bible reinforces such a view by referring to man, man and woman, and humankind simply as האדם, a general term that includes every aspect of who and what humans are.

Everything that God gives humans to do in the Eden narrative is a function of האדם as a whole. Describing these functions of human nature—biological/physical, relational, emotional/psychological, mental, volitional, spiritual—is beneficial for the sake of analysis, to better understand the human unitary entity. But if the example given in the Eden narrative is to be taken seriously, such analysis should always view these functions of human nature as functions of the one single human substance or physical body. The idea of sonship, as an explanatory complement to the *imago Dei*, does enforce the oneness of the human person. For to be a son, one generally has both some inward and outward characteristics of the parent—and these characteristics make up a whole person, not one divided into parts.

But how does this image and sonship make humans unique? On a most basic level, it is self-evident that the use of the word "image" in *imago Dei* shows that God originally created humans with

---

God—suggesting, as noted above, that the two terms 'in the image' and 'after the likeness' refer to the same thing" (*Genesis*, ch. 4, C.6.).

Based on semantic evidence, some commentators do see "image" as referring to humans' "outward resemblance" to God ("physical/material domain"), and "likeness" as referring to an "inward resemblance" to God ("spiritual/functional domain"). See Doukhan, *Literary Structure*, 63. However, such differentiation between "image" and "likeness" does not divide human nature or favor one domain over the other, it simply reinforces the notion of human unity by recognizing that the aspects of human nature are together meant to resemble God. Moreover, the Bible's first usage of these terms seems to indicate that no great technical distinction is meant between them. For even though Gen 1:26 uses both the terms "image" and "likeness" when describing God's intention to make האדם, Gen 1:27 uses only "image" in its account of God's creation of האדם. For a brief history of the distinction that has been understood between "image" and "likeness," see Gordon R. Lewis and Bruce A. Demarest, *Integrative Theology* (Grand Rapids, MI: Zondervan, 1996), 2:125-26.

analogy, a similarity, a likeness, to Himself, and with the potential to resemble Him in some way. The same is the case with "sonship." It points not only to a special bond between parent and child, but also to a certain similarity between them.[68] Because humans are created in God's image and endowed with God's sonship, they are endowed with a capacity to be similar to God in a way that animals cannot be, especially for those persons who choose to love and follow God, thus reflecting His beauty to His world.[69]

Conclusion

We have already seen how humans are called to model themselves after the *Elohim* and *YHWH Elohim* dimensions of God by ruling creation with wisdom and care and by being joined into close relationship with God, each other, and the rest of creation. In fact, rulership and relationship (of the depth that is revealed in this narrative) are the two mandates given to Adam and Eve in the key passage that introduces their existence as humans created in the image of God (Gen 1:26-28). All humans, even after sin, and as a definition of being human, are still created in God's image and have the capacity and responsibility for rulership and relationship. But in order to fulfill their divine mandates in a manner that truly reflects God's purpose, they must image the beauty of God in every dimension of who they are as humans. This is faithful to a unitary view of human ontology and to the depiction of human creation in the Eden narrative.

So how can and how do humans image God and His beauty in every function of their human nature (biological/physical, relational, emotional/psychological, mental, volitional, and spiritual)? In humans' *biological/physical function*, we know that God is not

---

[68] In the New Testament, God's children, created in His image, become even more transformed into His image as they behold Him, and when He returns they will be like Him, for they will see Him as He is (2 Cor 3:12-18; 1 John 3:1-3).

[69] This is not to downplay the intelligence or relationship to God that animals can possess (see, for example, Num 22 or Ps 148). Some animals may sometimes even surpass some humans in these ways. However, because humans are created in the image of God, according to His likeness, they have the potential to be more like God than the rest of creation, provided they walk according to God's ways.

mortal or dependent upon alimentary provision as humans are.[70] Yet humans' biological/physical function is what makes possible their capacity for work, especially the highly physical work given to them in the Garden of Eden. In doing well the work God gave them to do, Adam and Eve could image God in serving and keeping the creation He had created. Even in the "painful labor" (עצב) of birth, humans can in a small way understand the connection between self-giving sacrifice and the joy of new life—a truth that the life of the woman's Seed emulated. In all of the God-given work that humans have to do, they are to reflect the way in which God worked—wisely, mightily, tenderly, strategically, sacrificially, and lovingly. In so doing, they can experience the beauty and blessing of work that God made an indispensable part of their human nature.

In regards to the *relational function* of human nature, we have already seen how the oneness and plurality inherent in the marriage relationship reflects in a small way the oneness and plurality that is found in the relationship of the Godhead. This capacity and desire for intimate relationships is something that identifies God and also something that marks humans as made in His image (Gen 1:26-28). Since human creation began with just two humans who were joined in a marital relationship, this first human-to-human relationship had a sexual function (2:24, 25; 1:27, 28). However, this relationship also exemplified the human capacity to be engaged in a myriad of other social and societal relationships once more people lived on earth. All of these relationships image God, to the extent that they honor His laws and mirror the beautiful way He operates in relationships (especially seen through the depiction of Him as *YHWH Elohim* in Gen 2 and 3).

Next, the *emotional/psychological function* of Adam and Eve's human nature was on display before the Fall (in joy, peace, love, and openness) and after the Fall (in shame, blame, guilt, fear, deception, and subjection). That God the Creator also experiences emotions and various psychological states is evident in Scripture, and is also seen

---

[70] This paragraph speaks of how humans can reflect God in the biological/physical functions of their human nature. On the level of constitution, however, there is most likely a limited physical resemblance between God and humans. See, for example, Davidson, "The Nature of the Human Being from the Beginning: Genesis 1-11," in "*What Are Human Beings that You Remember Them?,*" 17-19, 21, 22.

in the Eden narrative. Much of this was brought out in the section above which spoke of God as *YHWH Elohim*. But even with a cursory glance at Gen 1-3, it is evident that God feels and displays a variety of emotions—a few of them being nurture and satisfaction in Gen 1, kindness, tenderness, love, care, and fairness in Gen 2, and gentleness, patience, severity, love, sadness, care, fairness, and kindness in Gen 3.[71] While it is true that because of God's perfect nature He does not experience certain human emotions like shame, or does not demonstrate other ones like revengeful blame, this does not negate the fact that He has the capacity to feel positive and negative emotions, as shown in the Eden narrative.[72] It follows, then, that part of His creating humans in His image was creating them to be emotional/psychological creatures. This is part of the beauty of what it means to be God and what it means to be His human children.

Additionally, even though God has given animals *mental, volitional, and spiritual capabilities*, humans' expression of these functions is the most akin to God's expression of them, and in this way they image Him. Take, for example, that while some animals have intelligence (including emotional intelligence) that might rival that of humans, humans are able to express such intelligence through writing or in self-reflection, like God and unlike animals.[73] Or that while some individual animals within a species may exercise their volition differently from even their own siblings, humans are far more able to choose their unique course in life, even when it goes

---

[71] Some of the verses that show these: Gen 1:2; 2:7-9, 16-18; the majority of chapter 3, especially verses 9-15, 20, and 24. Also, every occurrence of "it was good" in Gen 1 shows God's feeling of satisfaction over His created work.

[72] Admittedly, these statements about the emotions of God do not fit in with the classical Christian notion of the impassibility of God. However, in the Eden narrative God is seen to be capable of operating in the realm of physicality. See footnotes 31 and 32. Once this is established, it is possible to recognize God as having the emotions that the Bible shows Him to have.

[73] There are a number of animal species that can rival or surpass humans in certain aspects of intelligence. See, for example, a study that shows that some chimpanzees have better numeric recall than humans: Sana Inoue and Tetsuro Matsuzawa, "Working Memory of Numerals in Chimpanzees," *Current Biology* 17/23 (December 4, 2007): R1004, R1005.

against their own instincts or the pressures of their community.[74] Or that while animals can trust and praise God, there is no evidence showing that they understand deeper spiritual realities like justification and sanctification, or can choose salvation in the way that humans can.[75]

Furthermore, in light of humans' natures being created with such a potential to image God, God gives humans mandates that He expects them to fulfill in a manner that reflects Him and the beauty of His character. Not only (like animals) are humans to be fruitful, but they (unlike animals) are to teach their offspring to be image-bearers of God. Not only are humans to rule over the fish and the birds and the creeping things (1:28), but over the בהמה and over "all the earth" as well (1:26).[76] In this rulership, they are to reflect God's wise, compassionate, and salvific rulership, as exemplified in the Eden narrative, and thus image Him. Their ruling (1:26, 28—רדה) and subduing (1:28—כבש) must never be separated from the context of their serving (2:5, 15—עבד) and keeping (2:15—שמר) the entire estate with which God had entrusted them.[77] Such rulership, modeled by God, is intrinsically tied to a high capacity for relationships; and both the mandate for rulership and for human multiplication entail the harmonious development of every function of human nature in order to be most effective. In this, humans reflect the image, glory, and beauty of God to the world.

This is what gives humans their identity and makes them unique—this capability to be like God in every function of their human nature, this capability to represent Him and His beautiful character as His vice-regents and in relationship, and this capability to image Him in a way that no other creature can, for האדם alone are His children created in His image. The Eden narrative masterfully

---

[74] See Exod 21:29 about oxen that are "in the habit of," "tend to," or "are given to" goring humans, and the consequent price they pay.

[75] See, for example, Pss 104:27, 28; 148:7; 150:6 and Num 22:28-33. Again, for more on animals' relationship to God in the Old Testament, see Schafer, "You, YHWH, Save Humans and Animals."

[76] See footnote 10.

[77] God called His human image-bearers to the noble task of "shaping the creation into a higher order of beauty and usefulness" (Dan B. Allender and Tremper Longman, III, *Intimate Allies: Rediscovering God's Design for Marriage and Becoming Soul Mates for Life* [Wheaton, IL: Tyndale, 1995], 80).

reveals the beauty of what God is like so that we might be able to understand how His image is manifested.

In Gen 1-3, God is named as *Elohim* and *YHWH Elohim*, and we saw how characteristics of both those names are found in humans who image God and the beauty of His character. We also explored the notion of sonship and saw how human beings created as God's children relate to being created in His beautiful image, and how this enables them to fulfill their mandates of ruling and relating after His example. Most importantly, we saw how in order to comprehend the *imago Dei*, we must not look so much into ourselves, but outward, at the beauty of God as revealed in His Word. By doing so, we will better understand the original upon whose image we were created, and we will grow to reflect the beauty of His character ever more brightly "unto the perfect day" (Prov 4:18).

Glimpses of the Old Testament God: Vulnerability and Commitment

Daniela Gelbrich

Abstract

The article is about God and how he reveals himself in the Hebrew Bible. It focuses on his vulnerability and commitment towards human beings. The authors of the Hebrew Bible depict God as vulnerable because he is not afraid of being questioned by humanity and does not evade the possibility of being hurt by his creatures who have the freedom to abandon and reject him. In addition, he stays true to his commitment towards human beings, who finally abandon and reject him, by promising not to let go of them without ever imposing himself or forcing humans to stay. In fact, Israel is his covenant partner and is supposed to live in a relationship with him based on true mutual love and respect. Israel does not remain true to their commitment in that relationship, but God does, not leaving them to themselves but wooing them patiently and with tact all along the way. Relationships are complex in a broken world. The God of the Hebrew Bible remains committed to broken human beings despite the irrationalities of that broken world.

Introduction

While I have not had the privilege of personally working with Jo Ann Davidson, I have felt her deep passion for the Scriptures and God when I heard her share her thoughts on the use of the Hebrew root עָבַד ("serve") in the Jacob narrative at a meeting of the SDAIBC authors in Israel, on the shore of Lake Gethsemane. I would like to share some glimpses of the God of the Scriptures in honor of Jo Ann Davidson. These glimpses do not pretend to be exhaustive.

We live in a complex world. Life is challenging and we have to cope with brokenness and an ambivalent world every day of our lives. The God of the Scriptures has spoken to the hearts of human beings throughout the course of human history. To spark a little flame of hope amid the complexities of life in a world that is in constant search of meaning and identity, I would like to share two characteristics of Yahweh, the covenant God of the Hebrew Scriptures, namely vulnerability and commitment.

God is Vulnerable

According to one dictionary, vulnerability is the "openness to attack and hurt, either physically or in other ways," the "willingness to show emotion or to allow one's weakness to be seen or known," as well as the "willingness to risk being hurt or attacked." [1]

The library of the Hebrew Bible portrays a God who is willing to run the risk of being questioned, attacked, and thus wounded, in order to guarantee real freedom and true love in the universe. In fact, he takes the initiative and reveals himself to broken humanity, sharing his innermost thoughts, and letting his covenant partner (and finally the whole world) know what he feels in his heart. In other words, he makes himself vulnerable. The biblical authors paint God as a complex and profound being who is love.[2] Human history begins with God creating man and woman in his own image (Gen 1:27), giving them space to reign over the earth with wisdom and care (Gen 1:28).

The Hebrew Scriptures paint the picture of a vulnerable God. In fact, they emphasize his vulnerability right from the start. The Creator-

---

[1] Cf. all three aspects in the definition of "vulnerability" at www.dictionary.com (accessed June 18, 2022).

In today's cultural moment, being vulnerable is a popular topic of conversation. Brené Brown's TED-Talk entitled "The Power of Vulnerability" has been viewed over 53 million times to date. Reality proves again and again that it is not easy to be vulnerable and open to others in the face of an ambivalent world where evil wreaks havoc on all sides. The fear of being exposed to injury, scorn or rejection often wins out over the desire to be vulnerable. Human beings tend to put up their defenses and barricade themselves behind an invisible wall intended to protect them from the attacks and hurt perpetrated and caused by others. This can be understood in the face of the panoply of emotional wounds, and passive-aggressive violence, which are an integral part of our human reality. Cf. René Brown's TED-Talk on YouTube, https://www.youtube.com/ watch?v=X4Qm9cGRub0 (September 2, 2022).

[2] The New Testament authors explicitly state and underline that "God is love" (1 John 4:16b). He is not only loving but love. He epitomizes love. True love presupposes the idea of freedom. True love cannot be forced. It is interesting to note that the Old Testament already portrays God as a God of love. The prophets, for example, speak of the love relationship between God and Israel. God is Israel's loving and dedicated husband (cf. Hos 2; Jer 2:2; 31:3). In fact, the covenant relationship between God and Israel is based on mutual love (cf. Deut 6:4-5). God is also depicted as a loving father (cf. Hos 11:1-4; Is 63:16).

God chooses to be vulnerable to the human family he creates in his own image. The beginning of the Scriptures, and thus of the Hebrew Bible, sets the tone and the rhythm. However, before underlining God's vulnerability, the text speaks of a God who reveals himself through creation and considers every human being created in his image as unique.[3] In view of the uniqueness of every human being, it is unthinkable to consider human beings without freedom or free will. God endows them with the freedom of choice. God is free. Human beings, created in his image, are free. The biblical text asserts that human beings are even free to say "no" to God and his initial plan for humankind. God addresses himself to the first human beings in direct speech (Gen 1:28-30), which presumes the idea of dialogue. Man and woman are seen as valuable and appreciated partners of God who have the freedom to say "no" to the destiny proposed to them by God. True love rests on the foundation of true freedom, and true freedom includes the idea of risk, i.e., the risk of being rejected.

Genesis 2 states that God creates humans from the dust. In addition, God shares his life-giving breath with them. Woman is created by God as an equal partner of man.[4] Both of them are granted the freedom of

---

[3] Jacques B. Doukhan, *Hebrew for Theologians. A Textbook for the Study of Biblical Hebrew in Relation to Hebrew Thinking* (Lanham, MD: University Press of America, 1993), 209. Doukhan point outs: "God being conceived as unique (Deut 6:4), man who was designed to reflect Him was to be unique also. [. . .] This principle of individuality is particularly vivid in Hebrew psychology. The uniqueness of the human person makes him or her impossible to remain locked in a definitive category. Man is always free to be different and can say 'no' even to God (Gen 3:6; Gen 18:25; 1 Sam 15:11)." Doukhan mentions Bernard-Henri Lévy, *Le Testament de Dieu* (Paris: Grasset, 1979), 75-92. Lévy thinks that Israel is the only culture so far to have brought to life the concept of individuality.

[4] Man and woman, created in the image of God, are to reign over the earth (Gen 1:28). The Hebrew text relates the creation of man and woman in equal ways, utilizing about the same amount of space (words) for the creation of man and woman. Woman is to be a עֵזֶר (helper, NKJV) for man. Later, this Hebrew term is used for God who graciously intervenes to save someone in great need (cf. Gen 49:25; 1 Sam 7:12; Pss 10:14; 30:11). Furthermore, woman is a עֵזֶר כְּנֶגְדּוֹ ("a helper comparable to him," NKJV), underlining the idea of a worthy partner who is equal. Rashi comments on this choice of words by pointing out another possible translation of כְּנֶגְדּוֹ: "against him" ("Une aide qui soit face à lui. Si l'homme a du mérite, elle lui sera une aide. S'il n'en a pas, elle sera contre lui et le combattra") (Genesis Rabbah 17, 3.) Interpreted

moral choice, the freedom to eat from the tree of life and all the other good trees of Eden or the only forbidden tree in the garden (cf. Gen 2:8-9, 16-17). Put differently, they are free to question their Creator, and his love and integrity, by choosing to eat the forbidden fruit. Man and woman are free to reject his friendship. Love cannot be forced. It is a gift born of freedom, and it implies trust. The concept of free will seems to be so precious to God that he is willing to run the risk of being wounded and ultimately betrayed and abandoned by his creatures. He thus reveals himself as vulnerable, and the freedom offered to humanity bears witness to this vulnerability. Human beings have the freedom to ask questions about the integrity or intention of the Creator. The fear of being abandoned or rejected does not paralyze his love or actions. To summarize, the opening pages of the Hebrew Bible speak of a God who chooses to be vulnerable, who is willing to allow himself to be questioned, in the name of love and freedom.

The serpent is the first agent rooted in the biblical text who questions God's integrity. It doubts God's goodness and worthiness, portraying him as a restrictive, lying, self-centered and power-hungry God (Gen 3:1-5). The first humans place their trust in its charming discourse and distance themselves from their Creator by making a moral choice that will prove to be fatal. They eat the forbidden fruit, choosing to distrust their Creator and question his integrity. The consequences are sobering. They are naked and filled with fear (Gen 3:6-8). The reaction of the Creator-God who chooses to be vulnerable is surprising. Instead of bursting into rage because he has been questioned, sharply criticized, and wounded, the Creator-God goes in search of the first human family. He does not reproach them, treat them badly, or kill them because they have dared question him. He instead poses four open-ended questions to enter into dialogue with the man and woman who have just rejected him. He asks: "Where are you? Who told you that you were naked? Did you eat from the tree? Why did you do that?" (Gen 3:9-13). He invites them to grow aware of their acts and attitude.

God's vulnerability is real. He feels the wounds inflicted on him by humanity, the covenant partner he loves. These wounds are real. He

---

positively, "against him" would mean that woman is meant to be a worthy partner who reflects on life to challenge him with thoughts of her own, to make him grow by debating and exchanging ideas, by seeing things differently, complementing and enriching human existence.

faces them bravely and vulnerably and reacts admirably. Flying into a rage is no option in his eyes. He continues to respect the dignity and free choice of his interlocutors, while tactfully and delicately seizing the opportunity to communicate with them and make them think about their decision. The image that humans now have of God is distorted. They are afraid of God–one of the dysfunctions pertaining to human brokenness. In fact, they are afraid of God though the text considers him to be profoundly generous and loving. They begin to avoid God, though he regards human beings as true partners worthy of royalty. In fact, this God had just shared his royal dignity freely with them, giving them space and freedom. In summary, the Creator-God is wounded but remains calm in face of criticism and distrust. The text describes him as sensitively proactive, trying to reason with them while remaining deeply respectful of their choice.

The prophets follow this line of thought by highlighting the vulnerability of Yahweh, the God of the covenant. Yahweh is represented as a husband who is betrayed, abandoned, and deeply wounded by his covenant partner, Israel, with whom Yahweh lives in an exclusive and unique covenant relationship.[5] Despite the risks of freedom, Yahweh chooses to be vulnerable and opens himself to his covenant partner, so that the latter can understand his love for her.[6] But Israel continues to reject him and turn to other gods. The prophets give us a glimpse of a God who weeps, who is moved, and who is not afraid of being vulnerable.[7] He is wounded by rejection and unfaithfulness while remaining deeply concerned about his covenant partner, torn between his unfailing love for Israel and the pain provoked by Israel's

---

[5] Cf., e.g., the book of Hosea, which depicts Yahweh as a betrayed husband who cares deeply about his unfaithful wife but struggles with her callousness. He is torn between his desire to repudiate her (Hos 2:1-5) and his desire to stay based on his hope for her return (Hos 2:19-23).

[6] Abraham J. Heschel, *The Prophets*: *An Introduction* (New York, NY: Harper Torchbooks, 1962), 47. Heschel argues: "It is Hosea who flashes a glimpse into the inner life of God as he ponders His relationship with Israel. In parables and in lyrical outbursts the decisive motive behind God's strategy in history is declared. The decisive motive is love."

[7] See, e.g., Hos 11:8: "How can I give you up, Ephraim? How can I hand you over, Israel? [. . .] My heart churns within Me; My sympathy is stirred." Cf. also Jer 4:19 that describes the reaction of Yahweh's prophet, sharing Yahweh's heart.

rejection and neglect that seem to speak in favor of a painful separation.[8]

The vulnerable God of the Bible continues to see the face of broken human beings, respecting them deeply even if his integrity is questioned and he is rejected. Yahweh is considerate of the other.[9] He sees the face of the other as it is and clears a path to show humanity that his own face is not the one presented by the serpent. Because of the intrusion of evil, that respect for the vulnerability of the other is paramount. The God of the Bible is there for humans,[10] for every individual, taking a sincere interest in the biography of every representative of the human family.[11] God sees the face of the other and wants to promote life and not death. In fact, he declares "Thou shalt not kill."[12]

---

[8] Abraham J. Heschel, *The Prophets*, 44. Heschel underlines the tension between anger and compassion. Speaking of the prophets Amos and Hosea, Heschel points out: "Amos had proclaimed the righteousness of God, His iron will to let justice prevail. Hosea came to spell out the astonishing fact of God's love for man. God is not only the Lord who demands justice. He is also a God Who is in love with His people. [. . .] In the face of God's passionate love, the prophet is haunted by the scandal of Israel's desertion."

[9] Cf. Emmanuel Levinas, *Entre nous, Essais sur le penser-à-l'autre* (Paris: Grasset, 1991), 46. The philosopher thinks a lot about the other, promoting a move toward "being-open-to-the-other." He underlines that the face of the other "is the very identity of a being." God meets human beings at eye level. He takes them seriously, "being-for-the-other" without ever losing his identity. Cf. Terry A. Veling, *For You Alone: Emmanuel Levinas and the Answerable Life* (Eugene, OR: Cascade Books), 22-23.

[10] Every human being is unique in space and time and has a unique place in human existence. Cf. Jacques B. Doukhan, *Hebrew for Theologians*, 210; Terry A. Veling, *For You Alone*, 131.

[11] Terry A. Veling, *For You Alone,* xv. Veling refers to the parallels between the dedication of God to humanity and human dedication to the other. He states: "For Emmanuel Levinas, *Here I am* is 'a marvelous accusative: here I am under your gaze, obliged to you, your servant. In the name of God' (*GCM*, 75)."

[12] Emmanuel Levinas, *Ethique et Infini* (Paris: Fayard, 1984), 81. Cf. Jacques B. Doukhan, *Hebrew for Theologians*, 210. He notes that "killing a man means the destruction of what is unique in space and time–a kind of deicide. Thus killing stands as the contrary of love: as much as love is the affirmation of the difference, murder is its negation." The New Testament explains that the act of killing commences far before the act of taking

The vulnerable God and his reaction to the other who questions and wounds him by rejection or neglect can inspire us in the 21st century. We must live our lives and our relationships with others in a world that is broken. Being vulnerable to the other includes a risk. God took that risk. His conduct toward those who wounded him can serve as an example to us, and reassure us that God gives himself to us by revealing himself as vulnerable without ever losing his dignity or identity. His reaction to betrayal is an act of freedom and love that does not minimize the atrocity of evil. God will never be an accomplice to evil. Part of human maturity is also seeking dialogue, understanding the other's behavior, seeing his or her vulnerable face, and choosing love, all without losing our dignity or identity as human beings, and without glossing over evil. In the face of continual destructive abuse, we must set healthy and clear limits. But being vulnerable remains a goal to be achieved, especially because we know that every human being is broken, searching for meaning and identity in an absurd world.

Faced with the vulnerability of Yahweh and the Scriptures, which present a panoply of literary genres through which God makes himself known, and where God exposes himself to the risk of misunderstanding and rejection, human beings in an ambivalent world are invited to be inspired by God's vulnerability. In the absurdity of a broken world, every human being is invited to understand their constant fragility, their inevitable vulnerability, and the fact that they are exposed to criticism by others who have the painful freedom to question them. God has the inner greatness to allow himself to be questioned and distorted by humanity; he is vulnerable and does not use force to impose himself, all the while retaining his dignity and identity despite all the attacks on his person. He affirms his dignity while being vulnerable. His vulnerability does not erase his dignity.

The Scriptures invite broken humans to face their vulnerability while retaining and affirming their unequaled dignity as human beings. No physical or moral injury, no adversity or wounding, can erase human dignity. It is above all human categorizations. The God of the Scriptures reveals himself as vulnerable, incurring the risk of being distorted by the reader, but he retains his dignity and freedom to speak to human hearts despite all opposition. It is freedom and dignity to see

---

somebody's physical life (cf. Matt 5:21-24). Cf. Terry A. Veling, *For You Alone,* 29, who states that "Love is originary. The Good is primary. Life is on the side of love on the side of goodness."

the face of the other, the one who hurts, and to be aware of one's own dignity that goes beyond any human categorization. Human dignity and identity are anchored in the fact that every human being is created in the image of God. This vulnerable yet all-powerful God possesses a dignity that humanity cannot erase or destroy. God invites us to grow towards an intelligent maturity centered on the awareness of one's own vulnerability as broken human beings grappling with a broken world.

God Exhibits Commitment

Commitment and constancy[13] seem to be difficult in 21st century interpersonal relationships. Individualism and autonomy are highly praised. Relationships are often conflictual. For instance, the divorce rate in the US alone shows that people struggle to remain committed to their spouses. The Hebrew Scriptures paint the picture of a dedicated and deeply committed God who walks patiently with his covenant partner Israel and with all broken humanity. Despite human brokenness and weakness, God remains sincerely committed to the human family, who is in the grip of evil since the Fall.[14] The reality in which broken human beings exist is marked by ambivalence and the blurred philosophy of their self-chosen confidant, the serpent (Gen 3:1). Self-centeredness, hatred, violence, pride, invisible walls between human beings, and masks that must be worn to hide pain and weakness, whether physical or emotional, constitute an integral part of human existence.

Human beings are broken and torn between their deepest aspirations rooted in a world that God says is "very good," and the ambivalent reality in which they live. They long for justice but must face injustice. They yearn for true love, but are confronted with selfishness and the complexities pertaining to the dynamics of interpersonal relationships in a world that is struggling. They long for authentic and deep relationships but find themselves in difficult and often dysfunctional ones. And the virus of evil takes its toll. Paul

---

[13] In today's cultural moment, individualism seems to be sacrosanct. Our generation has a hard time committing to someone or something. Sacrificing one's autonomy for someone or something often sparks fear and people tend to refrain from it. They prefer to avoid it, i.e., to avoid the risk of real intimacy and commitment to another human being.

[14] Genesis 3 expounds upon the loss of Eden, humanity's initial residence, and the reality of exile, humanity's loss of innocence and undisturbed communion with God.

provides a very sobering description of the human situation by quoting thoughts from the Hebrew Bible:

> There is none righteous, no, not one; There is none who understands; There is none who seeks after God. They have all turned aside; They have together become unprofitable; There is not one who does good, no, not one. [. . .] Their feet as swift to shed blood; Destruction and misery are in their ways; And the way of peace they have not known; There is no fear of God before their eyes (Romans 3:10f.).

According to the biblical perspective, human beings are unable to save themselves, to alter the heartbreaking situation in which they find themselves trapped. The human family needs a Savior who is outside their dilemma and desirous of maintaining his friendship and covenant with human beings created in his image. Because of evil in the human heart, the image of God has been deformed and disfigured. The biblical text emphasizes that God aims to restore this broken image in human beings by saving them, caring for each individual human being, being sincerely interested in each human biography, and doing all in his power to restore his life-giving relationship with them. The God of the Hebrew Scriptures knows the complexity of broken human nature and finds a way to heal it. He is committed to the human cause, devoted, attached, loyal, and faithful.

God's relationship to humanity and Israel "is most commonly described as a covenant. The word 'covenant' conveys . . . permanence, steadfastness, and mutuality."[15] The God of the Hebrew Scriptures longs for reunion with wayward human beings created to live in a covenantal relationship with him. The biblical covenant between God and human beings who accept it is unique in human history.[16] Genesis

---

[15] Abraham J. Heschel, *The Prophets,* 50.

[16] The Hebrew noun בְּרִית is so far only attested in Hebrew. Cf. Gordon J. McConville, "בְּרִית", *New International Dictionary of Old Testament Theology and Exegesis,* ed. Willem A. VanGemeren (Grand Rapids, MI: Zondervan, 1997), 1:747. In order to explain the meaning of בְּרִית, McConville points to Akkadian: (1) the noun *biritu* (clasp, fetter), (2) the preposition *birit* (between), (3) a postulated verb *brh* II and its connection to the Akkadian *barû* (select for a task), and (4) the Hebrew root *brr* (something specially set apart). It is well-known that the biblical texts speaking of the covenant between God and Israel/humanity employ the six elements that are typical of the ANE. In particular, the Hittite vassal-treaty dating from the second millennium B.C.

15 can be regarded as one of the foundational chapters regarding the covenant. Inviting humanity into a covenant that God gives as a gift to them implies God's willingness to commit to broken humanity, whom he still considers to be a worthy covenant partner. God takes the initiative and calls Abram into a special and exclusive relationship with himself. Genesis 1-11 portrays the dilemmas and devolution of broken humanity in an ambivalent and complex world. Due to the Fall (Gen 3), humanity is severed from direct communion with God and fragmented (cf. Gen 11). The cohesion of the human family is therefore at risk.

In addition, since the Fall, evil has disrupted human flourishing. The call of Abram seems to be God's way of putting the world into order again, i.e., of restoring the losses humanity has experienced due to their deviation from loyalty to God.[17] Abram is invited to leave his country, his family, and his father's house, and to direct his steps towards a land that God will show him (Gen 12:1). The covenant is designed to restore broken relationships[18] and to maintain and continue the Adamic covenant in a world shattered by evil.

The book of Genesis relates seven encounters[19] between Yahweh, the covenantal God, and Abram (Abraham). God always takes the

---

with its six elements (titulary, historical prologue, stipulations, document clause, god list, blessings and curses) has strong parallels with that of Deuteronomy.

[17] E. A. Speiser, *Genesis*: *A New Translation with Introduction and Commentary*, The Anchor Bible Commentary (New York, NY: Doubleday, 1964), 1:115. Speiser writes: "This time, however, we are witnessing a covenant between the Creator of the universe and the ancestor of a nation ordained in advance to be a tool for shaping the history of the world."

[18] In the biblical perspective, God and human beings are deeply relational. God lives in community (cf. Gen 1:26; 11:7; Deut 6:4; Isa 6:8). Isaiah portrays a "communal God;" the Son given to humanity (Isa 9:6), the Spirit (Isa 63:10, 11, 14), and the Father (Isa 63:15, 16; 64:1), all of them working for the good of Israel/the human family. Human beings were also created to live in community. Due to the Fall, the relational concept designed by God was shattered to pieces. The vertical bond between humankind and God was broken, as well as the horizontal bond between man and woman or between human beings. The relationship to oneself was also damaged (shame, nakedness, guilt, the quest for identity, disordered love, and the disrupting reality of sin in one's life). Even the relationship of human beings to creation was broken (cf. thorns and thistles in Gen 3:18; with animals in Gen 9:2).

[19] (1) Gen 12:1-3 (לֶךְ־לְךָ), (2) Gen 12:7, (3) Gen 13:14, (4) Gen 15, (5) Gen 17, (6) Gen 18, (7) Gen 22 (לֶךְ־לְךָ).

initiative to meet Abram (Abraham). The first and last of these seven encounters is marked by the expression לֶךְ־לְךָ, commonly translated as "Get out." [20] In between these seven encounters, the biblical text describes the faux pas of Abram. After the second encounter, Abram goes down to Egypt to escape a famine in the land and pretends to be Sarai's sister instead of admitting to being her husband (Gen 12:10-20).[21] After the fourth encounter, Abram listens to the voice of Sarai, his wife, and takes Hagar, his wife's Egyptian servant, who finally gives birth to a son (Gen 16).

Despite these shady episodes in Abraham's life, Yahweh remains committed to Abraham. Genesis 15, within the context of the fourth encounter between Yahweh and Abram, portrays Yahweh as Abram's protector or shield.[22] The second part of chapter 15 describes the rather unsettling rite of an ANE covenant conclusion. It portrays Yahweh passing through the pieces of slain animals, expressing the idea that Yahweh assumes full responsibility for the covenant.[23] Passing through

---

[20] Cf. *The Brown-Driver-Briggs Hebrew and English Lexicon*, eds. F. Brown, S. Driver, C. Briggs (Peabody, MA: Hendrickson, 1994), 231.The Hebrew expression לֶךְ־לְךָ commonly translated as "Get out" ("Va-t'en," "quitte" in French) has been discussed from time to time. In the wake of Rashi, Jewish tradition understands this expression to mean "Go for yourself," i.e., for your good, for your happiness. Cf. Marie Balmary, *Le sacrifice interdit* (Paris: Grasset, 1986), 123, who translates לֶךְ־לְךָ with "Va vers toi" ("Go to yourself"), "adviens qui tu es" ("Become who you are," "Come to be who you are"). Cf. Danielle Ellul, *Apprendre l'hébreu biblique par les textes* (Paris: Les éditions du cerf, 2003), 84.

[21] This strategy will be repeated by Abraham. Cf. Genesis 20:1f.

[22] Tremper Longman, "מָגֵן," *New International Dictionary of Old Testament Theology and Exegesis*, 2:846-847. The term could relate to the Ugaritic word meaning "suzerain" (847). The idea of "suzerain" behind the Hebrew noun מָגֵן would underline the concept of covenant expounded in Gen 15.

[23] Frédéric Godet, ed., *La Bible annotée, A.T. 1 Genèse et Exode* (St-Légier: Librairie-Editions Emmaüs, 1985), 216. "Cette flamme et cette fumée font penser à la colonne de nuée dans laquelle l'Eternel se manifestait aux Israélites dans le désert [. . .] Remarquons que l'Eternel seul passe entre les animaux partagés. C'est lui qui prend l'engagement." The author identifies God as the one passing between the animal pieces, referring to the fact that the smoking oven and the burning torch allude to the pillar of cloud directing Israel in the wilderness. Cf. John Skinner, *Genesis, The International Critical Commentary*, eds. S. R. Driver, A. Plummer, C. A. Briggs (Edinburgh: T and T

the pieces signified that he would be slain to pieces in case the covenant between him and Abram was broken by him or Abram. It is interesting to note that the text does not state if Abram had to pass between the pieces. The text leaves the question open.

Yahweh commits to Abram. In other words, Yahweh pledges to stay faithful to this covenant at any cost to himself, even if his partner would break and trample upon it.[24] The biblical covenant relationship goes beyond our current idea regarding relationships. It implies intelligent and willing commitment to the covenant even if the other party breaks it. It is based on true love that clearly sees what may go wrong but is willing to stay, hoping that the offending partner becomes aware of their trespass and sincerely repents so that covenantal life may again flourish.

Later in biblical history, Yahweh reveals himself on Mount Sinai, giving his covenant to Israel. Yahweh unequivocally rehearses his willingness to commit to his covenant partner whom he loves sincerely and deeply.[25] There are several Hebrew roots that show Yahweh's unfaltering devotion and unflinching commitment to Israel, his

---

Clark, 1980), 283. "A fate similar of that to the victim is invoked on the violators of the covenant." Cf. also Richard Davidson ("Isaiah 53, Substitution, and the Covenant Curses—Part 2," *New England Pastor* [January/February 2010]: 12-13) on Isa 53 and Gen 15, who draws the same conclusion.

[24] Genesis 15:7-21 repeatedly mentions the idea of "darkness" (v. 12, "a great darkness," v. 17 "when the sun went down, and it was dark"). The New Testament describes the death of Jesus using the concept of darkness (cf. Matt 27:45, "from the sixth hour there was darkness all over the land unto the ninth hour;" cf. Mark 15:33 and Luke 23:44). In fact, the Son of God is slain, hanging on a cross, finally faring the fate of the animals slain to pieces. He did not break the covenant, but his partner (Israel/humanity) did. Nevertheless, he takes responsibility for it.

[25] Cf., e.g., Ex 19:4; Deut 7:7-8; Isa 43:4; 49:15; 54:7-8, 10; Jer 31:3. The figures of speech used to signify what God does for Israel accentuate his love for Israel. He bears Israel on eagles' wings. He brings Israel to himself (Ex 19:4). He finds Israel in a desert. He encircles him. He instructs him. He keeps him as the apple of his eye. He leads him like an eagle that stirs up its nest and hovers over its young, "spreading out its wings, taking them up, carrying them on its wings" (Deut 32:10-11). He teaches Ephraim to walk, taking them by their arms. He draws them with gentle cords, "with bands of love" (Hos 11:3-4, NKJV). He carries Israel through the wilderness, "as a man carries his son" (Deut 1:31). He spreads his wing over Israel and covers their nakedness (Ezek 16:8). He loves Israel with an everlasting love (Jer 31:3).

covenant partner. Two of them will be highlighted here. The first is found in the following statements:

> For the Lord your God is a merciful God, He will not forsake you (לֹא יַרְפְּךָ) nor destroy you, nor forget the covenant of your fathers which he swore to you (Deut 4:31, NKJV).

> Be strong and of good courage, do not fear nor be afraid of them; for the Lord your God, He is the One who goes with you. He will not leave you (לֹא יַרְפְּךָ) nor forsake you (Deut 31:6, cf. v. 8, NKJV).

> I will not leave you (לֹא יַרְפְּךָ) or forsake you (Josh 1:5, NKJV).

The *hifil* of the Hebrew root רָפָה is sometimes used in conjunction with hands, signifying the idea of letting one's hands fall, i.e., meaning "abandon."[26] Israel, Yahweh's covenant partner, is assured that Yahweh will not abandon them. Yahweh will not let go of Israel's hand. Yahweh is committed to Israel at whatever cost to himself. "The assurance of Yahweh's unfailing protective presence" is underlined by the expression לֹא יַרְפְּךָ and "constitutes the basis for an appeal to both the nation [. . .] and individuals [. . .] to be strong and courageous."[27] Yahweh will not fail his covenant partner. However, the biblical story shows that Israel fails Yahweh.

The prophets are shocked by Israel's unfaithfulness and ungratefulness towards Yahweh, their covenant partner. Israel is "a sinful nation, a people laden with iniquity" (Isa 1:4). They abandon Yahweh and deal treacherously with him, turning to other partners that seem more attractive to them. They commit adultery, abandoning Yahweh. "In the face of God's passionate love, the prophet is haunted by the scandal of Israel's desertion."[28] "Israel has forgotten his maker" (Hos 8:14). Yahweh is depicted as an abandoned and betrayed husband, wounded and hurting, longing for reunion and relational restoration with Israel, which means Israel must be willing to return to him. Because of his commitment based on true love, he remains faithful at

---

[26] K. M. Beyse, "רָפָה," *Theological Dictionary of the Old Testament*, 13:615. "In most cases the subject or object is a hand [. . .]; in this usage the expression is metaphorical."

[27] Robin Wakely, "רָפָה," *New International Dictionary of Old Testament Theology and Exegesis*, 3:1182.

[28] Abraham J. Heschel, *The Prophets,* 44.

whatever cost to himself. However, his love is not blind. He knows Israel. His love is rooted in himself because he is love and love is patient. He is "Yahweh, Yahweh, God, merciful and gracious, longsuffering and abounding in goodness and truth, keeping mercy for thousands, forgiving iniquity and transgression and sin, by no means clearing the guilty" (Exod 34:6-7).

God has a name: Yahweh.[29] André Lacocque considers it to be the "Revelation of Revelations,"[30] revealed to Moses in Midian (Exod 3) and on Mount Sinai (Exod 34). Yahweh is the God of the covenant, present and committed, doing what he says, liberating Israel from Egypt, bringing them into a relationship of love and freedom, and leading them finally into the true worship that is the essence of human flourishing. However, Israel is not faithful to their covenant with Yahweh and quick to worship other gods than Yahweh.[31]

In face of Israel's unfaithfulness and treachery, Yahweh "vacillates between compassionate lament and bitter accusation. [... This] testifies to the fact that God is wrestling with himself."[32] "Yahweh is 'emotional,' changing, affected. He repents (Gensis 6:6f.; Exodus 32:14; 1 Samuel 15:11, 35; Amos 7:3; etc.), and he laments (in Jeremiah 8:5, for instance, we read, 'Why then has this people turned

---

[29] The name Yahweh appears 6,823 times in the Hebrew Bible. Yahweh is God's name, a personal name implying a person with thoughts and feelings. Cf. André Lacocque, "The Revelation of Revelations," in *Thinking Biblically: Exegetical and Hermeneutical Studies*, eds André Lacocque and Paul Ricoeur, trans. David Pellauer (Chicago, IL: University of Chicago Press, 1998), 307. It is interesting to note that, statistically speaking, the occurrences of Yahweh (translated as "the Lord") increase steadily compared to the occurrences of Elohim (God), especially from Exodus onwards (see Helmuth Egelkraut, *Das Alte Testament: Entstehung, Geschichte, Botschaft*, 5th Edition [Gießen: Brunnen Verlag, 2012], 99, who notes that from Gen 1:1 to Exod 3:15 Elohim occurs 178 times and Yahweh 146 times, whereas from Exod 3:16 to the end of Pentateuch, Elohim occurs 44 times and Yahweh 393 times).

[30] André Lacocque, "The Revelation of Revelations," 307-329.

[31] After a couple of days without Moses (Israel's spiritual leader), Israel erects a molten image declared to be the god who brought Israel out of Egypt (Exod 32). This happened in spite of the fact that Israel had just declared: "All that Yahweh has spoken we will do!" (Exod 19:8).

[32] Hans Walter Wolff, *Hosea* (Neukrichen-Vluyn: Neukirchener Verlag, 1967), 151, as quoted by André Lacocque, "The Revelation of Revelations," 325.

away in perpetual backsliding?' cf. 12:7-13; 15:5-9; 18:13-17)."[33] However, he remains true to himself, reassuring Israel that he won't let them down (לֹא יַרְפְּךָ). "God's heart is not of stone."[34] Israel is invited to return to him, repenting and deeply aware of their trespasses, quitting their follies and returning to love Yahweh with all their heart, soul, and strength (cf. Deut 6:5).

However, if Israel wants to sever their ties with Yahweh, they are free to do so. Confronted with the prospect of such a painful separation, Yahweh is deeply stirred and moved. Love is painful if it is not reciprocal: "How can I give you up Ephraim? How can I hand you over Israel? . . . . My heart churns within Me, My sympathy is stirred" (Hos 11:8, NKJV). Despite the eventuality of unrequited love, Yahweh promises, לֹא יַרְפְּךָ, "I will not abandon you. I commit to you at any cost to myself, even if you abandon me." Yahweh is a God of commitment. The risk of being abandoned by his covenant partner Israel does not paralyze his love or actions toward Israel/humanity.

Another term regarding the biblical covenant is the Hebrew root גָּעַל. Michael A. Grisanti[35] argues regarding this Hebrew root that it:

> delineates a sad chapter in Israel's covenantal relationship with Yahweh. The heart of that covenantal relationship revolved around God's intent to be Israel's God (protector and benefactor) and his expectation that Israel would be his people (Lev 26:12), manifesting his character to the surrounding world (Exod 19:4-6). Yahweh promised to bless abundantly their obedience (Lev 26:1-3; Deut 28:1-14), but also to curse severely their rebellion (Lev 26:14-35; Deut 28:15-68). Part of that promised blessing was Yahweh's promise to put his dwelling place among them and the assurance that he would not abhor them (*g'l*, Lev 26:11).[36]

---

[33] Idem.

[34] Heschel, *The Prophets*, 2:73. He points out that "the ultimate meaning of history lies in the continuity of God's concern. His wrath is not regarded as an emotional outburst, as an irrational fit, but rather as a part of His continual care."

[35] Michael A. Grisanti, "גָּעַל," *New International Dictionary of Old Testament Theology and Exegesis*, 1:884-886.

[36] Ibid., 885.

Yahweh tells Israel, his covenant partner: "I will set my tabernacle (מִשְׁכָּנִי)[37] among you, and My soul[38] shall not abhor you (וְלֹא־תִגְעַל)" (Lev 26:11, NKJV). The root גָּעַל "signifies the transitive nuance, to consider something or someone as dung and filth." [39] The root in question also connotes the idea of rejection (Lev 26:15, 43, 44; Jer 14:19). Yahweh reassures Israel that he will not abhor/reject his covenant partner, but that he will live with them. Rendering גָּעַל with "reject" in Lev 26:11 instead of "abhor" (as most translations do)[40] seems to be more accurate.[41]

Yahweh reassures Israel that he will not reject them like a husband may reject his wife. He will set his tabernacle among them, and he will remain true to them. Israel's history shows that Yahweh stays committed to Israel despite their numerous and hideous backslidings. However, Yahweh's love for and commitment to Israel is not blind. He sees them as they really are and stays. He remains true to himself and to his promise, struggling in the face of Israel's unfaithfulness and rejection of him. Any relationship is doomed to break or get deeply unpleasant if one of the two partners involved starts to abhor or reject

[37] Leviticus 26:12, the following verse, highlights that Yahweh desires to walk (וְהִתְהַלַּכְתִּי) among Israel to be with them and to deliver them (cf. Deut 23:15). This Hebrew verb reconnects with Gen 3:8. Yahweh God walks (מִתְהַלֵּךְ) in the garden in the cool of the day to encounter the human family.

[38] N. F. Fuhs, "גָּעַל," *Theological Dictionary of the Old Testament*, 3:47. The "affective-intransitive meaning of *ga'al* has been abandoned almost completely in the OT. Remnants of this original meaning still appear in the regular use of *nephesh*, 'soul' (as the seat of feeling and emotion), as the subject of *ga'al* (with the exception of Ezk. 16:45)."

[39] Michael A. Grisanti, "גָּעַל," *New International Dictionary of Old Testament Theology and Exegesis*, 885. Cf. N. F. Fuhs, "גָּעַל," *Theological Dictionary of the Old Testament*, 3:48. "Idiomatically: 'to regard somebody as dirt.'" Cf. *TDOT* 3:47.

[40] The NASB renders גָּעַל with "reject," noting in a footnote that the literal rendering of the root is "abhor."

[41] The root גָּעַל is used five times in Lev 26 (vv. 11, 15, 30, 43, 44). Verse 11 states that Yahweh will not reject Israel. However, if Israel rejects his statues (vv. 15, 43), i.e., the life-giving values of Yahweh's kingdom, Israel will have to face the consequences (sooner or later). Human flourishing will not be possible. Evil will disrupt the good of life and destroy the beauty of relationships. The covenant between Yahweh and Israel will be in jeopardy. Nevertheless, Yahweh promises to remember them (v. 45) because of "the covenant with their ancestors" (v. 45). He remains committed to his partner.

the other partner because of a third party competing for love and devotion.

The Hebrew Scriptures portray such a situation. Israel loves other gods and rejects Yahweh and his kingdom, and Yahweh must deal with the pain of being rejected and despised. It is said that those who love deeply and most in a relationship suffer the most if their love is unrequited. But regardless of being neglected, rejected, and sidelined by Israel, Yahweh pledges himself not to abhor or reject Israel, his partner. He hopes for reconciliation, for a new start with Israel, and for them to return wholeheartedly to him, their covenantal partner. But he cannot force them or impose himself on them because love cannot be forced. He must wait, speaking gently to their hearts, without ever manipulating them or robbing them of the freedom of choice. Yahweh's commitment is real and deep. Yahweh stays true to his name. He is "God, merciful and gracious, longsuffering and abounding in goodness and truth, keeping mercy for thousands, forgiving iniquity and transgression and sin, by no means clearing the guilty" (Exod 34:6-7). He retains his unequaled dignity despite human attack and neglect. He does not gloss over evil, but he forgives and liberates from evil, and that is what he wants for Israel. His character is stable, consistent, and ongoing.

Conclusion

Yahweh's commitment to broken humanity is real and alive, even in the 21st century. We live in a cultural moment where commitment is rare. Human beings are afraid of committing, of sacrificing their autonomy for somebody else, of walking patiently with someone else. The Hebrew Scriptures are deeply honest about life in a world that has become full of evil. Life is complex and includes pain and the courage to face it bravely. The God of Israel, Yahweh, can serve as a reference of true commitment to other humans. All of us are broken and in need of forgiveness and healing. Broken human beings are hurting in a broken world. Rejection, neglect, mistreatment, abuse, and the wounds resulting from it are real in the realm of interhuman relationships. Yahweh and his unfaltering commitment to humanity is the only constant we have in life. Being anchored in him, human beings are destined to morph into men and women also committed to him and to others, seeing the face of the other, being there for the other, but without losing their individuality or becoming the plaything of others.

In the course of human history, Yahweh came down into human exile, into the reality of a broken world. He became flesh,[42] a brother of humankind.[43] His vulnerability and commitment to the human family were seen throughout his entire life and especially on the cross. He is the image of the invisible God, reminding humans of their unequaled dignity and worth as created in the image of God, as well as how to live in a broken world. The fear of being rejected and abhorred by humanity did not stop him. He is patient, totally aware of what is in the human heart, yet loving and gracious. Amid a complex world that humans must navigate, this God still speaks and sparks hope.

---

[42] "And the Word became flesh and dwelt among us, and we beheld His glory, the glory as of the only begotten of the Father, full of truth and grace" (John 1:14). The New Testament returns to the idea of Yahweh "dwelling," "tabernacling" among humanity (cf. Lev 26:11) to restore the broken relationship and grow in intimacy with humanity. The expression "full of truth and grace" is a retake of Exod 34:6-7. The Word is Yahweh made flesh.

[43] "He is not ashamed to call [human beings] brethren" (Heb 2:11-15).

Manifestations of God's Beauty through the Ministry of Presence in the Scriptures

Anna M. Galeniece

Abstract

The imagery of beauty is almost all-embracing in Scripture, as it starts with the beauty of the Garden of Eden and closes with the radiant glory of the heavenly Jerusalem in the last book of the Bible. As one considers the range and variety of things called beautiful by the biblical writers, we find confirmation that God "has made everything beautiful in its time" (Eccl 3:11, NKJV). However, some people may ask questions like how does the ministry of presence reveal God's beauty in human life, including His holiness? And what is meant by the term "presence" itself? Does it mean that the almighty and sovereign God imparts moral beauty to the soul, so that which is characteristic to God is also found in the life of His children? Could it be that through the relational presence of one's ministry, a person manifests the beauty of God in purity, consecration, love, humility, Christlikeness, etc.? To see how God's beauty was revealed in the life of an ordinary person in Bible times, this article will briefly focus on three selected women—Esther, Anna, and Dorcas—who will reveal some glimpses of God as the one who manifests His beauty through the incarnational-relational ministry of presence.[1]

---

[1] This chapter is dedicated to my dear teacher, colleague, and friend, Dr. Jo Ann Davidson, a Professor of Systematic Theology at Andrews University Theological Seminary in Berrien Springs, Michigan. From the moment I met her, she has become my inspiration as a theologian and musician, who has a great passion and skills for embedding the biblical aesthetic in her fundamental theological deliberations. I have learned from Dr. Davidson that I should never ignore aesthetic dimensions in my theological studies as I strive to understand the concept of ultimate truth. Moreover, Dr. Davidson is a prolific writer who has published multiple articles on different topics in the *Andrews University Seminary Studies* and the *Journal of the Adventist Theological Society*, and including such books as *Glimpses of Our God*, *Toward a Theology of Beauty: A Biblical*

Introduction

The ministry of presence[2] is viewed by most chaplains from merely horizontal and predominantly self-centered perspectives, while Scripture reveals a comprehensive approach to one's ministry of presence built on the vertical foundation. From the creation of the world to the redemption of people and the Second Advent, Emmanuel's revelatory presence[3] reveals the beauty of God's character and His purpose of salvation. His admirable example was reflected by a number of biblical heroes and heroines of faith, whose names are written in the book of life, even though not necessarily mentioned in the hall of faith (Heb 11).

This paper will examine three women. The first one is Esther, whose beauty was desired by King Ahasuerus, and who had committed herself to the King of the Universe. Her life was spared by the earthly king because she dedicated herself to the protective presence of God. This commitment won the victory for her, her family, and the whole nation. There is another woman, who stood in the doorway of the new chronological era,[4] who lived in the

---

Perspective, *Rediscovering the Glory of the Sabbath*, *Jonah: The Inside Story*, and many more.

[2] The ministry of presence is a comprehensive statement that encompasses not only God's presence on the vertical level, but also a reflection of God's presence through human instruments on a horizontal level. It is characterized by love, goodness, and truth, which like a shining, many-faceted diamond, is repeatedly manifested in the consecrated lives of God's children, who through their earthly walk faithfully reflect the beauty of their Creator and Redeemer. See also Winnifred Fallers Sullivan, *A Ministry of Presence: Chaplaincy, Spiritual Care, and the Law* (Chicago, IL: University of Chicago Press, 2019); Whit Woodard, *Ministry of Presence* (North Fort Myers, FL: Faithful Life Publishers, 2011).

[3] Isaiah foretold the birth of a son to be named Immanuel (Hebrew) or Emmanuel (Greek), meaning "God is with us," as a sign and reminder of God's abiding presence (Isa 7:14). Matthew referred to the prophecy of Isaiah and showed that it was fulfilled in the person of Jesus Christ. He emphasized that Jesus was born of a virgin and was, in a supreme sense, "God with us" (Matt 1:23).

[4] Daniel 9:24-27 contains a chronological roadmap that culminates with the redemptive death of the Messiah on the cross of Calvary—the event that has no equivalents and never will have. The sacrificial-redemptive presence of Christ on the cross changed everything, even dividing the human era in half. Today we use such terms as "A.D." and "B.C." "A.D. stands for anno

sustaining presence of God during her whole life. Because she dedicated herself to service in "the house of the Lord," Anna was allowed to physically "gaze upon the beauty of the Lord" (Ps 27:4)[5] and prophecy about the Redeemer. Her heart was thirsting for God's presence that equipped her to minister in the presence of Him. Lastly, a Christian disciple who gave herself fully to the widows and the poor in Joppa, reflected the presence of her Lord. Although Dorcas died, the community whom she served considered her death premature because God "has put eternity into man's heart" (Eccl 3:11). Her resurrection and the continuation of her active ministry of presence reveals the fact that the Almighty does "everything beautiful in its time" (Eccl 3:11). These are only a few examples of the biblical manifestations of God's beauty through the ministry of His relational presence, but provide plenty of evidence for His people to learn and follow Him in the 21st century.

Emmanuel: The Beauty of Beauties[6]

The Bible starts and ends with God's presence (Gen 2; 3; Rev 21:1-4), showing how and why He wants a personal encounter and close relationship with His people. The presence of the Triune God has three primary aspects; relational, revelatory, and incarnational dimensions find their most significant expression in the coming of Immanuel. "Behold, the virgin shall conceive and bear a Son, and shall call His name Immanuel" (Isa 7:14). This "mega theme" unites all the other major themes, "such as covenant, kingdom, creation,

---

domini (Latin for "in the year of the lord"); it is equivalent to C.E. (the Common Era) and it refers specifically to the birth of Jesus Christ. "B.C." stands for "before Christ." We also speak about the Old Testament and the New Testament. The cross of Christ serves as the chronological dividing line of the world's history.

[5] All the Bible texts are quoted from the NKJV.

[6] "Beauty is first of all an aesthetic quality that names what we find attractive, satisfying and excellent in an object or person" (Leland Ryken et al., *Dictionary of Biblical Imagery* [Downers Grove, IL: InterVarsity, 2000], 82). Concerning God's beauty manifested in innumerable ways, shapes and forms, see Jo Ann Davidson, *Toward a Theology of Beauty: A Biblical Perspective* (Lanham, MD: University Press of America, 2008); Richard M. Davidson, "The Sanctuary: 'To Behold the Beauty of the Lord,'" in *The Word: Searching, Living, Teaching*, ed. Artur A. Stele (Silver Spring, MD: Review and Herald, 2015), 1:15–16.

holiness, redemption, law and grace, sin and forgiveness, life and death, worship, and obedient living. It is indeed the cohesive center of biblical theology."[7] "I will dwell among the people of Israel and be their God. And they shall know that I am the Lord their God, who brought them out of the land of Egypt that I might dwell among them" (Exod 29:45-46). It is impossible to separate God's relational dimension from the fellowshipping and sustaining aspects of His presence that point to the culmination of salvation history, namely, to God's eschatological presence among His people.

The beauty of God's presence is seen both in the Old Testament and the New Testament. Both of them clearly demonstrate that God is simultaneously transcendent and immanent, and to ignore His self-revelation of either is to construct a new theology. The transcendent God, who abides in the realms beyond human understanding, and whose transcendence distinguishes Him from the created order is the One who revealed a glimpse of Himself in human flesh as a little baby, Emmanuel, or "God with us" (Matt 1:23). This God who is "in heaven above and the earth beneath" (Josh 2:11) decided to manifest the majestic and splendid glory[8] of His character through relationship with humanity for the sake of their redemption, rather than through the revelation of His grandeur and awesomeness not comprehensible by sinful human beings.[9]

---

[7] J. Scott Duvall and J. Daniel Hays, *God's Relational Presence: The Cohesive Center of Biblical Theology* (Grand Rapids, MI: Baker Academic, 2019), 1–2.

[8] It is impossible to describe or define the glory of God in human terms, as it manifests itself in countless forms and ways, including light (Gen 1:3; Exod 34:29; 1 Kgs 8:10), a pillar of cloud by day and fire by night (Exod 13:21), and through miracles like the Exodus (Exod 16:10). He shows His glory in wind, earthquake, thunderstorms, raising the dead, etc. (John 11:40; Rom.6:4). See E. F. Harrison, "Glory," in *The International Standard Bible Encyclopedia, Revised*, ed. Geoffrey W Bromiley (Grand Rapids, MI: Eerdmans, 1979–1988), 479.

[9] God's presence among people is powerfully revealed through the sanctuary message (Ps 77:13; Lev 16; Heb 8:1-5), the words of His encouragement and support (Exod 3:12; Josh 1:5, 6; Judg 6:12; Jer 1:8; Luke 17:20, 21), the very presence of Jesus Christ (Luke 4:17-19), and the presence of the Holy Spirit (John 14:16-18; Matt 28:20). For more information see Ángel Manuel Rodríguez, "God's Presence in the Sanctuary: A Theology of His Nearness," *Ministry* (Nov 2004): 16-17.

On the one hand, the glory, majesty, holiness, and righteousness of

In this sense, His theophany at Sinai (Exod 19:16-20; 20:18-21) pointed to the theophany of God on Golgotha, where God displayed the glory of His infinite sacrificial love for sinful humanity (1 John 4:9-12).[10]

The very nature and being of God is beauty, which can be summarized as "the sum and comprehension of all existence and excellence."[11] Moreover, there is indescribably harmonious functional beauty among the triune beings of Father, Son, and Holy Spirit.[12] Referring to God's beauty, Ryken and Hughes point out the "divine love within the Trinity" where "each person brings glory to the others," and the "beauty in the symmetry of God's divine perfections."[13]

The work of creation by the triune God speaks for itself (Ps 104). It involves the all-encompassing beauty on the earth, in the seas and in the skies; it includes the seen and the unseen (Isa 40:12-17). Everything that has been created emanates the power, wisdom, and majesty of God. The entire universe is captivated and awestruck with the grandeur of God (Job 38, 39).[14] The God of all perfection and beauty is the One who preconceived and created worlds and filled them with His own divine glory and perfection. But in the entire creation, there is nothing more beautiful, glorious, and wonderful

---

God function as one wholistic principle. On the other, it should be noted that the glory of the presence of God often is associated with the judgment of God (Num 16:46; Judg 5:5; Pss 34:16; 96:13; Jer 4:26; Ezek 38:20; Rev 6:16; 20:11).

[10] The Bible shows that the beauty and glory of the presence was the fundamental goal of the cross and the resurrection of Christ. The cross was the only way God could bring His creation back and restore the relationship with Himself broken by sin, so that one day men and women might experience His presence throughout eternity.

[11] Frank E. Gaebelein, *The Christian, the Arts, and Truth: Regaining the Vision of Greatness* (Portland, OR: Multnomah, 1985), 65.

[12] Mark Ward, *Biblical Worldview: Creation, Fall, Redemption*, ed. Mark L. Ward Jr. and Dennis Cone (Greenville, SC: BJU Press, 2016), 402.

[13] Philip Graham Ryken and R. Kent Hughes, *Exodus: Saved for God's Glory* (Wheaton, IL: Crossway, 2005), 1094.

[14] Gerard Manley Hopkins, "God's Grandeur," in *The Oxford Book of Christian Verse*, ed. Lord David Cecil (Oxford: Oxford University Press, 1940), 495. See also Abraham Kuyper, *Calvinism: Six Stone Foundation Lectures* (Grand Rapids, MI: Eerdmans, 1943), 156.

than human beings, which He made in His own image and in His own likeness (Gen 1:26, 27).

The greatest miracle of the active ministry of relational and revelatory presence was demonstrated before the entire universe when One of the three Persons of the holy Godhead, Jesus Christ, the matchless One, who is the Lord of all beauty, willingly took the form of fallen humanity to become the Redeemer and Savior of the world. There has never been a more beautiful human being than Jesus Christ, who is God incarnate, the very Son of God. The Bible clearly states that Jesus had no outward beauty. "He had no form or majesty that we should look at him, and no beauty that we should desire him" (Isa 53:2). His beauty was revealed in His perfect obedience to the Father, in His servanthood to people, in His sacrifice on the cross of Calvary, and in His glorious resurrection from the grave. The author of the book of Hebrews says that Jesus is "the radiance of God's glory" (Heb 1:3).

Despite the ugliness of sin and its destructive effects on God's nature and humanity, in and through Jesus every person is destined to be healed, re-created and to become beautiful. This is the very essence of the beauty of redemption and salvation. God invites men and women to come to Him as they are, all who have been stained and wounded by sin. Through His touch and special ministry of sustaining presence He can start to re-create their lives into something beautiful, even like the Edenic perfection. One day the process of re-creation and salvation will be completed, and on that day God's people will be presented before God the Father and all the unfallen worlds like a bride "without stain or wrinkle or any other blemish, but holy and blameless" (Eph 5:27). On that eschatological day, God's people will be more than beautiful as they will stand in the direct presence of their Creator and Redeemer and radiate the glory of God in the face of Jesus Christ. The secret of acquiring this beauty is simple: responding to Jesus' call, the redeemed received inner beauty, which originates only from the Spirit of Jesus Christ. Thus, God gives them a new meaning to life and a new nature to live that life.[15] "It has been the uniqueness and the perfection of Christ's

---

[15] Adrian Rogers, "Wedding Bells in Heaven," in *Adrian Rogers Sermon Archive* (Signal Hill, CA: Rogers Family Trust, 2017), Re 19:1–10.

moral beauty that have charmed even those who claimed to be His enemies throughout the centuries of history."[16]

The Bible contains many names of people who were faithful to God and reflected the beauty of their Savior Jesus Christ. As there are three things that often go together in the Bible (truth, goodness, and beauty),[17] this paper will focus on three outstanding women in the Bible who radiated the beauty of truth and goodness in their simple daily lives: Esther, Anna, and Dorcas.

Esther: Beauty Desired by the King

"So the King will greatly desire your beauty; because He is your Lord, worship Him" (Ps 45:11).

The biblical narrative about the lovely and beautiful (Esth 2:7)[18] Jewish young woman Hadassah, who was renamed Esther, fascinates readers and Bible scholars alike. The most likely time for her story is "in Nehemiah's day (Neh 2:1, 6)."[19]

The Bible is not in favor of praising outward beauty (1 Pet 3:3, 4), but it does not deny it either. Saul was a tall and handsome man (1 Sam 9:2). Joseph was handsome in form and appearance (Gen 39:6). A son of Jesse was a handsome person (1Sam 16:18). Sarai was a woman of beautiful countenance (Gen 12:11). Bathsheba was a woman very beautiful to behold (2 Sam 11:2). Leah's eyes were delicate, but Rachel was beautiful of form and appearance (Gen 29:17). Rebecca was very beautiful to behold (Gen 24:16). Abigail was a woman of good understanding and beautiful appearance (1 Sam 25:3).

---

[16] A. W. Tozer and Gerald B. Smith, *Mornings with Tozer: Daily Devotional Readings* (Chicago, IL: Moody Publishers, 2008), December 29.

[17] The three terms "truth, goodness, and beauty" could be capitalized, as each one of them is a perfect designation of Jesus Christ. See Exod 34:6; Pss 27:4; 100:5.

[18] Ellen G. White, *Daughters of God* (Hagerstown, MD: Review and Herald, 1998), 45, writes, "Esther was a beautiful Jewish girl, cousin of Mordecai, who took her into his home after her parents died and loved her as his own daughter. God used her to save the Jewish people in the land of Persia."

[19] J. S. Wright, "Esther, Book of," *The Zondervan Pictorial Encyclopedia of the Bible*, ed. Merrill C. Tenney (Grand Rapids, MI: Zondervan, 1976), 2:376.

However, when it comes to Esther, her beauty must have been much more pleasing and attractive than just her outward appearance. It is an attention-grabbing moment. According to the Jewish Talmud, Esther was of a greenish complexion, but she had a "thread of grace" that was laying upon her.[20] When a person's internal beauty is elevated, it will often become visible to others through the external appearance. According to Mangano, "The beauty of God's presence in the life of Queen Esther is forever remembered in the timeless question, 'And who knows but that you have come to royal position for such a time as this?'" (4:14).[21] While the Bible tells us that Saul was a tall and handsome man (1 Sam 9:2), it also portrays how his outward beauty did not reflect God's presence on the inside.

Hegai, the custodian who was in charge of the king's harem, duly noted Esther's beauty and assigned to her not only seven maidservants chosen from the king's palace, but also "hurried to begin her beauty treatments" [22] required for the appearance before king Ahasuerus[23] as soon as possible (Esth 2:9). This young woman obtained the favor of the eunuch who was highly experienced in preparing females to become the king's concubines. He "detected in

---

[20] Talmud Megillah 13a. The truth is that the word *yarok*, which the Talmud uses here, does not necessarily always mean "green" (See *Shulchan Aruch, Yoreh De'ah* 188:1). In fact, there is no consensus concerning her skin color. Regarding Esther, some do indeed explain *yarok* to mean a shade of green, while others explain it to mean more of a yellow-gold hue. See commentary of the Gaon of Vilna on *Tikkunei Zohar* 21. This seems to also be the understanding of the third Chabad Rebbe, the Tzemach Tzedek, in his responsum, *Even Ha'ezer* 427:1. However, in his *Ohr Hatorah*, on Megillat Esther, p. 18, it seems that he believed that she was a greenish color.

[21] Mark Mangano, *Esther & Daniel*, The College Press NIV Commentary (Joplin, MO: College Press, 2001), 14.

[22] Knute Larson and Kathy Dahlen, *Ezra, Nehemiah, Esther,* Holman Old Testament Commentary (Nashville, TN: Broadman & Holman, 2005), 297.

[23] Ahasuerus or Xerxes (Greek), the son of Darius I, was a Persian king who ruled from India to Ethiopia (Esth 1:1) during 486-465 B.C. He married Esther in the seventh year of his reign (Esth 2:16). See Merrill F. Unger, "Ahasuerus," *The New Unger's Bible Dictionary*, ed. R. K. Harrison (Chicago, IL: Moody Press, 1988), 37.

Esther a woman who could please the king"[24] and become the next queen; and a queen she became.

It is one thing to become powerful, have servants, and start a life of luxury and pleasure; but it is another thing to remember your humble beginning, your people, and the One whom you worship as King of Kings even amid prosperity and a heathen nation. Esther's cousin Mordecai dedicated himself to be a continual reminder to the queen by sitting "within the king's gate" (Esth 2:19, 21), which refers to the royal court where he "was busy in an administrative capacity within the palace."[25] Mordecai's ministry of personal presence to his young royal cousin not only saved the life of the king (Esth 2:21-23), but also generated deadly hatred from the king's prime minister Haman toward Mordecai and all the Jews (Esth 2:5, 6). The only way to unmask the seemingly well-planned plot to destroy God's people, was through the royal palace—the queen's approach to the king, which could be deadly if the king's golden scepter was not held out. But to go to the king required much more preparation than just adorning Esther's body with beautiful apparel. She needed strength to face the challenge, courage to meet her destiny, and the support of friends who would fast together for God's intervention.

In the context of the ministry of presence, being with someone is as equally important as doing something for that person. Even Jesus, being the Son of God, needed human beings to stay awake with Him during His agonizing hours of prayer in the Garden of Gethsemane (Matt 26:36-45). He needed their presence and their prayerful support.[26] In the same way, Esther needed the support of her people to fast with her and her maidservants (Esth 4:16). This Jewish queen "set herself and her people to the task of waiting upon God,"[27] whose name is not even mentioned in the book. However, this fact does not mean that God was absent in the lives of the Jewish people in Shushan and the rest of Persia. The very "fasting, which would

---

[24] Larson and Dahlen, *Ezra, Nehemiah, Esther*, 297.

[25] Ibid., 298.

[26] If Jesus in the Garden of Gethsemane needed the support of His disciples (Matt 26:36-46; Mark 14:34), how much more this support is needed by other human beings!

[27] Diana Schick, *The Challenge of Womanhood I: Studies on Women of the Bible* (Reston, VA: Creative Living International, 1995), 60.

include prayer, was part of the working out of God's plan" in the life of the queen and the whole nation.[28] Moreover, as Lockyer points out, "God may appear as if He is hiding Himself, but seen or unseen He ever accomplishes that which is according to His will,"[29] as was the case of the marriage of the Persian king to a Jewess. According to Persian law, a person in the royal line must take a wife "belonging to the seven great Persian families."[30] There is no explanation to this marriage other than God's providence for the future delivery of His people.

The three-day fasting requested by Esther was "an absolute fast in keeping with the dire situation that the nation faced." It was total trust in God's absolute power, authority, and capacity to do as He wishes.[31] It was persuasion that He would somehow demonstrate supernatural intervention in the dreadful situation that the Jews faced. True fasting does not involve a formal service of an outward behavior, but it is a deep heart-searching experience with "confession of sin, and earnest prayer."[32] The prophet Isaiah beautifully elaborates upon the deep meaning of this spiritual discipline in Isa 58. Also Daniel, when he prayed for his people, set his "face toward the Lord God to make request by prayer and supplications, with fasting, and sackcloth, and ashes" (Dan 9:3). In the same way, Ezra "fasted and entreated" God to answer his prayer for protection on the way to Jerusalem (Ezra 8:23). Ezra's fast

---

[28] Wright, "Esther," 2:380.

[29] Herbert Lockyer, *All the Women of the Bible* (Grand Rapids, MI: Zondervan, 1988), 52.

[30] Lockyer, *Women of the Bible*, 52. Esther's nationality was hidden from people in the royal palace; even her Jewish name Hadassah, meaning 'myrtle,' was changed to a Persian name, Esther, which means 'a star.'

[31] Larson and Dahlen, *Ezra, Nehemiah, Esther*, 322. In the Bible, fasting often functioned as an expression of a total or partial repentance (1 Sam 7:6; Dan 9:3; 2 Chr 20:3; Neh 9:1), or grief (1 Sam 31:13; 1 Kgs 21:27, 29; 1 Chr 10:12; Ezra 8:21). Moreover, "fasting is a means by which one denies one's own needs and focuses directly on his or her relationship with God and the world." See Mervin Breneman, *Ezra, Nehemiah, Esther*, The New American Commentary 10 (Nashville, TN: Broadman & Holman, 1993), 338.

[32] Ellen G. White, *Evangelism* (Washington, DC: Review and Herald, 1946), 165.

included the request for the people to be humbled before God and seek from Him the right way forward (v. 21).

There is a common saying that nicely explains the reason behind Esther's courage to face the challenge—you cannot give what you do not have. Before the young queen would "venture into his [the king's] presence as an intercessor" for her people and give herself to the mercy of the king of Persia, she needed to face the merciful King of the universe.[33] The situation was of utmost importance, as "both she and Mordecai realized that unless God should work mightily in their behalf, their own efforts would be unavailing."[34] So Esther turned to her only source of help, as she was deeply aware of her need for God's guidance. She desired to receive His wisdom and courage to act suitably.[35] She was willing to commit her life's plans to the plans of God in following His will. White nicely describes Esther's critical situation by saying that, "The crisis that Esther faced demanded quick, earnest action . . . . So Esther took time for communion with God, the source of her strength."[36] Without taking this time, neither she nor her nation would be saved from Satan's fury through the hands of Haman. Consequently, her presence in the presence of the Almighty God filled her with boldness and courage to stand in the presence of King Ahasuerus, who spared her life and the life of her nation.

Through this experience, Esther's character reflects "a woman of deep piety, faith, courage, patriotism, and caution, combined with resolution."[37] The biblical narrative describes her as a person of "clear judgment, of magnificent self-control, and capable of the noblest self-sacrifice."[38] These characteristics strongly testify of her inner beauty and full reliance on the Lord, and remind the Bible reader of a wise woman "who fears the Lord" (Prov 31:30). Esther

---

[33] Ellen G. White, *Prophets and Kings* (Boise, ID: Pacific Press, 1917), 601.

[34] Ibid.

[35] Gien Karssen, *Her Name Is Woman* (Colorado Springs, CO: NavPress, 1975), 117.

[36] White, *Daughters of God*, 46.

[37] Merrill F. Unger, "Esther," in *The New Unger's Bible Dictionary*, ed. R. K. Harrison (Chicago, IL: Moody Press, 1988), 378.

[38] J. Urquhart, "Esther" in *The International Standard Bible Encyclopedia*, ed. Geoffrey W. Bromiley (Grand Rapids, MI: Eerdmans, 1982), 2:156.

"was made of the fiber of heroes."[39] It is no wonder that from the beginning of Esther's involvement with the Persian king, she continued her influence over him for a long time (Esth 5-10). It would be fair to conclude that he was attracted to her inner beauty, and she was able to use this to do what was necessary for the salvation of her people. Moreover, Merrill Unger powerfully highlights her life by saying that "There must have been a singular charm in her aspect and manners since she obtained favor in the sight of all that look upon her (Esth 2:15)"[40] and this charm was nothing else but her God.

Anna: Gazing Upon the Beauty of the Lord

"One *thing* I have desired of the Lord, that will I seek: that I may dwell in the house of the Lord all the days of my life, to behold the beauty of the Lord, and to inquire in His temple" (Ps 27:4).

After centuries-long prophetic silence between the time of Malachi and the birth of Jesus, Anna was among those who broke this silence[41] with her prophecy about the "redemption in Jerusalem" (Luke 2:38). Who was this woman and why was her ministry so important to her contemporaries?

Anna is introduced by Luke as an elderly widow, and identified by the genealogical lineage of her father as the daughter of Phanuel of the tribe of Asher. This was a small northern tribe that was captured by the Assyrian army in the 8th century B.C. and was later assimilated among other nations. Nonetheless, the gospel writer

---

[39] Karssen, *Her Name Is Woman*, 117.

[40] Unger, "Esther," 378.

[41] An angel of the Lord originally broke the long silence by announcing to Zacharias about the birth of John (Luke 1:11-13). Jesus' birth was announced to Mary by the angel Gabriel (Luke 1:26-28). Then Joseph received an angelic message to not be afraid but to take Mary as his wife because she conceived by the Holy Spirit (Matt 1:19-21). After these angelic proclamations, God started again to use human subjects. Elizabeth, when seeing Mary approaching her, was filled with the Holy Spirit and spoke out blessings upon Mary and her Child (Luke 1:41-45). Even though she is not called a prophetess, her message was uplifting, and she saw prophecy as being fulfilled. Then, after the birth of John, Zacharias pronounced a prophecy in preparation for Jesus' birth and ministry. The very next person to be used by God in revealing His will was Anna (Luke 2:36-38).

highlights her ancestry lineage to Asher in order to testify about God's faithful remnant who returned back to Him (Isa 10:21, 22). Thus, Anna was a unique person that did not fit into the traditional Jewish cultural norms and standards, especially by not being from the tribes of Judah or Benjamin. However, Luke decided to include Anna in his gospel account through a very brief description, but with enough information about this devout woman, who against all odds loved the Lord with all of her heart and waited for His salvation.

Anna lived with her husband only seven years.[42] For some reason, his name is not mentioned in the gospel. It does not matter whether he was a godly man or not. The story that Luke depicts is not about him, but the widow Anna. This unusual detail about her widowhood may allude to the fact that her long lonely years were not spent in sorrow, self-pity, and isolation from society.[43] She dedicated herself to the One who could easily be blamed for taking her husband, devoting her life to and building her hope upon "the Mighty One . . . the perfection of beauty" (Ps 50:1, 2) who "had promised to be as a Husband to the widow."[44] Isaiah declares: "For your Maker is your husband, the Lord of hosts is His name" (Isa 54:5).[45]

Anna was included in the sextet of pious Israelites surrounding the miraculous births of John and Jesus. These were: Zechariah and Elizabeth—the parents of John, Mary and Joseph—the parents of Jesus, and Simeon whose "testimony concerning Christ"[46] Anna confirmed with her short declaration. These six persons epitomize both genders and all ages. Mary was the youngest, probably a teenager; Joseph was an adult; the parents of John represented older adults; and both Simeon and Anna were aged. The beauty of the

---

[42] Most probably Anna did not have children, or they had already died. If she had living children, she would have most likely dedicated herself to them and their support and care, instead of dedicating herself to the service of God. See Mark C. Black, *Luke*, College Press NIV Commentary (Joplin, MO: College Press, 1995).

[43] It is not clear whether Anna was 84 years old, or whether she was a widow for 84 years.

[44] Lockyer, *Women of the Bible*, 30.

[45] Other similar passages can be found in Isa 62:4; Hos 2:16; Jer 3:14; 31:32; Ezek 16:8, etc.

[46] Ellen G. White, *The Desire of Ages* (Boise, ID: Pacific Press, 1940), 55.

inclusivity of both genders and all ages speaks about the harmonious picture of God's people who were waiting for the Messiah's appearance despite the prevalent spiritual legalism and phariseeism.

The Bible tells the reader that this pious woman "did not depart from the temple" (Luke 2:37). Butler suggests that Anna "made the temple her permanent home: worship, prayer, and fasting, her occupation."[47] Her piety allowed others to see in this woman one who is worthy "to reside in one of the chambers of the women's court"[48] of the temple. This was not only a great privilege, but also a huge responsibility. According to Westerholm, the temple of God stood as a place 1) of sacrifice; 2) for prayer and praise; 3) for the consecration of persons and things; 4) for remembering the law of God; 5) for the union of the people; and 6) for the revelation of God.[49] While the sacrifices were assigned to Levites and priests, Anna may have participated in other responsibilities.

The Bible includes Anna among the godly female prophetesses. Timewise, she was in the middle between the four faithful prophetesses of the Old Testament (Miriam in Exod 15:20, Deborah in Judg 4:4, Huldah in 2 Kgs 22:14 and 2 Chron 34:22, and Isaiah's wife in Isa 8:3), and the four prophesying daughters of Philip (Acts 21:9) of the New Testament era. There are at least three more biblical accounts of prophetesses, but these have negative descriptions attached to their names or actions.[50]

Regarding Anna, it is clear that God uses people at any age, even an old woman who has given her heart to the Lord and willingly

---

[47] Trent C. Butler, *Luke*, Holman New Testament Commentary (Nashville, TN: Broadman & Holman, 2000), 33.

[48] Merrill F. Unger, "Anna," *The New Unger's Bible Dictionary*, ed. R. K. Harrison (Chicago, IL: Moody Press, 1988), 80.

[49] S. Westerholm, "Temple," in *The International Standard Bible Encyclopedia, Revised*, ed. Geoffrey W. Bromiley (Grand Rapids, MI: Eerdmans, 1979–1988), 765.

[50] Lockyer, *Women of the Bible*, 77. Noadiah was a fierce opponent of Nehemiah to the point that she intimidated him (Neh 6:14). Therefore, she is considered to be one of the false prophetesses. During Ezekiel's time, there were daughters of Jewish people who also prophesied, but they did so out of their own heart (Ezek 13:17). The last-mentioned biblical prophetess is Jezebel from the church in Thyatira (Rev 2:20). She was a forceful influential church leader who seduced God's servants into idolatry and wickedness.

serves Him. Her "fastings and prayers night and day" (Luke 2:37) were answered even though she had to wait for a long time. Habakkuk's message may have strengthened her in the waiting period, "For the vision *is* yet for an appointed time; but at the end it will speak, and it will not lie. Though it tarries, wait for it; because it will surely come, it will not tarry" (Hab 2:3). While her body was weakened by age, her spirit was strong, and she was directed by God to come "in that instant" (Luke 2:38) to the right place of the temple at the right time to find Simeon holding the promised Baby and blessing God for allowing him to see God's salvation (Luke 2:30). While Simeon met the Savior, it was Anna who met the Redeemer. White writes, "Also Anna, a prophetess, came in and confirmed Simeon's testimony. Her face lighted up with glory, and she poured out her heartfelt thanks that she had been permitted to behold Christ the Lord."[51]

Thus, Anna's continuous ministry of presence in the temple during her widowhood was not spent in vain. She fully dedicated herself to the ministry of presence in the house of the Lord. The Almighty answered her earnest prayers and provided her the unique privilege of seeing the Messiah. She was allowed to physically "gaze upon the beauty of the Lord" (Ps 27:4) and prophesy about the Redeemer. This inspired the old widow to become a powerful witness and missionary,[52] "the first female herald of the Incarnation"[53] in declaring the glad tidings "to all who looked for redemption in Jerusalem" (Luke 2:38). This prophetess was allowed by God to testify about Christ's incarnational presence and divinity in the temple,[54] and her message was addressed to all, men and women alike, who were waiting for the Messiah.

---

[51] Ellen White, *From Heaven with Love* (Boise, ID: Pacific Press, 1984), 30.

[52] See D. M. Pratt, "Anna," in *The International Standard Bible Encyclopedia, revised*, ed. Geoffrey W. Bromiley (Grand Rapids, MI: Eerdmans, 1979–1988), 128. In the context of the birth of evangelism, Roy Gane applies the female herald proclaiming "Behold your God" (Isa 40:9) to Anna, and the male herald (Isa 41:27; 52:7) to Simeon (Luke 2:25-35). For more information see Roy Gane, *Adult Teacher's Sabbath School Bible Study Guide: Isaiah* (Silver Spring, MD: General Conference of Seventh-day Adventists, 2021), 101.

[53] Lockyer, *Women of the Bible*, 31.

[54] White, *The Desire of Ages*, 231.

Dorcas: Everything Beautiful in Its Time

"He has made everything beautiful in its time. Also, He has put eternity in their hearts" (Eccl 3:11a).

A well-known Hellenistic Jewess of good reputation was called Dorcas by the Greeks, whereas to the Jews[55] she was known as Tabitha (Acts 9:36). This woman was a worthy disciple, a *mathetria*,[56] of Jesus. Her charitable and philanthropic life was filled with deeds of compassion and kindness. Dorcas did not strive for a leadership position in the church or society. She was content to do all she could for the sake of the needy. But, despite herself, this woman "became a great leader in an almost universal philanthropic cause"[57] by committing her life to the active approach of the ministry of presence, particularly to widows. The Bible is full of commands to not neglect the women who lost their husbands to death: "You shall not afflict any widow" (Exod 22:22); "Do not oppress the widow" (Zech 7:10); "Honor widows who are really widows" (1 Tim 5:3). James calls visiting "widows in their trouble" a characteristic of "pure and undefiled religion before God and the Father" (Jas 1:27).[58]

Dorcas was able to identify in the community those people, especially widows, who "needed comfortable clothing and who needed sympathy, and she freely ministered to the poor and the sorrowful. Her skillful fingers were more active than her tongue."[59] Her life and selfless ministry can be easily compared with the

---

[55] Merrill F. Unger, "Dorcas," *The New Unger's Bible Dictionary*, ed. R. K. Harrison (Chicago, IL: Moody Press, 1988), 316, 1247. Unger, in agreement with several Christian traditions, considers that Tabitha was a widow; however, the Bible does not indicate this.

[56] Beck states that the feminine version of the word disciple, *mathetria,* "is used only once in the NT, but the second-century Gospel of Peter applies it to Mary Magdalene" (D. M. Beck, "Dorcas," *The Interpreter's Dictionary of the Bible*, ed. George Arthur Buttrick [Nashville, TN: Abingdon, 2000], 865).

[57] Lockyer, *Women of the Bible*, 48.

[58] The Bible mentions the widows together with the poor and orphans. These three groups of people are usually marginalized in the sight of people, but they are precious in the sight of God. He cares for them, and demands His people do the same. See also Gary V. Smith, "Poor, Orphan, Widow," in *Holman Illustrated Bible Dictionary*, ed. Chad Brand, et al. (Nashville, TN: Holman Bible Publishers, 2003), 1311.

[59] White, *The Acts of the Apostles*, 131.

beautiful depiction of the woman of Prov 31:10-31. Consequently, both women displayed extraordinary energy. They willingly extended their help to the marginalized (Acts 9:36; Prov 31:20), were proficient in sewing (Acts 9:39; Prov 31:13, 19, 21-22, 24, 25), and performed good deeds to others, especially to those of their own faith (Acts 9:36; Prov 31:12, 30). Barclay points out that, "She was full of good works and of deeds of charity which she never stopped doing."[60]

In contrast to Esther and Anna, Dorcas is not said to have fasted, prayed, or prophesied; yet this quiet female disciple self-sacrificially served the Lord and His church with her beautiful heart and tireless hands. To this, White states, as mentioned above, that Dorcas' "skillful fingers were more active than her tongue."[61] The life of this woman can be described as a demonstration of Christian service that was not only exemplary to others, but also worthy to be mentioned in the Bible because of its long-lasting consequences.

Unfortunately, death and grief visit godly people the same way as the ungodly. Dorcas "became sick and died" (Acts 9:37). Traditionally, the dead body would be washed, anointed with nard, myrrh and aloes, then wrapped in a shroud, and buried on the same day or, in some rare occasions, on the following day;[62] but this was not the case with Dorcas. The Bible states that her body was washed by the believers and laid in an upper room (Luke 9: 37), where there was more privacy and quietness, suggesting that something still needed to take place. God allowed her death to happen as a

---

[60] William Barclay, *The Acts of the Apostles*, 3rd ed., The New Daily Study Bible (Louisville, KY: Westminster John Knox, 2003), 89.

[61] White, *The Acts of the Apostles*, 131.

[62] "The holy anointing oil was made from aromatic spices blended with oil (Ex. 30:23–25); certain temple officials had charge of the spices (1 Ch. 9:29). Hezekiah showed the spices and precious metals and oil in his treasure house to the Babylonian embassage (2 K. 20:13). Spices were used as cosmetics (e.g., by women in Est. 2:12) and at funerals, especially those of nobility (2 Ch. 16:14). The Canticles references to spices (4:10, 14; 5:1, 13; 6:2; 8:2, 14) indicate spices made from low-growing plants such as *Astragalus tragacantha* L., which can be cultivated in beds; thus, arborescent species such as sandalwood, cassia, and cinnamon are excluded here" (K. Harrison, "Spice," in *The International Standard Bible Encyclopedia, Revised*, ed. Geoffrey W. Bromiley [Grand Rapids, MI: Eerdmans, 1979–1988], 596).

demonstration of a Christian death that was fully mourned by others, especially by the widows.[63] The grief that these women experienced can be described as "the process of psychological, social, and spiritual reactions to loss."[64] But for them, this grief was short lived. While Christians put their ultimate trust in the coming resurrection (John 11:24; 1 Cor 15:22, 23), something extraordinary happened in Joppa that gave them hope for this resurrection at the end of time.

The believers, hearing that Peter had restored health to Aeneas in the nearby city of Lydda not long ago (Luke 9:32-34), cherished the idea of a greater miracle in Joppa. Gangel suggests that their immediate appeal for Peter to come "certainly makes it sound as though they anticipated a resurrection."[65] Thus, without question, the widows grieved for this beloved disciple of Christ because she was "so essential to the life of her believing community," and they could not "imagine life without her."[66] At the same time, the fact that "all who dwelt at Lydda and Sharon saw him [Aeneas] and turned to the Lord" (Luke 9:35) gave the believers in Joppa more hope for an occasion of spreading Christianity in their own region. And that is exactly what happened. According to Brooks, "As a result of Tabitha being raised from the dead, many people in Joppa believed in the Lord."[67]

---

[63] According to Worden, there are four tasks of mourning: (1) to accept the reality of the loss; (2) to process the pain of grief; (3) to adjust to a world without the deceased; and (4) to find a way to remember the deceased while embarking on the rest of one's journey through life. See J. William Worden, *Grief Counseling and Grief Therapy* (New York, NY: Springer, 2018), 41-53. It seems like the believers in Joppa accomplished only the first task because during the second task Dorcas was raised back to life.

[64] Mike Tucker, *Tears to Joy* (Nampa, ID: Pacific Press, 2018), 17.

[65] Kenneth O. Gangel, *Luke,* Holman New Testament Commentary (Nashville: Broadman & Holman, 1998), 147.

[66] Harrison, "Spice," 596.

[67] The resurrection of Dorcas is similar to the resurrection of Lazarus. "In delaying to come to Lazarus, Christ had a purpose of mercy toward those who had not received Him" (White, *The Desire of Ages*, 529). In a similar way, the resurrection of Dorcas was an open door for people in Joppa to accept the Christian message.

A powerful example of the demonstration of Christian resurrection took place.[68] "God saw fit to bring her [Dorcas] back from the land of the enemy, that her skill and energy might still be a blessing to others, and also that by this manifestation of His power the cause of Christ might be strengthened."[69] Peter, being taught by Jesus, followed His example of raising the dead. When resurrecting Jairus' daughter, Jesus put the mourners outside the house, "took her by hand and called, saying, 'Little girl, arise'" (Luke 8:54). In a similar manner, Peter put the mourners out, "knelt down and prayed. And turning to the body he said, 'Tabitha, arise'" (Acts 9:40). Both God's daughters received the gift of life back from Him who can do strange and unusual things, not for the curiosity of others but to convert and save lives. Thus, the family of Jairus[70] and many people in Joppa were brought "to the faith of Jesus."[71]

Ecclesiastes 3:11 states that God has put eternity in the hearts of human beings. This allows them to resist death at all costs; and there is nothing wrong with a fight for life. God Himself declared that He is "the Lord who heals you" (Exod 15:26). The Bible has numerous texts supporting the idea of wellbeing and health.[72] However, the

---

[68] In his teaching outline of the story, Gangel provides three demonstrations: (1) of Christian service; (2) of Christian death; and (3) of Christian resurrection. See Gangel, *Luke*, 152.

[69] White, *The Acts of the Apostles*, 132.

[70] Ellen G. White, *The Spirit of Prophecy* (Seventh-day Adventist Publishing Association, 1870), 2:322, 323.

[71] White, *The Spirit of Prophecy*, 3:324.

[72] The Old Testament characteristics of health include well-being, righteousness (Lev 19:36; Deut 25:15; Job 31:6; Ps 23:3; Ezek 45:10), obedience (Exod 15:26; Lev 26:14-16; Deut 5:32; Ps 38:3-8; Prov 3:7-8), strength (Ps 29:11; Isa 40:29-31; Dan 10:10; Zech 10:6), fertility (Gen 1:28; 17:16; Exod 13:26; Deut 7:12-14) and longevity (Gen 15:15; 25:8; Judg 8:32; Isa 65:20). It should also be noted that the Hebrew term *shalom* designates "completeness, wholeness, peace, health, welfare, safety, soundness, tranquility, prosperity, perfectness, fullness, rest, harmony, the absence of agitation or discord. *Shalom* comes from the root verb *shalam,* meaning 'to be complete, perfect, and full.' Thus, *shalom* is much more than the absence of war and conflict; it is the wholeness that the entire human race seeks. The word *shalom* occurs about 250 times in the OT (see Ps. 4:8; Is. 48:18; Jer. 29:11). In Ps. 35:27, God takes delight in the *shalom* (the wholeness, the total well-being) of His servant. In Is. 53:5, the chastisement necessary to bring us *shalom* was upon the suffering Messiah.

first part of Solomon's wisdom declares that God "has made everything beautiful in its time" (Eccl 3:11), and this notion includes even death. No matter how gruesome and horrible death is, Christians who have put their full confidence in the Lord have assurance that whether in life or death, God will make all things beautiful. This is what Paul states in Phil 1:21, "For to me, to live is Christ, and to die is gain."

For Dorcas, her resurrection meant a continuous life of service to others "that she might continue to make garments for the poor."[73] The same event had a slightly different meaning for the widows. Their grief must have been turned into rejoicing and laughter because they knew that they were not left alone and would continue to receive tangible and emotional support. The faith of other believers in Joppa was strengthened by seeing the miracle of God's power to resurrect someone to life. "Christ raised the daughter of Jairus by His own power; Peter invoked Christ's aid. . .With a word of command—'Tabitha, arise!' (compare Luke 7:14; 8:54; John 11:43)."[74] But the greater miracle that was performed in that city was

---

The angels understood at His birth that Jesus was to be the great peace-bringer, as they called out, 'Glory to God in the highest: and on earth peace, goodwill toward men!' (Luke 2:14-17; compare Is. 9:7)" (Jack W. Hayford, ed., *Spirit Filled Life Study Bible* [Nashville, TN: Thomas Nelson, 1997], Na 1:9).

The following five Greek words describe the comprehensive nature of health in the New Testament: (1) *hugies*–the quality of soundness derived from a proper balance of the whole being (Luke 5:31; 7:10; 15:27); (2) *eirene*–a state of peace or tranquility (Rom 5:1; Col 1:20; Phil 4:7); (3) *zoe* –life (John 3:16; 10:10; Rom 1:17; Gal 3:11); (4) *teleios*–perfect, mature, complete (Matt 5:48); and (5) *soteria*–the condition of being safe and sound (Luke 1:69, 71, 77; 19:9; John 4:22). The New Testament usually describes health as life, blessedness, holiness, and maturity. For more information see John Wilkinson, *The Bible and Healing* (Grand Rapids, MI: Eerdmans, 1998), 9-30.

[73] Ellen G. White, *Education* (Boise, ID: Pacific Press, 1903), 217.

[74] Jack W. Hayford, ed., *Spirit Filled Life Study Bible* (Nashville, TN: Thomas Nelson, 1997), Na 1:9. There were ten resurrections in the Bible, in addition to Jesus' resurrection: (1) The son of a widow from Zarephath was raised by Elijah (1 Kgs 17:17-24); (2) the Shunamite's son was raised by Elisha (2 Kgs 4:20-37); (3) a man tossed into Elisha's tomb was raised by God (2 Kgs 13:21); (4) the son of a widow from Nain was raised by Jesus (Luke 7:11-17); (5) Jairus' daughter was raised by Jesus (Mark 5:35-

the fact that "many believed on the Lord" (Acts 9:42). Thus, the sickness and death of the godly disciple Dorcas became the most beautiful event in the life of a number of people. The one who gave her wholehearted ministry of presence to the widows and the poor, was herself visited and ministered to by the presence of the Almighty God through His servant Peter.

Conclusion

From the creation of the world to the redemption of God's people at the Second Advent, Emmanuel's active presence reveals the beauty of God's character and His purpose of salvation. The majestic attributes of His divine nature were reflected by a number of biblical characters of faith, whose names are written in the book of life. Esther, whose inner beauty outshone her physical beauty, had committed herself to the King of the Universe by dedicating herself to the presence of God. This commitment saved her, her family, and the whole nation. Another woman, Anna, who continually lived in the presence of God by dedicating herself to service in "the house of the Lord," was privileged to "gaze upon the beauty of the Lord" (Ps 27:4) and prophesy about the Redeemer. A Christian disciple, Dorcas, dedicated herself fully to the widows and the poor in Joppa. She, too, reflected the ministry of the presence of her Lord. Her sudden death ended with glorious resurrection and the continuation of her active ministry for the needy.

It is not a coincidence that the names of these three women are found on the pages of the sacred Scriptures. These few biblical examples of God's beauty, goodness, and truth manifested in the lives of common people provide powerful evidence for the blessings of the ministry of presence. Today every child of God is called to live and minister in the sustaining presence of Jesus so that everyone will be ready for the fast-approaching day of the eschatological

---

43); (6) Lazarus was raised by Jesus (John 11:1-44); (7) Dorcas was raised by Peter (Acts 9:36-41); (8) Eutychus was raised by Paul (Acts 20:7-12); (9) The individuals at Jesus' crucifixion were resurrected by God (Matt 27:51-53); and (10) Moses was resurrected by God (Jude 1:9). See "The Ten: Resurrections in the Bible (Other than Jesus')," *Adventist Record* (April 12, 2017), accessed on February 15, 2021, https://record.adventistchurch.com/2017/04/12/the-ten-resurrections-in-the-bible-other-than-jesus/.

harvest. That day will culminate in the eternal presence and glorification of Jesus and the salvation of the redeemed. Moreover, then they will see and praise the presence of His majestic beauty face to face (Mark 14:62; Rev 22: 4, 5).

God's Love for Animals in the Torah: Are They Among the "Poor"?

A. Rahel Wells

Abstract

This paper focuses on the connections between the poor and animals in the Torah, and argues that many of the same elements of human responsibility towards the poor correlate with the responsibility towards non-human animals. Thus, although non-human animals are never said to be "poor" in the Torah, the connections between the two groups indicate their dependence on humans for their needs, as well as God's heart of love towards them.

Introduction

Commands to care for the poor abound in the Torah.[1] Interestingly, God also indicates that the poor will always be present, perhaps to remind everyone of their need to bless others and not be so focused on themselves. However, the Torah indicates that we are to seek to eradicate poverty, and that God desires to do this among his people. Kaminsky notes that Deut 15 sets forth the ideal (no poor), but then states the reality (poor always there) and then gives guidelines on reaching towards the ideal.[2]

In addition, although non-human animals are not the main focus of the Bible, God also makes clear that he cares for them, and asks humans to do the same. My mother, Jo Ann Davidson, is a lover of animals. She taught me from a young age to value and care for all of God's creatures. My research on God's care for animals is a natural extension of all that she embodies and practices.

---

[1] The various words for "poor" occur many times in the Torah, but only 11% of the times the words occur are in the Torah. Scheffler argues that this is because the focus of the Torah is indeed on caring for the oppressed, but it does this through narrative as well as law. Eben Scheffler, "Of Poverty Prevention in the Pentateuch as a Continuing Contemporary Challenge," *Verbum et Ecclesia* 34 (2013): 2.

[2] Joel S. Kaminsky, "'The Might of My Own Hand Has Gotten Me This Wealth': Reflections on Wealth and Poverty in the Hebrew Bible and Today," *Interpretation: A Journal of Bible and Theology* 73 (2019): 11.

Treatment of the Poor

Although there are many specific elements of how the poor are to be treated, they can be grouped in three main categories: physical/material provision; treating fairly; and having a proper heart attitude towards them.

The first main aspect of how people are to treat the poor involves providing for them physically and/or materially. On a yearly basis, the poor are to be allowed to glean from the fields (Lev 19:9, 10; Deut 24:19, 21). Rather than leaving the grain to rot, or coming back to take every little piece, the poor were to be allowed to take all that remains for their own sustenance. In addition, during the jubilee, people are to share food with them, especially the produce of the harvest (Exod 23:11; Lev 25:6). And this is not a typical sharing of food, but an injunction to leave the land fallow, so that whatever grows in it is to be for the needy (*'ebyon*) in Exod 23 and for the servants and sojourners in Lev 25. This is also to apply to the vineyards and olive trees, which did not need to be seeded to produce in abundance, unlike the field.

Even part of the tithe paid by every household is to be given to the poor (Deut 14:28-29; 26:12, 13). When a person is rich, they are to be more generous to the poor, rather than hoarding everything to themselves (Deut 15:7-11). If the poor are in need, they are to be lent whatever they need (Num 22; Deut 15), indicating that help for the poor is of greater importance than accumulating wealth. For example, as Scheffler notes, Lev 23:22 indicates that the people who were to be generous to the poor were not necessarily wealthy themselves.[3]

Secondly, the poor are to be treated fairly, and not to be taken advantage of, even when helping them. Usury is forbidden, so no interest could be collected from the poor (Exod 22:25; Lev 25:36). This stipulation protected them from unscrupulous people taking advantage of their need and making money off their inability to pay back quickly. In addition, when the poor gave their cloak as their pledge, one was to return it to them at the end of the day, since they often gave their only garment, and that is what kept them warm (Exod 22:26-27; Deut 24:10-13).

The laborers were also to receive their wages at the end of the day, rather than having to wait, and this was especially crucial for the poor as this would often mean they could actually eat and survive (Lev 19:13). Deuteronomy 24:15 takes it a step further and notes that "you

[3] Scheffler, "Poverty Prevention," 8.

shall give him his wages on the same day, before the sun sets (for he is poor and counts on it), lest he cry against you to the LORD, and you be guilty of sin."[4] Thus, it is not just a matter of helping the poor, but is a matter of right and wrong to not pay the laborers their due, especially if they are poor. God will hold people accountable.

In addition, the bond servants are to be set free in the jubilee year (Lev 25:38-42, 47-54; Deut 15:12-15). Also, the poor could recover their property in the jubilee year (Lev 25:25-30). In this way, whatever means had been taken from them in disadvantage would return to them, and they would be able to start afresh with their land and freedom intact. Any slave who was freed is also to receive supplies and means to live when they depart, not just literal freedom (Deut 12:12-18).

The third way that people are to look at the poor is to have a heart change. They are not to close up their hearts to the poor but are always to be willing to lend to the poor, so much so that "there will be no poor among you" (Deut 15:4). The temptation would be to harden one's heart and shut up one's hand against the poor, reasoning that it would be an inconvenience or hardship to share with them (Deut 15:7). Instead, the people are to lend to the poor whatever they need (Deut 15:8). This is especially true as the sabbatical year and jubilee years are coming close, since the poor would automatically be taken care of at that point, and the Israelites would also want to preserve what they have for the upcoming time of need.[5] But Moses warns the people to "take care lest there be an unworthy thought in your heart and you say, 'The seventh year, the year of release is near,' and your eye look grudgingly on your poor brother, and you give him nothing, and he cry to the LORD against you, and you be guilty of sin" (Deut 15:9). This is not a neutral matter, as it becomes sin when people hoard their belongings and shut off their compassion. This whole passage is filled with language of the heart, noting that "you shall give to him freely, and your heart shall not be grudging when you give to him" (Deut 15:10).[6]

---

[4] Unless otherwise noted, all biblical quotations are from the ESV.

[5] Kaminsky ("Might of My Own Hand," 11) notes the second point, and also points out that by blessing others, they open up the chance to be continually further blessed by God.

[6] This is also likely because wealth brings a measure of security, which is only an illusion. It can keep people from focusing on God being the origin of all their wealth (Kaminsky, "Might of My Own Hand," 10).

As noted in Lev 25:35, the Israelites were also to bring the poor to live with them if needed: "If your brother becomes poor and cannot maintain himself with you, you shall support him as though he were a stranger and a sojourner, and he shall live with you." This would prevent people from feeling superior due to their greater wealth. The sojourner, fatherless, and widows (who would all likely be among the poor) were also to take part in all the feasts, implying that those who had more means would provide for them in this time as well (Deut 16:11, 14).[7] In the next chapter, even though it would be God's ideal for there to be no poor in Israel, Moses notes that "there will never cease to be poor in the land" (Deut 15:11), likely due to the people's lack of compassion.

In many of these cases, God indicates that He hears the cries of the poor people when they are unfairly treated, and shows compassion on them (cf. Exod 22:27). The reason that Israel is to treat poor people so kindly is because they also were poor, sojourners, and servants, and God rescued them. They are to remember their origins (Lev 25:38, 42, 55). As a result of this, they are also to make sure justice is done for the poor, and not to favor the rich (Exod 23:2-6).

These three main categories of care for the poor are to be done even though people can be poor for a multitude of reasons. Most of the time, it is not their fault, and they were oppressed in some way, but Proverbs makes clear that sometimes poverty comes from laziness.[8] In addition, sometimes people do not plan to prevent poverty and become poor as a result.[9] But no matter how one became poor, it was incumbent on the Israelites to help them.[10] Similarly, as we will see, non-human animals are also to be treated according to the same three basic principles of care.

---

[7] Scheffler ("Poverty Prevention," 8) also agrees that the specific categories were chosen to give direct examples of who the poor are, and that servants could be used as a representative of other groups of poor people.

[8] Kaminsky ("Might of My Own Hand," 12-15) discusses these different possibilities.

[9] Scheffler, "Poverty Prevention," 3.

[10] For more discussion on this, see Fook-Kong Wong, "A Reflection on the Nature and Theological Basis for Poverty and Debt Laws in the Pentateuch," *Review and Expositor* 111 (2014): 187-195.

Treatment of Non-human Animals

In general in the Torah, while less important than humans, non-human animals are also important to God. Non-human animals are considered "persons" according to the biblical definition. They are called *nepesh khayah*, which is often translated as "living soul" for humans and "living creature" for non-human animals, but is the same phrase (cf. Gen 1:21; 2:7). Non-human animals eat the same food, breathe the same air, have the breath of life just like humans, and are considered as flesh along with humans. In Gen 1, non-human animals are blessed and told to be fruitful and multiply and fill the earth. Non-human animals are also involved in covenants with God (Gen 9), are to keep the Sabbath (Exod 20; Deut 5), and are not to touch Mount Sinai along with humans (Exod 19:13; 34:3).

Non-human animals are considered part of the household in Israel, similar to the servants and sojourners living in various households. The plagues and deliverances fall on non-human animals and humans alike (Gen 6-8; Exod 8-11). Non-human animals are also responsible and accountable for various things. They are not to kill humans, and will have the death penalty if they do (Gen 9:5-6); they are also killed if they commit bestiality (Lev 20:16). In Num 8:16, YHWH seems to consider non-human animals as part of the children of Israel. In multiple places, non-human animals are considered part of the household (cf. Exod 8-11; 20:8-11; Josh 7:24).

Humans are also to be caretakers of the earth and all its creatures, acting as God's representatives on the earth, ruling it as he would if he were in our place. The Hebrew verbs (*radah* and *kabash*) in Gen 1:26-28 do not give license to abuse, but demand a just and wise rule over God's creation. Genesis 2:15 reiterates this principle of care for all creatures by using Hebrew verbs for humanity's care of the garden that are also associated with the priestly care of the temple, seeming to indicate the importance of this task.

Multiple laws indicate that humans should show compassion towards non-human animals and treat them fairly and kindly, with many similarities towards how humans are to treat poor people. Indeed, specifically in relation to the poor, non-human animals are often included in the care provided or are considered to need similar treatment.

First, non-human animals are to be provided for physically similar to the poor. Non-human animals and the poor come together most clearly in Lev 25, where the year of jubilee was to be patterned after the weekly Sabbath. During that time, the produce was not to be harvested at all, but left for the servants, the sojourners and all the domestic and wild non-human animals to eat (Lev 25:6-7). This would be more than gleaning, or sharing the produce, but would involve actually leaving it for them, and trusting that God will take care of the owner of the field by bringing an extra harvest in the sixth year (Lev 25:20-22).

Exodus 23 reflects a similar situation. They are to sow and gather produce for 6 years, "but the seventh year you shall let it rest and lie fallow, that the poor of your people may eat; and what they leave, the beasts of the field may eat" (v. 11). This was also to apply to the vineyards and olive groves. In the next verse, Moses makes clear that the reason for resting on the Sabbath day is "that your ox and your donkey may have rest, and the son of your servant woman and the alien may be refreshed" (v. 12). Here the non-human animals are mentioned first, not necessarily because they are more important, but perhaps because they were most likely to be exploited or oppressed. In addition, the word for non-human animal rest here is *nuakh*, which is elsewhere used for God's rest (Exod 20:11), and implies emotional and spiritual rest, not just physical.[11] Thus, part of the way that Israel was called to care for the poor and the non-human animals involved providing emotional rejuvenation, not simply a cessation of labor. A provision for non-human Sabbath rest would likely ensure humane treatment of non-human animals on other days as well.[12] So this provision for the poor and the non-human animals on the sabbatical year brings together the notion of caring for physical needs and spiritual needs at the same time.

While Exod 23:12 does not mention the poor, in light of v. 11 it seems that they would be implied by the servants and strangers as is also the case in Lev 25. Most often, people became servants because they were poor, as evidenced by being able to regain the land they had lost at the time of the jubilee (Lev 25). So, the non-human animals are to receive the food from the year of jubilee, along with the poor. And non-human animals are to be able to rest on the Sabbath, along with the poor.

---

[11] See my article, A. Rahel Schafer, "Rest for the Animals? Nonhuman Sabbath Repose in Pentateuchal Law," *Bulletin of Biblical Research* 22 (2013): 167-186.

[12] C. Meyers, *Exodus* (The New Cambridge Bible Commentary, Cambridge: Cambridge University Press, 2005), 163-166.

Similarly to the poor, non-human animals are also not to be taken advantage of. Non-human animals are worthy of their labor, and are not to be prevented from eating while they work (Deut 25:4). This would be connected with giving the wages on the same day to the poor; since eating throughout the day is part of the normal habits of oxen, it is thus comparable to wages for humans. Paul quotes this passage in 1 Corinthians, to indicate that those who work need to be paid, even if it seems that they are doing it out of the kindness of their hearts. Further supporting this connection between working humans and animals, historians note that an ox could be substituted for any laborer in rabbinic thought at that time.[13]

Various other laws prescribe kindness and care for non-human animals, even while they are working (e.g., Exod 23:4-5.)[14] Deuteronomy 22:1-2 states that "you shall not see your brother's ox or his sheep going astray and ignore them. You shall take them back to your brother. And if he does not live near you and you do not know who he is, you shall bring it home to your house, and it shall stay with you until your brother seeks it. Then you shall restore it to him." When non-human animals are lost, they are to be taken back to their owners. But if you cannot find the owner, you are to care for the non-human animal until you can figure out who it belongs to. While this is also a kindness to the owner, the basic immediate need is that of the non-human animal, which is not to be ignored. This even applies to the donkey of your enemy (Exod 23:4).

In addition, Deut 22:4 notes that "you shall not see your brother's donkey or his ox fallen down by the way and ignore them. You shall help him to lift them up again." This is a direct help for the non-human animal who is burdened. Rather than leaving the non-human animal there to be in pain or struggle, you are to help the non-human animal while it is working. The implication may also be that you relieve some

---

[13] For further discussion, see my article, A. Rahel Schafer, "'Does God Care About Oxen?': Another Look at Paul's Use of Deuteronomy 25:4 in 1 Corinthians 9:9," *Journal of the Adventist Theological Society* 21 (2010): 114-132.

[14] D. Block sees a triangular interrelationship between God, earth, and all living creatures. Humans are the linchpin that interconnect all three, governing the world for God as his representatives ("All Creatures Great and Small: Recovering a Deuteronomic Theology of Animals," in *The Old Testament in the Life of God's People: Essays in Honor of Elmer A. Martens* [ed. J. Isaak; Winona Lake, IN: Eisenbrauns, 2009], 283-305).

of its burdens. Once again, this is also a help to the owner, but that does not negate the immediate help for the non-human animal and not beating it while it is down. This is corroborated by Exod 23:5, which notes that even for the donkey of an enemy who is lying under a heavy burden, "you shall refrain from leaving (*'azab*) him with it; you shall rescue (*'azab*) it with him," implying that the help is more than just getting the non-human animal up again (by using the verb *'azab* two times, with opposite connotations).

This could be in contrast to the story of Balaam, who tortured his donkey and beat her severely when she lay down under him, even though she was trying to protect him. God makes it very clear that these cruel actions towards the donkey eclipsed his greed in going to curse Israel, and were even worthy of death, although his own donkey protected him from it, despite his abuse of her (Num 22).[15] It is also interesting to note that Exod 23:6, the next verse after the injunction to help up a burdened donkey, talks about not perverting justice to the poor in a lawsuit, further connecting non-human animals with the poor.

Third, people are also to show compassion towards non-human animals and have a heart change in this regard. Although there is not a direct statement on this as with the poor, one can see this in several ways by implication. Baby non-human animals are to remain with their mother for a time, showing compassion towards the creaturely bonds (Exod 22:30). Sacrifices are to be limited compared to the ancient Near East and what Solomon does in actuality. When non-human animals are eaten, the blood must first be drained, to respect the life of the non-human animal (Gen 9:3; Lev 17:10-11; Acts 15), and the original diet did not include any non-human animals at all (Gen 1:29-31).

The Sabbath connection is another crucial element, which would affect non-human animals as well (Exod 20:8-11; 23:11-12; Deut 5:12-15). They are not to work just like the humans are not to work, even though there would be a temptation to make them work since they are "just animals." In spite of the fact that non-human animals were crucial for the day-to-day survival activities of harvesting crops, threshing grain for bread, etc., the Sabbath commands seek to ensure that non-

---

[15] See my dissertation on this passage: A. Rahel Schafer, "'You, YHWH, Save Humans and Animals:' God's Response to the Vocalized Needs of Non-Human Animals" (Wheaton College, PhD Diss., 2016).

human animals are not abused or overworked.[16] The Sabbath rest is to pertain to the non-human animals as well, partly due to the connections with creation (Exod 20), which is when non-human animals were made also, partly due to the connection with redemption (Deut 5), which is where non-human animals were rescued also, and partly due to the need for rest which all creatures have (Exod 23).

Interestingly, unlike humans in Exodus 23 (the Hebrew verb *shabat* is used for humanity's Sabbath rest in Exod 23:12), the non-human animals are to be rejuvenated on the Sabbath by the same verb that is used for YHWH's rest in Exodus 20 (*nuakh*). This special connection between YHWH and non-human animals implies that YHWH places a high value on all his creatures, not just humanity.

In addition, all non-human animals are blessed by Sabbath rest, including domestic and even wild non-human animals, through their connection with the sabbatical year (Lev 25).[17] The notion of care even

---

[16] See Oded Borowski, *Every Living Thing: Daily Use of Animals in Ancient Israel* (Lanham, MD: AltaMira, 1999). However, this leads to the tension between viewing Sabbath as giving rest to laborers (both human and non-human animal), and viewing Sabbath as the cessation of trying to provide for oneself one day a week.

Additionally, this raises the question as to whether non-human animals are held responsible on some level for keeping the Sabbath, as they appear to be for other commands of YHWH (e.g., Gen 9:5-6; Exod 19:13; 21:28; 34:3; Lev 20:15-16). This is not to deny that the main concern of Sabbath is humans, but that does not eliminate concern for non-human animal rest as well. This cannot be compared to the modern Jewish use of a stove on Sabbath, because non-human animals are living creatures. The land and rocks are not told to rest in the commandments, even though they were a crucial part of the economy as well.

[17] Although Leviticus does not reiterate the Sabbath commandment in the same manner as the Decalogue, observance of the Sabbath is assumed in several instances, and is mentioned more specifically in regard to the festivals and the Day of Atonement (Lev 16:31; 19:3, 30; 23:3, 8, 11, 15-16, 32, 38; 24:8; 26:2). However, in comparison to Exodus and Deuteronomy, the concept of the sabbatical year seems to take on a greater significance in the Holiness Code (Leviticus 19-26). J. Milgrom notes parallels between this passage and Lev 23:3a (*Leviticus 23–27: A New Translation with Introduction and Commentary*; Anchor Bible 3B [New York: Doubleday, 2001], 2157), while F. R. Kinsler connects the Exodus to the Jubilee and the care of creation ("Leviticus 25," *Int* 53 [1999]: 395-399). See also G. J. Wenham, *The Book of Leviticus* (Grand Rapids, MI: Eerdmans, 1979).

for the non-human animals further removed from contact with humans makes it clear how much YHWH cares for all of his creatures.

Also somewhat connected to the Sabbath, land goes into rest during the sabbatical year and the exile (Lev 25), which would imply rest for the non-human animals as well. Clearly the land is not alive in the same way as oxen or donkeys, but it is also deserving of some sort of Sabbath rest, perhaps inclusively representing all life contained on it.[18] This could be compared similarly to when the land returns to the original owner in the jubilee year.

Treatment of Non-human Animals as the Poor: Reflections across Scripture

These basic principles of caring for non-human animals in similar ways as humans are to care for the poor are reiterated throughout the rest of the Bible. Due to space constraints, I will only focus on a few passages about non-human animals and how these principles play out.

Humans are called to care physically for non-human animals. But even when they do not, non-human animals cry out to God, and he hears them and provides sustenance for them. God responds to their needs in Ps 104, Joel 2, Ps 147, and Job 38-41. God provides food for the lions in Ps 104:21, and water and food for the suffering non-human animals in Joel 2. In Ps 147 and Job 38, God gives food to the baby ravens when they cry out to him.

In the New Testament, when non-human animals are in need, Jesus instructs us to take care of them, even when doing so on the Sabbath requires what would normally be considered work. In Luke 13:15, Jesus mentions the well-being of oxen on the Sabbath who need water to drink, and therefore promotes the healing of humans on the Sabbath as well. By mentioning the loosing of oxen from their stalls in order to give them a drink, this passage seems to assume that the oxen were not working on the Sabbath (as commanded in Exod 20:8-11; 23:10-12; Deut 5:12-15), but remained in their stalls resting from their labors.

[18] Leviticus 26:31-44 also includes the concept of Sabbath rest for the land, but non-human animals are not specifically mentioned in relation to Sabbath in that passage. It is important to note that the Hebrew verb in this passage is *ratsah* ("to restore/make amends") which implies that the land is not actively participating in repose and rejuvenation, but is being restored from human abuse and overuse. In light of this, it seems that YHWH cares for all of his creation, but that living creatures take priority over plants and land masses.

Non-human animals are also not to be taken advantage of. In the new earth, there will be no fear or violence between humans and non-human animals (Isa 11:6-9; 65:25; Rev 21-22), implying that should be the goal now as well. The prophets condemn cruelty to non-human animals, even if indirectly (Isa 46:1; Hos 4:1-3). Non-human animals are involved in additional covenants with God (Job 5:23; Hos 2:18). Psalm 36:6 states that YHWH saves both humans and non-human animals (*behemah* here, usually referring to larger land animals). In Jonah 3:7-8, non-human animals are to fast along with humans and cry out to God for salvation from the destruction of Nineveh, which he graciously provides.[19]

The New Testament has a similar view of non-human animals and the poor; using similar language for our responsibility towards both (Luke 3:11; 14:3; Acts 6:1; Gal 2:10; James 2:15-16). In response to the accusation that his healing on the Sabbath broke the fourth commandment, Jesus replied in Matt 12:11 that sheep (or oxen and donkeys in Luke 14:5) could be lifted out of a pit on the Sabbath. Jesus' argument depends upon the spirit of non-human animal rest and care that is portrayed in the Sabbath commandments of the Torah, and his reasoning is actually dependent on the similarities between humans and non-human animals, rather than highlighting the differences. So, even in Jesus' day, the importance of rest and repose for non-human animals on the Sabbath was maintained, reflecting the spirit of care for all creatures shown clearly in the Pentateuch.[20]

Humans are also to have a compassionate heart towards non-human animals. In Prov 12:10 the righteous person "knows the soul" (*yada' nepesh*) of his non-human animal, similar to how Israel is to "know the soul" (*yada' nepesh*) of the sojourner (Exod 23:9). The sojourners were

---

[19] See Schafer, "You, YHWH, Save Humans and Animals." Job 12:7- 10 implies that non-human animals know that God is in charge and directing events of the world, even the lives of every living thing.

[20] In the New Testament, the church realized the value of the jubilee principles, and attempted to make them applicable at all times, as they shared everything in common, helped the needy, and supported freedom from slavery (Acts 2:42-46; 4:34-35; 5:14-16; Gal 3:28; Col 3:11; Phil 15-17). Jesus reiterates the heart-changing intention of the law in Matt 23:23, when he states that justice and mercy are inseparable from acceptable tithing. Paul implies that we should not become destitute ourselves in order to help the destitute, but that we should give as much as we are able, not just what is required (2 Cor 8:12-14).

part of the vulnerable class of people along with the widows and the orphans, and they were most likely to be poor, even though all of them may not have been poor. This idea of soul knowledge is usually translated as fulfilling the needs of the non-human animal, but the connection with the Torah here indicates that much more is involved. The non-human animals have personalities and passions, emotions and experiences.[21] Righteous people will really get to know them and provide love and companionship, not just food and water. Even anecdotally, when one has had a pet, it becomes clear that they each have their own wishes and way of living life. Research has shown that this is true of wild non-human animals as well; including small mammals like squirrels.[22]

All creatures worship God, sometimes better than humans do (Isa 1:3; 43:20; Jer 8:7; Job 12:7-10), but the destruction of the earth is portrayed as due to human sin, and affecting non-human animals through no fault of their own (Rom 8:21-23; Rev 11:18). Thus, our level of compassion should be even higher as a result. And as noted above, when humans do not show compassion for animals, God hears the cries of non-human animals when they are in need and responds to help them (cf. Joel 1-2; Ps 147; Job 38). Additionally, in Isa 13:20-22 and 34:10-17, land is ultimately given to the non-human animals because the people were not faithful.[23]

---

[21] The noun *nepesh* is used broadly to describe everything from personhood to specific individual desires. E. Brotzman notes ten semantic range categories for *nepesh*, and although it is not clear which meaning is referred to here, this passage surely refers to more than the basic needs of food and water that many would automatically assume by the usual English translation of "life" ("Man and the Meaning of *nepesh*," *BSac* 145 [1988]: 400-409). More than just making sure the non-human animals live (or are humanely slaughtered), a righteous man knows the "soul" (as it were) of his non-human animal: the desires, appetites, inner living being, even emotions, passions and personality.

[22] See the recent article on squirrel personalities: J. R. Aliperti, et al, "Bridging Animal Personality with Space Use and Resource Use in a Free-Ranging Population of an Asocial Ground Squirrel," *Animal Behavior* 180 (2021): 291-306.

[23] A. Rahel Wells, "'The Porcupine Shall Possess It': Legitimate Land Acquisition by Non-Human Animals in Isaiah 34," (Paper presented at the virtual Humanimal Conference, March 9, 2023).

In at least one place, non-human animals are actually called "poor." Psalm 34 discusses those who fear the Lord, and how they have no need (*makhsor*). In contrast, the psalmist notes that the young lions (*kefir*) are poor (*rush*) and are hungry (using the verb *ra'ab*), while those who seek (*darash*) the Lord do not lack (*khaser*) any good (*tob*). One could read this in a multitude of ways, including that the young lions are not seeking God, or that their lack is due to human sin. But the words for the lack (in vv. 10, 11 [9, 10]) for humans, and for lions (*rush* in v. 11 [10]) differ, suggesting that a direct comparison here between humans and non-human animals may be misplaced. In addition, the lion is called poor (*rush*) and hungry (*ra'ab*), and in many other passages God shows concern for the poor (cf. Ps 72:12, 14; Prov 21:13) and feeds the hungry (cf. Pss 107:9; 146:7; Prov 20:13). Thus, because lions would die without prey (cf. Job 4:8-11), this verse may be better translated "even strong lions are sometimes hungry," just as God's people sometimes face hunger in spite of such promises.[24]

Furthermore, when compared to Ps 34:8 [7], Ps 145:16 and Ps 104:20 suggest that God fills the desires of all his creatures; these verses parallel Ps 145:20 where God fills the desires of those who fear him, and Ps 111:5 where God provides prey (*terep*) for those who fear him.[25] Similarly, in Ps 123:2 the eye of the servant looks to the hand of his master, and people are to look to God to show mercy. In Ps 104:27, all wait on God (cf. Ps 145:15), God opens his hand, and they are filled with good (cf. Pss 65:10-12 [9-11]; 136:25). God is also the one who directly gives food to the young lions, as in Job 38:39, where God hunts prey for the lion and fills the young lion (*kefir*) with sustenance (*khit*). Psalm 104:21 indicates that the young lions (*kefir*) seek (*baqash*) their

---

[24] In Jer 14:5, 6, other non-human animals suffer from lack of food as well. Compare Isa 32:6, where only the fool keeps the hungry (*ra'eb*) unsatisfied, contrasting God's provision to animals in many other places. Note also Isa 9:19–20, where only the wicked are hungry (*ra'eb*) and not satisfied. Thus, perhaps here the lions suffer because of wicked humans, or this may hint at the possibility for accountability in predators.

[25] Almost all occurrences of the word *terep* involve the prey of lions/wolves, or are used metaphorically as if wicked humans were predatory beasts. Thus, it seems that God is actually providing prey for lions, and suggests that non-human animals may be included in other passages about those who fear him. The only exceptions are Prov 31:15 (calls food in general *terep*), Mal 3:10 (calls the food to bring to God's house *terep*), and Job 24:5 (calls the donkey's food *terep*).

food from God; in this psalm, lions are the only ones to seek God, as humans do not do this.[26] When considering the roar of the lion in Ps 104, it seems to both call out to God when in need, as well as give thanks to God for the food; since the roaring is the finite verb, and it does two things as a result (the infinitives). Thus, while Ps 34:8-11 [7-10] may initially seem to portray lions as lacking and suffering hunger, in contrast to those who seek God and will not lack, further examination indicates that this is not accurate and that God provides for all of his creatures.

Conclusion

Although not enumerated fully here, the Torah makes clear differences between the poor and non-human animals. For instance, the poor are humans, so are more valued, with many more commands to help them, and specific categories of poor are named. In addition, the motivation for helping the poor is due to God rescuing Israel out of slavery.[27] However, animals are often more vulnerable and oppressed even than the poor, as they have no voices that humans understand and so are even more likely to be exploited.

Thus, while God views care for the poor as a high priority in the Torah, humans are also called to care for non-human animals in similar ways, with a caring responsibility (perhaps even towards their very inward beings) and humane treatment. Although non-human animals are not equal to humans in the sacredness of their lives, in many other ways non-human animals have the same privileges as humanity. Specifically, this similarity is shown in the application of the sabbatical year (connected to the blessing of the Sabbath) to the wild non-human animals as well as domestic creatures.

According to the Torah, all are to work, which would include non-human animals and the poor (cf. Exod 20:8-11). However, though individuals may work hard to stay out of poverty, the Torah indicates that there will be times when both humans and non-human animals

[26] Further study could include examining whether in certain biblical passages humans do not seek God, while non-human animals or lions do (compare Pss 14:2; 53:3 [2]; Isa 65:10).

[27] Other ancient Near Eastern sources note the importance of caring for the poor. However, the Bible is unique in the motivations and scope given. See Emmanuel O. Nwaoru, "Poverty Eradication: A Divine Mandate," *African Ecclesial Review* 46 (2004): 198-214.

need additional help from other humans.[28] Although non-human animals are not as important as humans, the many connections between how the poor and non-human animals are to be treated indicates the importance of ethical treatment of both groups. Non-human animals are never considered to be "poor" in the Torah, but they are to be provided for physically, not taken advantage of, and to experience a heart attitude of compassion from those in better economic situations.

[28] As previously mentioned, this chapter does not deal with the causes of poverty, since it does not ultimately matter in God's call to help the poor and non-human animals.

Appendix

Tributes to Jo Ann Davidson from Colleagues, Former Students, and Friends

I remember the first class I took with Jo Ann Davidson—Great Controversy, Covenant, Law, and Sabbath. After greeting us with her winsome smile she announced, with a twinkle in her eye, that our daily devotionals would be taken from the book of Revelation. She then looked off into the distance and began to recite the first chapter by heart. With thespian intensity, spiritual conviction, and rapturous delight her words transported me to the island of Patmos. I beheld Jesus and tears filled my eyes. In awe I wondered to myself, *who is this woman*? Of course, I knew Dr. Davidson had taught many years with my father, Fernando Canale, in the systematic theology department at Andrews University. In fact, when I considered doing a doctorate in systematic theology, I was encouraged by the assurance that there was at least one brilliant lady who had successfully trudged the road ahead of me—and that alone commanded my respect and admiration. But when I sat in her classes and experienced her passionate love for Jesus and His words in Scripture—the grand meta-narrative to which we connect our own—it was impossible to not love her back. As such I am delighted that my dear professor, a godly woman and excellent systematic theologian, is being honored with this festschrift. May it be a small taste of the day when Jesus Himself will celebrate His daughter for her beautiful life of devotion to His cause.

Silvia Canale Bacchiocchi
PhD student
Seventh-day Adventist Theological Seminary, Andrews University

I was introduced to Jo Ann Davidson while working on graduate degrees at Andrews University. Her husband was a member of my dissertation committee and thus Jo Ann and I were introduced during that time. Our quests to earn PhD's overlapped and through the years of engaging at professional conferences, or on the TOSC dealing with the ordination of women, I have been blessed by her scholarship and friendship. Jo Ann's seemingly boundless energy is inspiring. Her call to see theological significance in aesthetics invites us to balance our intellects with a Godly appreciation of beauty. Finally, her caring heart and words of affirmation and encouragement have been a great blessing to me. I am thankful God has raised her up within the ranks of SDA scholars.

Stephen Bauer, PhD
Professor of Theology and Ethics
Southern Adventist University

Jo Ann Davidson has been a significant pioneer for women in Adventist theological studies. Her unique contribution on the aesthetic nature of Scripture, in reclaiming the philosophical concern for aesthetics, brings a renewed perspective to the field of biblical interpretation. Humanity made in God's image, nature, and the beauty of the Bible as a literary masterpiece, all point to the truth and beauty of our Creator God. This hope inspires us to not merely live for the afterlife, but to find joy and beauty in the present created world. Joy can also be seen and felt in Davidson's passionate preaching. I have vivid memories of her preaching with fervor, passion, and boldness in the seminary chapel at Andrews University. I recall her sharing her personal journey to professorship which began with her love of learning. Her early struggles, and bravery to step into a male dominated field, have helped other women to move forward in their calling. A memory that I have of her preaching in chapel one day was when she said that study is the highest form of worship. We must never think that we are wasting time when we study God's Word or engage in study and preparation of the mind. This validation of education helped my perspective as a Ph.D. student to see immense value in the studies I was completing at that time. Her inspiration went beyond what she said, and her appreciation of beauty was also reflected in the care and modesty she took in her clothing and deportment. I feel privileged to have been blessed by the ministry of Jo Ann Davidson.

Katrina Blue, PhD
Associate Professor of Theology & Christian Spirituality
Pacific Union College

Dr. Jo Ann Davidson: Woman of Beauty

Heartiest congratulations to you, Dr. Jo Ann Davidson, on this well-deserved *festschrift!*

It is my joy to pay tribute to your life and legacy and to celebrate you, daughter of the God of beauty.

You might recall that we first met during my second year at the Seventh-day Adventist Theological Seminary in 2013 in a seminar on Narrative Theology (THST 649). In that seminar with you, I chose to study, and write a paper on, the book of Ruth. Imagine that—studying about such a world-changing woman of faith, courage, and resilience with one of similar ilk! Dr. Davidson, in your class I learned through the study of Ruth that God often works in ways we cannot imagine; that He creates beauty—not always against, but often through, that which might be perceived as beauty's antithesis.

You epitomize God's exceeding abundance beyond what we can ask or imagine! In this sometimes-challenging epoch for God's daughters you have, by God's grace and empowerment, lived a beautiful life as an author, beloved wife and mother, child of God, leader, mentor and model, pianist, professor, scholar, Seventh-day Adventist Christian, and all-time woman! You always carry yourself with dignity and poise.

Dr. Davidson, thank you for being a model and inspiration to all God's daughters everywhere. Thank you for being a mentor. I still recall the afternoon you made time to talk through potential directions for my dissertation with me after spending the entire day pressing grapes and bottling grape juice! It has been a blessing for me to "sit at your feet."

Thank you so much for your legacy of beauty and for always inspiring me toward the beautiful life that God has made possible for all!

Wishing you God's continued blessings and beauty,
Jenifer Daley, PhD
Administration Pastor
Pioneer Memorial Church, Andrews University

Jo Ann Davidson is a trailblazer in many areas—as a theologian, seminary professor, and scholar of beauty—to name a few. I would like to focus on how she joins a distinguished group of missionary kids who have blessed this church and the world with service that began in childhood. When missionary families go overseas, as Jo Ann's family went to Singapore, not only the parents go as missionaries, their children go too. Missionary kids also have a role and a witness as they grow up in places where they are obviously different. They are shaped in ways unlike their peers in their home cultures. That shaping can result in people, like Jo Ann, who seek to serve all their lives, who have a worldview that increases creativity, and who productively work for good in the world. Jo Ann's biblical study of beauty, a topic not widely explored by Adventists, underscores that creativity. Her prolific writing on theological issues reveals her dedication to productivity. And her involvement in the life of the seminary, not only teaching but helping with many other activities, shows a servant's heart. Arriving at Faculty Retreat to receive our room assignments from a welcoming, and very organized, Jo Ann, or seeing her with apron on at the new student dinners or leading out in Sabbath evening vespers are small examples of how I personally witnessed her willingness to serve in any capacity. Thank you, Jo Ann, for being part of that illustrious group of missionary kids who are outstanding examples of truly lifelong service.

Cheryl Doss, PhD
Retired Director
General Conference Institute of World Mission

Dr. Jo Ann Davidson was invited to speak to my church for two women's retreats. Her exposition of the Sabbath and the character of Jesus Christ was so moving, it brought tears to many of our eyes. As a well-known scholar, professor, but most importantly, a woman who passionately loves God, she has brought many closer to Him. As

Proverbs 31 exclaims, "Give her of the fruit of her hands; and let her own works praise her in the gates!"

Arlyn S. Drew, MD, MBA, PhD
Adjunct Professor of Theology and Christian Philosophy
Seventh-day Adventist Theological Seminary, Andrews University

Dear Jo Ann,

Your contributions to Adventist theology and scholarship have impacted an entire generation of pastors and theologians, and in particular women in ministry for the Seventh-day Adventist Church. Your impact and influence have transformed many lives. It has been an honor to share a teaching ministry with you in our department at the Seminary. May God continue to richly bless your ministry.

Denis Fortin, PhD
Professor of Historical Theology
Seventh-day Adventist Theological Seminary, Andrews University

Dr. Jo Ann Davidson has made a unique and pioneering contribution to the Seventh-day Adventist Church and its Theological Seminary at Andrews University. Her scholarly writing, teaching, and passionate presentations all around the world have been developing a legacy for all Adventists and a role model especially for women who are called and gifted by God to work in the area of theology. Dr. Davidson's special contribution is not in spite of her being a woman, but partly because of her female perspective. Not only is she a fine theologian by any standard, having overcome some gender prejudice along the way; she additionally enriches our understanding by bringing to our attention important concepts that we have missed or neglected, such as the biblically significant theology of beauty. I am thrilled that she is honored by this volume and that its contributors demonstrate such a wealth of Adventist female theological expertise that is rapidly growing for the benefit of our Lord's end-time mission.

Roy E. Gane, PhD
Professor of Hebrew Bible and Ancient Near Eastern Languages
Seventh-day Adventist Theological Seminary, Andrews University

I remember Dr. Davidson's strong animal advocacy in the classroom with really strong theological arguments, but what stands out was when I stepped into her office to argue a grade on a paper. . . [I had] done this many times before and I know the way to a teacher's heart is kindness, respect, hard work and understanding or empathy to their plight in grading papers. I was so sure that she would change my grade, because in my eyes I put in the effort and the sermon I wrote was '40 minutes' long. . . well. . . little did I know this tough cookie who had such a heart for animals was such an experienced scholar that she deconstructed my whole sermon and proved to me in no uncertain terms how my sermon was junk and how gracious she had been with her grade. . . No arguments, no bad feelings, just pure AWE at the brilliance of such a scholar. . . yet she was funny, approachable, kind, and loved Dick. . . there was not one day in class that she did not speak about Dick and her love and admiration for him. Dr. Davidson is class!

Brian Gonzalez, MDiv
Seventh-day Adventist Theological Seminary, Andrews University

It is a beautiful privilege and pleasure for me to give a tribute to Dr. Jo Ann Davidson who is a specialist in the theology of beauty, as is evident in her research and publications on that subject. I have been JoAnn's colleague at Andrews University for almost 20 years since 2004 when I joined the faculty of the Department of Theology and Christian Philosophy. Her contributions to our deliberations during faculty meetings have always communicated a wealth of wisdom. In addition, I am inspired by her example of service to Christ in the classroom, in the society of scholars, and in service to church leaders and members. JoAnn's students and colleagues honor her as a faithful servant of God and a trusted friend to humanity. At the same time, the full impact of her words and actions is known only to God who called, equipped, and ordained her for gospel ministry through the spiritual gift of scholarship. Dr. JoAnn, we thank God for you, and we claim His promise to continue blessing you and making you a blessing.

Martin Hanna, PhD
Associate Professor of Systematic Theology
Co-Editor, Andrews University Seminary Studies
Director, Theological Center for Interdisciplinary Dialogue
Seventh-day Adventist Theological Seminary, Andrews University
Pastor, All Nations Church, Berrien Springs, MI

As a female responding to the call of God, I was plunged into the masculine world of the Seventh-day Adventist Seminary at Andrews University. Although many of the male staff were very supportive of females in ministry, it was wonderful to discover that amidst all the testosterone, there was also a female scholar in the Theology and Christian Philosophy Department. From the outset, I was impressed by Jo Ann Davidson's passion for Jesus, Scripture and the Sabbath. It is through this passion that I gained a new appreciation of the Sabbath and the joy it could bring. Jo Ann also ignited an interest in narrative theology, ecotheology, and the beauty of scripture which continue to inform my current views and research. In addition, I was blessed to benefit from her mentoring. Although Jo Ann had a busy schedule, she carved out time to catch up with me twice a semester during my doctoral studies. I appreciated her interest and care as I was being prepared for my own leadership role.

Today I recognize and celebrate the pathway that Jo Ann blazed as the first Seventh-day Adventist woman to obtain a PhD in systematic theology, the first female academic hired in the Theology and Christian Philosophy Department at Andrews University, and the first female president of the Adventist Theological Society. Thank you, Jo Ann, for courageously stepping into those roles and showing those of us you taught, along with so many other females, that leadership in theology is not solely a male domain, but also possible for females.

Wendy Jackson, PhD
Head, Avondale Seminary

Dear Dr. Jo Ann Davidson,

An inspirer. A caring scholar. An enthusiastic and engaging teacher. These three characteristics describe a glimpse of how seriously you utilized your God-given potentials to change the lives of your students. Your teaching styles allowed me to appreciate the power of reason and are empowering. In your classroom, you intentionally created a safe learning environment that encouraged critical thinking.

My mind cannot detach itself from the great souvenirs I kept from your class, Understanding the Christian World, that I attended in 2007. I learned how to reach my brothers and sisters in the Roman Catholic, Protestant, and post-denominational churches. I gained a solid theological ground on how to be an effective evangelist. Had it not been for your class, my first evangelistic series in Quebec would have turned into a mess. I was able to preach my first evangelistic campaign to a Muslim community.

In fact, I preached in a bowling place night after night. The title of my evangelistic campaign about social issues in Quebec was "*La solution aux accomodements raisonable.*" I had never before seen an evangelistic title without Jesus's name. It was a shock for me. I finally addressed the social issues on how to accommodate differences with respect and love. At the end of the series, those who attended realized that only Jesus could bring respect and love in Christian community. Five Muslims came forward and received baptism. Pastor Jean Hercule who sent me was so proud and the church pastor called me, "Little Apostle Paul."

Your teaching insights prepared me for my first evangelistic meeting in Quebec and shaped my understanding on how to do ministry in a diversified context. You have a unique [ability] to welcome all cultures. I often heard it from other students, "she is real." You made us feel authentically supported when you said to the class, "Please let me know how I can be helpful."

In addition, your enthusiastic nature is unique. I understand why Ellen G. White says, "An important element in educational work is enthusiasm." I cannot recount one time that you came to class with a negative spirit. Your positive spirit controlled the whole classroom environment. Your class was a sanctuary. When a student (from Haiti like myself) was dealing with personal issues, you stopped the class and took time to pray for her. You are amazing!

I often do not take time to express my gratitude for the support from others. So, I want to thank you, Dr. Jo Ann Davidson, for imprinting your taste of knowledge, your sense of humor, and your love for teaching in me. I am now making a great difference as a mathematics and bible teacher at DePaul Academy dealing with youth at risk.

Thank you for being a genuine teacher. Thank you for seeing great potential in your students. Thank you for being you, a woman of God. Thank you for being one of the few great female teachers out there. May you continue to inspire others to achieve greatness for Jesus.

With gratitude,
Ernst Jacques, MDiv
Seventh-day Adventist Theological Seminary, Andrews University

To be recognized with a *Festschrift* after a long and fruitful academic career—what an honor! But to be done so as a theologian of beauty is truly splendid. Dr. Davidson's efforts to bring this "forgotten transcendental" (von Balthasar) to the forefront of Adventist attention is commendable on many fronts. For one, we are naturally attracted to predications or descriptions of things as vivid, graceful, elegant, balanced, integrated, synthetic, coherent, and holistic—all of which are aesthetic categories *par excellence*. But more pertinently, theological aesthetics goes to the heart of the Christian faith in that no discussion of, let's say, worship, sanctification, or eschatology is possible without some recourse to notions such as desire, attraction, and glory. And if Jonathan Edwards is correct in identifying benevolence as the primary beauty of moral agents, and if, accordingly, the highest form of beauty is God's self-giving love in his acts of creation and redemption, then the Sabbath, which is Dr. Davidson's other longstanding scholarly interest, represents a perfect counterpoint to her reflections on beauty. In fact, it is the triangulation of aesthetics, worship, and ethics, particularly as it concerns animal rights and environmental justice, that I consider one of the most salient features of her scholarly legacy. For these and other reasons, I feel honored to be her colleague in the Department of Theology and Christian Philosophy at Andrews University.

Grace and peace,
Ante Jeroncic, PhD
Department of Theology and Christian Philosophy
Seventh-day Adventist Theological Seminary, Andrews University

Jo Ann Davidson has done many wonderful things in her personal and professional life. But apart from her homemaking, mothering, music making, studying, teaching, preaching, and writing, she has been a friend and an encourager. Jo Ann is an authentic person who lives on the outside what she is on the inside. Her passion for truth sparks in her eyes. Her face reflects the intense earnestness of her longing for God. I am blessed to reflect back to her in words the way I have experienced my friend. "Thank you, Jo Ann!"

Brenda Kiš
Brenda's late husband, Dr. Miroslav Kiš, was a dear mentor and colleague of Jo Ann's and with this tribute we also honor his memory.

Dr. Davidson was synonymous with the Theology and Christian Philosophy Department when I first entered the seminary in the fall of 2006. Although I never had the pleasure of taking one of her courses, my friends all had wonderful things to say about her classes. She was and still is known for the passion and intellect she brings to the study of theology.

As the first woman hired to work in the Theology and Christian Philosophy Department at the seminary, Dr. Davidson has been an example and role model for female students and theologians. Her contributions go far beyond the classroom through her scholarship, publishing, and leadership in the Adventist Theological Society.

Thank you Dr. Jo Ann Davidson for being who you are, and for serving God with your amazing talents!

Amanda McGuire-Moushon, PhD
Assistant Dean for Graduate Education
School of Graduate Studies & College of Education and International Services, Andrews University

Dr. Jo Ann Davidson was one of my first teachers at the Seminary. And she was one of the best teachers I have ever had. She brought a rare combination of passion and exceptional competence to the classroom. She was always well-prepared and she expected her students to be also.

I had the privilege of taking a number of classes from her, including her outstanding Seminar in Narrative Theology, which opened my eyes to the beauty and importance of biblical narrative. I loved her classes and learned so very much in each one of them. I was inspired by her teaching to greater love for our great God and a desire to study more and more to know Him better. And, I continue to be inspired by Dr. Davidson in many ways.

I am extremely grateful for her excellent pioneering work as a scholar and teacher in our church. And, at a more personal level, I will be forever grateful for the positive and deeply formative impact she has had on my own life, first as my teacher and also as a colleague. Along my own journey, she has encouraged me countless times and I am so thankful for her.

What a privilege it has been to learn from Dr. Davidson and work alongside her, a great scholar and teacher and mighty servant of the living God, who exemplifies the best of what it means to be a teacher-scholar who unashamedly loves and faithfully follows Christ.

Blessings,
John C. Peckham, PhD
Research Professor of Theology and Christian Philosophy
Seventh-day Adventist Theological Seminary, Andrews University
Associate Editor, Adventist Review Ministries

I am grateful for this opportunity to express my thanks to Jo Ann for the many ways she has served as a model for me and many other Seminary faculty women and students during her ministry here at the Seminary. I have so much appreciated her always evident passion for beauty, expressed not only through biblical and theological research and writing but also through her meticulous care for the environment she creates around her. (For my own mother, another great lover and creator of beauty, she was an all-star hero.) I have also learned much from the way she pours her whole self—intellectual, relational, emotional, and spiritual—into her speaking and teaching. What an amazing impact she has had on people in this way. And when she takes on a task, rest assured it is done with excellence. Jo Ann has smoothed and lighted the way for us who have followed after, and we are indebted to her courage and dedication.

Teresa Reeve, PhD
Associate Professor of New Testament Contexts
Seventh-day Adventist Theological Seminary, Andrews University

Dr. Jo Ann is a well of deep spiritual sweetness and profound theological insight. She has invited us to know Jesus and walk breathing in His beauty, finding inexpressible joy that is lived out in passionate witness. I can't wait to live next door to her in heaven.

With love from a Texas student and pastor who has been blessed by her friendship and the fellowship of shared ministry,

Lynn Ripley, MDiv
Seventh-day Adventist Theological Seminary, Andrews University

For the past 20+ years I have known Dr. Jo Ann Davidson as a colleague on the Biblical Research Committee, a little more recently as a professor coworker at the Seventh-day Adventist Theological Seminary, Andrews University, and most recently as the head elder of the Eau Claire Seventh-day Adventist Church where I have become the pastor. Throughout all these experiences and roles she has been a gracious and cheerful friend in the work of the Lord. I am pleased to add my tribute to her many years of service and dedication to family, students, and church. May the Lord continue to bless her with strength and service for His mighty Name.

Thomas R. Shepherd, PhD, DrPH
Senior Research Professor of New Testament
Seventh-day Adventist Theological Seminary, Andrews University
Pastor, Eau Claire and Dowagiac Seventh-day Adventist Churches

Dr. Jo Ann Davidson is a professor, a scholar and a motivational speaker. I love the passion she demonstrates in narrating the Old Testament narratives. The Narrative Theology seminar is one of the best classes I had with her. She is always enthusiastic and full of zeal. I came to grasp the reality of who God is and how He deals with His people more from the biblical narratives than from the doctrinal classes. Praise be to God for the privilege of learning from such a caring and God-fearing professor.

God's peace and love be with you always,
Sussie Stanley
PhD Student
Seventh-day Adventist Theological Seminary, Andrews University

Dr. Jo Ann Davidson has been an inspiration to me as a theologian and as a Christian woman and mother. She paved the way for many of us women in higher education. During my PhD studies I was encouraged knowing that there was another woman who was successful in her doctoral studies and achieved excellence. It gave me courage and hope to continue pursuing my PhD degree. When I was teaching Biblical Greek, I met Dr. Davidson's daughter, now Dr. Rahel Wells. After getting to know Rahel, I appreciated Dr. Davidson also as a wonderful Christian mother. She raised her daughter to believe in herself as a woman scholar, along with helping her develop a good Christian character. Thank you, Dr. Davidson, for your contributions in the field of theology and in the field of Christian living.

Lena Toews, MAEd, MA, PhD
Religion Division
Union College, Lincoln, NE

I did not have the privilege to take a course with Jo Ann, but I was blessed to have her visit some of my classes and also listened to her every time she lectured on the campus. I was moved by her reading of Genesis 22. The passion with which she explained the meaning of "Hineni!" deeply impressed me. I followed her at every lecture she gave at professional meetings. Her focus on beauty and aesthetics was a missing piece for me, a rational archaeologist. My studies have been transformed by a new sensitivity and admiration for aesthetics. Last, but not least, I appreciate her care for the world that the Lord has given us. The creation of the Lord must be celebrated and appreciated. Thanks!

Efraín Velázquez II, PhD
President, Inter-American Adventist Theological Seminary

Jo Ann,

You have blessed me in so many ways through the years! First as the mom of Jon, one of my good friends from my time at Andrews. I will always remember the way you modeled love, hospitality, and family worship the times I spent an evening or afternoon at your home. It was through that relationship that I learned of your Sabbath seminar where you and Dick taught me for the first time the way the Jews celebrate the Sabbath through your own testimony from your time in Israel. And that was all BEFORE I enrolled in the seminary. While I worked on my MDiv you were always a smiling face and an encourager. You even attended my wedding! Finally, the last semester I was there I got to experience you as a professor! I love systematic theology and I thoroughly enjoyed our time in class two days a week. You truly are a Proverbs 31 woman in every way! Thank you for your ministry! Thank you for your love! Thank you for being an example of a life well lived!

Love and blessings,
Travis Walker, MDiv
Pastor, Daytona Beach Seventh-day Adventist Church
Daytona Beach, FL
Host of the Adventology Podcast

In the fall of 1998–just as "Net '98" kicked off–my family moved to Berrien Springs, MI. I was 6 years old. Unknowingly, I found myself plunged into a world full of theologians. It was only years later, as a theology student at Walla Walla University, that I began to associate the names I had grown up around with the theological work they had done. For me, these can never be just names; they are the faces of people who gathered over haystacks, around living rooms, and put up with my and my brother's abounding childhood energy at seminary retreats.

Today, as a woman in pastoral ministry, I have come to appreciate in a special way the women who trod the halls of the Seminary before me. I feel so very blessed to have grown up knowing Ellie Economou, Leona Running, Nancy Vyhmeister, and Jo Ann Davidson. At the time, I did not know what God had planned for my life. I did not yet appreciate the things they had overcome to be there. And, I did not know that Dr. Davidson's specialty–systematic theology–would become my own favorite area of theological study. What I did know was that she spoke with confidence and taught from her heart. I knew that she was energetic and passionate about sharing the meaning and specialness of the Sabbath. I knew that she was kind.

The fact that I did not get to take a class from Jo Ann during my MDiv coursework was and is disappointing (I did sign up for one, but something sadly intervened). Our communications during my seminary studies convinced me that her kindness, energy, and vivaciousness remain unchanged. Several of her books sit proudly on my bookshelves–including a well-marked, well-loved copy of *Jonah: Wrestling with the God of Second Chances*. I am continually thankful for God's willingness to extend second chances and to be the author of our life narratives. That the narrative of my life has overlapped just a bit with that of Dr. Jo Ann Davidson is something I count as a privilege. Thank you, Jo Ann, for all you have done and continue to do through your writing, teaching, and being. Thank you for how you have–knowingly and unknowingly–paved the way for energetic six-year-olds to grow up seeing a possible future for themselves in the world of Seventh-day Adventist theologians.

With much appreciation and love,
Macy (McVay) Weir, MDiv
Seventh-day Adventist Theological Seminary, Andrews University

Wow! Dr. Jo Ann Davidson is an inspirational professor and passionate human being. Her love of God and all His creatures great and small was communicated in class at times with tears restrained and an unwavering conviction in her voice. I was moved by her presentations and continue to benefit from her instruction. I had the privilege of being in a class she taught during my MAPMin.

Grace and peace to you and your family,
Brandon Westgate, MAPMin
Seventh-day Adventist Theological Seminary, Andrews University

Words cannot [express] the impact that Dr. JoAnn Davidson has had on my life and time while at the Seventh-day Adventist Theological Seminary. Dr. Davidson, while in her Principles of Christian Ethics class, gave me some advice in regard to a paper I was writing and then she stated, on a personal note, that I should consider pursuing a Ph.D. in the area of Christian Ethics. I have never had a professor take such an interest in my future career, or ever share such a personal note about their desire for me to pursue something that will benefit not just me, but the mission of the church as a whole.

Dr. Davidson's classes have been a most wonderful blessing to me personally. I sense the Holy Spirit in her classes and feel being drawn closer to Jesus. I greatly appreciate her ministry in my life and I am thankful to have been a part of her classes and to be able to say that I was blessed to be taught by her in my time at the seminary.

Brody Woodard, MDiv
Seventh-day Adventist Theological Seminary, Andrews University

It is with pleasure that I have the opportunity to reflect on my appreciation for my professor and friend, Dr. Jo Ann Davidson. Unlike some of her students at the Seventh-day Adventist Theological Seminary, my memories of her go back to my childhood. Jo Ann, her husband (Dr. Richard Davidson), and her children (now grown) are family friends of my parents and family. So it truly is a special delight to celebrate her influence upon me for an enduring period of time–from my childhood through to the completion of my own academic studies and beyond. And I can also fondly recall that the Davidson household was a frequent source of hospitality with delicious food abundantly present.

Jo Ann's specialty is the theology of beauty and I can affirm that in the two courses I took with her, focusing on the Sabbath and biblical narratives, there is much beauty to be found! Many philosophers and theologians have sought for beauty in my own area of focus, that of natural science and religion. And while both Jo Ann and I heartily affirm that God's creation is indeed beautiful in its aesthetic design, there is a special beauty that can only be seen through God's other special creation, and that is humanity, the reality of language, and that most special of creations, the Sabbath, a "tabernacle in time." Alongside this, the biblical narrative as a whole, and specific narratives, depict a very special kind of beauty, which grows the more we immerse ourselves in the story the biblical text is sharing, which is something Jo Ann loves to do. I can warmly share that her course lectures, delivered with an enthusiasm and energy only Jo Ann can provide, were a tremendous blessing to me, and truly provided some of my most memorable moments at the Seminary.

It is an unfortunate fact of history that much of the work of theologians through the ages has been of a rather dry sort, as "dry as the hills of Gilboa" in its attractiveness. Jo Ann, and her students (many of whom are also women), have sought to brighten and bring color to the work of theology. For this contribution I am most grateful!

With warmest wishes for God's continued blessings,
Michael F. Younker, PhD
Historical Research Specialist
Archives, Statistics & Research (ASTR)
General Conference of Seventh-day Adventists

Made in the USA
Monee, IL
27 June 2024

60851231R00193